# TASK FORCE

John Parker, a journalist and former Fleet Street editor,
has undertaken many investigative projects in his writing career
with topics ranging from the Mafia to Northern Ireland.
His numerous books include several military bestsellers
including *S.B.S., The Gurkhas, Commandos* and *Desert Rats.*

# TASK FORCE

## The Inside Story of the Ships and Heroes of the ROYAL NAVY

JOHN PARKER

First published in 2003 by
HEADLINE BOOK PUBLISHING

This edition published 2005 by Bounty Books,
a division of Octopus Publishing Group Ltd
2–4 Heron Quays, London E14 4JP

ISBN-13: 9780753712962
ISBN: 0 7537 1296 2

A CIP catalogue record for this book is available
from the British Library

Printed and bound in Great Britain by MPG Books Ltd

# Contents

# Acknowledgements

Readers of my previous books in this series will appreciate that the narrative relies heavily on the personal testimony of many former servicemen, especially those at the scene of particular events and important and crucial moments in history. This is especially so in a century of outstanding Royal Navy activity recorded here and I am once again deeply indebted to those whose contributions, obtained through personal interview or from archive material, bring these episodes to life in a manner that is simply impossible by merely recording the dry history of events. Apart from interviews I have conducted, a major source of material has been the vast collections housed at the Imperial War Museum, London, and especially those acquired and maintained by the IWM Sound Archive. The latter principally consists of tape-recorded interviews obtained over many years, and includes contributions from those able to recount events dating to the beginning of the twentieth century, which is also the starting point for this book. Most of the famous missions of all the services are covered and provide a coruscating and unique insight into some of the most heroic military adventures examined within these pages. Below is a list of principal tapes and transcripts consulted at the IWM Sound Archive with the accession number in brackets for those who might wish to pursue these references, along with principal dates of service.

Adshead, Gilbert (660) 1909–22. Alder, George T.C. (10674) 1938–45. Anderson, Oliver (7072) 1939–45. Ball, Fred C.A. (13293) 1939–53. Bayly, Patrick U. (12590) 1938–52. Bowen, Frederick T. (8181) 1939–45. Briggs, Albert E.P. (10751) 1938–56. Brockman, Ronald (18781) 1938–59. Brown, Leo E. (13581) 1917–43. Clarkson, George M. (679) 1915–37. Cockburn, James (8860) 1939–45. Collett, Roger G.P. (20499) 1940–52. Cross, Stanley R. (17235) 1939–45. Darling, Larratt C. (19916) 1941–71. Denham, Henry M. (10869) 1915–45. East, Rupert D. (10806) 1936–53. Fairbanks, Douglas jnr (8258) 1940–5. Gates, John H.B. (9335) 1939–45. Gaynor, John (8246) 1938–45. Gibson, Donald C. (9696) 1939–45. Goddard, Victor (303) 1910–20. Goldspink, Ernest W. (760) 1908–20. Goldsworthy, Frank (11245) *Daily Express* journalist 1941–60. Haig, George E. (735) 1912–18. Hardy, Frederick L. (8190) 1939–45. Harris, John D. (13765) 1939–45. Hill, Ronald C. (20271) 1946–56. Hutchison, F.G. (10888) 1937–54. Instance, Howard J. (11904) 1939–45. Jenkins, Harold G. (10490) 1936–45. Joughin, T.A. (10905) 1938–45. Kemp, Frederick R. (10503) 1921–45. Kingsmill, Charles M. (9735) 1939–45. Lazenby, Charles H. (664) 1916–23. Lewis, Roger C. (10670) 1939–45. Longhurst, Victor H. (2165) 1939–45. Lucas, George F. (11620) 1939–45. Marr, Geoffrey T. (10150) 1939–45. McMullen, Colin W. (10975) 1938–45. Mills, Charles P. (11767) 1939–56. Mott, John W. (10791) 1938–45. Napier, John (11322) 1936–56. O'Neill, James (11443) 1936–45. Perry, Clifford W. (11615) 1932–52. Reading, R.G. (4840) 1940–5. Redman, Donald R. (20145) 1945–52. Reynolds, Edward J. (10779) 1934–45. Scott, P.M. (11244) 1940–5. Shaw, Robert J. (9764) 1916–45. Siggins, Harold E. (9297) 1939–45. Smith, Richard G. (8663) 1939–45. Sparks, William E. (8397) 1939–45. Sweet, William F. (718) 1915–19. Terry, George A. (685) 1910–18. Tevendale, A.H. (770) 1920–45. Thornton, F.E. (16701) 1939–45. Walters, Leonard V. (12788) 1938–56. Warner, Alfred H. (10778) 1938–45. Wellman, Derek (12886) 1940–4. Young, Walter G. (9405) 1939–45.

Online searches can now also be made via the IWM's all-embracing new website, at www.iwmcollections.org.uk

# Prologue

It was a different kind of war, the first full-blown conflict of the twenty-first century, horrific, awesome, shockingly fascinating and played out in every detail on television. And a British Task Force of more than 30 ships and fleet submarines laden with assault aircraft missiles and an amphibious force of 4,000 Royal Marines from 3 Commando Brigade played a significant role in Gulf War II to depose the Iraqi dictatorship of Saddam Hussein. The Royal Navy ships were led by pride of the British fleet *Ark Royal*, whose battle group included the helicopter assault carrier *Ocean*, three Type-42 destroyers, two Type-23 frigates and two minehunters, backed up by the ever-present Royal Fleet Auxiliary, bearing all the necessary supplies, ammunition and paraphernalia of war. They were in action from the commencement of the battles, notably with the contribution of British fleet submarines firing Tomahawk cruise missiles in the early stages of the bombing campaign against Saddam's murderous regime and in the massive humanitarian effort that followed.

These operations will be described fully in the chronology of these chapters, but what the world witnessed in those days of awe in March and April 2003 was striking in a particular and noteworthy element: the whole operation was conducted with remarkably few casualties among the forces of liberation, and many of those who were sadly lost in the campaign, and especially among the Royal Navy Task Force, were brought down by so-called 'friendly' fire. The high technology and precise nature of modern warfare were demonstrated in all their incredible power, and these aspects provide a striking contrast to earlier conflicts that will be examined and recalled in the ensuing pages by men who were there in the thick of it, back in the days when great battleships, whose names were familiar to every schoolboy, took the frontline of maritime warfare in an era when the Royal Navy was the most powerful and potent force in the world.

The big, capital ships have long been replaced by the nuclear-powered fleet submarines and carrier-based aircraft and helicopters to deliver their massive bombardment of destructive capability, so evident in modern times in operations in the Gulf, Afghanistan and against the Milošević regime in the former Yugoslavia. In a past age, though well within living memory, it was all so different, especially in the potential for great loss of life among the crews when the great ships went head to head, and when a single enemy bomb or torpedo could kill and maim hundreds on board, or send a ship to the bottom in minutes with no hope of escape. In this regard, there are few accounts more poignant than that of Ted Briggs, from Redcar, Yorkshire.

He fell in love with the battle cruiser HMS *Hood* when he first saw her as a boy when the ship paid a pre-war visit to the town, one of many public relations exercises that the finest ship in the Royal Navy undertook at home and abroad. She stood off the mouth of the River Tees, proud and belligerent, the brass on her decks polished and glistening in the sunshine, and her guns, huge and menacing, presented an awesome sight. Local fishermen were charging five shillings (25p) a time to row people around the ship, but Ted's mother couldn't afford the fare, and so he just stood and stared: 'I had never seen anything so powerful and beautiful in my life, and I knew then I wanted to join the Royal Navy.'

There were three battle cruisers built in that class at the end of the First World War and which were among British front-line ships in the Second World War – *Hood, Repulse* and *Renown* – and of the three *Hood* was the finest. She had the reputation of being the most powerful warship in the world, the epitome of British sea power, and the grace of her lines brought acclaim from all who saw her, especially when she was travelling at full speed, when the wash came up either side of the quarterdeck. By some quirk of fate, *Hood* was the first ship that Ted Briggs joined after his entry into the Royal Navy. He enlisted on 3 March 1938, two days after his fifteenth birthday, and within three years he would find himself at the very epicentre of one of the great and most tragic dramas in modern naval history. He had completed his basic training at the infamous HMS *Ganges*, the huge shore-based naval school at Shotley, Suffolk, the strict but fair introduction to life in the Royal Navy for all young lads wishing to join the Senior Service. The pay was 5s. 3d. a week for a second-class boy and 8s. 9d. for a first-class boy, of which they were allowed to keep one shilling a week pocket money and the rest was put in the bank until they were 18. Ted joined as a seaman and chose to specialise in visual signalling, which in those days involved flashing, semaphore, Morse flag and flag signal, and was ready for posting in the early summer of 1939. It is as well now that he takes up the story:

Much to my surprise and much to my delight, I was sent to *Hood*. It was entirely different from training. You were treated as one of the ship's company and, although the discipline was still there, it was more relaxed. As boys [around 110 of them] we had our own mess deck and you were kept segregated as much as possible within the confines of the ship. The older personnel treated you with rather amused tolerance. I joined her in June, just as *Hood* had finished her refit in Portsmouth. It was a very crowded ship. The wartime company was 1,421 but the main problem was sleeping billets. There were not enough sling billets [for hammocks] and so you slept where you could, either on the mess deck tables or on the deck. We sailed to [the naval base of] Scapa Flow and from there at the beginning of September and we were actually at sea when the declaration of war was made.

The captain broadcast that we were at war and as flagship of the ships at sea we made the general signal to fleet to commence hostilities against Germany. One of the jobs I had was making that signal by semaphore from the director of

*Hood.* We knew that the Germans were constructing big battleships, like *Tirpitz* and *Bismarck*, but we didn't know the size of them. Under the international convention prevailing at the time, they were supposed to be only 35,000 tons but in actual fact they turned out to be 50,000 tons and more.

Most of our early days were spent covering Atlantic convoys. They had their own anti-submarine escort, but the capital ships were stationed between the various convoys so they were able to go to their assistance if they came under attack. The first real action we saw was shortly after the commencement when the submarine *Spearfish* was damaged and the Home Fleet went to sea to escort her back in the hope of tempting the German fleet to come out. The German fleet didn't come out, but the German air force did and the carrier *Ark Royal* and *Hood* were singled out for attacks. *Ark Royal* consistently had many near misses. They got a very near miss on *Hood* which peppered the port side with shrapnel. I was on the flag deck and actually watched the Heinkel that dived on us. I saw this black object leave the aircraft, and it didn't register with me what was happening until it exploded just at the side of us and I realised we might easily have been hit.

Thereafter, *Hood* joined the often frustrating task of protecting the Atlantic convoys, although she did not see a great deal of action until June 1940, when she was detached to Gibraltar and joined Force H as the flagship under Vice-Admiral Sommerville on his mission to sink the French fleet at Oran and then returned to Scapa Flow, rehoisted the flag of Vice-Admiral Whitworth and resumed patrols. There were a number of chases, including hot pursuit of the German battle cruisers *Scharnhorst* and *Gneisenau*, which had broken out into the Atlantic, but they reached the safe harbour of Brest and *Hood* spent time patrolling there as part of a constant blockade of the port.

On 20 May 1941 news that *Bismarck* had completed her trials and had ventured out of the Baltic reached *Hood*. She was sighted at Bergen in company with a heavy-class cruiser, *Prinz Eugen*, and that was the beginning of the hunt for *Bismarck* in which Ted Briggs, then two months past his eighteenth birthday, was at the centre of the action in his duties in the compass platform from where Admiral Holland controlled the chase:

We sailed from Scapa Flow at night on 21 May 1941. Visibility had closed down and the aircraft couldn't keep contact. There was a flying boat at Scapa which went wave-hopping to Bergen. When he arrived there, the harbour was empty. Meantime, the cruisers, *Norfolk* and *Suffolk* were patrolling up and down the areas where the ships were likely to break out. *Suffolk* sighted *Bismarck* and a heavy cruiser and reported to the Admiralty. We intercepted the enemy reports and the admiral ordered complete radio silence, and we turned to intercept the two ships. It was estimated we would be in a position to engage at 2 a.m. on the morning of 24 May. *Bismarck* realised she had been sighted by *Suffolk* but was apparently unconcerned since the ship represented no real threat. However, *Norfolk* joined *Suffolk* and stationed themselves on either quarter of the enemy ships and carried on reporting their movements. *Bismarck* then decided she would try to chase them off, turned, came straight in and fired.

The two cruisers turned and got out of the way. They had radar but it was very much in its infancy and could only scan forward, and consequently they lost contact. Admiral Holland in *Hood* made the mistake of assuming that *Bismarck* had turned back because she had been located. But in fact she had resumed course, and we went to action stations at midnight. Meanwhile, the destroyers were rapidly dropping back because they couldn't maintain our speed of 28 knots. Holland made a signal stating that he would continue on without them. Consequently, when the action took place the destroyers were 50 miles astern.

We regained contact with *Bismarck* on our radar at 3 o'clock on the morning of 24 May. She was about 30 miles off our starboard bow and she was steaming at 29 knots towards the Atlantic. Admiral Holland decided to maintain a parallel course until the weather moderated. He also knew what we didn't – that when *Hood* was built, a lot of armour had been sacrificed for speed. So our deck armour was thin and vulnerable and he had to get in as close as he possibly could during the action so that the fall of shot would be a flat trajectory rather than a high plummeting effort from a longer range. Whereas our maximum gun range was originally 20 miles, but reduced to 17 because of her age, the maximum effective gun range was now about 12 miles.

He turned towards the enemy ships at about 4 a.m. We had *Bismarck* sighted at about 20 miles on the starboard bow and moved into the 12-mile range. There was an atmosphere of excitement and tension and apprehension. It was something we'd been waiting for. There wasn't a man aboard that ship who doubted her capabilities, and when action stations began those below decks were given a running commentary of what was going on by the padre, over the intercom, in a calm, matter-of-fact way: 'We have just sighted the two topmasts of the two enemy ships and will be opening fire very shortly . . .'

There was fear, yes. But my main fear was of showing fear. But it was mainly excitement. We opened fire, again fine on the starboard bow and consequently the after guns could not be brought into action. So we could only use the for'ard gun turrets. The *Prince of Wales* was on our starboard quarter and could also only use her starboard gun turrets. But we had made the mistake of assuming that *Bismarck* was the leading ship. In fact, the leading ship was *Prinz Eugen* and so we had to shift target as soon as the mistake was realised. We fired about six salvoes, the third of which hit *Bismarck*'s oil tanks and caused one of them to leak. She'd obviously been taken completely by surprise. Although she knew two cruisers were shadowing her, she had no idea there were two capital ships in the vicinity because we had been keeping radio silence. *Bismarck* replied, and her gunnery was extremely accurate.

*Bismarck*'s third salvo went over. The next salvo fell short and the fifth salvo hit us. It sounded like an express train coming through a tunnel and hit at the base of the mainmast. I was on the compass platform from where the admiral was conducting the battle, so I knew what was going on. We couldn't see aft because of the enclosed bridge. All we knew was that we had been hit, because the ship shuddered and we were thrown off our feet. The gunnery commander went out on to the starboard wing of the bridge and reported to the captain that there was a fire around the four-inch ready-use shell lockers, the secondary armaments, and there was exploding ammunition going up there.

What struck me at the time was the unreality of it all. It seemed as if it wasn't happening. It seemed as if you were watching a film. The captain ordered that the fire should be left until all the ready-use ammunition had exploded and the boat deck should be cleared of all personnel. By that time, we'd got into the range we wanted and the admiral ordered both ships to alter course to bring the after guns into action. Just as he did so, the next salvo hit us. That penetrated into X and Y magazines. Again the ship shuddered and we were all thrown off our feet. All I saw was a gigantic sheet of flame which shot round the front of the compass platform. Until that time, it had been a fairly calm atmosphere. The admiral was sitting in the captain's chair at the front of the compass platform, the captain was standing close behind, the squadron gunnery officer was on the wing of the compass platform, the navigating officer and officer watch were at their positions and Midshipman Bill Dundas was standing by the phones.

Everybody else was at the rear of the bridge. It was very calm, and when the gunnery officer reported the hit, it was just as if he was giving a normal routine report. I have stressed the unreality, and it was – it just didn't seem as if such a thing could be happening to us. The fear was there, without doubt, but control of that fear is something that one was forced to do.

After the hit, you heard the screams and noise resulting from the carnage. The ship started listing to starboard, then righted herself and then started going over to port, and carried on going over. At the same time, the quartermaster reported, 'Steering gear gone, sir,' and the captain ordered the change-over to emergency conning and by that time she was going over. We realised that she wasn't coming back. There was no order given to abandon ship. It wasn't necessary. She'd gone over about 45 degrees when we realised she wasn't coming back and started to make our way out. I started to make my way to the door of the compass platform, and as I got to that door with the gunnery officer in front of me, the navigating officer stood to one side to let me go ahead.

I was about halfway down the ladder to the admiral's bridge when I was dragged into the water. I realised there was a deck head above me and I just had to get away from it as fast as I could. I also felt myself being dragged down. Again, you can get to such a stage when you can't do anything, and I felt myself being dragged down and down and down, and I just couldn't do any more; I couldn't do anything about it. I felt quite a feeling of peace; it sounds ridiculous, I know, but it was a feeling of peace and calm. Then I suddenly shot to the surface and I came up and looked around: the ship was vertical with the water and B turret was just going under so that the two for'ard turrets and the whole of the bow were vertical with the water and about 50 yards away from me. And I panicked and swam as fast as I could away. The water was covered with a four-inch-thick layer of oil.

There were lots of three-foot-square Carley life-saving rafts floating around and I managed to get on one of these. And then when I looked around, she'd gone; the mighty *Hood* had sunk without trace. There was a fire on the water with all the oil around and again I panicked and paddled away, sprawled on the Carley raft. Fortunately, when I looked around, the fire had gone out. There were two others on Carley rafts, and we swam towards each other, Midshipman Bill Dundas and Able Seaman Bob Tilburn. We managed to hold on to each other's rafts for a while. We saw *Prince of Wales* disappearing still firing, because a ship in action won't stop to pick up survivors. She had apparently reported to the Admiralty: *Hood* sunk, very little hope of survivors.

It was now desperately quiet, calm almost. But we couldn't understand it. There was no one else splashing around, not a soul. I also saw in the distance the tops of the three funnels of one of our cruisers and they then disappeared. We floated around, and after a while hypothermia set in and I just wanted to go to sleep. Tilburn said he could hear a flying boat, and we looked up and there was a Catalina approaching. We waved and shouted and splashed the water, but they didn't see us. The next thing I knew was Bill Dundas shouting. There was a destroyer ahead. I looked up and saw *H27* approaching, and I started shouting and the other two joined in with me. Well, there were two destroyers and apparently the commander-in-chief just couldn't believe that there was little hope of survivors and he'd sent them to search the area and so we were picked up. We were unable to move they dropped scrambling nets over the side and seamen jumped in to help us up.

The chief bosun's mate threw a rope and I hung on to it. He shouted, 'Don't let go of that.' And I shouted back, 'You bet your bloody life I won't.' Anyway, we were pulled out, our clothing cut off, and wrapped in blankets. Bill Dundas was taken to the wardroom and myself and Bob Tilburn were taken to the sickbay. When we came round a bit, we were taken to the mess deck and applied with lots and lots of rum to warm us up, and it also had the effect of helping me dispose of the oil I had swallowed by throwing up.

It transpired we were the only three survivors [out of the ship's company of 1,421]. Bill Dundas had managed to get out by kicking out one of the armour-plated windows on the compass platform. How he managed it, God alone knows, although he did sprain his ankle. Bob Tilburn had the most miraculous escape. He was on the boat deck and went over on the port side. One of the roof aerials which had broken loose tangled round his legs under water and he had to take his knife out to cut himself free.

We were taken to Reykjavik, where we landed up at the military hospital. The padre came to see us and we sent telegrams to our relatives. We were informed that we would be sent back to the UK in one of the ferries which operated between Iceland, *Royal Ulsterman*. We were put aboard her the following day, segregated into cabins, Bob and I in one and Bill in the other, and told we had not to talk to anyone. When we got back to Greenock, we were met by an officer, taken to the night-train bound for London and again told we should not talk to anyone about the sinking. We were met at the station in London by an officer in a car and taken to the Admiralty at about six in the morning, given breakfast and told that we were going to be interviewed by the Second Sea Lord, Vice-Admiral Whitworth. When we were ushered into him, he had tears in his eyes. He remembered me from when he was on *Hood*.

We all gave our versions, and we were told again not to talk to anyone until the court of inquiry, three months later. We also told him how we were dragged down and then shot to the surface and they came to the conclusion that a boiler had burst under water and we got caught in an air bubble and came up with that. But there wasn't another soul [who survived], not another living soul, and the only thing that we can think of was that most of those on the upper deck would have been killed or maimed by the first hit and those below decks wouldn't have stood a hope. Those on the upper deck would have been taken care of by suction.

As to the weaknesses in the ship's armour, we knew nothing about that. I don't think many people did, with the possible exception of the senior officers. But it was always intended that that weakness should be rectified, but in peacetime she could never be spared from flag-waving duties and in wartime it was impossible because of the length of time it would have taken to get the job done.

As to her sinking, it was always intended that *Hood* and *Prince of Wales* and the two cruisers would take on *Prinz Eugen* and the destroyers would come up behind to carry out torpedo attacks as necessary. But things moved with such bewildering rapidity when battle was joined. From the time we opened fire to the time *Hood* was fatally hit was about five minutes and she went down in three minutes from the time she was hit to when she disappeared.

Ted's story is just one of many displaying the unique courage of men (and now women) at sea in the ensuing pages . . .

# CHAPTER ONE

## Britannia Rules . . .

There was not a shadow of doubt. As the world turned into what would become a catastrophic century in terms of wars and the potential for the annihilation of mankind, Great Britain and her dominions were protected by the most powerful navy the world had ever known. It would get better, too, in the years leading up to the First World War, as Kaiser Wilhelm II of Germany began to show increasing belligerence towards the political hierarchy of first his grandmother Queen Victoria, then his Uncle King Edward VII, and finally prepared to go to war against his cousins, Tsar Nicholas of Russia and the British monarch, George V. Over that period of time, the navies of Germany and Great Britain were being built up to enormous potential, a race that had been urged on the Germans by their monarch, who had been a regular observer, courtesy of his family connections, of the traditional Spithead Reviews of British naval strength.

The new British King George V also had a particular interest in furthering the cause of the Royal Navy. It had been his life as a young prince and it was his first commander and great friend of Edward VII, Jackie Fisher, who was to kick-start the Royal Navy towards its greatest strength at the beginning of the twentieth century. Fisher was appointed First Sea Lord in 1904, and his good friend Winston Churchill, who later became his boss as

First Lord of the Admiralty, gave him full credit for the formation of 'a great and powerful Royal Navy that would be capable
of withstanding a confrontation with any other of the world's
most potent seagoing forces'. Fisher was, however, deeply dis-
trusted by many in the naval hierarchy, who regarded him as a
vain and indiscreet man, although it has to be said that he had
made known his intentions to attack the snobbish old boy
network that ran the Victorian navy like a yacht club. As an
avowed reformer, he had also promised sweeping changes to
improve the lot of the seamen who, at the turn of the twentieth
century, were still abysmally paid and generally treated like dirt.

Fisher produced the blueprint for modernisation in every
respect, although he would be criticised later for not having
followed through with a plan as to how this great force could be
most effectively deployed. On taking up the task, Fisher finally
discarded some of the older ships – fine vessels though they were –
that he believed were totally outmoded for the modern warfare
that he envisaged. There were still ships in use in the fleet that
dated to the Crimean War and beyond, and he was determined to
replace them with a fleet whose speed and power would be
unmatched anywhere in the world – and Britain, following the
golden age of the Industrial Revolution, was well placed to achieve
this aim.

At the apex of his plans was the dreadnought revolution, the
introduction of battleships with unrivalled potency (see below)
which he forced into being. Churchill was still Under-Secretary at
the Colonial Office as this development came to pass, and he
recalled early encounters with Fisher in his book *The World
Crisis*:

[He was] at the height of his reign [as First Sea Lord]. We
talked all day long and far into the night. He told me
wonderful stories of the navy and of his plans – all about
dreadnoughts, all about submarines, all about the new education scheme for every branch of the navy, all about big guns
and splendid admirals and foolish, miserable ones and about
Nelson, and the Bible . . . I could have passed an examination
on the policy of the then Board of Admiralty.

Big guns, dreadnoughts, torpedoes and submarines were all Fisher's fascination. As soon as he became First Sea Lord he began his programme of major reforms throughout the Royal Navy, ranging from improving the notoriously inhumane treatment of men below decks to upgrading the education and training of officers and men. The hardware, however, was the focus for his greatest upheaval both in terms of the type of ships and the manner in which they might be deployed. As described in this author's earlier book, *The Silent Service,** he forced through these developments in surface vessels in tandem with the creation of Britain's first submarine fleet, demanded research to increase torpedo ranges and, above all, sought dramatic improvements in the accuracy, range and capacity of the navy's big guns.

He wanted to out-gun the world, and at the forefront of his plans was the great new battleship class led by HMS *Dreadnought* in which King Edward VII, along with all the other seafaring nations of the world, showed great interest. Ships, after all, had been the playthings of monarchs for centuries, and it was their navies that had provided the key to unlock power and wealth as their respective governments set about forming an empire for them to rule over.

It was a link that generated a quintessentially British style about the Royal Navy, with its traditional virtues of discipline and courage, and calmness under fire. Although at the beginning of the twenty-first century that 'special' relationship is something of a fading memory, and some would say irrelevant to modern times, the history *was* glorious, and exceedingly bloody, and before going on to examine Fisher's contribution, it is as well to remind ourselves of some of the defining events in a thousand years of history in which seaborne warriors from Great Britain helped forge the destiny of the nation, and the world.

The most effective lesson of all – never to be forgotten – was learned in 1066 when King Harold's warships on patrol in the English Channel returned to port after he ran out of money and

---

* *The Silent Service: The Inside Story of the Royal Navy's Submarine Heroes,* Headline, London, 2001.

could not afford to pay the sailors. Duke William of Normandy took immediate advantage of this state of affairs, dashed across the Channel to land at Pevensey Bay in Sussex, and thus became William the Conqueror. The great navies, however, began appearing in the sixteenth century, led by James IV of Scotland, whose fleet, created to patrol the Western Isles, was led by a massive new ship, *Great Michael*, which carried one of the largest arsenals ever seen. Not to be outdone, Henry VIII set about creating his own Navy Royal, as he called it.

His own pride and joy would be *Mary Rose*, built between 1509 and 1511 and one of the first ships able to fire a broadside. She generally carried a crew of 200 sailors, 185 soldiers (the first marines) and 30 gunners, and became a leader in that era of blood, guts and thunder. After a long career in which she was engaged in most of Henry's wars, *Mary Rose* sank accidentally in the Solent during an engagement with the French fleet in 1545. Her wreck was discovered in the nineteenth century and was finally raised in 1982 and is preserved in Portsmouth. By the time of his death in 1547, Henry VIII's fleet had grown to 58 vessels with a substantial array of docks and warehouses.

The more swashbuckling adventurers, however, appeared under Elizabeth I, who more or less privatised naval enterprise, producing personalities such as Sir John Hawkins and Sir Francis Drake, and their famous battles with the French and the Spanish. Most notable, of course, was the great British response to the arrival of the Spanish Armada in 1588 when the Navy Royal and the privateers combined to ensure an heroic victory. The British simply stunned the opposition with the brilliance of their tactics, the steadfastness under fire and the rather gentlemanly imperturbability that allowed Drake to finish his game of bowls.

It was another Elizabethan sailor, Sir Walter Raleigh, who insisted: 'Whosoever commands the sea, commands the trade of the world, commands the world itself.' It was a quotation that remained to the fore among successive British administrations thereafter, as the beginnings of empire gripped the imagination of seafarers and investors alike. The seventeenth century saw larger galleons with more guns, led by the latest English ship, *Sovereign of the Seas*, built for Charles I. The first ship with three gun decks to carry her 102 guns, she remained the most powerful vessel in the world for many years. When the Civil War broke out in 1642, the navy remained loyal to Parliament and was rewarded by Cromwell's creation of the largest fleet Britain had ever seen.

By 1652 the navy continued to expand, and changed battle tactics successfully to assemble in long lines, each of three squadrons, which set the form for decades hence, and indeed were used in the First World War. King Charles II inherited a substantial fleet of almost 160 ships in the 1660s, a development that saw the creation of the Royal Navy that exists in the twenty-first century – although, curiously enough, on a far lesser scale. Britain was not without her reverses, by any means, and suffered losses in both European waters and in the Americas.

The French Revolutionary Wars and the Napoleonic Wars also provided the scenario for considerable activity, which ultimately took the French navy to full stretch, and although these wars dragged on for years, the remarkable successes of the Royal Navy placed the British in good heart for the future. Napoleon's ambitions had been constantly frustrated by the Royal Navy's harassment of his ports and ships. Horatio Nelson, meanwhile, came to prominence for his contribution to the British defeat of the Spanish fleet at St Vincent in 1797. The following year, Nelson's charismatic management of the British fleet in the Battle of the Nile in 1798 became an oft-quoted example of tactical brilliance in launching a surprise attack on the disengaged side of the French fleet. He found his eternal place in history for himself and his ship, HMS *Victory*, during the 1805 Battle of Trafalgar, when his fleet demolished a superior joint force of French and Spanish ships. Although he was killed at the hour of victory, Nelson saved Britain from invasion by the French, once again reinforcing the belief that, come what may, the Royal Navy was the indispensable defender of the British Isles.

Historically, success in naval battles relied first and foremost on the tactics of fleet commanders. Equally, however, historians of the day recognised that the decisions of the commanders merely established the basis of what might be a great victory. The eventual outcome came down to the skill of the gunners and the strength, courage and sheer fighting willpower of the men themselves, and that had always been a brutal, deadly and horrendously bloody affair, very much a case of the survival of the fittest. In this particular sequence of battles, the British tars had 'fought like dogs' to achieve victory over their French and Spanish counterparts, whose desperation and determination were equally evident, but in the end were overcome. As one historian of the day recalled: 'Willpower and courage must always accompany tactical art and science and often dominate the outcome of battle.' When it came to it, the men were not simply fighting for their lives, but for their ships, and that in many respects was surprising because in theory they ought not to have been concerned about loyalty, only self-preservation.

These great ships were manned by a motley collection of seamen often drawn from the dregs of society, collected from jails or infamously press-ganged into service and who were subsequently whipped and cajoled into handling cannon, rope and sail. Dr Johnson famously recorded: 'Why, Sir, no man will be a sailor who has contrivance enough to get himself into a jail, for being in a ship is being in a jail, with a chance of being drowned!' As recruits to the navy were largely impressed men, no leave was granted to prevent 'running'. The only consolation was that in home ports 'wives' were allowed on board, but most were prostitutes who brought venereal disease with them.

Only the upper deck enjoyed fresh air. The lower decks were all enclosed, and daylight and ventilation were by hatches and gun ports that could be opened only in fine weather. Lighting was by candle. The ship's company was housed mainly on the gun decks, while midshipmen and other lesser crew members, such as the surgeon's mate, were housed on the lowest deck, which was below sea-level and had no ports. Extracts from the *Handbook for Royal Navy Medical Officers*, assessing causes of disease and death among sailors, provide a disturbing insight into conditions.

There was severe overcrowding between decks, and a space of only 36 centimetres was allowed between beds and hammocks. Rats were a constant nightmare. Punishments were appalling, with flogging a daily occurrence and keel-hauling not uncommon. The diet consisted chiefly of salt-beef or pork, oatmeal, biscuits, beer and occasionally cheese. There were no fresh provisions except on rare occasions, and after a short while much of the food became rancid, with the badness disguised by salt, and biscuits were alive with weevils. Water taken on board in casks rapidly became foul. Pay was negligible, and a levy of sixpence a month was demanded to the 'Chatham Chest' for the treatment of the sick and wounded. The experiences of Tobias Smollett, who served as surgeon's mate in HMS *Cumberland* in 1739, are recounted, and in particular his own accommodation on the lower deck among the holds for stores, rotting food and vegetable matter and bilges where foul stagnating water accumulated. Open braziers used in an attempt to dry the decks added fumes to the already poisoned atmosphere. The handbook quotes this description of life at sea in bad weather:

> During such furious storms the spray of the sea raised by the violence of the wind is dispersed over the whole ship; so that people breathe as it were in water for many weeks together. The tumultuous waves incessantly breaking upon the decks, and wetting those who are upon duty as if they had been drenched in the sea, are also continually sending down great quantities of water below; which makes it the most uncomfortable wet lodging imaginable; and from the labouring of the ship, it generally leaks down in many places, directly upon their beds. There being no fire or sun to dry or exhale the moisture, and the hatches necessarily kept shut, this most stagnating confined air below becomes most offensive and intolerable. When such weather continues long, attended with sleet and rain, as it generally is, we may easily figure to ourselves the condition of the poor men; who are obliged to sleep in wet clothes and damp beds, the deck swimming with water below them; and there to remain only four hours at a time; till they are again called up to fresh fatigue, and hard labour, and again exposed to the washing of the sea and rains.

The overcrowding was often exacerbated by the need to accommodate fighting men as well as sailors, and for extra numbers taken on board for longer journeys to allow for 'inevitable wastage' from sickness and death. A ship carrying 100 guns or more and varying from 2,000 to 6,000 tons might have a crew of nearly 1,000 men, while a 60- to 80-gun ship would have 750 men on board at the outset, of whom a quarter might fall victim to disease alone, not counting other causes of death at sea. Diseases of all kinds were rampant, many brought on board by men pressed into service or collected from prisons. Scurvy was the scourge of sailors right up to the end of the eighteenth century, and the cause and transmission of some diseases remained unresolved until early in the twentieth century.

George Anson who, as First Lord of the Admiralty from 1751 to 1762 organised the Royal Marines, encouraged investigations into scurvy much earlier in his career when, in 1741, during his voyages around the world, he lost 292 men and had only 214 of his crew remaining on his return. Such a toll on Royal Navy personnel was not uncommon until naval surgeon James Lind, while serving on a 74-gun ship, *Salisbury*, carried out controlled experiments and observation at sea on the causes and treatment of scurvy, finally proving the value of fresh fruit and vegetables. It was not until 40 years later that Lind's recommendations were put into effect.

Other common killer diseases included malaria, dysentery and typhus, or jail fever, the last carried by the many men brought from prisons, lousy and in rags. Because no uniforms or clothing were issued by the navy and without any facilities for bodily cleanliness, disease spread rapidly. In 1795, for example, *Invincible* lost a third of her crew to typhus within a month of setting sail. Initially, the cause was thought to originate from the impure air below decks, and these were only added to by the practice of fumigation by odious-smelling sulphur. The transmission of the disease by the body louse from person to person was not discovered until 1909 – although Lind had spotted the connection in his report more than 150 years earlier when he suggested a period of isolation for incoming crews. He wrote:

The most effectual preservative against this infection during a press would, perhaps, be to appoint a ship for receiving all ragged and suspected persons; their stay in her, however, should be short, as soon as they are stripped of their rags, well washed and cleaned, they should be supplied with new clothes and bedding and be sent on board the receiving guard ships. Such of their apparel as appears tolerably good ought to be cleaned, or if necessary fumigated with brimstone, and returned to them, but it will be absolutely necessary to destroy all filthy rags and all such clothes as are brought from Newgate or other prisons.

The image of Captain Bligh, especially that portrayed by Charles Laughton in *Mutiny on the Bounty*, therefore rightly prevails in modern times. Even so, many commanders were exceedingly anxious to sail a relatively happy ship, so that a crew eventually moulded together, bound by loyalty to each other, because at the end of the day the greatest loss of life came from the great battles at sea, as the two sides engaged in a war of nerves, and then broadside to broadside, when nerves and willpower were stretched to breaking point. 'The cries of the wounded rang through all parts of the ship,' remembered a seaman on board HMS *Macedonian* during the Anglo-American war of 1812 in a scrap with an American frigate. 'The crew fought like tigers . . . our men kept cheering with all their might. We kept shouting and fighting.'

The American frigate was a new type of warship that came into widespread usage in the second half of the eighteenth century as the leading shipping nations sought protection from pirates for their merchantmen and fishing fleets. The Americans built some very large 44-gun frigates at the turn of the nineteenth century and in 1812, having seen them in action, Britain commissioned ships of the same design. The frigates became of special use in American and Far Eastern waters, and as Great Britain gradually and effectively assumed supremacy of the seas the Royal Navy increasingly found itself in the role of world policeman.

Warships were now to be regularly dispatched to sort out local difficulties in Britain's expanding empire, and additionally humanitarian and scientific projects were added to their repertoire, following on from Captain James Cook's incredible journeys of discovery and cartography in the late eighteenth century. In the nineteenth century the British Admiralty undertook extensive cartographic surveys which provided the basis for global shipping charts, sent warships to clean up pirate-infested waters in various parts of the globe and, after the abolition of slavery in Britain in 1833, despatched men-o'-war to intercept slavers off the coast of Africa from where the trade still flourished with shipments to other parts of the globe, including America until 1865.

The term 'gunboat diplomacy' also came into play as the guns became more powerful, allowing shore bombardment to take its place as a major mode of naval warfare, notably during the Crimean War in the 1850s and at Sweaborg against the Russians in the Gulf of Finland in 1855. In the latter action, the Royal Navy's bombardment lasted almost four days, annihilating the enemy positions with no losses to the ships involved, while at Alexandria in 1882 the rebel forces of Arabi Pasha were bombarded for six days. At the same time, another major development occurred when both the French and British navies built armoured vessels, known as 'ironclads', for shore bombardment, on the grounds that they would be less susceptible to the molten metal shells designed to set fire to wooden ships.

Britain's first iron-hull ship was HMS *Warrior*, which can still be seen today at Portsmouth. Commissioned in 1861, *Warrior* was the first ship of the industrial age, bringing together technological innovations such as the use of iron and steel and the introduction of steam power, albeit on a limited basis because of the shortage of coal and the restricted distance a ship could travel before needing to take on more fuel. Even so, Britain advanced so quickly that there were few threatening challenges to the Royal Navy and, equipped with an unrivalled lead in the Industrial Revolution in the eighteenth and nineteenth centuries, Britain pressed ahead with replacing all her wooden-hull ships with ironclads, progressively using thicker armour and bigger guns, mounted in revolving turrets. Bows were also strengthened to enable the greater use of ramming tactics, although it also led to a number of serious peacetime disasters in which ships were accidentally rammed, in fog for example, and sunk.

Among those involved in such an incident was the huge new battleship *Iron Duke* (the first of three to bear that name). She weighed in at 6,034 tons, had a complement of 450 men and came into service in 1871, taking the starring role as flagship of the Commander-in-Chief, China, and becoming the first capital ship to use the Suez Canal. On her return to Britain in 1875, she accidentally rammed and sank her sister ship, HMS *Vanguard*, off the Kish Bank, Dublin Bay, in fog. *Vanguard* sank within an hour, but all hands were rescued. After a number of refits, *Iron Duke* was eventually cut down to become a coal hulk before being sold for scrap in 1906.

From the early nineteenth century, Britain's mercantile marine expanded rapidly in quantity, quality and capability. The standardised introduction of steel for armour for battleships also gave rise to the appearance of large armoured cruisers of almost equal size to battleships, but faster and more powerful. One other welcome side-effect of the improvement in the seagoing stock was in the death rate, which fell dramatically aboard ironclad ships, and the decline continued as shipboard technology required the recruitment of men capable of being trained to new skills, and with marines who were at last being trained specifically for their role. They were especially required to protect Britain's now vast network of trade routes and her massively enhanced merchant fleet.

Another newcomer to the navy scene was the first British-built torpedo, introduced in 1870. A crude form of sea mine, it was first encountered by the Royal Navy during the Crimean War when two paddle-steamers were damaged. During the 1860s naval engineer Robert Whitehead invented a device capable of delivering an underwater charge initially just a few hundred yards. It was subsequently perfected into the familiar cigar-shaped model that could travel under water and strike the target beneath the water line. The frigate HMS *Shah* fired the first Royal Navy torpedo to be launched in anger in 1877 against a Peruvian ironclad, *Huascar*, and very soon many nations were equipping themselves with small, fast torpedo boats designed to attack enemy ships from close range.

The British Admiralty, having provided the world with the prototype torpedo, now had to hurriedly put together plans to combat them. They came up with the idea of specially designed fast ships to destroy the torpedo boats before they could attack. The first two, *Havoc* and *Hornet*, were built in 1893, and eventually the title of 'torpedo boat destroyers' was shortened simply to destroyers and their role was extended to become scouts and screens for fleets of battleships and battle cruisers – thus a new type of ship was born.

These developments in the second half of the nineteenth century coincided with Britain's huge industrial advances in which shipbuilders and allied trades and professions took a commanding lead over the rest of the world. The technology and innovative design of both warships and merchant vessels put the nation well ahead of her rivals in virtually every level, and apart from being a world leader and exporter of ships to the rest of the world, the Royal Navy was well equipped to meet any challenge. Even so, a political pact between Russia and France exposed a weakness – and indeed complacency – among the navy of Queen Victoria, in that the joint navies of the two countries exceeded the power of the British fleet.

The naval hierarchy took flak from commentators who criticised their lack of intelligence about opposing navies, and for snobbery and smugness resulting from several decades of relatively unchallenged dominance. In the end, the British government ordered a review and in 1889 passed the Naval Defence Act, authorising a massive building programme to put the Royal Navy on comparable terms with the world's next two largest navies, although ironically when the time came for action it would not be the French who were the enemy.

Now, for the first time, a complete revamp of naval thinking was called for, and the Royal Corps of Naval Constructors was given the task of spearheading the design and manufacture of a new generation of battleships and cruisers that were to be unrivalled anywhere in the world. Never had the navy been blessed with such an expansive and futuristic programme of shipbuilding, and Britain had the industrial might to turn out these new monsters in record time. The new plans would call for the building of 70 new ships and new dockyards over the final decade of the nineteenth century. There was no mention of submarines in these plans, even though numerous experimental craft had already been built by other nations. However, when the Americans successfully built a prototype of a craft under the name of *Holland I* after its designer, the Royal Navy ordered five submarines costing £35,000 each.

They were just 64 feet in length with a beam of 12 feet, had just one torpedo tube and were powered by a rather dangerous petrol engine and a battery-powered motor for underwater propulsion.

The arrival of submarines in Britain was still a decade away when a great demonstration of Britain's naval power was staged to celebrate Queen Victoria's Diamond Jubilee in 1897. But they were hardly missed. The incredible pace of change in ship design and construction, the massive conglomeration of mechanical structure that powered them and the potency of the big guns were apparent for all to see. Without withdrawing a single vessel from any of Britain's overseas stations, more than 150 warships were mustered for a spectacular display during Victoria's jubilee celebrations – four lines of ships, stretching for 25 miles, and including 22 battleships and 42 cruisers. The Germans were already taking copious notes and would continue to monitor closely the construction of this fleet of steel during the years ahead, as Wilhelm II brought his entourage to the various events hosted by the British royal family – especially the Spithead Review – where he (and his spies) saw for themselves the might with which Britain was equipping herself.

Even that show of might was not enough for Sir John Fisher, a renowned technocrat among the naval hierarchy who was soon to be charged with taking the British capability to an even higher level. Fisher was already a man of influence and power when he was appointed to the role of First Sea Lord in 1904. Born in Ceylon in 1841, he entered the navy at the age of 13 on board HMS *Victory* at Portsmouth. He was a midshipman in the Crimean War and in China (1859–60), where he took part in the capture of Canton. Promoted to captain (1874), he commanded various ships and the gunnery school and took a prominent part in the bombardment of Alexandria (1882) as commander of the battleship *Inflexible*. He was commandant of HMS *Excellent* when the future king, 20-year-old Prince George, joined his company.

On his elevation to First Sea Lord, he made no secret of his determination to shake the navy to its foundations, with modernisation at every level, and he became the hero of the lower decks by insisting on making life more acceptable down below. There would be greater emphasis on education and training, creating opportunities for promotion on merit and ability rather than social standing or the old boy network, and ridding the hierarchy of its 'yacht club' attitude to life in the Royal Navy – all of which raised the hackles of many of the top brass. These changes fundamentally altered the social order of the Royal Navy, although it would take years before the old ways were fully eradicated, especially those relating to the culture of punishment and heavy-handed discipline which was still endemic in the navy well into the twentieth century, even though such punishment was, in theory at least, regulated by law.

In 1871 the Admiralty issued instructions by circular letter (of 18 December) that corporal punishment was to be inflicted only in cases of (1) mutiny and (2) using or offering violence to a superior officer. A circular letter of 16 September 1879 directed that no commanding officer was to award a sentence of corporal punishment exceeding 25 lashes. On 10 January 1881 a Bill to abolish corporal punishment was presented to the House of Commons. This was withdrawn on 12 July 1881, but on 3 August 1881 the Admiralty issued instructions that the power of commanding officers to award corporal punishment was suspended until further orders. Administrative action was taken in 1881 to advise court-martial-convening authorities that corporal punishment was not to be awarded without Admiralty approval. Curiously enough, this order did not include the punishment of boys at the navy's education establishments, and that continued for many years hence.

It was, however, still no picnic for young men entering the service. Chief Petty Officer George Terry recalls in his tape-recorded memoir for the Sound Archive of the Imperial War Museum that at the age of 11, in 1904, he entered Greenwich Preparatory School for Marine Training to follow in the footsteps of his father. He recounted that quite soon after enrolling he suffered a hefty caning of 12 lashes after getting mixed up with six boys who left school early to go to a fair:

> We were hauled before the captain and were stripped of our merit badges. He then told us that as an example to the other boys we would get 12 cuts of the cane each. We were taken

into the schoolroom and lined up in front of two marine sergeants who gave us six each. The skipper stood and watched. By heck, they were a real dozen and I have the marks on my backside to this day [almost 70 years later]. We could hardly walk. When we got up to our quarters, where we were supposed to prepare our beds and sit down for prayers . . . well, we couldn't sit down, and the other boys had to get hold of us and ease us down on to the floor for prayers and then lift us up and put us to bed. That went on for over a week. It was the one and only time I was ever excused going to church.

George stuck it out, but at the end of his education at Greenwich he failed the test for the marines on medical grounds. During the training, he had suffered a hernia that required an operation. But having passed through the marine school, he was subsequently passed for the navy, which he did not want:

I didn't want to go. I was really disappointed. My father was a marine and I'd set my heart on it. But I'd signed a contract, and my dad said I should go. In the end I was glad I did. So in 1908 I was sent to HMS *Ganges*, the shore-based training school, and it was a hundred per cent better than Greenwich. The food was marvellous, the sports facilities were very good and we were paid sixpence a day. I had never received any money before, and it went up when I joined *Leviathan*, the flagship of the training squadron, in 1909. That was a real experience for us young lads, and the beginning of my life in the Royal Navy. I never looked back.

There was another beating early on – six cuts of the cane for under-age smoking – and then George Terry had his first encounter of 'coaling', the loading of coal on to the ship, an operation in which every member of the ship's company, including the chaplain, took part. And on his very first voyage, he witnessed a mutiny by the seamen:

We set off for Gibraltar as part of our training, and while we were there we did gunnery practice off the Balearic Islands. It was a reduced crew because we were a training ship, but many of the duties had to be carried out as normal. That included coaling. When we came back from gunnery practice, we had to coal the ship. There are two ways that is done: either loading the coal from a collier ship, when we had to attach the coal sacks to derricks that would swing them across into our coal hold, or we had to load it manually from the wharf. It was bloody hard work and everybody on board had to get involved, including the padre. The only ones who didn't were the telegraphists, because they said the coal dust affected their ears. If the coal was on the wharf, we would have to carry it from there in wicker baskets or sacks; someone would put it on your shoulder and you'd walk up the gangway and on board to the coal bunker and tip it in. Now, we did this every time we pulled into harbour, obviously, because without it we'd just stop. If you'd got a couple of thousand tons of coal to move, you'd know about it when you were finished. It was very dirty work. There wouldn't be anywhere in that ship where there wasn't coal dust by the time you'd finished. It was slightly easier to coal a ship from a collier, or tender, because the coal was bagged up in the ship and lifted out by a derrick into the receiving ship, but of course the coal still had to be manhandled by the receiving crew, both sides of the operation.

And then, of course, we had to clean up. Well, on this particular occasion in Gibraltar, the commander, a bit of a twerp, came round afterwards for his inspection and wasn't very happy. Reckoned the deck was in a mess and the coal not stacked correctly and wanted it done again. It was already early evening, just after tea. We were all called on deck before the commandant, but the seamen – the ship's reduced crew of around a hundred – refused to turn out. They were warned again, and still nothing, so the skipper called in the navy police and the marines. We were still kept standing on deck during this time, while the seamen were eventually brought up and questioned. Most of them refused to speak. Anyway, the upshot was that six ringleaders were court-martialled, and got sentences of up to two years for disobeying an officer's orders.

Complaints about coal dust and grime also demonstrated the vast change in the need and desire for personal hygiene in the Royal Navy that had occurred in a relatively short time, and especially since the introduction of modern conveniences that came with steam-powered ships had their effect. Although ragged and diseased recruits were by then pretty well screened out, many, of course, did come from homes where even running water was a luxury. When a true appreciation of Lind's discoveries half a century earlier that personal cleanliness on board ship was essential became apparent, it began to become an obsession in the Royal Navy, and even then certain infections and parasitical conditions were unavoidable, especially because try as they might the presence of rats on board ship remained a problem for many years to come.

William Sweet, in his recollections for the Imperial War Museum, found the need for cleanliness one of the most memorable experiences when he first joined the boy recruits' training ship *Impregnable* at Portsmouth in 1914:

Before we went on board, we took off our boots. And we never put them back on again until we went ashore – however long that might be – and for the rest of the time on board we'd be barefoot. It was then scrubbing down, cleaning out, and I must say the deck and the woodwork were, oh, dazzling, and they meant to keep it that way. Only the instructors wore shoes. And then, washing . . . as soon as you got up in the morning at 6 a.m., you had to wash in tubs of cold water. Without fail. They you'd be scrubbing down – scrubbing a section of the deck, which your class had to keep clean. Then you'd go down to breakfast and afterwards there would be a morning inspection of the whole ship's company by the captain. You had to be exceptionally clean. And we had to have a bath two or three times a week and as soon as you had a bath you were inspected. Well, it taught you how to keep yourself clean.

Many of these improvements to life on board ship came into being during the early part of Jackie Fisher's term as First Sea Lord and were later taken up by Winston Churchill on his appointment as First Lord of the Admiralty in October 1911. Fisher's greatest contribution to the effectiveness of the then still Edwardian Royal Navy, however, was to convince the Admiralty, and subsequently the government who would foot the bill, that the Royal Navy had to upgrade its battleships and take full advantage of new steam-turbine technology. There was a race on, between Britain and Germany, and the Royal Navy had to ensure that its superiority was maintained.

Edward VII and Churchill were among those who ardently supported that view, and Fisher won approval to build *Dreadnought*, the prototype of a new class of battleships that revolutionised naval construction and made all preceding battleships obsolete. She was immediately copied by Germany, and Fisher persuaded the British government to begin the construction of eight dreadnoughts, although the original was herself made obsolete within a dozen years by the progression of technology in building the remainder, and subsequently the successors, the even more ambitious *Queen Elizabeth*-class battleships.

The original dreadnought technology was an amalgamation of a number of ideas already in existence that together enabled the creation of the largest, fastest and most powerful battleship the world had ever seen. Just as *Warrior* had been built 50 years earlier to scare Britain's enemies, so *Dreadnought* was built in the record time of just over a year and launched in 1906 to spearhead the revitalisation of the Royal Navy in response to Germany's own ambitious programme. Everything about *Dreadnought* was bigger and better, and newspaper reports of the arrival of this giant of the seas captured public imagination like no other.

The revolutionary aspects came with the use of turbine power and the introduction of big guns, a combination that was to dominate the world's navies for the next 35 years. *Dreadnought* displaced 18,000 tons (more than 20,000 tons fully loaded), was 526 feet long and carried a crew of about 800. Four propeller shafts, powered by steam turbines instead of the traditional steam pistons, provided what was then an incredible top speed of 21 knots. Her firepower was also revolutionary. At a time when battleships usually mounted only four big guns and an array of smaller weapons, *Dreadnought* carried as its main armament ten 12-inch guns in five twin turrets. In addition, 24 three-inch quick-firing guns, five Maxim machine guns and four torpedo tubes were added for fighting off destroyers and torpedo boats. This represented a 250 per cent increase in gun power on predecessors.

Fisher's next task was to create an even faster big-gun cruiser, the *Invincible* class, which was a dreadnought-type armoured cruiser but with only eight 12-inch guns which meant that with less weight the ship could rely on her speed of 25 knots for protection. The theory was that *Invincible* could simply avoid punishment from enemy ships by racing out of range, which, in war, proved not to be the case; as will be seen. The basic flaw was in the lightness of her armour, which was easily penetrated by bombs.

The problem was that Fisher was a man in a hurry. He took over as First Sea Lord at the age of almost 64, and to some extent his task was a combination of personal ambition and what he saw as a very grave need to return the Royal Navy to its world-beating status. He knew he had only half a dozen years or so to make an impact before he retired at the age of 70 in 1910, and he succeeded in pushing through massive changes – but at a pace that did not always allow time to discover some of the flaws in technical and tactical developments. It is no exaggeration to say that in many respects he split the navy from top to bottom with his controversial and outspoken assault on the status and working practices of the Royal Navy as a whole.

Churchill, watching then from his position at the Home Office, was certainly of the view that the drawbacks were outweighed by the dramatic impetus, technology and strength that Fisher brought to the management and effectiveness of the navy, and he would write later that he was utterly convinced that these factors contributed to a German defeat in not one but two world wars. Not least in importance was creating a career structure and promotion possibilities previously unheard of in the Royal Navy.

Churchill himself became a champion of these changes when he assumed the role of First Lord of the Admiralty in October 1911, having sought the advice of Fisher before proceeding. In his biography of his father, *Young Statesman, 1901–1914*, Randolph

S. Churchill wrote that in naval matters Fisher had been Churchill's mentor. Thus, the very first thing the new First Lord did on reaching his office was to seek counsel from his friend, and on 23 October 1911 he wrote: 'I want to see you vy much. When am I to have that pleasure? You have but to indicate your convenience & I will await you at the Admiralty.'

Pay and conditions of disciplinary treatment were among Churchill's early priorities. Having overseen social reform in his earlier duties at both the Board of Trade and the Home Office, he took up what he described as Fisher's 'vigorous assault' on the navy. He considered that pay was the most pressing item. It had remained almost unchanged for 60 years, and he persuaded Lloyd George at the Treasury in Asquith's government to allow the pay of older able seamen to be raised by 3d. a day to 1s. 11d. and that of petty officers by 6d. a day to 3s. 2d. It was less than he had campaigned for, but it was well received by the men.

Churchill then moved on to the thorny issue of naval discipline. He set up a committee under Admiral Brock and after thorough investigation, with written and verbal evidence from across the spectrum of naval personnel, recommended major changes in the administering of punishments by commanding officers. A complete overhaul in the internal administration of ships was quickly introduced. Promotion was also studied again, and whereas a number of elderly warrant officers were commissioned as a reward for long service but never went to sea as officers, Churchill introduced a scheme by which for the first time young warrant and petty officers could be given educational training ashore and then sent to sea as officers. This was an immediate success and was later expanded, much to the delight of the lower decks whose talents were at last to be revealed and recognised.

Churchill also pursued other major advances that were under way when Jackie Fisher retired in 1910. He had left a legacy of big ships and big guns, and another on the drawing board with more revolutionary assets was the massive *Queen Elizabeth*-class battleships armed with 15-inch guns but fuelled by oil instead of coal, once again stealing a lead over Germany. He had also pushed ahead with submarine development, particularly in the use of diesel engines, which was a great stride both in efficiency and safety. But there was one further aspect that Fisher studied, and which Churchill initiated, which in turn brought a rapid and long-lasting contribution to the strength and capability of the Royal Navy.

He introduced the idea that the British Senior Service should join the new era of flight. As early as 1909, when the British army somewhat tardily took responsibility for the formation of an air force, the navy was already looking at ways of equipping itself with both airships and aeroplanes. By 1911, water-borne takeoffs and landings had been successfully achieved with planes adapted with skis in place of wheels – which Churchill christened 'seaplanes' – and in January 1912 a plane actually took off from a platform built over the forecastle of the battleship HMS *Africa*.

By the end of the year, approval had been obtained to convert the old light cruiser *Hermes* into a 'parent ship' for naval aircraft, which in fact became Britain's first aircraft carrier. The navy, now officially with its own flight wing under the title of the Royal Naval Air Service, placed *Hermes* in the annual review of ships in 1913, but sadly one of the seaplanes ran out of fuel and had to be rescued by a German ship – not that it made much difference. The Germans had long been aware of the British air operations, both with the navy's efforts and those of the Royal Flying Corps. Churchill ordered continued work and trials to perfect seaborne aircraft, and at the end of that year gave approval for the commissioning of a ship capable of carrying ten light planes, but the overall complement of naval aircraft went much deeper, as Churchill himself recorded in *The World Crisis*:

> The War Office claimed on behalf of the Royal Flying Corps complete and sole responsibility for the aerial defence of Great Britain. But owing to difficulties of getting money they were unable to make any provision for this responsibility. Seeing this, and finding myself able to procure funds by various shifts and devices, I began in 1912 to form under the Royal Naval Air Service flights of aeroplanes as well as seaplanes for the aerial protection of our naval harbours, oil tanks and vulnerable points. In consequence, I had in my own hand on the eve of the war fifty efficient naval machines or

about one-third the number in the possession of the army. The War Office viewed this development with disfavour and claimed they alone should be charged with the responsibility of home defence. When asked how they proposed to discharge this duty, they admitted sorrowfully that they had not got the machines and could not get the money. They adhered, however, to the principle.

It was the final piece of the complete overhaul of naval thinking controversially instigated by Fisher and his committee of reformers, and continued under Churchill's administration.

Nor had the navy seen the last of Jackie Fisher.

# CHAPTER TWO

## And So to War . . .

In a dozen years, the Royal Navy had changed beyond recognition. The colourful traditions of Queen Victoria's navy had been virtually obliterated, not without howls of protest, although there remained a large number of ships built during that era which, in the event of war, would have to face an enemy whose capital ships would blast them out of the water. The pace of change had been incredible: dreadnoughts, submarines, aircraft carriers, not to mention the technology that brought turbine power, big guns, long-range firing and wireless telegraphy. Supremacy was claimed, but the Royal Navy had not been seriously tested in battle for almost a hundred years, and the German fleet gathering its own momentum across the North Sea was looking menacingly ready to mount such a challenge, in which case all previous concepts of naval warfare would be of little value.

To some extent, Jackie Fisher had left a gaping hole in the handbook of tactics and strategy, but before he retired he did set in motion important steps to reorganise the navy into three distinct operational fleets in order to diminish the risk to older ships. The first fleet contained all the latest hardware led by the dreadnought battleships, along with cruisers, destroyers and torpedo boats. The second was classed as an operational reserve: strong but older ships, manned by reduced crews in peacetime, but kept at a state of permanent readiness. The third element comprised the oldest and least potent ships.

An emergency mobilisation plan to test the effectiveness of bringing these three parts into operation in the event of war had been prepared and would be staged when the latest new battleships had been released into service. Churchill's warnings of the possibility of early war with Germany continued to bear fruit in terms of his naval budget. Four capital ships were laid down in British shipyards in 1911 with another four scheduled for the 1912–13 programme. Approval had also been given for the recruitment of thousands of additional seamen. King George V, who succeeded to the throne on the death of Edward VII in April 1910, took a great interest in these remarkable developments in a navy that now bore little resemblance to that in which he had served for 15 years. Nor was he backward in making his views known on issues ranging from senior appointments to the naming of new ships. The latter caused some lengthy and heated exchanges of correspondence between himself and Churchill when, for example, the names *Africa*, *Liberty*, *Assiduous* and (somewhat mischievously) *Oliver Cromwell* were suggested by Churchill for the new ships laid down in 1911.

The King would accept only *Africa*, and he proposed *Delhi*, *Wellington* and *Marlborough* for the remaining three. Churchill agreed to *Marlborough*, changed *Wellington* to (the second) *Iron Duke* and opposed *Delhi*. The King wrote back, through his secretary, insisting that he would prefer to keep *Delhi*, to mark India's change of capital, and Churchill finally accepted that suggestion. A similar exchange followed over the next batch of four, and once again the name *Oliver Cromwell* appeared on Churchill's list. The King was furious and dictated a blunt refusal. Churchill came back with the response that Cromwell was one of the founders of the navy and 'scarcely any man did so much for it'. After further exchanges, the King made it clear he had no intention of giving way, and Churchill eventually accepted his suggestion of *Valiant* and so Oliver Cromwell remained without the honour in the name game.

With new ships coming into service, the Test Mobilisation was scheduled for the summer of 1914. By pure coincidence, events abroad suddenly made this trial imperative. On 28 June 1914 Archduke Franz Ferdinand of Austria-Hungary was assassinated while on a visit to Sarajevo. To a public and political arena in Europe then, as now, already hardened to bloody outrages in the Balkans, the ramifications were not immediately recognised. Indeed, it was initially viewed as an irrelevance in terms of European peace and, at that moment, had no bearing on Churchill issuing orders for the Test Mobilisation, which would take the form of a grand review of the entire British fleet massed at Spithead. The ships began assembling there on 18 July 1914, and the event was staged to perfection. King George took the salute aboard the royal yacht *Victoria and Albert* on 20 July and on a balmy summer's day the miles of marine might – virtually the entire stock of the Royal Navy – steamed past: 26 dreadnought battleships and battle cruisers, 38 pre-dreadnoughts and 123 cruisers, 228 destroyers and a multitude of lesser craft and submarines, together numbering in excess of 400 ships.

Churchill described it as 'incomparably the greatest assemblage of naval power ever witnessed in the history of the world'. The fleet then put to sea for exercises and completed the Test Mobilisation on 23 July, after which the ships prepared to disperse to their home ports or stations, or go on leave. At least that was the plan, but even as they turned for home a general alert was issued to all ships; all leave cancelled; all commands to remain on high alert and await further orders. On 24 July the assassination of a relatively unimportant Austrian royal suddenly escalated into a crisis of unexpected proportions.

The Austrian government issued a blunt ultimatum to Serbia, demanding that an Austrian force should enter the country to search for those who may have plotted the archduke's murder. The ultimatum came like a thunderbolt to the governments of Europe, especially when the German Kaiser, Wilhelm II, pledged his support for Austria before leaving for his annual yachting holiday in Norway. It seemed that even he was not quite expecting events to turn so quickly, but within the week the Kaiser returned home to declare war on his cousin, Tsar Nicholas II of Russia, who had sided with Serbia. On 3 August the Kaiser signed a similar order against France, and the following day Wilhelm's British cousin,

King George, was informed by Prime Minister Herbert Asquith that Britain was at war with Germany. The news brought cheering crowds thronging into the streets, given that the popular news-papers had been whipping up something of a frenzy of anti-German feeling. This aspect alone was to have an unexpected and quite remarkable effect on the management of the Royal Navy at its most crucial moment in history.

The story dated back to the retirement of Jackie Fisher. Between then and 1913, Churchill had lost two First Sea Lords, one who resigned over differences with the First Lord on pay and manning, and the other who retired after only months in the job because he was 'feeling unwell'. In the meantime, Churchill had controversially appointed a brilliant young naval officer known to all as Louis Battenberg as Second Sea Lord. The problem with Louis, in the British navy, was that he was a German prince who spoke with a strong German accent, a fact which had already held back earlier promotion. The Battenbergs came from a minor princely house linked to the mighty Hesse dynasty. There was much contact between them and the British royal house, which still traded under the family name of Saxe-Coburg-Gotha. It had been Queen Victoria's dream that the inter-relationship across the royal houses of Europe would eventually bring peace and stability, which of course it did not.

Prince Louis of Battenberg spent much of his early life in Britain through his connections with the British royal family and subsequently joined the Royal Navy. He also married Princess Victoria of Hess,* daughter of Queen Victoria's third child Princess Alice in her marriage to Grand Duke Louis IV of Hesse. As such, Prince Louis became a cousin by marriage to the future King George V, and they served together as officers in the navy. George left to assume the mantle of Prince of Wales while Louis rose to the rank of vice-admiral in spite of the aura of hostility that emanated from some of his colleagues, a young man with a foreign accent and connected to royalty who advanced rapidly. Yet many admired him, and Churchill's appointment of Prince Louis as Second Sea Lord was applauded by Lord Selborne, a former

* Prince Louis of Battenberg and Princess Victoria were also the grandparents of Prince Philip, future consort of Queen Elizabeth II.

First Lord, who wrote that Louis was 'the ablest officer the navy possesses and, if his name had been Smith, he would 'ere now have filled various high offices to the great advantage of the country, from which he has been excluded owing to what I must characterise as a stupid timidity'.

Such praise did not wash with some elements of the British press and certainly not the public. Soon after war was declared, agitation against all things German erupted, particularly over princes linked to the British royal family, who were resident in England but had German titles. German businesses were attacked and 'spies' were suspected everywhere. Then, as two German battleships, *Goeben* and *Breslau*, slipped the Royal Navy net at the outset of the war and sailed on to Turkey, newspapers rounded on Prince Louis, by now promoted to First Sea Lord, all but accusing him of treachery and pointing out that in spite of his British residency he had maintained his strong family connections in Germany. But then, so had the British royal house. In fact, the German ships were sighted by a British cruiser squadron, but in confusion over the interpretation of a telegram from Churchill instructing the Grand Fleet not to challenge enemy ships of greater firepower unless they were certain of success, the battleships were left to proceed on their journey.

The pressure relating to Louis Battenberg's German ancestry, however, was such that he resigned immediately, and King George was obliged to condone what amounted in reality to the dismissal of an in-law whose capacity he much admired, not to mention the family relationship.* King George was at the same time forced to

---

* Subsequently, the King ordered a review of all Germanic connections within his family, which resulted in name changes, both his own and others resident in England. The monarchy adopted the name of the House of Windsor. Battenberg changed his name to Mountbatten and soon after was given the title of the first Marquess of Milford Haven. His younger son, Louis, already at naval college, suffered similar taunts to those of his father but recovered later in life to rise to high office and leadership in the Second World War when Churchill, by then Prime Minister, appointed him to positions that his father was denied, resulting in his becoming Earl Mountbatten of Burma. The eldest of the Battenberg children, Princess Alice, married the impoverished Prince Andrew of Greece, and their youngest child Philip married the future Queen Elizabeth II in 1947.

give his assent to the appointment of Prince Louis' successor of First Sea Lord to lead the Royal Navy into battle.

The selection of a suitable candidate for the role was one which caused Churchill considerable anguish. In the end he settled on demanding the return of Jackie Fisher, who was then 74 years old and had been out of office for almost five years. The choice was not a popular one with the navy, or the King. According to his biographer, Harold Nicolson, Fisher was a man in whom George V now 'placed little reliance'. Nicolson quoted an entry in the King's diary for that day:

> October 20, 1914: Spent a most worrying and trying day . . . At 11.30 saw Winston Churchill who informed me that Louis of Battenberg had resigned his appt. as First Sea Lord. The Press & Public have said so many things against him being born a German, & that he ought not to be at the head of the Navy, that it was best for him to go. I feel deeply for him: there is no more loyal man in the Country. Churchill then proposed that Lord Fisher shd. succeed him as First Sea Lord. I did all I could to prevent it & told him he was not trusted by the Navy & they had no confidence in him personally. I think it is a great mistake. At the end I had to give in with great reluctance.

Other detractors pointed out that Fisher had aged, and his opinions changed from day to day. Prime Minister Asquith was questioned on the appointment and replied that he gathered from Churchill that there was no one else suitable and that the Admiralty Board (consisting of four of the navy's most senior officers) was weak and incapable of initiative. King George did not let his protest rest there. He later wrote to the Prime Minister: 'I should like to note that, while approving the proposed appointment of Lord Fisher as First Sea Lord, I do so with some reluctance and misgivings. I readily acknowledge his great ability and administrative powers, but at the same time I cannot help feeling that his presence at the Admiralty will not inspire the Navy with that confidence which ought to exist, especially when we are engaged in so momentous a war. I hope that my fears may prove groundless.'

Churchill was given the benefit of the doubt as the Royal Navy entered the fray against this unfortunate background of inter-necine conflict and rivalry. However, Britain did have a numerical advantage in terms of ships. In August 1914 the Royal Navy had 26 capital ships ready and another 13 under construction, while Germany had 18, with nine being built. What soon became clear, however, was that the strategy of both navies was to steer away from direct confrontation, and certainly they wanted to avoid a head-to-head between the massed ships in the style of great naval battles of the past. The British approach was chiefly to protect their trade routes and merchant ships, while the Germans kept their fleet pretty well out of sight and concentrated their efforts on spreading minefields on British routes, making occasional attack-ing sorties with two or three ships, but focused heavily on building their submarine fleet in the hope of picking off some of Britain's finest ships without exposing Germany's own new hardware to risk.

The British naval strategy initially was to keep a heavy presence of its big guns in the North Sea to keep the Germans bottled up by blocking the exits at the Strait of Dover and between Scotland and Norway so that the Kaiser would think twice about risking any large-scale manoeuvres by the German fleet. Commanded by Admiral John Jellicoe, the Grand Fleet was to operate largely from the naval base at Scapa Flow, in the Orkney Islands. The desolate site offered good natural protection, studded with numerous islets and almost entirely landlocked. It became a place of high activity, as Midshipman Robert John Shaw recalls. He was one of ten children of a country vicar, with three brothers (all subsequently killed in the war) and six sisters. He joined the Royal Navy College, which was housed in the converted stables of Queen Victoria's house on the Isle of Wight. He then went to Dartmouth Naval College, by then the accepted route for those intending a career in the Royal Navy:

At the beginning of the war, Dartmouth was cleared out completely of all cadets aged 15 and over. They were all transferred for duty aboard ships of the fleet, and in my case I became a midshipman on one of the early

39

dreadnoughts, *Hercules*, which was coal fuelled. We were keen to get into the war, doing all we could to get into the ships that we felt would be in the limelight, such as battle cruisers and so on. Luckily, I did not get to a cruiser; in my group of 78 from Dartmouth, 16 were in fact killed at the Battle of Jutland [see Chapter Three] when they were only 16 years old. *Hercules* was an early pre-war battleship after *Dreadnought* herself. There was only one other similar one in the fleet, *Colossus*, which had on board a sub-lieutenant at that stage [the King's second son, Prince Albert] who later became King George VI.

The Grand Fleet spent all its time up at Scapa when not at sea on exercises or looking for the Germans for a scrap. Every three months, squadrons in turn went down to Invergordon, basically for a change of scenery. There was nothing at all at Scapa, although the fleet commanders later built a golf course on one of the islands. But the fleet was always at four hours' notice to go to sea, and occasionally, if there were potential threats, two hours'. Eventually we were there waiting to go to sea straight away if it became necessary. Also, every time we came into harbour, a collier pulled alongside for us to take on fuel. As usual, everyone in the ship's company would participate, going into the collier's hold, loading up sacks, and for hours afterwards the ship was always full of coal dust, you couldn't help breathing it in. We never really got rid of it.

The first significant encounter between the two navies came on 28 August 1914, when a strong British force of cruisers, destroyers and submarines entered German home waters off Heligoland Bight. The British contingent was known as the Harwich Force, which for this operation comprised two light cruisers, *Fearless* and *Arethusa*, with two flotillas of destroyers, and they set out to raid German shipping located close to the German naval base at Heligoland. The 1st Battle Cruiser Squadron was sent to give further weight to the attack, sailing from the naval base at Scapa Flow under the command of Vice-Admiral Sir David Beatty. His squadron consisted of the battleships *New Zealand* and *Invincible*, plus three battle cruisers. The Harwich Force began the action by sinking two German torpedo boats, but the Germans responded by rapidly deploying six light cruisers whose joint firepower left the Harwich ships substantially outgunned and under incessant fire, and, with *Arethusa* heavily damaged, the Harwich commander signalled for assistance from Beatty's squadron, then some 25 miles to the north.

Beatty arrived within the hour and immediately opened fire, sinking three German cruisers – *Mainz*, *Köln* and *Ariadne* – and damaging three others. The remaining German ships turned and ran for cover in the mist, leaving 1,200 of their men dead or captured, against just 35 British fatalities. The Admiralty was delighted with the result of this first battle of the war and issued a directive in the following terms:

For each ship which was engaged in the recent action in the Heligoland Bight, whether damaged or not, the words 'Heligoland August 28th 1914' are to be painted in gold letters in some convenient place. Further, in the case of HMS *Arethusa* (which was damaged after some particularly noteworthy action) My Lords have decided that the following verses are to be engraved upon a brass plate and fixed in a conspicuous place in the ship:

> Come all ye jolly Sailors bold,
> Whose hearts are cast in honour's mould,
> While English Glory I unfold,
> Huzza for the 'Arethusa'!
> Her men are staunch
> To their fav'rite launch,
> And when the foe shall meet our fire,
> Sooner than strike, we'll all expire
> On board of the 'Arethusa'.
>
> And now we've driven the foe ashore,
> Never to fight with Britons more,
> Let each fill his glass
> To his fav'rite lass;

A health to our Captain and Officers true,
And all that belong to the jovial crew,
On board of the 'Arethusa'.

Thereafter, the Germans were somewhat timorous with their big ships, sending out only hit-and-run squadrons until their submarine fleet was large enough to spearhead the assault. This enabled the expanding British Expeditionary Force to be ferried across the English Channel to France with barely a hitch. In fact, it was this uninterrupted service protected and managed by the Royal Navy that Churchill highlighted as a major contributing factor to the eventual Allied victory over the Germans, although for tens of thousands of parents and wives it represented a moving platform along which their sons and husbands were being herded to horrific experiences and death as war in the trenches ground on to one of appalling attrition.

By early autumn the Germans began to see success through U-boat attacks and their policy of mass dispersal of mines. On 22 September a single submarine sank three British cruisers within an hour off the Netherlands. Hundreds of seamen survived this first initial attack, but no sooner had they been picked from the water by a cruiser that had escaped destruction than it, too, was sunk by a torpedo, throwing them into the sea again, with heavy losses. The mining of the seas around Britain, however, was also hitting shipping routes badly, and not just warships. The light cruiser *Amphion* was the first British warship to be hit, on 6 August, but a number of fishing vessels and neutral ships sank after striking mines in the North Sea, leading the British Admiralty to protest that Germany was laying them indiscriminately, using merchantmen rather than expensive warships to do so. Britain had refused to lay mines, claiming it was still possible to keep the sea lanes open to commerce. Other early casualties of this strategy included the torpedo gunboat HMS *Speedy*, which struck a mine 30 miles off the east coast, the cruiser *Pathfinder* and the liner SS *Runo*, which sank off Hull with 300 Russian refugees on board; most survived due to prompt rescue by a nearby fishing fleet. Britain's biggest loss to mines in the North Sea, however, occurred on 27 October when one of the navy's newest battleships,

*Audacious*, was sunk. She was a *King George* V-class super-dreadnought and had only completed her sea trials a matter of months earlier, carrying the latest powerful 13.5 inch guns. Later investigation revealed that she had fallen victim to mines laid only three days earlier by the German minelayer *Berlin*, a converted liner, close to shipping lanes off the north coast of Ireland. Having disposed of her cargo of 200 mines, *Berlin* headed for home but suffered mechanical problems and the German crew was forced to offer themselves and their ship into internment at Trondheim, Norway.

The sinking of *Audacious* occurred at the time the Grand Fleet was using a base on the coast of Northern Ireland while new anti-submarine defences were being installed at Scapa Flow. After breakfast on 27 October, the heavyweight 2nd Battle Squadron, consisting of the super-dreadnoughts *Centurion*, *Ajax*, *Audacious*, *King George* V, *Orion*, *Monarch* and *Thunderer*, left port for exercises at sea. As they rounded the coast, *Audacious* struck one of *Berlin*'s mines, blasting a hole in the starboard side and killing a number of men in the engine room. Her commander, Captain Dampier, attempted to turn and head back to base, but the damage was too great to contain the flooding and eventually all engines stopped. All but essential crew were evacuated while efforts were made to put *Audacious* under tow with the light cruiser *Liverpool* and two destroyers, but the towlines parted and the giant vessel sank lower into the water. The rescuers battled for eight hours until early evening, when the order was given to abandon her. Just before nine that night, *Audacious* capsized and sank. This was indeed a major blow, and was not revealed until after the war, at least not in Britain. However, American travellers on board the liner SS *Olympic* took photographs of the stricken ship which were published in US newspapers.

There was an appalling accidental tragedy, too, destroying HMS *Bulwark*, the fifth ship to carry one of the most famous names in British naval history. She was a 15,000-ton twin-screw armoured battleship, launched in 1899 and once commanded by Captain R.F. Scott, who later came to fame as the Antarctic explorer. She exploded while taking on ammunition off Sheerness on

26 November 1914. There were only 12 survivors from a ship's company of 750. The explosion shocked a nervous British public, who were being warned to expect the possibility of aerial bombing from Zeppelin attacks, but in fact the next move by the Germans was totally unexpected and brought panic down the east coast of England.

On 15 December three battle cruisers of the German High Seas Fleet set off on a sortie across the North Sea under the command of Rear-Admiral Franz von Hipper. Evading the Royal Navy's protective shield, they loomed out of the mist and began bombarding the seaside towns of Scarborough, Whitby and Hartlepool. Over 200 shells rained down on the towns, killing more than 100 civilians and injuring 400 others. Many buildings, including resort hotels and churches, were damaged. Two destroyers in the British flotilla arrived to drive the Germans off but were also hit, with several seamen killed. In the following month Hipper set out on a similar mission, but this time his sortie was intercepted by the British in what became known as the Battle of Dogger Bank.

Hipper led a force comprising three battle cruisers, the armoured cruiser *Blücher*, which was claimed to be the most powerful in the world, four light cruisers and a number of torpedo boats. Their intentions were uncovered by the British Admiralty's deciphering service 'Room 40', and the Harwich Force of light cruisers and destroyers under Commodore Tyrwhitt was sent to intercept from the south, and Vice-Admiral Sir David Beatty came from the north with his battle cruiser group consisting of his own ship *Lion* followed by *Tiger*, *Princess Royal* and, bringing up the rear, the older *New Zealand* and *Indomitable*. At daybreak on 24 January, the German flotilla was spotted off the coast of Great Yarmouth, and the Harwich Force moved in. The Germans squared for battle when their light cruiser *Kolberg* signalled the sighting of the British light cruiser *Aurora*. Both opened fire and took a couple of hits. The German commander was convinced that the British opposition consisted of the light enemy units from Harwich and had already turned to engage them when Beatty's battle cruisers appeared on the northern horizon.

Hipper decided to make a quick exit, and a running battle developed across the North Sea with Beatty's battle cruisers pursuing at fast pace, reaching 27 knots, while the Germans were held back by the slower *Blücher*, which eventually dropped out of the line and fell within range of the British guns and torpedoes. The Germans returned fire and nominated Beatty's ship as the prime target and scored a dozen hits in quick succession. *Lion* was out of the fight and dropped back. The damage to Beatty's ship was so severe that he had no power or wireless contact. A signalling error during the transmission of his orders to the rest of his ships sent them in the wrong direction towards *Blücher*, thus allowing the rest of Hipper's flotilla to make a run for it.

*Blücher*, meanwhile, had taken heavy punishment and was further hammered until the battle cruiser rolled over and capsized on Dogger Bank. A photograph taken from a battleship became one of the most famous naval shots of the era, showing hundreds of sailors either in the water or clambering on the overturned hull of the ship. Unfortunately, the British rescue operation to collect survivors had to be called off when a Zeppelin 1.5 and a seaplane appeared overhead and began bombing the British ships. The Germans suffered almost 1,000 casualties and 189 captured, while the British recorded losses of 15 killed and 32 wounded.

Both British and German battle groups went home with their tails between their legs. The actions of neither on that day could be classed as a successful outcome. The Germans had lost a great ship and taken heavy casualties but had inflicted only repairable damage on the enemy. For Beatty, it was even more of a horror story. True, they had sunk *Blücher* (see first picture section) but nothing else had gone right: the best ships had been allowed to get away, highlighting signalling errors and, more important, the poor accuracy of the British gunnery units. During the engagement, well over 1,100 shells were fired by the British group, yet fewer than half a dozen hits were recorded against ships other than *Blücher*.

First Sea Lord Jack Fisher was not happy. He spotted the statistics immediately, but worst of all they had allowed the German squadron to escape. Beatty took some of the flak for his administration, though it did not appear to do him any harm in the long term. Whatever the shortcomings, it was a victory: a German ship lost and the others high-tailing it back to port. Similarly, Hipper was criticised for taking *Blücher* in the first place.

One lesson the Germans did greatly profit from, however, was that concerning the damage caused to one of Hipper's ships, *Seydlitz*. The barbette of the rear gun turret took a direct hit and the resultant fire caught hold of the store of shell propellant. The flames shot into the turret itself, and into the second turret, killing both turret crews, 154 men in all. An investigation revealed the cause and the effects, which were in fact not uncommon. But the German navy commanders took steps to reduce the amount of propellant kept in the gun turrets to curtail the risk of explosion. As will be seen from later eyewitnesses' accounts from the Battle of Jutland, it was a lesson that the British were slow to take up. In fact, this battle showed up a number of flaws on both sides to which the Germans probably paid greater attention than the British.

These, then, were the developments in home waters, but there was even more dramatic action abroad on the high seas involving the Germans' most powerful surface force under one of their most revered naval officers, Admiral Graf Maximilian von Spee. He was leading a squadron of Germany's fastest and most powerful cruisers, including *Scharnhorst*, *Gneisenau* and *Nürnberg*, which had been operating in the eastern waters of South-East Asia. Spee's group moved without serious challenge across the Pacific Ocean, and another of Germany's fastest ships, *Emden*, joined the squadron in August 1914 but later moved on to cause havoc in the Indian Ocean.

For months, these cruisers were a threat to merchant shipping on the British trade routes and to troopships on their way to Europe or the Middle East from India, New Zealand or Australia. *Emden* had been especially successful, sinking merchant ships in the Bay of Bengal, bombarding Madras in September and then moving on to cause further mayhem in the approaches to Ceylon – all of which were vital routes for Britain. By the end of October, *Emden* had been credited with the single-handed sinking of 15 Allied ships. Her luck ran out off the Cocos Islands on 9 November 1914 when she was caught by an Australian squadron and sunk by the cruiser *Sydney*.

Admiral von Spee, meanwhile, moved across the Pacific in September towards the South American coast for her transport vessels to take on supplies and coal. Off the Chilean coast, the group was joined by two additional cruisers, *Leipzig* and *Dresden*, an accumulation of five exceedingly potent ships under Spee's command. Not unnaturally, British naval intelligence began to suspect that some new action on the vital trade routes around the west coast of South America was being planned. This was eventually confirmed by intercepted radio communications, and the Admiralty in London decided to send the only squadron available in that region, the West Indies patrol group under Sir Christopher Cradock, which at that time was in the Atlantic patrolling the eastern coastline of South America.

Cradock was not, at that time, told of the strength of Spee's force and was undoubtedly given the impression that he could take the Germans on. In any event, he had to: those were his orders. But as he would soon discover, his squadron of old tubs would be hopelessly outclassed by the Germans. Cradock's own flagship was the ageing cruiser *Good Hope*, which had just come out of the reserve fleet and was manned by an inexperienced crew. He had the armoured cruiser *Monmouth*, which was notoriously under-armed for a ship of her size and too slow to make a quick getaway should the need arise – and it certainly would. Next was the armed merchant cruiser *Otranto*, which was a converted liner with eminently visible vast smokestacks, especially in silhouette, and was also short on gunnery strength. Only the light cruiser *Glasgow* was up to date and well equipped and carried a well-trained crew.

To strengthen this totally outgunned force, the Admiralty sent another ancient battleship *Canopus*, also from the reserve stock, entirely manned by reservists who, courageous though they were, had never fired the ship's guns in anger. Worse, *Canopus* developed engine trouble on the way and could travel at only 12 knots. One other armoured cruiser, *Defence*, was also supposedly on her way to join the patrol, but in fact never arrived at the rendezvous point in the Falkland Islands, where Cradock was to establish his base.

At the end of October Cradock sent *Glasgow* on an intelligence-gathering mission along the Chilean coastline, where she picked up radio transmissions between one of Spee's ships, *Leipzig* and her collier. On 1 November Cradock sailed to make his challenge, although he must have known in his heart of hearts that London had sent him on a fool's errand that would surely end in the sacrifice of his brave sailors, many of whom should not have been put in this position in the first place. Just off the coastal town of Coronel, 300 miles south of Valparaiso, they made contact and Cradock formed his line of ships, which comprised his own inaptly named *Good Hope* along with *Monmouth, Glasgow* and *Otranto*. *Canopus* was still limping behind. When he spotted the opposition, Spee had formed a battle line of *Scharnhorst, Gneisenau, Leipzig* and *Dresden*. His fifth, *Nürnberg*, was still some 30 miles north.

The British line turned towards the Germans at about 1930 and found themselves silhouetted against the setting sun. They made the approach, but at 11,500 yards the German armoured cruisers opened fire. *Scharnhorst* hit the British flagship with her third salvo and a wall of flame shot skywards. *Monmouth* was also hit immediately by *Gneisenau's* guns. Once they had found their range and with the flames presenting an easy target, the German ships let rip before the British really had a chance to mount an effective reply. Shell after shell hit the two British cruisers, while *Leipzig* and *Glasgow* also engaged and *Dresden* took on *Otranto*. The latter realised the hopelessness of the situation and pulled back out of the line, leaving *Dresden* free to join *Leipzig* against *Glasgow*.

Just 20 minutes after the battle began, Cradock's *Good Hope* was wrecked by a magazine explosion. She went down in minutes without survivors. *Monmouth* was also crippled and listing to port. She was already beyond help when *Nürnberg* arrived to join the battle, and five more shells finished her off. She, too, sank without survivors. *Glasgow*, meanwhile, had taken half a dozen hits but was still operational and pulled out to fight another day. Slow-coach *Canopus* was also warned to turn back, and so three ships were saved. The cost of this mismatched mission, now in history as the Battle of Coronel, was 1,600 British lives, a bloody nightmare for the seamen – and the Royal Navy's first major defeat for almost a century.

The shock in London was immense and immediately a revenge attack was planned, with First Sea Lord Fisher and Churchill personally involved. A British force, strong enough to hunt down and sink the German squadron, was ordered to prepare immediately under the leadership of the eminent and – this time – more aptly named Rear-Admiral Sir Doveton Sturdee. He would take two modern battle cruisers, *Invincible* and *Inflexible*, each equipped with eight 12-inch guns, and no fewer than six other cruisers. All were to rendezvous off the Brazilian coast and then sail south to the Falkland Islands. It was an impressive sight: *Invincible*, *Inflexible* and the cruisers HMS *Bristol*, *Carnarvon*, *Cornwall* and *Kent*. To these were added the remains of Cradock's squadron, *Glasgow* and *Canopus*, already at Port Stanley, as well as the armed merchant cruiser *Macedonia*.

Apparently unaware of the strength of the newly arrived British force, Admiral von Spee was already moving south towards the Falklands to perform what he believed would be a second great victory. Sturdee's squadron arrived at the Falkland Islands on the evening of 7 December 1914. Coaling was commenced at once so that the ships would be ready to begin the search for the enemy the next day. At 8 a.m. on the following day a signal was received from a station on shore that a four-funnel and two-funnel man-o'-war, in sight from Sapper Hill, were steering northwards. The following recollections of Captain J.D. Allen, on HMS *Kent*, provide a commentary of the opening stages of a battle that was to last over 12 hours:

Just under half an hour after the signal was received, *Kent* was under way and steaming down the harbour past the flagship. A general signal had been made for all ships to raise steam for full speed. The flagship signalled to *Kent* to proceed to the entrance to the harbour and wait there for further orders. From aloft we could now see over the land . . . the German cruisers *Gneisenau* and *Nürnberg* approaching the harbour. We hoisted three ensigns, including the silk ensign and Union Jack which had been presented to *Kent* by the ladies of the county of Kent and which we had promised to hoist if ever we went into action.

*Gneisenau* and *Nürnberg* came steadily on towards the harbour until they were only 14,000 yards from *Kent*. . .

Suddenly we heard *Canopus* open fire on them with her 12-inch guns across the land, and we saw the shell strike the water a few hundred yards short of the German ships. This must have surprised them, as *Canopus* was hidden behind the land. About this time also they must have caught sight of the tripod masts of *Invincible* and *Inflexible*, as they immediately turned round and made off. We could now see the smoke of three more cruisers coming up from the southward: these were *Scharnhorst*, *Dresden* and *Leipzig*. *Glasgow* was now coming down the harbour, and soon afterwards *Invincible* and *Inflexible* came out, followed by *Cornwall* and *Carnarvon*. The admiral now signalled to *Kent* to proceed and observe the enemy's movements, keeping out of range. Off we went at full speed ahead in the direction of the enemy's ships, clearly in sight to the south-east, hull down.

Presently *Glasgow* came along at full speed and passed us, then out came *Invincible* and *Inflexible* sending up great columns of black smoke, then *Carnarvon* and *Cornwall*. It was a magnificent sight. It was a glorious day, just like a fine spring day in England, a smooth sea, a bright sun, a light breeze from the north-west. Right ahead of us we could see the masts, funnels and smoke of the five German cruisers, all in line abreast and steaming straight away from us. At 10.20 a.m. the signal was made for a general chase, and off we all went as hard as we could go. It was only a question of who could steam the fastest. *Invincible* and *Inflexible* were increasing speed every minute, and soon passed *Kent*. They were now steaming at 25 knots and were rapidly gaining on the enemy . . .

The continuing drama of this action is covered step by step in the formal report of the action by Rear-Admiral Doveton Sturdee to London:

The two leading ships of the enemy, *Gneisenau* and *Nürnberg*, with guns trained on the wireless station, came within range of *Canopus*, who opened fire at them across the low land at a range of 11,000 yards. The enemy at once hoisted their colours and turned away. At this time the masts and smoke of the enemy were visible from the upper bridge of the *Invincible* at a range of approximately 17,000 yards across the low lands to the south of Port William. A few minutes later the two cruisers altered course to port, as though to close the *Kent* at the entrance to the harbour, but about this time it seems that *Invincible* and *Inflexible* were seen over the land, as the enemy at once altered course and increased speed to join their consorts.

The signal for a general chase was made . . . [and with] the enemy maintaining their distance, and [after almost two hours of cat-and-mouse manoeuvres] the action finally developed into three separate encounters. The fire of the [British] battle cruisers was directed on *Scharnhorst* and *Gneisenau*. The effect of this was quickly seen and [after a battle lasting almost 90 minutes] *Scharnhorst* caught fire forward . . . and *Gneisenau* was badly hit. The effect of the fire on *Scharnhorst* became more and more apparent . . . There was a large [shell] hole in her side, through which could be seen a dull red glow of flame. At 4.40 p.m. *Scharnhorst*, whose flag remained flying to the last, suddenly listed heavily to port, and within a minute it became clear that she was a doomed ship; for the list increased very rapidly until she lay on her beam ends and disappeared.

*Gneisenau* continued a determined but ineffectual effort to fight the two battle cruisers. At 5.08 p.m. the forward funnel was knocked over. She was evidently in serious straits, and her fire slackened very much. At 5.15 p.m. one of *Gneisenau*'s shells struck the *Invincible*; this was her last effective effort. She turned with a heavy list to starboard, and appeared stopped, with steam pouring from her escape-pipes, and smoke rising everywhere. About this time I ordered the signal 'Cease-fire', but before it was hoisted *Gneisenau* opened fire again, and continued to fire from time to time with a single gun. At 5.50 p.m. 'Cease-fire' was made [but ten minutes later] *Gneisenau* keeled over very suddenly, showing the men gathered on her decks and then walking on her side as she lay a minute on her beam ends before sinking. Prisoners of war from *Gneisenau* report that, by the time the ammunition was expended, some 600 men had been killed or wounded. The surviving officers and men were all ordered on deck and told to provide for themselves with hammocks and any articles that could support them in the water.

When the ship capsized and sank there were probably some 200 unwounded survivors in the water, but owing to the shock of the cold water, many were drowned within sight of the boats and ships. Every effort was made to save life as quickly as possible, both by boats and from the ships; lifebuoys were thrown and ropes lowered, but only a portion could be rescued. *Invincible* alone rescued 108 men, 14 of whom were found to be dead after being brought on board; these men were buried at sea the following day with full military honours.

The enemy's light cruisers, *Dresden*, *Nürnberg* and *Leipzig*, turned to starboard to escape . . . In accordance with my instructions, the *Glasgow*, *Kent* and *Cornwall* at once went in chase of these ships . . .

*Nürnberg* and *Leipzig* both came under heavy and sustained fire from British ships and both eventually sank, the last to go being *Nürnberg*, sunk at 7.27 p.m., and as she went down a group of men were waving a German ensign attached to a pole. Just 12 of the crew of the two ships were rescued, but only seven survived. British casualties from the entire operation this time numbered just 25. *Dresden*, meanwhile, managed to get ahead of the action due to her superior speed and in the fading light and closing weather escaped, for the time being at least. She was eventually caught and sunk off the Juan Fernández Islands on 14 March 1915, and her demise also marked a virtual end to Germany's attacks on British trading routes using surface vessels.

Instead, on 2 February Germany began its U-boat assault on supply routes around the British Isles and announced to all foreign shipping that if they got in the way they, too, would be sunk. Indeed, in the first month two American ships were sent to the bottom amid strong protests from Washington. Britain continued with its surface blockade of ships passing through the English

Channel and the North Sea as a tactic against Germany, and in the first 12 months of operating this policy British patrol ships halted and boarded for inspection more than 3,000 vessels, of which 743 were sent into port for examination. Outward-bound trade from Germany was brought to a complete standstill.

The Germans' retaliation with their submarine blockade was considerably more ruthless. On 30 January 1915 two Japanese liners, *Tokomaru* and *Ikaria*, were torpedoed without warning. In the face of mounting international protest, the Germans then insisted that they would treat the waters around the British Isles as a war zone in which all merchant ships would be destroyed, enemy or not. In the first week of the campaign, seven Allied or Allied-bound ships were sunk out of 11 attacked, but 1,370 others sailed without being harassed by the German submarines. But despite Britain's increasingly effective anti-submarine measures, including nets for battleships, armed merchant ships, depth bombs and hydrophones to locate submarine engines, the U-boat campaign gradually grew in its successes.

However, the sinking by a German submarine of the British liner *Lusitania* off the coast of Ireland on 7 May 1915 was a catastrophe from which the Germans, to this day, have not been forgiven. The ship, from New York to Liverpool, carried 2,000 civilian passengers, of whom 1,198 were drowned; they included many Americans. Even so, the US did no more than lodge a formal protest and stick to its policy of neutrality, which it continued to do even after the sinking of another liner, *Arabic*, five months later.

The German Grand Fleet, on the other hand, seldom ventured into the open after the destruction of Admiral von Spee's squadron in the Battle of the Falklands. It was a respite seriously needed by the Royal Navy, in that since the turn of the year it had become embroiled in a major battle elsewhere, one that remains among the most controversial campaigns involving the British military in the entire twentieth century.

# CHAPTER THREE

## Daring and Disaster

Further action in foreign parts was to form the focus of world attention on the Royal Navy as 1914 ticked into the New Year, and with it came a major split in the most senior of ranks. First Sea Lord Fisher was to have a very serious falling out with his great friend the First Lord, Winston Churchill, over unfolding developments in the eastern Mediterranean. It was, to be precise, the Dardanelles fiasco that caused the rift and, at its climax, brought a temporary halt to what the newspapers had described as Churchill's meteoric career. Fisher had angrily told the First Lord: 'Damn the Dardanelles. It will be our grave.' No one listened, and it would indeed become the place which saw half a million Allied and enemy casualties in one of the most ill-conceived campaigns of the war.

Britain's attention to the Dardanelles had been somewhat limited prior to the war, and in August 1914 diplomats bungled the chance of a pact with Turkey, which in turn then signed a treaty with Germany. This in effect gave the Germans virtual control of the Dardanelles, the long and narrow strait between the Aegean and the Sea of Marmara, which is connected to the Black Sea by the Bosporus. In return, Turkey received German military advisers, weapons and two brand-new ships, *Breslau*, a light cruiser, and a magnificent battle cruiser of 22,600 tons, *Goeben*, whose escape from Germany and into the Mediterranean past British patrols was in part responsible for the furore that led to the resignation of Louis Battenberg soon after the outbreak of war. The ships were harboured at Constantinople, and just to demonstrate whose side they were on the Turks unleashed their new big guns and sent them forth to bombard Russian Black Sea ports before returning to the safe haven of home waters.

Germany had long realised the potential benefits to the Allies if they ever took control of the Dardanelles. On 8 August 1914 navy minister Admiral Alfred von Tirpitz stated that 'should the Dardanelles fall, the war has been decided against us'. Consequently, the Germans decided to bolster Turkey's defence of the strait by dispatching 400 naval mine warfare experts, under the command of Vice-Admiral Guido von Usedom, who were hidden in the ranks of the Turkish military so as not to disrupt the Turks' continuing claim of neutrality. They were fooling no one, especially when the German experts began mining the strait in the most effective manner, under the overt leadership of the German navy's Rear-Admiral Wilhelm Souchon, who commanded the cruisers *Goeben* and *Breslau* and had now been seconded to the position of commander-in-chief of the Turkish navy.

On 27 September 1914 the Turks closed the strait by completing the minefields, effectively blockading all the Russian Black Sea ports to imports of necessary war supplies and halting exports of wheat to Europe and the United Kingdom, where they were especially needed. More than 120 Allied merchant ships were locked up in the Black Sea when the Turks sealed access to the Sea of Marmara and in turn into the Mediterranean through the Dardanelles strait and Aegean.

By the winter of 1914 the Russians were threatened by the Turks in the Caucasus and appealed to the British for some relieving action. Although it would stretch resources, Britain was happy to oblige – or at least Churchill and the British War Cabinet were. The British Cabinet was of the opinion that if Russia were strengthened, it would also help the Allies to overcome the horrendous stalemate on the Western Front and set free the grain-carrying ships bound for Britain.

Finally, the British War Cabinet approved an operation to open the Dardanelles strait using only a strong Royal Navy Task Force, including some heavyweight firepower. In theory, the ships were supposedly to go in with all guns blazing via the Mediterranean and the Aegean and blast their way through to the Black Sea. The plan was the brainchild of the Secretary of State for War, Field Marshal Horatio Kitchener. He argued that a successful naval assault on the Dardanelles would be equivalent to winning a campaign, and equally such a mobile force could be disengaged if it became necessary. Munitions Minister David Lloyd George agreed, and so did Prime Minister Herbert Asquith. 'One must take a lot of risks in war,' Asquith declared, 'and forcing the Dardanelles presents such a unique opportunity that we ought to hazard a lot elsewhere rather than forgo it.' At first Churchill did not like the plan, but later he fell in behind the others.

First Sea Lord Jack Fisher did not. In fact, he was horrified and saw huge dangers to his ships as they attempted to run the gauntlet of the heavily defended approach to the Marmara Sea from the Aegean. He also pointed out to Churchill that the Dardanelles strait had for centuries provided the Turks with a natural defence to Constantinople. It had become a focal point of history in that no attacking enemy craft had successfully negotiated the Dardanelles for a hundred years, although many had tried. It provided an easily defended passage, 40 miles long, running south out of the Marmara at the Gallipoli Peninsula into the Aegean Sea and on to the Mediterranean.

The geographical hazards of the Dardanelles provided the infrastructure for a superb defensive position. Although several miles from shore to shore at its widest points, the Dardanelles produced a natural rat-run 12 miles upstream from the Aegean known as the Narrows. The passage contained a dogleg hazard reducing to just over a mile in width. It was there that Alexander moved his armies by a bridge of boats in 334 BC and where it was swum in legend by Leander and in reality by Byron. The rocky banks of the strait were strewn with forts and fortified bunkers containing around 150 guns ranging from six to 14 inches in calibre. There were shore-mounted torpedo launchers, mobile howitzers, floating and fixed minefields and huge anti-submarine nets.

In December a large flotilla of British and French ships assembled off the Greek island of Limnos. It consisted of the new super-dreadnought HMS *Queen Elizabeth*, 16 pre-dreadnought battleships, a battle cruiser, five cruisers, 22 destroyers, 32 mine-sweeping trawlers, a seaplane-carrying ship and initially six small B-class submarines. This was the first time a submarine force had been used on such an operation, and for them it was a task fraught with danger. The type sent to the Dardanelles were based on the earliest of British submarines, originally designed for the defence of home waters. But their commanders made a big impression and their heroics matched those that some of the newer, larger boats were soon to follow. In all, it sounded an impressive force, but given that the capital ships required constant protection, 22 destroyers were barely enough to go round, and there was already a shortage of ammunition – a setback that was felt on both sides in the dash to keep up supplies to the disastrous events on the Western Front.

By then, the Germans were already one step ahead. Their own officers had moved in to take command of the fortifications and minefields of the Dardanelles and because of the shortage of ammunition had decided to depend heavily on the mining of the strait, a decision that was to have an early impact on the ability of the British force to make any headway. They created a defensive shield of 350 mines fixed in ten lines at intervals on the approach to the narrowest part of the Dardanelles and positioned these heavily mined areas so that they coincided with the guns of the forts. Where there were no forts, mobile guns were moved in. The effect would be a massive fireworks display from these emplacements and forts every time an enemy vessel as much as turned towards the Dardanelles strait.

To test the water, the minesweepers went in first, at night, followed by the submarines, whose crews were soon to discover that the sweepers were not especially effective against the minefields laid by the German technicians. The minesweepers were converted English trawlers still crewed by civilian fishermen. They operated in pairs of boats 500 yards apart, sweeping with a single 2.5-inch wire and a one-ton, twelve-foot-long 'kite' to regulate the wire's depth. They were also fitted with steel plating for personnel protection. It was very much a hit-and-miss affair, as would soon be discovered, and it was a submarine that made the first run under Lieutenant Norman Holbrook and his 12-men team in submarine *B11*. On the morning of 13 December 1914 he threw caution to the wind and decided to have a go at a hit-and-run raid. He warned his chaps that they might end up lunching with the fishes and then made a dash into the strait as fast as the little craft could carry them, for around 12 miles. He got through minefields at Sari Siglar Bay and there came upon the Turkish battleship *Messudieh* at anchor. What happened next is described in the citation for Britain's highest honour, the Victoria Cross, awarded to Holbrook the following week:

> For most conspicuous bravery when in command, he entered the Dardanelles and, notwithstanding the very difficult current, dived his vessel under five rows of mines and torpedoed the Turkish battleship which was guarding the minefield. Lieutenant Holbrook succeeded in bringing the *B11* safely back, although assailed by gunfire and torpedo boats, having been submerged on occasion for nine hours.

There were several other such high honours awarded for the brave efforts of the submariners.* They were trailblazers who, with extraordinary skill and courage, set the standard for the development of submarine warfare of a kind never previously imagined in the Royal Navy, although already well developed by the German U-boat commanders. The reverse side of the coin, as ever, took its toll. On 14 January 1915 the French submarine *Suphir* attempted a second run but she was lost with all hands just beyond the Narrows.

The minesweepers were brought forward again and managed to penetrate six miles inside the strait, attempting to clear the area of mines ahead of the decision to move in the big ships and fire the opening salvoes ahead of the great surge to storm the Dardanelles. The movement began on 19 February, when the ships from the Allied flotilla shelled the shore approaches at the mouth of the

---

* Recorded in greater detail in *The Silent Service*.

Dardanelles. The assault started with a long-range bombardment followed by heavy fire at closer range, and as the navy flotilla edged closer the outer forts were abandoned by the Turks as the shells began crashing into the masonry.

As the bombardment progressed, the Turks fell into disarray and soldiers were running, until three British ships struck mines and sank and the opening barrage in Britain's grand plan did little more than cause panic among the Turks for a while. The scene was witnessed by Henry Denham, then a midshipman in the battleship *Agamemnon* (named after the legendary Greek king), having joined the navy in 1910 as a cadet. His battleship, launched at the same time as *Dreadnought*, had four 12-inch, ten 9.2-inch guns and a secondary armament, two converted anti-aircraft guns and half a dozen torpedo tubes, but a rather steady speed of 17 knots. He recalled the events at the Dardanelles in a tape-recorded memoir for the Imperial War Museum:

The outbreak of war did not take us by surprise. We knew it was coming and in fact we were looking forward to it. The Germans were certainly not feared, seen more as a rival. We looked forward to fighting them in our youthful years, and had contempt for them. My duties were in the crow's-nest, a tiny little makeshift platform at the very top of the foremast, really rather frightening. When the guns fired if you were on your way up, the foremast vibrated violently. You have a very commanding view of our gunfire.

I was 17 when we moved to the Dardanelles. We were bombarding either gun placements or enemy troops. We had a wonderful view of the targets. We could see the fall of shot, which is what I was there for on my lookout post. We travelled up the strait towards the Narrows, which was as far as we could get. There were mines all over the place, and there was not a great deal of room to manoeuvre. From what I could see, the bombardment was quite effective, but also there was a lot which was rather wasted. We also took a great deal of incoming fire from the enemy, and had quite a few people killed. Quite a lot of damage was done to the ship. We were hit about 50 times in all. There was always fear of enemy submarines, very much so, about halfway through the campaign. Torpedoes were in use, and there were a number of attacks, and several ships sunk by torpedo. The destroyers came in to drop depth charges to attack the submarines, although it wasn't always very accurate. If one came to the surface, we might try to ram them.

The issue was that if we could knock out Turkey, it would be the beginning of victory. Morale was always pretty good, but the question of progress varied from optimism to dire pessimism. As the Turks got more and more help from the Germans, so they got stiffer in their resistance and our task became more and more difficult. I'm now fairly sure that if we had been able to push on fairly quickly at the beginning of things, we might have succeeded.

In fact, the early push soon collapsed. Bad weather delayed further progress, and it was 25 February before the outer forts overlooking the Dardanelles were silenced by the navy bombardment. Those further inland were simply out of range of the ships' guns. Withering enemy fire, however, continued to disrupt the minesweeping operations. The trawlers were continually being withdrawn, and although the crews had already been applauded for their heroic work it was a fact that under fire during night-time operations they were missing mines, or if they had been withdrawn early, the German spotters were laying new batches. This aspect alone was to prove fatal to a third of the Royal Naval Task Force preparing to make a major thrust into the Dardanelles.

London was growing impatient. The British naval commanders were themselves being bombarded – with a flurry of telegrams demanding explanations about the slow progress. First Sea Lord Fisher who, although against the Dardanelles operation itself, remained determined to back his men to the hilt and try to ensure that they were not cut to pieces. Fisher discovered, however, that the naval commander on the spot, Admiral Carden, found the strain of decision-making extremely stressful, and in the second week of March his doctor confirmed that the commander was on the verge of a nervous breakdown. He was sent home to England and replaced by his deputy, Vice-Admiral Sir John de Robeck, who immediately responded to Churchill's demands for action and ordered the Allied fleet to prepare for an immediate return into the attack to force the Dardanelles. On 18 March, two days after he took over, 18 ships entered the Dardanelles. The fleet included *Queen Elizabeth, Lord Nelson, Agamemnon, Inflexible, Ocean, Irresistible, Prince George* and *Majestic* from Britain and the *Gaulois, Bouvet* and *Suffren* from France. Henry Denham in *Agamemnon* recalled:

> We set out full of enthusiasm. It was a terrific sight, these huge ships making a lot of smoke and blasting away at the shoreline batteries and troop positions. We made fairly good progress and then the first tragedy occurred. The French ship *Bouvet* hit a mine, which blew a hole in her port side, and she just keeled over, capsized and disappeared in a great cloud of smoke and steam. Soon afterwards, another two went down, both victims of mines: first *Irresistible* and then *Ocean*, which had been standing by to take on survivors. But it was a double hit for *Ocean*. After she struck a mine, almost immediately she was hit by shelling, and this giant of a ship went down very quickly. Even so, I believe we had the good fortune to see most of the men from the two ships rescued.

*Ocean* had a particular place in recent naval history, and the name is still in use in the Royal Navy in the twenty-first century. She was designed to be able to transit the Suez Canal, had served on both the Mediterranean and China stations and at the outbreak of the war was dispatched to the East Indies for the protection of the Persian Gulf convoys. In January 1915 she defended the Suez Canal against the Turks and then sailed to take part in operations in the Dardanelles. It had been a long journey for her crew before they joined a squadron comprising two of *Ocean*'s sister ships, *Albion* and *Goliath*, along with *Irresistible, Majestic, Triumph* and *Vengeance*. The day of her demise was also a bad day for the squadron to which she was attached: as well as *Ocean* and *Irresistible*, *Goliath* was also sunk and *Albion* had to retire from action, all hit within the space of two hours with more than 700 casualties.

Although the naval bombardment had cleared the outer forts again, there was no breakthrough in the strait and within five days of commencing the operation de Robeck decided to abandon any further attempts to force the Dardanelles. Instead, he now informed Churchill that he felt convinced that a naval force alone could not succeed in capturing the Gallipoli Peninsula. He suggested it could be achieved only with a large body of troops making an assault with naval support. In this he was supported by General Sir Ian Hamilton, commander of the Allied troops in the region, who had made his headquarters on the Greek island of Limnos. Back in London, Jackie Fisher was still of the opinion that the navy should withdraw from the scene altogether. He was convinced that the Dardanelles was a suicidal place to be for the Royal Navy, and it would be worse for unprotected troops, especially in the flyblown heat of the coming summer. 'More than that,' Fisher wrote, 'what is there to gain? Nothing that is tangible at present, nor worth the high cost we will have to pay.'

His protestations, made privately to Churchill, were disregarded, and the British War Cabinet continued on its ultimately disastrous path. Leaders of the Greek army told Kitchener that the invasion plan would be murderous, with so many natural hazards, sheer rock, forts and, if it was a drawn-out fight, extreme heat in the coming summer months and cold in winter. They said he would need an army of 150,000 men to occupy the Gallipoli Peninsula. Kitchener replied that half as many could take it, and the final figure was indeed 76,000 men. And so the final act in this great military tragedy was set in motion.

The British 29th Division joined the force made up of troops from Australia and New Zealand, along with a lesser contingent of French colonial and Foreign Legion troops. Later, 20,000 more troops, including the 29th Brigade of Gurkhas, were hauled in as Allied casualties began to mount horrendously, and midway through the campaign five more divisions of reinforcements were shipped in. Troops were pulled in from around the Mediterranean and Middle East, and from Britain, and the Turks were quickly aware that a great movement of men was under way. It took almost two months to complete and thus all elements of surprise had been lost. By the time of the Allied landings, 60,000 Turks had been strategically positioned on the high grounds above the landing points, all in place long before the Allies had even brought ashore their main body of men. In order to take them on, the Allied troops would have to climb treacherous terrain, with sheer rock, deep ravines and dense jungle growth, while above them, protected by rocky outcrops, the Turks began picking them off like a duck shoot.

Young Henry Denham, still on board *Agamemnon*, recalls how the Royal Navy led the task of ferrying in the invasion army whose intention was to capture the Gallipoli Peninsula, while at the same time continuing its bombardment of gunnery positions. Nor was it merely a case of shipping in the men. The navy had to equip itself with suitable landing craft to handle a massive supply chain for the land army as well as shifting more than 5,000 mules and horses, 2,500 vehicles and 2,000 artillery pieces over the coming months:

To collect the troops, their equipment, ammunition, food, vehicles, artillery and animals and ship them out all took time, many weeks, and it was astounding that they were able to move them so quickly. They had to be landed by force and under horrendous fire with all their equipment. By then, the Germans were already giving assistance with ammunition, guns and men. I was there throughout the Dardanelles campaign [during which he celebrated his seventeenth birthday] in charge of a picket boat at one of the landing points. We had armoured plating around the wheel so that if you were steering the bullets could not hit you. They were steam, of course, fast little boats with a crew of about six or seven, and we had to take on coal at least once a day. We did a great deal of towage work, towing the men and equipment into landing points while under fire and bringing back the wounded.

We took many, many casualties in the landing [of troops] which was supposedly going to solve everything. But of course it did not. When we came close in, we were under heavy fire, but the steel plating protection was very good. Even so, there was no lack of spirit, either on our part or the men going in. The landings were all straight on to open beaches. Often the landings were at night because there were no protection or jetties and the men had to wade ashore up to their waist while they being shot at. They were very exposed. They were very vivid scenes, especially at what became known as Anzac Cove [where the Australian and New Zealand forces were landing].

The stage was set for fierce fighting, which began officially on 25 April 1915 and dragged on in a bitter war of attrition to which there seemed no end. From day one, the Gallipoli adventure looked ill-judged, badly managed and doomed to failure, although one of the outstanding features of this campaign – the high morale and courage of the men themselves – was evident from the beginning. From the very first day of the landings, casualty figures were appalling, and there were many acts of heroism by sailors, especially those who had the task of taking the troops ashore. In one ship alone – HMS *River Clyde* – five members of crew were each awarded the Victoria Cross for heroic action at what was known as V Beach (see first picture section).

It began when Sub-Lieutenant Arthur Tisdall, aged 24, hearing wounded men on the beach calling for help, jumped into the water and, pushing a boat in front of him, went to their rescue. He found he could not manage alone, but with help from other naval personnel he made four or five trips from the ship to the shore and was responsible for rescuing several wounded men under heavy and accurate fire. Ironically, he was himself killed two weeks later on a similar operation and was awarded his medal posthumously.

Tisdall's skipper, Commander Edward Unwin, 51, of *River Clyde*, left the ship and under murderous fire attempted, with the help of four other crew members – Midshipman Wilfred Malleson, 18, George Leslie Drewery, 20, George McKenzie Samson, 26, and William Charles Williams, 26 – to get the flat-bottomed lighters into position to transport men and equipment ashore. He worked until, suffering from the effects of cold and immersion, he was obliged to return to the ship for treatment. He then returned to his work against the doctor's orders and completed it. He was later attended by the doctor for three wounds, but once more left the ship, this time in a lifeboat, and rescued three men, wounded, in the shallow water.

Midshipman Drewery also worked away at securing the lighters under very heavy rifle fire. He was twice wounded in the head but continued his work and twice subsequently attempted to swim from lighter to lighter with a line. Malleson was also involved in the work of securing the lighters under very heavy rifle fire when Drewery, through sheer exhaustion, failed to get a line from lighter to lighter. Midshipman Malleson swam with it himself and succeeded. The line subsequently broke and afterwards he made two further unsuccessful attempts at his self-imposed task. George Samson, meanwhile, worked all day under very heavy fire, attending the wounded and getting out lines to the lighters, and was eventually seriously wounded himself. This left William 'Billy' Williams at the work of securing the lighters. He held on to a rope for over an hour, standing chest deep in the sea, under continuous fire. He was eventually dangerously wounded and later killed by a shell while his rescue was being effected by the commander, who described him as the 'bravest sailor I have ever met'.

In London, First Sea Lord Fisher came under increasing pressure to order his battleship fleet positioned in the Aegean to resume their efforts to force the Dardanelles. He refused point-blank to override the decisions of his admirals on the spot and subsequently resigned on 14 May 1915. The Royal Navy battleships did not resume attempts to force the strait, but kept up bombardment in support of the troops. Instead, the battle commanders brought in their most modern submarines to attempt to reach the Sea of Marmara.

On 25 April, the same day that Australian and New Zealand troops landed on the beaches, Lieutenant-Commander Hew Stoker, Irish-born captain of the Royal Australian Navy submarine *AE2*, successfully dodged the mines and shells to become the first to reach the Gallipoli Peninsula, although it was a close-run affair. En route, he miraculously weaved his way through two minefields and was then spotted by a Turkish destroyer, which attacked. He was forced to dive and remain on the bottom for almost 13 hours while ships overhead searched for him.

The crew was choking for air when Stoker finally managed to bring the submarine to the surface. Although damaged from depth charges and shells, Stoker finally steered his fragile craft onwards and into the Sea of Marmara. Virtually overnight, enemy ships were curtailed substantially and, buoyed by Stoker's success, Lieutenant-Commander Edward Courtney Boyle was dispatched in his boat, *E14*, with a crew of 30, half of them British and half Australian, and successfully reached the Sea of Marmara on 27 April. The *AE2* was subsequently sunk after suffering heavy shelling from the Turkish torpedo boat *Sultan Hissar*, but the crew managed to escape before she went down and were picked up and taken into captivity by her attacker. Boyle also succeeded in reaching the Sea of Marmara and remained there until 15 May, sinking two gunboats and a transport ship before returning to the Aegean. News of the breakthrough brought jubilation in London and the award of a Victoria Cross for Boyle.

With great skill and daring, British submarines went on to make many further sorties through the Narrows and into the Sea of Marmara and caused havoc among Turkish shipping. Most notable were the activities of Lieutenant-Commander Martin Nasmith and his crew in *E11*. On their first mission, they sank one large Turkish gunboat, one ammunition ship and four supply ships, for which Nasmith, too, was awarded the VC. On a later patrol Nasmith remained in the Sea of Marmara for 47 days, a record equalled by no other commander in the First World War. During the entirety of the Dardanelles campaign, 13 Allied submarines completed 27 passages through the strait. Seven were sunk, but the scorecard was somewhat uneven: the Turks lost two battleships, a destroyer, five gunboats, 11 transports, 44 steamers and 148 sailing boats. The Royal Navy's submarines also recorded a similar level of success in the Baltic operating from Russian bases, a campaign which continued until the Russian Revolution brought their activities to an end after inflicting great damage to iron-ore convoys from Sweden to Germany.

The submariners' efforts in the Dardanelles were one of the few bright spots in an appalling conflict. By the end of August the Allies had lost over 40,000 men, and the situation grew worse by the day as the winter months set in. Casualties through disease and sickness in the months of October and November were almost as high as those wounded and killed. Literally hundreds were drowned in their trenches, many simply froze to death and dozens lost one or both feet through frostbite, while the stalemate of battle remained solid.

In October General Hamilton, who had directed this ground war from the outset, was relieved of his post and was replaced by General Sir Charles Munro. He personally toured all three fronts where battle continued and was appalled by what he saw. He made an immediate recommendation that the Gallipoli expedition should be halted and the Allied army evacuated. In London, his report instigated immediate political upheaval. Winston Churchill resigned as First Lord of the Admiralty, his career temporarily in limbo. Newspapers reported that he was bitter 'about not having clear guidance from the Admirals before launching the attempt to force the Dardanelles'. Asquith's Liberal government was replaced by a coalition, and an end to the Gallipoli fiasco was finally in sight.

Henry Denham had survived the onslaught. Like so many other young men in the operation, he had shown remarkable courage, engaged as he had been for months in ferrying troops and supplies to the landing points and returning with the wounded and dead:

When the campaign was brought to an end, morale was surprisingly still very high, especially among the troops. We were rather sad, but I think it was realised there was no alternative but to call it off. The enemy was getting stronger and we were not. It was realised it was stalemate. The enormity of the transport effort of carrying everything out from England had been simply immense, and also we had now become involved with another enemy on the mainland, after Bulgaria came into the war against us. We had to have troops in Macedonia, based on Salonika, and the whole expedition became so vast that we really were almost unable to support it from the homeland. Sea transport became very great indeed, and it was a tremendous effort, but we had lost a number of ships because the German submarines were increasing in number. So, after about nine months of incredible bravery and heroism on the part of all concerned, the evacuation at the end of 1915 had to be planned and it went very successfully, unbelievably so.

The final act to retrieve the remaining 90,000 men, 4,500 animals, 1,700 vehicles and 200 guns turned out to be one of the great successes of the whole campaign. What seemed a logistical nightmare to its planners was carried out to perfection and with few casualties under the noses of the Turkish forces. The evacuation of all Allied personnel began on 7 December and was carried out at night, while by day the activity ceased and the naval fleet gave the impression they were still operating as normal. At night, the evacuation continued while a line of ships turned searchlights on the enemy trenches. The last of the men left Helles on 9 January 1916.

Almost half a million Allied troops had been drawn into the Gallipoli campaign, and losses had been heartbreaking. The British suffered 205,000 casualties, of whom 43,000 were killed; there were 33,600 Anzac casualties, with more than 12,000 killed, and 47,000 French casualties, of whom 4,800 died. Turkish casualties were estimated at around 280,000, with 65,000 killed. If there was any defence for the ridiculously high cost of the campaign, it could be seen in other areas, in that the action distracted the Germans from opening another offensive in France and weakened the Turks enough to help the British seizure of Palestine in 1917. British submariners had also kept up the pressure, and the effect on Turkish supply lines was catastrophic and seriously affected Turkey's capacity elsewhere in other theatres.

For the rest of the war, the navy kept up a blockade of the Dardanelles, and almost towards the end some unfinished business was dealt with. The two German-built ships, *Breslau* and *Goeben*, whose secondment to Turkey had in effect started the whole business, ventured down the Dardanelles and into the Aegean on 19 January 1918. They ran straight into an Allied minefield. *Breslau* was hit and sank immediately; *Goeben* was severely damaged but managed to limp back towards the Narrows. She was bombarded by Royal Navy aircraft, which scored 16 direct hits but failed to sink the ship. To make sure of her demise, the submarine *E14*, now captained by Lieutenant-Commander Geoffrey White, was dispatched into the strait to make a torpedo attack. The story of his journey was to be told in the *London Gazette* in May 1919:

On 21 January 1918 the battle cruiser *Goeben*, which had been mined while attempting a raid against Mundros, ran aground off Nagara Point in the Dardanelles. Repeated air attacks failed to achieve any noticeable results and at dusk on 27 January HM submarine *E14* [formerly Boyle's boat when he won his VC] under the command of Lieutenant-Commander G.S. White left Imbros in the desperate hope of torpedoing her. Despite being caught in the anti-submarine nets, White succeeded in bringing *E14* up to Nagara only to find *Goeben* had [been towed away] during the night. There was nothing White could do except to reverse course and start back down the strait. When off Chanak he sighted and fired at a large merchantman, but the torpedo exploded prematurely and *E14* was badly damaged. For two hours the submarine continued her dived passage towards the open sea but finally she became so flooded as to be uncontrollable. White gave the order to surface in the hope of making a final dash clear, but *E14* was hit by gunfire from the shore batteries. With no hope of escape White altered course towards the shore to give his crew a chance of safety, but was himself killed by shellfire shortly before *E14* sank.

Lieutenant-Commander White, who had a daughter he had never seen and two sons, was posthumously awarded the Victoria Cross, which was received by his widow at Buckingham Palace on 2 July, her late husband's birthday. His submarine, *E14*, also had the distinction of being awarded the VC twice. That four of the five VCs awarded to submariners in the First World War related to their exploits at the Dardanelles demonstrated the extent of their contribution.

Apart from many examples of particular heroism in the Dardanelles campaign, there were other aspects in the Royal Navy's experience there that went into the history books as among their greatest successes of the war – one being that of bringing forth the new technology that Churchill and Fisher can be especially credited for. The rapid development of submarines was the prime example, in which the navy had progressed from a standing start of relatively few boats capable of anything other than guarding home ports to initiating a fully fledged attacking force whose courageous crews would be capable of taking on the most arduous challenge. The results, as we have seen in a sample of the operations above, set the targets for further advancement.

That was one of the most important 'firsts' that the navy brought into play. The others concerned the use of aircraft. Again at the behest of Churchill, who utilised the navy's skills and experience in dealing with manufacturing contracts, exacting standards were set to create the Royal Naval Air Service, which had greater diversity and often better aircraft than the Royal Flying Corps. It was also the development of seaplanes, with their floats instead of wheels, and the Royal Navy's experimental flights that in part contributed to the foundation of the international Schneider Trophy race for seaplanes which Britain won in 1914 in a Sopwith. With a prize of the then huge amount of £1,000, it was meant to encourage progress in civil aviation but ended up by becoming a contest primarily about speed, and by the end of the First World War aircraft were reaching speeds of 150mph. From Britain's point of view, the Schneider Trophy race led to the development of an aircraft that would make a major contribution to the defeat of the German air force in the Second World War – the Spitfire. Apart from being used regularly on reconnaissance and artillery-spotting missions over Turkish positions in the Dardanelles, the RNAS conducted early experiments in the use of aircraft for bombing missions and also made the first-ever successful aerial torpedo attack.

# CHAPTER FOUR

## Come Out and Fight!

There had been battles sure enough, but the fact remained that for the first 18 months of the war the British Grand Fleet as a whole had spent most of that time at Scapa Flow sending out patrols across the North Sea to keep the German High Seas Fleet bottled up in home ports, leaving the Germans to rely on its expanding and efficient U-boat force to harass Allied shipping. The British fleet commanders, meanwhile, remained ready for action, constantly training and exercising for the big event, a head-to-head with the German fleet in a battle, if it ever came, that was being billed as the greatest naval engagement of all time. A shoot-out between the opposing dreadnoughts, hurling one-ton shells by the score at each other to determine who ruled the waves, was the subject of much speculation. The outcome might ultimately determine the victor in the wider conflict.

When that prospect finally moved towards reality, 17-year-old Midshipman Robert Shaw was sitting on a gun turret of his ship, *Hercules*, steaming towards the scrap that became known as the Battle of Jutland.

There was a real sense of occasion, because the Grand Fleet had not been in direct action at all and we all hoped that this was going to be a modern Trafalgar. I don't remember being scared by it; just excited, in spite of the fact that by then my three brothers had already been killed in France, in the army. Morale was very high. Everyone was very eager to have a go. When we came close to action, my station was in a gun turret. There was considerable speculation about how we would fare. Sailing south, as the fleet was, we were all thrilled with the idea of going into action. As we approached Jutland itself, we were all closed up at action stations and I was sitting on top of the turret at the time. In the distance, which was a bit misty, I saw a flash of gunfire on the horizon and thought 'Oh dear, something's happening now' and didn't worry very much until within a few seconds there was the most enormous splash alongside the ship. We had been near-missed and I quickly ran down the turret. A few splinters came on board and within minutes we were firing ourselves at the German fleet in the distance.

The young Shaw had witnessed one of the first shots in the drama of Jutland that had begun to unfold on the afternoon of 30 May 1916 when Admiral Reinhard Scheer, commander-in-chief of the German High Seas Fleet, finally led his ships forward for the long-awaited confrontation. The German architects of naval battles had devised a plan to entice elements of the British fleet into a manoeuvre through which they could achieve a separation from the Grand Fleet under the overall command of Admiral Sir John Jellicoe and by such a division could go on to victory. The target for separation was Admiral Sir David Beatty's squadron of battle cruisers, then operating from Rosyth out of the Firth of Forth.

It was to be achieved by sending five German battle cruisers and four light cruisers from Wilhelmshaven under the command of Rear-Admiral Franz von Hipper, who last encountered Beatty at the Battle of Dogger Bank. This advance party was intended to lure Beatty into a chase across the North Sea and into the hands of Scheer, who had positioned the rest of his fleet off the southern coast of Norway. If all had gone to plan, Beatty would have been trapped and sunk, prior to the engagement of the Grand Fleet. As German ships moved to take up their positions late in the afternoon of 30 May, the British intercepted a signal, only partly decoded, which alerted them to some kind of German movement, although the precise details were still not clear. Jellicoe reacted immediately and by midnight the entire British Grand Fleet was at sea heading for a confrontation off the south-western coast of Norway.

The Grand Fleet, sailing from Scapa Flow, were still 50 miles away to the north on the afternoon of 31 May when Beatty, joined by four *Queen Elizabeth*-class battleships of the 5th Battle Squadron, realised he was closing on the enemy. But he dashed into the fight without waiting for the slower battleships. His battle cruisers were also faster than the enemy's and his guns had a longer range. He was presented with a choice: at 19,000 yards he could have bombarded Hipper's ships but instead chose to move in to 14,000 before opening fire. But in the running battle that developed, dangerous ammunition handling practices (see below) in all the British battle cruisers (except the flagship *Lion*, which had been modified) led to first *Indefatigable* and then *Queen Mary* blowing up as soon as they took a hit. At that point, Beatty made his famous remark: 'There seems to be something wrong with our bloody ships today.' He was saved from further loss at that point by the accurate gunnery of the accompanying battleships.

Now it was Beatty's turn to spring the trap. Having pursued Hipper to the point of contact with Scheer's High Seas Fleet, Beatty turned northwards to lead the Germans towards Admiral Jellicoe's oncoming Grand Fleet. As they steamed to meet head-on, the Grand Fleet switched to its battle formation, as Robert Shaw explained: 'It was after six in the evening . . . The fleet, which had been approaching in six lines, re-formed into a single line abreast, ships end to end, under Admiral Jellicoe. It was getting dark and misty, and there was a great deal of confusion. Those of us closed up down below had no real idea of what was going on.'

Through the manoeuvre of turning his battle fleet into an end-to-end line, Jellicoe calculated that he would be firing broadside on with all guns blazing towards the German ships while they could only return fire with the forward guns of their lead ships. It was a tactical move, known as 'crossing the enemy's T', which naval tacticians had long ago promoted as providing initially, at least, overwhelming firepower to the oncoming straight line. Even with this advantage, the British were unable to make the most of what was described in a later analysis as a 'lambs-to-the-slaughter' situation. The inferior quality of the British shells and the superior strength of the German ships allowed the enemy to turn without far greater wounds than were in fact inflicted.

Their leading ships, the battle cruisers *Lützow* and *Derfflinger* and the battleship *König*, survived broadside shelling from ten British battleships yet remained operational throughout the initial exchanges. It was only then that Scheer realised he had himself fallen into Jellicoe's trap, and as he contemplated his next move the ships of the two fleets blasted away at each other, almost 600 heavy guns between them, with the Germans outnumbered in average weight of fire-power by almost two to one. Scheer's fleet faced annihilation and soon after 6.30 p.m. he decided to pull back and to escape the British onslaught. He ordered all his ships to make a 180-degree turn, a difficult manoeuvre in an exercise let alone under heavy fire, but it was completed with incredible precision to allow the great escape to take place into a smoke screen laid by German destroyers steaming across their rear. At 6.45 p.m. Jellicoe's fleet had lost contact, but Scheer's troubles were not over yet.

The British Grand Fleet now lay between the German fleet and their home ports, and so just before 7 p.m. Scheer made another sharp detour, hoping to get past the British fleet but instead ran straight into a fresh bombardment and he was forced to re-engage. The flagship *Lützow* sustained fatal damage in a duel to the death with the British battle cruiser *Invincible*, which later also blew up when one of the German salvoes hit a gun turret. Many other ships on both sides were sunk or damaged at this time, and in desperation Scheer at one point ordered his cruisers and destroyers ahead to mount what was in effect a line-abreast charge against the British ships.

Behind them, Scheer's battleships fell into a state of confusion amid the smoke and gunfire as they tried to follow Scheer's orders for another reverse turn. Jellicoe, probably expecting a torpedo broadside from the oncoming destroyers, gave the order for his own fleet to turn away, and so by 7.45 p.m. the two battle fleets steamed apart at a combined speed of around 35 knots, at which point the Germans made a dash for home and were never to come face to face again. Robert Shaw explained:

> Soon after that we lost touch with the German fleet completely. They dropped first northwards and then escaped to the stern of us. We steamed around for some hours, and then we turned around and went back home. It was getting light by then, past three in the morning. On the way, we saw a Zeppelin fly over us and fired at it but didn't do any damage as far as I could tell. It wasn't until we arrived back into Scapa that we in the gun room heard the news. Being two or three decks down, we had no idea what was going on up top or that three battle cruisers had been sunk. And, of course, the first thing we did was to coal the ship in case it was necessary to go to sea again. A collier drew alongside and every member of crew had to help load up . . .

At around the same time, the German fleet arrived in their own home ports and there they stayed. Behind them, the scene at the Battle of Jutland was one of smouldering desolation and death. A newspaper commentator of the day described it thus: 'All the theories of a century's peace were being put to the test amid the roar of battle and the flashes of the most powerful guns ever fired in anger at sea. Tonight, the sea is reported to be awash with bodies. One steamer alone spotted 500, but there are many tales of heroism . . .'

Indeed there were, and many that never became known, because in the heat of battle, although thousands of men were killed outright, many others simply drowned because of the impossibility of launching rescue parties. A number of the actions were of such merit as to receive the highest accolade, the Victoria Cross.

Commander Edward Bingham, 34, of the destroyer HMS *Nestor*, was awarded the medal for leading his division in their attack, first on enemy destroyers and then on their battle cruisers, where he came under murderous fire. Followed by the one remaining destroyer of his division (HMS *Nicator*), he closed to within 3,000 yards of the enemy to reach a favourable position for firing the torpedoes. While making this attack, *Nestor* and *Nicator* were under constant fire from the secondary batteries of the High Seas Fleet. *Nestor* was subsequently sunk, although Bingham survived and went on to attain the rank of rear-admiral.

Boy First Class John Cornwell, aged 16, became one of the youngest-ever recipients of the VC for his heroic stand as part of a gun crew on HMS *Chester*. Although severely wounded early in the battle, he remained alone at a most exposed post with the gun's crew dead and wounded around him. He continued firing virtually to the end of the action and was then himself killed.

On Beatty's flagship, *Lion*, Major Francis Harvey, 43, was mortally wounded and the only survivor after an enemy shell exploded on the gun house in which his team were operating. With great courage, he remained to ensure that the magazine was flooded, an action and presence of mind that saved the ship from blowing up. He died with that knowledge shortly afterwards.

Commander Jones, of HMS *Shark*, led a division of destroyers to attack the formidable German Battle Cruiser Squadron and in the course of the attack *Shark* was disabled by heavy shellfire and was drifting helplessly between two enemy fleets. Commander Jones was badly wounded in the leg, but with the help of three surviving seamen he kept the midships gun firing until he was hit again by a shell which took off his leg. He continued, however, to give orders to his gun's crew until *Shark* was hit by a torpedo and sank. Commander Jones was not among the survivors.

In the light of the curious way in which the battle ended, controversy would last for years as to who, exactly, won. Britain declared herself the winner by a mile, because it was the Germans who gave up and ran for home. In fact, Jellicoe's fleet suffered greater losses: three battle cruisers, three cruisers and eight destroyers sunk, with 6,094 officers and men killed. The Germans lost one battleship, one battle cruiser, four light cruisers, five destroyers and 2,545 officers and men.

The general opinion, outside Germany, was that the Grand Fleet emerged in better shape, and retained supremacy in the oceans of the world, and Germany did not feel inclined to challenge that proposition again throughout the remainder of the First World War. As one commentator wrote, the 'High Seas Fleet has assaulted its jailer but is still in jail'. It was a painful exercise on the part of the jailer, and the British fleet accepted that there had been many failings, not least of which was the tendency of the battle cruisers to blow up on taking a hit that might otherwise not be of a crippling nature. Robert Shaw explained:

> Our large number of losses was [somewhat self-inflicted] because of poor protection between the gun and magazines. Magazines blew up due to the trail of cordite from the turret down to the magazine. The Germans had already dealt with that problem, but it was only after Jutland that all magazines on British ships were given another layer of protection, and in fact when that was being done in *Hercules* one of the bulkheads near one of the magazines got warm through a fire in the engine room and preparations were made to flood the magazine in case the ship blew. There were at least two ships which had blown up in harbour.

There were other failures – in signalling, in accuracy and in the quality of shells – all of which were given urgent attention. But in fact the German High Seas Fleet did not venture out again for battle, and instead the German navy now concentrated heavily on submarine warfare as its main arm of attack and redirected its efforts against the merchant fleet, rather than the Royal Navy, in a bid to starve Britain of vital supplies and food. This action was further enhanced when the United States entered the war in April 1917, to which Germany reacted by reinforcing its policy of unrestricted submarine warfare – in other words, any ship was fair game in areas Germany declared to be a war zone – from which it had pulled back after the sinking of *Lusitania*.

With almost 120 U-boats operational, the German war planners set a target of 600,000 tons of shipping to be sunk each month and calculated that if that was achieved, Britain would be out of the war within six months. The target was far exceeded, rising from 180 ships sunk in January 1917 to 430 in April, the latter amounting to a catastrophic 850,000 tons. In response, the Allies immediately brought in the convoy system of transporting food and raw materials. This had been mooted on several occasions, but some strategists felt that to gather ships together provided a bigger target for the U-boats and also tied up much-needed destroyers for protecting the convoy. But under the unrestricted warfare edict issued by the Germans, convoys became very necessary, especially for the Atlantic crossing and through the Mediterranean.

The Royal Navy provided warships to form a protective screen around the merchant vessels so that to get within striking distance the U-boats had to risk getting within range of the destroyers' guns, torpedoes and depth charges. The convoy system brought dramatically swift results, and consequently the tonnage sunk by U-boats was curtailed to more manageable levels. In May 1917 the tonnage dropped to 500,000 and by the end of the year was less than 200,000 tons a month. The building programme for replacement merchant ships also began to outstrip the losses for the first time for many months.

In the meantime, all aspects of anti-submarine technology were being improved and minefields massively extended, and Admiral Roger Keyes, who made his name in the Battle of Jutland to become the youngest admiral in the fleet, took command of the Dover Patrol of fast boats equipped with searchlights to harass any U-boats using the English Channel to get out into the Atlantic. To avoid the patrols, the submarines were forced to dive to a depth that put them at risk of hitting submerged minefields. The U-boats therefore had to take the longer route around the north of the British Isles. This passage was also made more difficult in the early summer of 1918 when American and British minelayers put out more than 60,000 mines over a 200-mile passage of the North Sea between Scotland and Norway, so as to further block U-boat access from Germany to the Atlantic. These measures combined to form an exceedingly effective shield against the German U-boat campaign.

There remained, however, one major area of weakness in this vast panoply of measures against the U-boats, and it centred on the Belgian coastal town of Zeebrugge, which in turn led to a submarine base at Bruges, reached by an eight-mile-long canal. The access point at Zeebrugge was a heavily defended mole, a curving wall 40 feet high and 80 yards wide stretching one and a half miles out into the sea brimming with German guns. The base provided a perfect haven for ocean-bound U-boats, and in 1917 U-boat commanders began using the Zeebrugge hideaway, thus dodging the North Sea minefields.

On his arrival to command the Dover Patrol, Keyes was presented with the urgent task of tackling the Zeebrugge problem. His answer was an ambitious and risky plan to take a large force across the English Channel and, while marines launched a diversionary assault on the German fortifications, three ancient cruisers, *Thetis*, *Intrepid* and *Iphigenia*, filled with concrete would be scuttled in the Bruges canal, thereby blocking German access. Meanwhile, an equally ancient submarine packed with explosives would be steered to a point close to a viaduct connecting the Zeebrugge mole to the mainland. At a given point, the five-man crew would evacuate in a skiff, leaving the boat to sally forth on automatic pilot, with a timer set to detonate the explosives and blow the construction to pieces to prevent the Germans from reinforcing their troops at the mole once the fighting had begun. The key to the success of the whole operation was the landing of the diversionary force at the Zeebrugge mole. The raiding party would be ferried in aboard a fourth redundant cruiser, *Vindictive*, engage the German defenders and withdraw as soon as the cruisers had been scuttled. Around this main body of ships would be a flurry of smaller craft laying smoke screens.

It all sounded too far-fetched for many of Keyes' senior officers at the Admiralty, but in the end he won approval and set about gathering his force, drawn from the Royal Navy, the Royal Marines and the submarine service. Admiral David Beatty, who by then had succeeded Jellicoe as commander of the British Grand Fleet, was only too willing to participate. Almost two years had passed since the Battle of Jutland, and his ships had been waiting in vain at Scapa Flow for the German High Seas Fleet to venture out. In fact, there had for many months been a general murmur of discontent among other units, notably the army, and a sarcastic aside among the military hierarchy and newspaper commentators in London – 'What's the Grand Fleet doing today? Exercising again?' – was not uncommon, especially when there had been bad reports from the battlefields. The men themselves were also becoming bored, to the point that additional sports facilities had been laid on for them.

Beatty sent 200 volunteers, young, unmarried sailors with no dependants, who were to be joined by a detachment of Royal Marines. They spent three weeks training while Keyes put together his mini-fleet for the operation. An early problem was discovered after *Vindictive* had been fitted with additional armour to shield the raiding force from German guns on the approach to the mole. She would not safely accommodate the large assault force. Keyes therefore commandeered two civilian ferryboats, *Royal Daffodil* and *Royal Iris II*, which for years had been carrying passengers across the River Mersey in Liverpool. They were thought to be ideal for the Zeebrugge raid because of their capacity for passengers and their shallow draught, which would allow them to sail over minefields and navigate the shallow waters close to the mole. *Iris* and *Daffodil* sailed to Chatham dockyard, where they were fitted with additional metal armour to protect the men as the ships came within range of the German guns. The three old cruisers, *Thetis*, *Intrepid* and *Iphigenia*, were stripped and filled with concrete. Then came two submarines, *C1* and *C3*, which were to be modified to take the explosive charges and which were to be operated by skeleton crews.

Another crucial addition was the assembling of a posse of fast motorboats from the Dover Patrol whose task was to lay dense smoke screens using a new concoction developed by Commander Brock, of the Brock Firework Company. The boats would also remain on hand to pick up survivors from the attack. The whole group assembled north of Harwich, ready to sail at 5 p.m. on 22 April 1918, a motley collection of 76 vessels, including the new destroyer *Warwick* with Admiral Keyes aboard, and in total carrying 1,760 men.

As they steamed towards the Belgian coast, the fast motor launches raced ahead to begin laying their huge smoke screen in front of the mole. It worked well initially, but by the time the attacking ships arrived the wind direction had suddenly changed and had blown the smoke away. The ships were spotted immediately and the Germans sent up a series of star shells, which lit up the skies over the whole area covered by the incoming attackers. Undaunted, they sailed on into murderously heavy shellfire from the German positions, which killed a number of men even before they had reached the landing point. *Vindictive* bombarded the emplacements, but the German guns on the mole were presented with easy targets. Even so, *Vindictive* arrived alongside the mole just after midnight on St George's Day but had difficulty in holding her position and the ferryboat *Daffodil* was moved alongside to hold her firm, taking hits from German shells which exploded in her engine room. *Daffodil's* engineers managed to keep her coal-fired boilers burning while holding *Vindictive* for the assault team to disembark. Those on *Daffodil* herself were thus unable to disembark and none took part in the raid. *Vindictive* was badly mauled by a direct hit, which killed or wounded half the assault force aboard as they prepared to disembark. Others had a difficult time when the shelling also smashed the gangplanks that had been specially built to give them a quick exit from the ship. Those aboard *Iris* did get ashore relatively unscathed, and the weakened force stormed off towards its objectives, the first task being to silence the guns mounted on the end of the mole.

As the troops charged the mole, *Vindictive* could provide cover only from a machine gun perched high on the ship's superstructure, as all her heavy guns were below the level of the mole. This was manned by Sergeant Albert Finch, who was soon spotted by the Germans and under fire himself. He was severely wounded but amazingly carried on firing. On the ground, the assault force soon became involved in close fighting. The party's youngest member, Albert McKenzie, 19, who had volunteered from the fleet battleship HMS *Neptune*, described the scene in a letter to one of his brothers, which is now in the Imperial War Museum.

Well, we got within 15 minutes' run of the mole when some marines got excited and fired their rifles. Up went four big star shells and they spotted us. That caused it. They hit us with the first two shells and killed seven marines. They were still hitting us when we got alongside. There was a heavy swell on, which smashed all our gangways but two, one aft and one forward. I tucked the old Lewis gun under my arm and nipped over the gangway aft. There were two of my gun's crew killed inboard and I only had two left, with myself three. I turned to my left and advanced about 50 yards then lay down. There was a spiral staircase which led down into the mole and Commander Brock fired his revolver down and threw a Mills bomb. You ought to have seen them nip out and try to get across to the destroyer tied up against the mole, but this little chicken met them halfway with the box of tricks, and I ticked about a dozen off before I clicked. My Lewis gun was shot spinning out of my hands and all I had left was the stock and pistol grip which I kindly took a bloke's photo with it, who looked too business-like for me, with a rifle and bayonet. It half stunned him and gave me time to get my pistol out and finish him off. Then I found a rifle and bayonet and joined up with our crowd who had just come off the destroyer.

All I remember was pushing, kicking and kneeing every German who got in the way. When I was finished I couldn't climb the ladder so a mate of mine lifted me up and carried me up the ladder and then I crawled on my hands and knees inboard.

The last paragraph of the letter referred to the return to the ship, but McKenzie's recollections were somewhat blurred. He had been severely wounded, and his exploits were such that he was awarded the Victoria Cross – on the recommendation of his Royal Navy comrades. In fact, the raiding party suffered heavy casualties from the very beginning and had been unable to achieve several of its goals simply because they did not have enough fighting men. Even so, they had completed what they set out to do, which was to stage a massive diversion while the three old cruisers were moved towards the entrance to the canal, where they were to be scuttled. Unfortunately, one of them hit an obstruction before entering the mouth of the canal, and the remaining two ships were too small to make a complete blockage. None the less the sunken ships provided a sufficient hazard to make the canal unusable by the U-boats, and after the war it took a salvage company almost a year to clear the wreckage.

As they began to sink, their crews were picked up by the fast launches. Meanwhile, the two old submarines *C1* and *C3*, packed with explosives, also hit problems. They were to be towed by destroyers towards a rendezvous point five miles from the viaduct, but *C1* came adrift and was delayed and so Lieutenant Richard Sandford, commander of *C3*, decided to go on alone. Discarding the use of the automatic pilot, he and his crew gingerly steered a course to the viaduct. As he neared the viaduct, star shells burst overhead, providing the German gunners with near-daylight conditions to take range and fire. Sandford held a steady course and made it to the target, ramming the bows of the submarine into the side of the masonry.

Overhead there were howls of laughter as German troops on the viaduct mistakenly believed that the submarine had become accidentally stuck. Those who survived the next few minutes would know differently. With the time fuse set, Sandford led his five crew members out into the motor-driven skiff to make their escape. As they did so, they came under a hail of fire. Sandford took two bullets, and three of the others were also wounded. The skiff's motor was also hit, so they had to paddle their way out until they were picked up by a picket boat driven by Sandford's brother. As they clambered aboard the mother ship, they witnessed the satisfying blinding flash as their exploding submarine brought down the centre struts of the viaduct, which then collapsed.

The assault team was also to make its escape, called back to the ships by a Morse code 'K' sign sounding on *Daffodil*'s siren. The men were allowed ten minutes, and those who didn't make it were left behind to be taken into captivity or to be buried. The whole operation from the time *Vindictive* pulled in to her moving out took 70 minutes. Even as they drew away, they took heavy fire from the Germans. In all, 176 men were killed in the operation, 75 of them by a single shell, which hit the ferryboat *Iris* as she pulled away from the mole. A further 28 died later from their injuries, 386 were wounded, 16 others were reported missing and 13 were taken prisoner.

Back at Dover, the survivors of the raid were greeted with a heroes' welcome. King George sent Roger Keyes a telegram: 'I most heartily congratulate you and the forces under your command who carried out last night's operation with such success. The splendid gallantry displayed by all under exceptionally hazardous circumstances fills me with pride and admiration.'

Keyes was awarded a knighthood by the King and given a grant of £10,000 by Parliament. An unprecedented number of medals was awarded to the men, including eight VCs, but even more remarkable was the method of selection. Keyes argued that there were so many deserving examples of heroism that he wished to invoke the little-used Clause 13 of the Victoria Cross Warrant, which allowed members of a particular unit to nominate one of their colleagues to be awarded the VC to represent them all. This was to be achieved by applying the social divisions in the Royal Navy at that time, which allowed officers to vote for their own candidates and the naval ratings and marines to do the same.

Four nominees were named under this procedure, and Keyes himself selected four other VC candidates, along with a recommendation for the award of 21 DSOs, 29 DSCs, 16 medals for Conspicuous Gallantry, 143 medals for Distinguished Service and 283 names to be Mentioned in Dispatches. He also submitted 56 names for immediate promotion for service in action. The extent of his list of awards sent the hierarchy at the Admiralty into apoplexy. They objected to the selection by ballot and retorted that never had such a large number of awards been suggested for an operation of such duration. Some even made the point that with the huge numbers of deaths occurring in France and elsewhere in land-based actions of great importance, this might be felt as an extravagant gesture. Keyes stood his ground and wrote back complaining of the Admiralty's 'infernal rudeness'.

The upshot was that most of the awards he requested were granted. After the war the Anglo-Belgian Union erected a memorial at the shore end of the Zeebrugge mole in the form of a figure of St George and the Dragon on the top of a tall column. People from all over England, Belgium and France subscribed to the memorial, which was unveiled by the King and Queen of Belgium on St George's Day in 1925.

The symbols of maritime power: the great battleships of the Royal Sovereign class designed at the beginning of the twentieth century to maintain the Royal Navy's command of the oceans of the world, but already being overtaken when they came into service in 1915. The modernisation was pushed through by First Sea Lord Jackie Fisher (*right*) and the then First Lord of the Admiralty, Winston Churchill

Smoke from the stacks of the British and Allied fleet at the beginning of the disastrous attempt to force the Dardanelles in 1915, initially planned as a naval operation, but which descended into the tragedy of Gallipoli. *Below*: the V-beach where shiploads of equipment and thousands of men and animals came ashore

IWM:A191

Coal-burning ships remained in service well into the twentieth century, and whether at sea or in harbour every member of the ship's company, including the padre, took a hand in manhandling the tons of fuel into the hold. It was a filthy job, and coal dust flew everywhere, requiring even more elbow grease when it came to scrubbing the decks

*Above:* Hundreds of men scramble over the side and walk down the hull of the *Blücher*, Germany's most powerful warship, sunk by the British in January 1915. Unfortunately British attempts to rescue survivors had to be called off when Zeppelin bombers appeared

A bird's eye view of the big guns of *King George V* which was among the first major warships commissioned in time for the Second World War, a major improvement on the First World War types, especially in her firepower and armour

*Above:* The Royal Navy's air service, later the Fleet Air Arm, experimented with numerous seaborne aircraft projects. In the early 1920s, this M-class submarine was converted to become the world's first submersible aircraft carrier

Until the Navy was allowed more escort aircraft carriers – often the only means of protecting Atlantic convoys – various methods were tried to protect merchant ships. This catapult contraption had one major flaw: there was no means of recovering the aircraft

*Left:* The escort carrier HMS *Avenger* with six Hurricanes aboard, introduced on to the Arctic convoys in 1942

*Above:* Early casualties of the Second World War: the *Graf Spee* scuttled after a ferocious fight with British ships, notably *Exeter* (*left*) in what famously became known as the Battle of the River Plate

CROWN COPYRIGHT/MOD

*Below:* A great loss to the British meanwhile was the first great aircraft carrier *Ark Royal* which was torpedoed in the Mediterranean in November 1941 and sank after a fourteen-hour struggle to keep her afloat. All but one of her 1,400 crew were saved – a rare occurrence indeed

IWM: A6332

CROWN COPYRIGHT/MOD

CROWN COPYRIGHT/MOD

*Above:* One of the great maritime dramas of all time was played out in May 1941 when the great *Hood (top),* pride of the British fleet of the interwar years, was engaged in the hunt for the mighty *Bismarck*, Germany's newest and most powerful warship. *Hood* was sunk with the loss of all but three of her 1,461 crew. *Bismarck* was then hunted down in a massive operation by the Royal Navy, and was herself sunk with the loss of more than 2,000 men

*Right:* Another great disaster for the British was the loss of two ships sent to protect Singapore from the Japanese: *Repulse* and the brand new *Prince of Wales*, both were sunk in action in December 1941. Here crew from the latter scramble over the side into a waiting destroyer which then had to pull away as the ship went down

IWM: HU2675

IWM. A8603

IWM. A6872

*Above:* The light cruiser *Penelope* was re-christened HMS *Pepperpot* after she limped away for repairs with dozens of holes and severe damage elsewhere following a series of engagements around Malta in 1942

Ice cold in the Arctic: a typical winter scene on one of the escort ships protecting supply convoys to Russia

IWM: A29715

*Left:* The hazard of landing under fire: a Seafire aircraft crashes into parked planes on the flight deck of *Indefatigable* during operations against Japanese kamikaze pilots

# CHAPTER FIVE

## The Scuttling

Although submarine warfare flourished around the British Isles, the Atlantic and the Mediterranean in the final months of the war, the stalemate between the two great fleets of the high seas remained unresolved to the end. In that regard, Jutland had settled nothing and Britain, by default, still ruled the waves in spite of having the bloodier nose. The German High Seas Fleet thereafter was never seen collectively again in any confrontational mode and thus remained an undiminished force, hiding away in home ports as the war approached its final stages. Similarly, apart from a number of losses in other actions in the wider field of operations, Britain's mightiest ships also remained unassailed and had continued to spend most of their time exercising rather than fighting, much to the chagrin of the fleet's exceedingly bored sailors and thoroughly battered and exhausted soldiers on the Western Front.

As already noted, the German U-boat campaign against Allied shipping peaked in 1917 but then went into decline, although U-boats remained a constant danger to the British merchant fleet and, to the end, succeeded in compromising the supremacy of the British fleet. Even so, the fleet's very presence in Scapa Flow, combined with the massive coastal defensive operations now in place under the auspices of the Royal Naval Air Service, continued to enhance Britain's blockade of Germany. Considerable hardship was at last being inflicted on the German nation as a whole in terms of food shortages, but more significantly in the effect on the morale of German troops in the field. By mid-1917 the RNAS operated from 123 bases around Britain's coastline, mostly for reconnaissance and observation through the use of conventional aircraft, seaplanes and a considerable and effective airship fleet. The last had been successfully used to complement the onslaught against U-boats, especially in providing sightings for the incoming convoys, and by 1916 the new versions were more adequately equipped for bombing submarines.

The RNAS had also continued to relieve the pressure on the overstretched Royal Flying Corps whose commitments in support of British troops had expanded massively since 1915. Such were those demands that the RNAS provided a multi-tasked service operating largely as a land-based unit in conjunction with the RFC on a wide range of air warfare tasks. Under some of the far-sighted schemes implemented during Churchill's era, the RNAS was also better equipped in many ways and, surprisingly perhaps, was the first of the two to commission heavy-duty aircraft specifically for night bombing missions.

At the same time, conventional land-based Sopwith Pups made the first-ever takeoff from the deck of a ship. An old liner, *Campania*, was converted as a seaplane carrier for the Grand Fleet, but the seaplanes attached to the ship had to put down on the water and be lifted back on board. An experimental deck landing by a fighter took place in 1917 on the partially converted light cruiser *Furious*, and the experiments proved that wind directions around the superstructure of the ship affected takeoff and landings, as Robert Shaw, whom we last met as a midshipman aboard *Hercules*, explained: 'I was by then a sub-lieutenant on *Royal Sovereign*, and a takeoff ramp was built for an aircraft over the aft gun turret. Air currents, of course, are vital to an aircraft taking off and, shielded by the superstructure of the ship, there often wasn't sufficient wind for the lift and the aircraft simply dropped into the sea.'

Eventually, an old liner, *Argus*, was converted to resolve this problem and joined the Grand Fleet in 1918 with a long clear deck so as to operate torpedo bombers both taking off and landing. It was the first step towards the arrival of true aircraft carriers, culminating in the formation of a squadron of Sopwith Cuckoos. Although the squadron did not become operational until towards the end of the war, this development alone marked the beginning of the end of battleship dominance at sea and, like all innovations in the nursery of the First World War, the repercussions down the decades of the twentieth century were immense.

All these new procedures demanded an ever-increasing degree of professionalism and skill on the part of the men who were at the sharp end. And although the atmosphere of a high-octane sport that had pervaded the early days of flight still miraculously remained, new recruits were for the first time facing a far more intense level of training and discipline, with a meaningful curriculum that entailed rather more than a few flights in an aeroplane. The new threat of formation flying for mass-bombing raids had also suddenly appeared on the horizon and, with the RNAS a principal defender of Britain's shores while the RFC centred its aircraft over the battle fronts, calls for greater preparedness to meet this threat were being voiced loud and clear as early as spring 1916. The *Daily Mail* picked up the mood of the politicians and public alike when it began a resounding campaign: 'Hit Back! Don't Wait and See!'

The threat first appeared in the form of the Zeppelins, but big bombers became a reality in 1917 when the Germans began rolling out twin-engined Gotha 'pusher' biplane bombers to begin a series of daylight raids over London, followed soon afterwards by night-time bombing. They began with lone aircraft, and then for the first time with craft in formation. The first major effort in May of that year saw 23 Gothas bound for London, only to be turned back by poor weather. A month later, 20 bombers set off from Germany, 14 of them reaching London to dispose of a total of 72 bombs concentrated on a single square mile of the city, killing 162 and injuring 432. Great damage was also caused to property.

Now, the RNAS found itself overstretched and under fire for the lack of an effective response to German bombing raids over British cities, and the RFC had to divert men and machines badly needed elsewhere into home defences, deploying a force of 12 squadrons with 110 aircraft while the RNAS was fully deployed around the coast, running observation and fighter squadrons against both airborne and seaborne attacks. When the next big German raid of bombers occurred on 7 July 1917, 78 aircraft of the RFC and 17 from the RNAS took off to intercept them.

The defensive force included 21 different types of fighter aircraft, including some of the very latest. Even so, only one of the attacking bombers was shot down because the bombers were able to maintain great height. In September they switched to night-time bombing, the first of these running on six consecutive nights. As the war ran its course, the casualties on the ground mounted: 557 killed and 1,387 wounded in 51 airship attacks; 857 killed and 2,058 wounded in 52 aircraft bombing raids. The figures, though not huge, had a frightening effect on the British public, and demands for greater action became more vocal. Finally, the War Office began to get a grip, but it was well into 1917 before organisation and ingenuity took hold among the Allied attacking forces across the Channel to begin serious bombing raids on German targets. In 1917 competition for aircraft between the two British air forces of the RFC and the RNAS, together with dissatisfaction with Britain's overall effort in the air following German bomber attacks on London, led to the decision to create a unified Royal Air Force. This took place in 1918, by which time aircraft, both shore- and ship-based, were playing a major role in all forms of naval warfare both in the Grand Fleet and in the convoy escort role. However, the Royal Navy was about to lose control over the air force set up by Churchill.

The beginning of the Gotha bombing raids over London and talk of experimental armadas had been a defining event, confirming once and for all that the island status of the United Kingdom was no longer a relevant factor in the nation's defence against aggressors. Although invasion of her shores was by no means unheard of, Britannia still ruled the waves and, by and large, maintained control of the great moat that surrounded fortress Britain. Suddenly, almost without warning or comprehension, the Grand Fleet, with its battleship-led dominance of the nation's coastlines, had lost its claim to being the sole provider of defensive measures. Far greater dangers were now imminently possible unless Britain could have control of the air, too.

The War Cabinet demanded an immediate inquiry into home defences after the Gotha bombing raids and appointed a committee to make the study, under the chairmanship of the respected South African politician Lieutenant-General Jan Christian Smuts, who had arrived in the country recently to attend an imperial conference. The first report, which appeared within three weeks, criticised the totally inadequate anti-aircraft defences in Britain's major cities.

A follow-up report shortly afterwards dealt exclusively with the organisation of Britain's air forces and Smuts pulled no punches. He assessed that they were an organisational mess, riven by backbiting and rivalry among the top brass. He also examined the topical issue of bombing enemy cities and had no hesitation in saying that aviation was on the brink of playing a much greater role in war. Britain, he insisted, should aim for nothing short of air supremacy, just as she had maintained supremacy at sea, and he prophetically outlined his vision of future combat:

> As far as can at present be foreseen, there is absolutely no limit to the scale of its future independent war use, and the day may not be far off when aerial operations with their devastation of enemy lands and destruction of industrial and populous centres on a vast scale may become the principal operations of war, to which the older forms of military and naval operations may become secondary and subordinate.

Officers and men of the said military and naval forces reacted with acrimony and disbelief. Smuts' theories were tantamount to heresy – much the same reaction, incidentally, as many naval commanders had given to the arrival of submarines. Nor was there even the slightest hint of alacrity as a result of Smuts' report, and the RFS and RNAS were conjoined in their forced marriage to bring the Royal Air Force into being on 1 April 1918. Even its new Chief of Air Staff, the army's former RFC stalwart, Major-General Hugh Trenchard, warned the government that they should not expect too much of the new service, and privately told army commanders in France that 'ministers are quite off their heads as to the future of possibilities of aeronautics for ending the war'.

At the time of the merger, the RNAS had 67,000 officers and

men, 2,949 aircraft and 103 airships. This contingent was deployed on Britain's home-defence airfields and coastal stations as well as a number of squadrons operating on the Western Front. The combined RAF force meant that the Allies had increased its air force substantially to around 7,500 of some 24 different types. America's entry into the hostilities brought an additional 1,481 combat aircraft over the coming months. With the additional capacity, special training in night flying was set up for both bomber pilots and observers and their fighter pilots flying with them for protection.

The strengthening came not a moment too soon. In that same month of April 1918, Germany began a big new offensive on the Western Front, aided by massive reinforcements of troops and machines following Russia's exit from the war in the wake of the 1917 revolution. While the Grand Fleet played its part by enforcing the blockade of Germany, the air assault would now include the introduction of heavy-duty bombing raids into Germany itself as well as effective low-offensive day and night bombing raids on enemy communications, transport, shipping and troop positions. The great battles of the final months of the war now proceeded, at huge cost to both sides, and by July the Allies had the enemy on the run until, at the end of October, the Germans made overtures towards peace.

Even as armistice talks were under way in November 1918, which required Germany to given an undertaking to abandon submarine warfare, the U-boats carried on regardless, sinking the transport *Leinster*, with 600 civilians on board, and the cruiser *Britannia*. Without a doubt, however, the importance of the battleship in the First World War was fading long before the first signs of an armistice began to appear, and in the final throes German sailors mutinied at Kiel, refusing to take orders from their officers, as the general air of revolution in the wake of the Russian experience gripped European states.

Even so, the German fleet as a unit of power and might remained a great threat to the Allies both in terms of present and future danger, and when peace negotiations finally began the German navy was placed at the top of the list for instant neutralisation. Never, said the Allies, would this powerful fleet be allowed to remain in existence. This was just one of the conditions in the terms demanded by the Allies in their provisional armistice agreement placed before the Germans on 11 November 1918. Their list was harsh and punitive in every respect, and one that remained a festering sore among Germans – and Corporal Adolf Hitler in particular – for years to come.

The Germans were to surrender their complete fleet of warships and U-boats and a long list of other hardware which included 2,000 warplanes, 5,000 heavy guns, 30,000 machine guns, 5,000 locomotives, 150,000 wagons and 5,000 assorted lorries – all to be delivered up to the Allied nations who would then share the spoils among themselves. The reparation was insignificant compared with the cost. The Royal Navy alone had lost 1,069 ships, including auxiliaries such as colliers and minesweepers, against Germany's total of 362.

The terms therefore demanded that the German High Seas Fleet, comprising 74 warships, would deliver itself to Admiral Sir David Beatty, commander of the British Grand Fleet, to be interned in British waters until the peace agreement was finally signed. Additionally, 39 serviceable U-boats were to be brought to the Royal Navy destroyer base at Harwich, and another 200 in various states of completion or repair were eventually destroyed where they lay in German shipyards.

Such a move, or course, was sacrilege to Kaiser Wilhelm II, who once said 'Our future lies upon the water'. His beloved ships had been kept safe and sound throughout, but now the Kaiser's own future was bleak, although not quite so desolate as that of his Russian monarchical cousin who had been shot along with his entire family. The Kaiser was merely forced to abdicate and fled the country on 10 November 1918, leaving behind him a nation gripped by revolutionary fervour. Across Germany, as in the once-mighty Austro-Hungarian Empire of the Hapsburgs, the princes and dukes of the ruling class were being dumped in favour of republicans and revolutionaries.

Surrender of the German fleet was to be made on 21 November 1919, with all ships and their skeleton crews steaming to Rosyth and then on to internment at Scapa Flow until the terms of the armistice and declaration of peace had been agreed by the nations involved. The event caused great interest among the British public not only for the historic occasion but for the sheer spectacle. This account in the *Daily Mail*, by the naval historian H.W. Wilson, who had sailed on board *Royal Sovereign*, part of the Grand Fleet under the command of Sir David Beatty, which was sent to escort the German ships back to Britain, captured the mood of the times:

There was no excitement but only a pleasurable anticipation of memorable events when this afternoon Admiral Beatty's orders were issued that the immense fleet under his command was to prepare for sea. The ships lay motionless on the grey water in the falling light of a winter afternoon, searchlights busily flashing out their mysterious messages over the sea, across which the German force to be handed over for internment was already making its way towards us at ten knots. Wireless instructions were sent to it, and questions asked by the German commander were answered. Many wondered what were the feelings of its officers and men.

In the Grand Fleet there was a general doubt whether some officers or some ships might not try a last stroke and prefer to perish in smoke and fire rather than accept this end of ignoble submission. The German crews were known to have no stomach for fighting, but there will always be desperate men to be reckoned with, therefore very special precautions were taken. The Grand Fleet was to approach the Germans with cruisers and fast craft ahead. It was to be formed up in two immense lines six miles apart, and between them the Germans were to proceed to internment exactly as two policemen, one on either side, conduct a malefactor to the police station.

The cruiser *Cardiff* was charged with the duty of directing the German ships' movements and was to steam at their head. If there was any attempt at treachery, the gap separating the German line from either of the lines of Allied ships was too great – three miles – to permit the use of the ram, and gave our ships a good chance of eluding a torpedo. Before the Germans were met, all crews in all ships were to be at action stations ready for battle, and were to remain at these stations till further orders were issued. Overhead, watching the

Germans, the aeroplane squadrons from local stations were directed to fly. Thus provision was made against surprise and treachery. The whole [available] strength of the Grand Fleet was to be employed – five battle squadrons (the fourth, of King Edward's pre-dreadnoughts, was otherwise employed, and here and there ships were absent from the squadrons docking and refitting). The 6th Battle Squadron, of five lattice-towered American super-dreadnoughts, was there under Rear-Admiral Rodman. There were two squadrons of battle cruisers and six of light cruisers, with eight flotillas of destroyers, a gigantic force overwhelming in its superiority.

The order in which the Germans were to meet us was [they were to be in a single line with intervals of 600 yards between each ship's bow and the next astern]: five battle cruisers, nine battleships, seven light cruisers and 50 destroyers. The German ships were ordered to have their guns in the fore and aft position, in which they could not be trained upon our ships without attracting instant attention. They were to steam due west at a speed of ten knots to the meeting place, which was off the Firth of Forth, 56 degrees 11 minutes north latitude and 1 degree 20 minutes west longitude, and the leading ship was to be at the rendezvous at 8 a.m.

After being escorted to the Firth of Forth they were to anchor off Inchkeith. Two examinations of them were to be carried out – the first by a small number of officers to make certain that their magazines were empty, as Admiral Beatty's instructions required; the second, a complete and careful search as a precaution against booby-traps and tricks of any kind, a work necessarily demanding hours of attention, as every compartment would have to be thoroughly inspected.

Somewhere about 3 a.m. we weighed anchor and, with our battle squadron leading the line, put to sea. It was a cloudy night but fine and without mist. The great black hulls swept silently through the water. We passed under the gigantic girder work of the Forth Bridge and our topmasts, which had been lowered, seemed to scrape it. All arrangements were made for the possibility of an attack by submarine or destroyer. We went silently through the many booms, which protect the Firth, the outermost near May Island. On the upper bridge the night defence officer took up his position at the director, which controls the searchlight and guns for anti-submarine defence.

But out of the still, black water no enemy showed as two long lines of British and American warships steamed at 12 knots to the rendezvous. The only sound to be heard was the officer of the watch giving the steering orders. 'Follow *Resolution*' (our next ahead), 'Steer 78' (degrees of the compass), 'Steady', '76', 'Don't give her too much helm'. Pointers waved gently backwards and forwards on the dimly lighted dials which decorate the upper bridge. The ship far below was dark without a glimmer of light, and in front her forecastle looked from this height (87 feet above the water) like a flat iron; and the *Resolution*, ahead of us, was nothing more than a dim black mass.

Down there all was still as death, but for the occasional fall of feet, the note of the bugle-calls now and again, and the gentle hum of the machinery. Dawn came of this day, the most wonderful in naval history and destined to witness such unparalleled events. The Germans were late; they had been delayed by trouble in the condensers of one of their ships. The clouds were lifting and gave promise of perfect weather. About 8, the German Fleet was 40 miles off. At 9.30 they were in sight. We were flying the White Ensign from every possible place in every ship – a precaution taken before going into battle. 'Is it peace, Jehu?'

All glasses on the bridges were turned on the Germans, now very faintly to be seen on the horizon. Mist still hung despite the bright sun. We were present at one of the tremendous moments of history – such a moment as when Caesar crossed the Rubicon and changed the destinies of the world. It was peace. Slowly, at a speed of ten to 11 knots, the Germans came on, down the great lane of warships prepared to escort them, led by the British cruiser *Cardiff* and by one of our airships, as when a criminal surrenders himself submissively for execution.

They looked in admirable order. They kept perfect station.

They moved with clockwork regularity. They carried the German flag for the last time, and the German commodore's broad pennant flew at the main of the *Seydlitz*. Silently, dejectedly they came on in the midst of the silent escort, with no salutes and no dipping of the flag. Their paint gleamed with a curious copper-red glint in the sun so that it might have been the stain of blood though their general colour was a greenish grey, somewhat darker than ours. Behind the battle cruisers were the battleships, nine great vessels magnificently built and keeping perfect station like the battle cruisers. The *Friedrich der Grosse* carried the rear-admiral's flag, a black cross and two balls on a white ground, hoisted at her topmast.

The procession was funereal in its solemnity. That a great fighting force should surrender in this fashion was something of which the world had never dreamed, something which four months ago most men would have pronounced impossible. Now came this signal from Admiral Beatty as we neared the anchorage: the Grand Fleet met this morning at 9.20 five battle cruisers, nine battleships, seven light cruisers and 49 destroyers of the High Seas Fleet, who surrendered for internment and are being brought to the Firth of Forth. At 11.40 he signalled: the German flag will be hauled down at sunset today and will not be hoisted again without permission.

At 12.30 came what may be said to be the last signal of the naval war: negative man action stations. I hear that of the 50 German destroyers which were on their way over to surrender, one, *V30*, struck a mine and sank. The cruiser *Köln* was delayed by condenser troubles and was towed by one of the German battle cruisers some part of the voyage. The return of the fleet with its prizes to the Firth was one of the most splendid spectacles which man can imagine. For miles the lines of British ships crossed the sea, moving with exquisite precision, with paint and brass work, or so much of it as is tolerated in our modern navy, sparkling in the sun, with the glorious White Ensign flying and the signalmen busy with their rainbow hoists of signal flags.

There was no exultation or desire to trample on a fallen enemy, but a feeling of heartfelt satisfaction that the victory had been gained and the war won, though at the price of cruel losses. So, as in Nelson's day, the British navy has been at once the sword and shield of freedom. As *Royal Sovereign* anchored east of Inchkeith we saw the German vessels which had been sent in ahead of us at close quarters. At a distance they had seemed resplendent in the sun, but now they looked distinctly shabby and out at elbows. Officers and men stood in crowds on their decks watching us anxiously and showed no signs of great depression.

The ships of the First Battle Squadron, and *Royal Sovereign* among them, cheered Admiral Beatty as they passed his flag-ship, the immense *Queen Elizabeth,* and he stood there in the evening sun waving his hand in this last ceremony of the Grand Fleet. At sunset the German flag was hauled down and the admiral made a final signal: It is my intention to hold a service of thanksgiving at 6 p.m. today for the victory which Almighty God has vouchsafed to His Majesty's arms, and every ship is recommended to do the same.

The German ships were again thoroughly inspected and two days later were escorted to Scapa Flow, 200 miles from Rosyth, where they were to be interned until the peace treaty was signed, which in the event would be months away. That the ships were likely to be given back to the German nation – as many of the officers and men aboard them desperately hoped would be the case – was already a wholly improbable notion. They were the subject of argument as to which nation should have which ships among the Allies: Great Britain, France and the United States. Skeleton crews, numbering upwards of 3,000 men, were kept aboard the interned ships for care and maintenance while the rest were sent back to Germany in transport vessels. In fact, speculation as to the German fleet's eventual transfer to Allied nations would, in the event, prove to be utterly wrong, but then few could have imagined the dramatic events that were to be witnessed in Scapa Flow that would send virtually the entire High Seas Fleet to the bottom.

In the meantime, these were tedious and soul-destroying times for the German crews left aboard their ships. There was little to do, and in the bleak anchorage of the Flow the once-proud ships were slowly becoming enveloped in an air of malaise and shabbiness. The crews were not allowed ashore, and food and fuel were delivered by tender vessels. Sub-Lieutenant Robert Shaw on *Royal Sovereign* now found himself at the very epicentre of events unfolding at Scapa Flow:

> There were no British guards on the German boats, but there were usually a few patrol boats and other ships of the Grand Fleet that stood guard. The German fleet was an important part of the armistice peace negotiations, and the ships were still classed as interned rather than captured vessels and would remain so until the armistice was ratified and the peace agreement signed, and although we did not know it then, this would take months to achieve.
>
> Parties from our fleet went aboard each ship. They were in a pretty messy state, I must say, but then the ships' companies had not been used to living on board because in their home ports they generally had onshore accommodation. But as the weeks passed, rats and cockroaches flourished, and quite a few sailors became ill. I was placed in charge of a captured German trawler which we used for patrolling, to make sure there were no communications with each other and to ensure nothing untoward was happening. It was a pretty desperate time for all concerned.

Conditions on board grew worse in the coming months of inactivity in Scapa Flow while negotiations continued at the Palace of Versailles in Paris over the final wording of what would go down in history as a somewhat infamous peace treaty. The Allies spent much of the time quarrelling over the terms of the treaty, which eventually ran to 200 pages, 75,000 words long with 400 separate clauses. The French wanted Germany partitioned, while the British Prime Minister, Lloyd George, fighting a general election at home, was demanding financial reparation 'to squeeze the German lemon until the pips squeak'. The final settlement called for territory of seven million square kilometres of German territory to be surrendered to neighbouring states, plus a provisional compensation payment of 20 million gold marks. But the terms of the overall package were described by Lloyd George as being 'so harsh that we shall have to fight another war again in 25 years' time at three times the cost'. His words were, of course, proved to be an exceedingly accurate assessment.

The Germans refused to sign the treaty and held out for almost two further months until, in the third week of June 1919, they caved in and accepted the terms almost without further negotiation. There was, however, a last-minute delay over the final signing, and in the meantime the entire British Grand Fleet left Scapa Flow on 21 June for exercises in the North Sea, leaving just two destroyers and the smaller patrol vessels on guard duty. As the British fleet pulled away, German Rear-Admiral von Reuter, in command of the interned fleet, would claim he gained the impression that the armistice had run into trouble, having read of such a possibility in newspapers (which were five days old when they were handed to him) and that no agreement was possible on the part of the Germans, in which case his orders were to scuttle the fleet. He said he was unaware that on 21 June the armistice had been extended to allow last-minute changes to the treaty, but he assumed the sudden and surprising departure of the British Grand Fleet from Scapa Flow was somehow connected with the treaty negotiations in Paris. His version of events would be challenged by interrogators later, that in fact his motives were the reverse of those claimed – and that he ordered the scuttling because he believed that the armistice was being signed on that day and that on no account were the Allies going to get their hands on his ships. The plan, it was said, had been prepared long ago in expectation of such an eventuality.

Whatever his motives, one of the most staggering and spectacular events in naval history began to take shape shortly before noon under the sunshine of a midsummer's day, when the stately German fleet was gently swaying at anchor, just as it had every day since arriving there in November. Having watched the British fleet disappearing over the horizon, Reuter moved rapidly to a decision that shocked the world. He signalled from his flagship *Emden* to the rest of his fleet a single word: Scuttle. The skeleton crews were well aware of what was now expected of them. They dashed to their prearranged stations, opened all sea cocks, portholes, torpedo ports, internal doors and in some larger ships laid explosive charges. They then made for their boats and headed for the nearest land.

Within an hour, the scene was one of staggering desolation, with ships sinking in clouds of steam, foam and spray. Robert Shaw, from *Royal Sovereign*, was one of the few British sailors to witness the event:

I was left behind with the trawler patrolling the fleet and I was embarking coal ready to go out when one of the destroyers left behind rushed by and said: 'Look what's going on.' I was horrified to see that the German ships were starting to sink. It was an incredible sight, and by the time I arrived with my trawler the German caretakers were leaving them in small boats. I was about to take some of them aboard when my wise old chief petty officer warned me against it, since we were only a crew of eight against so many, and we were in a captured German ship. So we put these boats under tow and sailed on towards the bigger ships, the first of which turned turtle and sank even as we approached. We then went on to the cruiser the *Nürnberg*; she was still upright. I went on board to attempt to stop her sinking by closing watertight doors, at the same time picking up stuff which was nice. I have a German officer's sword, for example, and later on, of course, we were accused of looting.

That ship thus did not sink [she was later towed to shallow water by a destroyer] but I did see boatloads of German sailors heading for one of the islands, so I went back into the trawler and steamed towards them, firing a revolver over their heads. I finished up with a number of boats in tow when the Grand Fleet came back [after a hasty U-turn] and I pulled alongside my mother ship, *Royal Sovereign*, with all these German prisoners. The commander said he wasn't going to have them on board, although he was eventually persuaded to do so by his captain.

By then, many of the German ships were sinking, one after the other. Some sank more quickly than others, but that was more to do with the fact that many of the sailors simply did not know what was happening. There was undoubtedly a good deal of friction between officers and men and probably only the officers were aware of what had been planned. When it came actually to scuttling the ships, it had to be done in a hurry, all the holes, so to speak, down below, such as the torpedo ports and so on, had to be opened up to fill the ships so that they'd sink. The whole operation was supposed to be coordinated so that they all sank together, but it didn't turn out quite like that. Some sank quickly, others just turned over, some settled in shallow water with parts of their structure exposed and some did not sink at all. Meantime, the crews took to their boats and made for the nearest land.

The Grand Fleet was signalled to return immediately and had come charging back into Scapa Flow soon after 2 p.m. on 21 June. Beatty quickly realised that there was little they could do to halt the scuttling of their precious charges, said to be worth £70 million. There were angry scenes as German crews were picked up, and nine Germans were killed that day and ten others wounded – the last casualties of the war – as marines were called out to help round up the fleeing sailors.

Scapa Flow was crowded with small boats full of the men, many of whom were taken aboard HMS *Victorious*. One German officer reportedly came aboard wearing his sword and attempted an impressive ceremony of handing it over, but the British receiving officers were having none of it. Another officer who had been in command of a division of the interned destroyers said: 'Peace was signed today. We had our orders and have carried them out.' This confirmed that they were unaware that the armistice had been extended by 48 hours. It was also evident that the German crews had been ready for departure from the amount and variety of possessions they had carried with them. Some of the sailors were staggering under the weight of their bundles.

One other fact was also apparent: that officers and men coming aboard the British ships were unrepentant and seemed anxious that none of their ships stayed afloat, and in that they were not dissatisfied with the result. By the end of the day, only three German warships and a dozen or so destroyers remained afloat. The remainder were either wholly or partly submerged, leaving great ghostly hulks of superstructure littering Scapa Flow. Robert Shaw explained:

> Subsequently, every ship in the Grand Fleet appointed a salvage squadron to attempt to salvage some of those which were still relatively upright, bearing in mind they were a major hazard to our own ships. *Royal Sovereign* went up to a battleship that was perfectly upright but settling somewhat because one could see the water was not far from the open scuttles. A destroyer was attempting to tow her away, but the battleship still had her anchor down and wouldn't shift. I planned to go alongside and try to place a charge to blow up the cable. Just as we pulled alongside, the cable attached to the towing destroyer parted and she shot ahead. We did manage to get a salvage party on board, but by then the water level was up to the ports and eventually she did sink to the bottom.
>
> For quite a time thereafter, my mother ship was looking after one of the battleships that had settled in shallow water with salvage teams back and forth. In fact, very few of the Germans ships survived, and they rested on the bottom until they were eventually salvaged for their metal. Oddly enough, almost exactly 19 years later, in 1937, I was in Scapa in the *Vindictive*, which was by then the cadets' training cruiser; they were just attempting to lift one of the last ships to be salvaged. The diver who was in charge of the salvage operation actually came on board to give the cadets a lecture on how to salvage the ships.

Rear-Admiral von Reuter was questioned by the naval authorities and British intelligence officers on the issue of whether the scuttling of the German fleet had been preplanned to coincide with the signing of the peace agreement. Reuter had returned to Berlin in May, pleading ill-health, but he came back after just a week. With the benefit of hindsight, and with Scapa Flow now the graveyard of sunken ships, the British investigators questioned whether he was given orders there and then by the German Admiralty that the fleet had to be destroyed at all costs, even if there was loss of German life. A copy of detailed orders for sinking the ships was found aboard his flagship, albeit signed by the Kaiser at the start of the war, which gave instructions that no warship was to fall into enemy hands.

Reuter told his interrogators that he believed from what he read in a newspaper that the armistice had been terminated and circulated his order to his ships by making unobserved signals to begin the scuttling procedures. In fact, after the 48-hour delay, the armistice was finally signed on 28 June 1919, and the Great War that had cost almost ten million lives was officially ended. As Germany woke up to the stringency of the Treaty of Versailles, the nation went into a week of public mourning, not least for the fate of their once mighty naval fleet.

The graveyard that was Scapa Flow was a desolate place, with hulks of the few beached ships close to the shore giving way to the sight of masts, funnels and superstructures of the sunken ships. Initially, the Admiralty's answer to those who enquired of their eventual fate was: 'Where they are sunk, they will rest and rust. There can be no question of salvaging them.' It was a premature assessment that could not stand. The wrecks were not only a shipping hazard, but they had considerable value as salvage, especially those that were not fully submerged. Some of the ships still upright and undamaged were salvaged by the Royal Navy, but in 1922 commercial companies were invited to tender for the bulk of the salvage operation, which was indeed a massive project that was still not fully completed by the beginning of the Second World War, when it was halted. The whole operation, the largest of its kind in history, required incredible foresight and new skills on the part of the salvage people, but over the years all but eight of the big ships were raised from the sea-bed, towed to harbour and cut up for scrap metal.*

So ended one of the great dramas of the First World War, but Scapa Flow became more than just an historic place of dead ships. It also became a symbol of German patriotism, and when their navy rose again under Hitler's Third Reich, revenge in that very place would become one of its first objectives.

---

* The subject of media attention throughout this daunting process, years later the Scapa Flow wrecks spawned a new local industry – wreck diving – and in modern times Scapa Flow became a world-famous dive site.

# CHAPTER SIX

## Managing the Empire

The 'war to end wars' had in reality merely set the scene for the next one and facilitated the emergence of revolutionary powers that would keep the world on edge of a potential holocaust for almost the rest of the twentieth century. The hopeful millions who danced in the streets, believing Armistice Day to be the dawning of a new era in world peace and security, were, of course, to be hopelessly betrayed. The euphoria was short-lived, and in any event bound up with grief for the millions of dead and a generation of young men wiped out. The killing had stopped, but the wrongs that had resulted in such appalling desolation would not be resolved so quickly.

Politically, the most noticeable difference was that the aristocratic rulers and their great dynasties of Europe had been wiped out or dethroned. Of the three principal players, the cousins Tsar Nicholas of Russia, Kaiser Wilhelm of Germany and King George of England, only the last remained *in situ* and on occasions even his crown had wobbled. The Russian Empire remained intact in terms of its territory but was now under the Communist rule of Lenin's Bolsheviks. But monarchical imperialism had gone for ever. The German Empire dissolved into the Weimar Republic, the vast Austro-Hungarian Empire amassed by the Hapsburgs through war and marriage over a thousand years was now carved up into four nations, the Ottoman Empire was destroyed and all the great European economic landmarks of the pre-war world were left to vagaries of the disunited and shambolic policies of the victors who could not even agree among themselves. Central and Eastern Europe were in turmoil as revolutionary groups attempted to fill the political void, while civil war still raged in Russia. On a wider front, the war also marked the beginning of the end for the great British Empire whose influence at the turn of the century covered almost a third of the world's land surface and whose populations after the First World War became increasingly gripped by national fervour which, over the next half-century, blew away the vestiges of colonial power amassed over four centuries of mercantile adventure.

The end of the war also meant that the Royal Navy had to begin an immediate reinforcement of its stations in far-flung parts to service and sustain Britain's global commitments, especially where nationalistic uprisings threatened. First, however, there was some unfinished business around Europe that required both old-style gunboat diplomacy and humanitarian effort to resolve. The first ran on immediately after the armistice, and within a month of leading the German High Seas Fleet to surrender at Scapa Flow, HMS *Cardiff* was among the British warships dispatched immediately to what became known as the Intervention War, which ran for almost two years against the Red Russian factions.

The British were engaged in a number of small campaigns in the Arctic Sea when a force was landed to help Russians who supported the Allied cause. A good deal of fighting ensued, and a number of British soldiers were subsequently interned and, when no positive results were achieved, a British political team was sent to oversee a withdrawal of the Allied force. Similarly, the Royal Navy supported a large Allied force of 90,000 men landed in December 1919 to help bolster the Cossacks' stand against the increasingly triumphant Red Army in the Caucasus. Even the arrival of a contingent of RAF and British tank detachments failed to rescue the mission and the force was withdrawn within three months, leaving the region in a state of anarchy, with nationalists and Bolsheviks fighting one another prior to a ruthless advance by the Red Army to gain control. The Royal Navy placed a strong presence in support of these Allied operations, and the humanitarian effort to aid the thousands of White Russians fleeing the country, especially in the Black Sea and the Baltic. Charles Henry Lazenby was a seaman on *Emperor of India*, part of the British fleet's 4th Battle Squadron, which had moved to the Mediterranean and then into the Black Sea. The squadron operated out of the British base of Malta. For Lazenby it was his first experience at sea, having come through the navy's training school for boy seamen at Greenwich and then into HMS *Ganges*, the land-based boys' training centre at Shotley, near Harwich. On this first voyage, at the age of 16, he found himself heading for a first-hand insight into the Russian Revolution:

It turned out that thousands of White Russians were fleeing from the Red Army, coming down south to the Black Sea ports. There were some British merchant ships loaded with army supplies, mostly clothing, boots and stuff like that, and when we arrived we all went ashore to clear all this stuff out of the holds and convert them into space for passengers. We also took refugees on our ship. We packed a lot of them in, more than was best in the interest of sanitary arrangements. We roped off an area for'ard for our men and an area aft for the officers to come on deck, but the remainder of the deck was crammed with Russian refugees. We made latrines for them; a long plank with holes over buckets and a screen around them, one each side, but it was an awful mess after four days' using them.

The refugees were also in an awful condition. I guess some of them must have marched for many days, if not weeks. They were worn out. Their boots were worn through, they were up to their waists in mud, some of them. Few had any possessions, nothing with them at all. We loaded up with refugees and just as we were ready to sail the Red Army's shore batteries opened up on us. They just riddled one funnel with a bit of shrapnel. But we replied with full-calibre 13-inch guns. There was a terrific noise from the guns going off, and these poor people on the fo'c's'le were just underneath the muzzles. They must have almost split their eardrums. We took them off to Mudros, where we built a refugee camp with stuff we brought up from Malta: tents, bedding, blankets, cooking utensils and all that sort of stuff.

We made a subsequent trip to Malta for more equipment and we built further tents and accommodation for them. We then moved on to Constantinople, which was then under Allied control after the war. There was an American warship there, a big French warship, a Portuguese warship and, always, a British warship. We weren't going to be left out. Conditions in the city were pretty grim. The sultan's palace had been burned to the ground. The place was overcrowded with Russian refugees. We always imagined that every girl was a White Russian princess, you know, who'd come down and sold all her jewellery to escape. It was a wild and dangerous place, though. When we landed we had to have our side arms on. We weren't allowed out alone; we had to go in groups of four.

Constantinople was swamped by 100,000 fleeing White Russians and was placed under the protection of the Allies, who declared it a demilitarised zone. But the Turkish situation was rapidly running out of control. Across the country, tens of thousands were killed in genocidal attacks as the nationalists under their leader Mustapha Kemal Atatürk began a concerted effort to reclaim their country from the Armenians and Greeks who had moved in as a result of the war. Britain's response was confused and confusing. Royal Navy battleships and aircraft carriers were called on to protect British troops who were ashore on both sides of the Bosporus and were called on to bombard Constantinople to prevent a takeover by the nationalists. The British ships then rejoined the humanitarian action in evacuating thousands of refugees when the ancient commercial city of Smyrna, which had been in Greek hands since the end of the war, was set alight and reclaimed by Kemal. Then the experiences in the Dardanelles temporarily returned to haunt Westminster when British forces came under fire at Chanak, the fortified town at the narrowest part of the Dardanelles on the Asiatic side which had been unsuccessfully bombarded by the British in 1915. Now, for a whole month, it looked as if it would become another flashpoint as Kemal poured his nationalist forces into the surrounding countryside. Only a last-minute peace conference averted a new confrontation, when the sultan agreed to leave Turkey. He was spirited away to Malta in the battleship *Malaya* and the crisis ended. Within a year, all British forces had been extracted from the region.

Thereafter, Malta once again resumed its importance as a naval base and port of call for ships bound for the east. It had been in British hands since 1814 and remained one of Britain's most important bases. The Mediterranean Fleet also possessed the most up-to-date ships, responsible for maintaining the vital trade route to the Far East through the Suez Canal. The island had a tradition among officers of a yacht club atmosphere that had lingered from Victorian days. It was also one of the most favourite places for shore leave for all experienced seamen and for the entourage of tradesmen, craftsmen – and girls – who followed the fleet. It was a real eye-opener for the young Charles Lazenby, to watch his shipmates – and their officers – at work and at play in a scenario that reverted to post-war activity with remarkable speed and alacrity.

The behaviour of British seamen in foreign ports was generally more relaxed, because they would have more freedom. They wouldn't be hampered by home ties or anything like that and the temptations were much greater. I mean, there was nothing laid on for them apart from the pubs. There was a very nice opera house but what sailor wanted to go to an opera house? In fact, we called Malta the place of the three Ps: pubs, priests and prostitutes. And they were all more prolific than in Chatham. But many of them were not Maltese girls. There were a lot of English girls out there, brought out as dance hostesses and that sort of thing only to find that there'd be no other work for them except in bars or prostitution.

The men were allowed all-night leave from 4.30 in the afternoon to 7.30 the next morning, which was established while in port at home for married men, so that they might get home to see their families if they lived locally. In far-flung places, the same system operated but, of course, there were no wives around, except for officers. Boys weren't allowed all-night leave. You'd get ashore in the evening, but you were given a deadline to be back on the ship. There was a lot more leave-breaking on overseas stations than at home and quite a good deal of drunkenness. Attempts were made to smuggle beer into the ship, because all we had aboard was our daily tot of rum. The punishment for bringing beer on would be three days in the cells. For breaking your leave you were punished by a scale of deprivation of pay and leave. If you were an hour over your leave you'd lose a day's pay or a day's leave, that sort of thing. Malta depended heavily on the British navy. We had a repair depot there, and a fully operational dockyard facility.

We even had a Maltese canteen manager, Maltese cooks for the officers, and the Maltese also had a contract for collecting all the swill from the ship – all the food refuse. They used to pay for the privilege and they'd take it ashore, and you could see them on the front queuing up to buy this stuff for food. It was all our refuse! They were also employed by the ship to take us ashore in their own boats and bring us back again. They'd line up and take us ashore. And when we wanted to come back we just hailed one like you'd hail a taxi, and it would bring us back.

There was a lively sports calendar as well at Malta. We often had dances, and some of the officers had their wives out there. And there were British residents who had their ladies and friends out there. Regattas also played a very important part in the sporting and recreational life of the ships. A lot of time would be spent preparing – probably we'd begin preparing for the next regatta soon after the current one had finished. They'd start training the crews physically, with weightlifting and that sort of thing, but also preparing the boats. The officers would pick out the fittest men; they'd probably have a few runs in the boat, see who was the best oarsman. They gave them as much practical training as they could in the boats themselves. In the evenings they'd often pipe away racing boats' crews to go and practise. But, of course, when we were at sea they couldn't do the practice very well and so they used a rope pulley with a big weight on it. The oars were attached to that and they'd pull that and pull this weight up as they pulled and as they recovered, you see, they'd drop the weight on to a mat.

The preparation of the boats was pretty meticulous. There were strict rules about it. You were not allowed to interfere with the structure of the boat at all. You could strip the paint off it, you clean the bottom of the boat, sandpaper it down, but you were not allowed to blacklead it, which was a favourite dodge. There were several classes of boats on a ship. The battleship carried a pinnace [ship's tender], which was 42 feet long, and a launch which was exactly the same. But usually the launch had a motor in it and the pinnace was a sailing pinnace. So they used the pinnace, and we probably had three cutters – 30-foot cutters, 12 oars – two whalers with seven oars, three one side, four the other. And then there were the gigs and the galleys, very long and thin boats with very small beams. They were much faster; they were really the captain's boats. They were all used in the regattas, and it was great sport between the ships stationed in Malta, just as it was in the summer back home in England.

By the early 1920s, when most of the skirmishes associated with the war had been cleared up, the Royal Navy returned to what might be described as 'normal' duties, although there remained a number of areas that required a touch of the gunboat diplomacy that only the navy could provide. There were also urgent problems requiring attention, the first of which was drastically to cut the size of the overall fleet, which far exceeded peacetime needs, especially as the number-one enemy had been put out of action for a few years hence. Thousands of 'hostilities-only' officers and ratings, as well as a large number of career seamen, were let go as bankrupt Britain – like most nations involved in the war – had to severely prune their military commitment, given that having just fought a war they could safely do so without fear of another conflagration of such proportions arising in the foreseeable future. Dozens of obsolete ships and submarines were scrapped and work on almost 30 ships of various calibres ordered during the war years was also halted, many simply being scrapped and cut up. At least half the remaining stock of ships was also moved into a reserve state. In terms of personnel, the strength of the Royal Navy was cut from 380,000 men in 1919 to a mere 90,000 by 1932, much of the reduction falling under what became known as the Geddes Axe. The then First Lord of the Admiralty, Sir Eric Geddes, as chairman of the Committee for National Economy, brought swingeing cuts to the navy, and once again the pay and conditions of the men suffered badly as new rates of pay introduced were lower than those of 1919.

Even so, Britain's naval commitment necessarily remained greater than that of any other nation in the world because of her continuing colonial ties, and in these unsettled times, coupled with the rising tide of national fervour in so many areas within the British sphere, the Royal Navy's overseas commitments were as strong as ever. Ships and aircraft were scattered around the globe largely for the protection of British imperial interests and trade routes, and that protection remained a vast undertaking, even for the Royal Navy. There were Royal Navy commitments in the Mediterranean, Africa, East Indies, West Indies and China, along with naval bases in Malta, Singapore, Hong Kong and South Africa.

China was a centre that required some old-fashioned gunboat diplomacy as the central government collapsed and local warlords and bandits were well equipped to challenge British naval units on the country's great rivers, such as the Yangtze, where the navy maintained permanent patrols with relatively small gunboats, given the narrowness of the rivers at certain points. There were some ferocious exchanges at Wanxian on the Yangtze in 1925, followed by numerous actions over the next five years at Canton, Hankow, Nanking and Shanghai – all names that were to figure prominently in British naval activity as the local wars threatened British interests and businesses. In September 1926, for example, *The Times* reported 'grave news reaching London from the Yangtze River front in the civil war in China . . . In a gallant action, Royal Navy gunboats rescued five British merchant officers held by 600 Chinese soldiers on board a ship in the Yangtze. In the fight

13 British sailors lost their lives.' The place was not far from the spot 23 years later when, as will be seen, the Royal Navy crew of a gunboat became national heroes in what was thereafter to be known as the Yangtze Incident (see Chapter Fourteen).

But other forces were also worryingly present in China. Even before the decade of the 1930s was out, Churchill among others was warning in London that the China Station, where a reasonable force of ships and men was maintained, would be wholly outnumbered and isolated by Japanese ambitions in that region, and thereafter a policy of appeasement rather than confrontation was the solution adopted by British governments who simply could not afford to contemplate a further build-up of forces in the East.

In addition, there were patrols of international shipping routes in the Atlantic and the Indian Ocean used by Britain's merchant fleet, and occasional one-off operations to impose some gunboat discipline in times of waywardness, standing off Calcutta during the Indian riots of 1927, landing three platoons of marines and sailors to quell labour riots in Trinidad and sending the warships *Queen Elizabeth* and *Ramilles* to administer some light bombardment in the wake of riots in Egypt in which British interests were targeted. In this last role, the navy was increasingly called on to police areas where nationalistic tendencies began to become restless which, by their very nature, could only grow worse down the years. There was to be no loosening of the grip on the Empire, not yet at least.

To this end, and in spite of dire financial straits, Britain was now the only mercantile nation that constantly maintained large squadrons of warships abroad, whereas navies of other countries sent visiting ships. The principal role in all this was to maintain and protect British influence and businesses and generally to protect the colonies and protectorates which otherwise might feel inclined to opt for self-government or attract the attentions of other nations. As in times past, this meant long periods of foreign service for Royal Navy crews, separated from their wives and families. For the British government, it was also a hugely expensive operation to maintain and defend the overseas bases. The whole exercise began to take on the aura of King Canute, and many in government were turning increasingly towards curbing even further the expenditure on overseas stations. In consequence, when war came again the overseas bases had all suffered several years of neglect, especially Malta, whose defences were almost totally ignored and suffered badly in consequence. Of all the overseas bases, only Singapore had been fortified and expanded to meet the threat of Japanese expansionism. It was the key to Britain's continued ability to defend her interests in the Far East, but even that would in the event prove to be woefully inadequate.

The truth was that Britain could no longer afford a navy on the scale required to meet such demands while maintaining a strong presence around the British Isles, which was worrying because there were signs of a new arms race emerging, with Japan and America challenging the British standard of having a more powerful navy than the next two nations. In fact, the two-nation parity rule that decreed that the Royal Navy should have more ships than the combined total of the next two most powerful navies finally had to be dropped, and when the opportunity came for negotiations between the big powers to place international limits on battle fleets, Britain was only too happy to join in. But in fact she was soon to find herself considerably disadvantaged by international agreements first set in place in 1922 at a Naval and Disarmament Conference in Washington, and at subsequent meetings to administer the size of the national fleet of Britain, France, Japan and America. British delegates made the ground-breaking concession that in effect finally gave up Britannia's claim to rule the waves by accepting parity with the United States Navy in capital ships and limits on tonnage for lesser warships, with Japan not far behind.

This was merely a recognition of Britain's financial inability to match her competitors, but always when politicians talked of agreements over armaments, history showed that this was a pointer towards the ambitions of those who were, in fact, attempting to strengthen their military power. It was also an ironic truth, at that time, that the pride of the Japanese fleet were ships commissioned from British shipyards but built to Japanese specifications and were, in fact, the most powerful warships in the world. In the short term, however, the Washington conference did enable a clause curtailing Japan's navy to an agreed limit which did not exceed that of the British and the Americans. In the long term, of

116

course, that limit was eventually cast aside. At the same time, the Royal Navy was empowered to produce only two 35,000-ton battleships equipped with 16-inch guns to be built in the coming decade.

Overall, this meant that the Royal Navy relied on a fleet which contained a substantial portion of obsolete ships. The important cruiser squadrons, for example, were well used and tired out after the war. Replacements were restricted by the naval conference because Britain already had more ships than did other nations, and, because of financial constraints, replacements were slow to come through for ageing destroyers. The result was that Britain was still forced to rely on mighty but outdated dreadnoughts of First World War vintage which were easily outclassed and outgunned by other nations. Even the super-dreadnoughts of the *Queen Elizabeth* and *Royal Sovereign* classes did not match the firepower of the Japanese, and these were ships with a fairly long life expectancy.

Exactly the same problems gripped the Royal Navy submarine fleets. Literally dozens of boats were scrapped after the war and, although excellent advances had been made in the technology of submarine warfare, Britain did not have the financial muscle to develop her submarine fleet on the desired scale. The Admiralty anguished over its budgets and where best to deploy its resources and eventually came up with a proposal that shocked everyone. British delegates to the Washington conferences on disarmament put forward an astonishing proposal, calling for a worldwide ban on submarines. Their case was presented in an argument strung around the morality of underwater warfare, which had long been opposed by the traditionalists in the Royal Navy. At the turn of the century, submarines had been described by Admiral Sir Arthur Wilson, then Third Sea Lord, as 'underhand, underwater and damned un-English – certainly no occupation for a gentleman'.

Needless to say, Britain's proposal received no support from the other three nations who formed the policies for international maritime armaments, and Britain found herself relying on submarines built during the First World War for the bulk of her fleet well into the 1930s. Nor was that the end of the story. No longer did the maritime nations have to consider only attacks from the surface and submarine fleets of other navies. The third element came in the form of the arrival of the very real and potent threat from aircraft carriers, which came quickly to fruition from the final months of 1918. The possibilities for expansion in this form of naval warfare were evident at the time Field Marshal Smuts produced his report for the amalgamation of the Royal Flying Corps and the Royal Naval Air Service in 1917, and which the Admiralty fought tooth and nail to stop.

The Sea Lords argued that apart from the fact that the Royal Navy had built up a strong and well-equipped air force which it did not want to lose, aircraft carriers would soon become a major element of all the major navies. That prediction was already becoming a reality by the end of the war and would advance rapidly in the 1920s. The Admiralty was overruled and all aircraft operations were placed under RAF control – even those aircraft flown from ships. This meant that although the navy was sailing ships, the ships were carrying aircraft over which the navy effectively had no operational control.

Even worse, in the eyes of many senior planners at the Admiralty, was that almost the entire echelon of air-trained and experienced officers and most of the fliers were transported wholesale to the RAF, leaving few to plan the future needs for aircraft-carrying operations at a time when other navies – those of Japan, America and Italy in particular – were developing advanced types of aircraft specifically for carrier operations.

The Admiralty was also thwarted in its own plans to expand its carrier force, first by the limitations of the Washington Treaty and then by the financial constraints prevailing in the 1930s, and thus its hopes of building a dozen carriers were gradually downgraded to a trickle of make-do-and-mend alternatives. The First World War carrier *Argus* was followed by *Eagle* and the purpose-built *Hermes* in 1924, but they were designed for the toy-like aircraft that were in use at the time. The remainder of the carrier fleet consisted of conversions, such as *Glorious*, originally designed as a large cruiser, *Furious* and *Courageous*. Plans to build four major front-line carriers were delayed at every turn, and by 1937 only one, *Illustrious*, had arrived into service, and with it the Admiralty finally won total control of its aircraft with the formation of the

Fleet Air Arm. It was a wholly unsatisfactory situation that had dragged on for almost two decades without resolution so that, when war came again, Britain was seriously lagging in the aircraft-carrier business, both in the size of its ships and the totally outmoded aircraft that they carried. But then, in those difficult years of dire financial troubles, passing through the General Strike, the Wall Street crash and economic crises of gargantuan proportions in Britain, military spending was far from the government's lists of priorities.

Hard up and heavily in debt to the United States, the nation's financial malaise and industrial unease eventually spread to the workforce of the Royal Navy, in what famously became known as the Invergordon Mutiny. The run-up to this event was the great political crisis of 1931, when Labour Prime Minister Ramsay MacDonald sacked his Cabinet when the majority refused to back his draconian spending cuts and formed a National Coalition Government with the Tories and Liberals. Amid cries of 'Traitor!' by his Labour colleagues, MacDonald pressed on with the measures demanded by the banks.

One of the proposals which caused most grief among Labour MPs was a ten per cent cut in unemployment benefits and similar reductions in pay for public services. There was a particular problem with this scheme as it applied to the Royal Navy, in that while officers would barely notice the alterations, the majority of ships' companies would be badly hit. To add to the problem, a poorly worded statement was issued to all ships, stating that on government orders pay rates would revert to 1926 levels. At 6 a.m. on 15 September 1931, the crew of the battleship *Rodney* refused orders and went on strike, followed successively by men in other ships of the fleet as word passed down the line until all radio communications were shut down.

The marines, normally the enforcers of naval discipline and order, made it clear that they would not move against the strikers, or mutineers as they were called by officers as they shouted threats through loudspeakers that the miscreants 'would get no further than the end of a rope'. But the men ignored them. On the flagship *Nelson*, the seamen physically prevented the officers from putting the ship to sea. As Leonard Wincott, a seaman from HMS *Norfolk*, explained: 'The ships were under our complete control. We carried out all the essential duties, such as food supply, the cleaning of our living quarters, the provision of safety men and fire parties at night-time. The services of the officers were not required, and they were completely ignored and shunned by us.'

The mutiny achieved quick results. Within 24 hours the Admiralty capitulated and restored part of the wage cut. But the mutiny inspired other working-class resistance, and on 20 September the government was forced into unprecedented emergency measures, devaluing the pound and in turn being forced off the Gold Standard. In the wake of the Invergordon protest, a massive demonstration against wage cuts took place in Hyde Park, consisting of civil servants, teachers and postal workers. On 7 October the National Unemployed Workers' Movement led a demonstration of 50,000 unemployed in Glasgow. The next day 30,000 did likewise in Manchester, followed by another demonstration of 60,000 in Glasgow.

In the Royal Navy there were to be reprisals. Some 397 sailors were purged as troublemakers, and not just from the Atlantic Fleet, showing that there was widespread support in other ports. The Communist Party's *Daily Worker* naturally supported the mutineers. Its offices were raided, and its printer, business manager and an editorial board member arrested under the Incitement to Mutiny Act of 1797. But an investigation failed to uncover any Bolshevist subversion among Naval personnel, and the Admiralty was forced into a review of pay and conditions on the lower decks.

The Invergordon Mutiny, fascinating though it was as an element of British naval history, turned out to be no more than a little local difficulty that barely rated a mention in the scale of importance in the events unfolding elsewhere. The Nazis were on the march in Germany, Mussolini was rattling his sabre in Italy, the Japanese were in control in Manchuria, Churchill was warning at every opportunity that war was inevitable, and the Royal Navy, along with the Royal Air Force and pretty well all other elements of the British military, were falling further and further behind in their aspirations to rearm and replace their woefully outmoded principal elements of battle.

In the navy's case, quite apart from its shortcomings in the area

of aircraft carriers, the wake-up call in relation to its own effectiveness came when the Germans launched the first of three new
'armoured ships' that had completely and utterly outwitted the
international statesmen who had compiled the statutory limits on
the size of ships Germany could produce. In effect, these were
supposed to prevent Germany from building any battleships that
had the potential for matching the capital ships of the nations
involved with the Washington Treaty. But the Reichsmarine
secretly produced designs for the Panzerschiffe – the deadly
'pocket battleships' that were to cause Britain so much grief at the
start of the war. Officially, they were within the 10,000-ton limit
set down by the Allies, but they possessed 11-inch guns which had
the potency to threaten Britain's capital ships and cause havoc
among the lesser ships of the fleet. They had been specially built
for long-range raiding operations, which again was in breach of
the Versailles agreement. The British equivalent in the 10,000-ton
range was the County-class cruisers – *Norfolk*, *Suffolk* and so on –
which were comfortable ships, with eight-inch guns and lightly
armoured and, as one analyst commented, were 'splendid for a
world at peace'.

The Japanese were also cheating, quoting the tonnage of their
ships at 30 per cent below the real figure. In effect, therefore, a
naval conference in London in 1930 to extend international limits
on battleship construction until 1936 only really affected the
ability of the Royal Navy to expand, because as the world's largest
navy at the time of the original agreement, it was at its agreed
tonnage of warships – albeit with a large proportion of its ships
old and ill-equipped for modern warfare, as was very quickly to be
proven at the outbreak of war.

Even the leeway granted to Germany was not sufficient for
Hitler when he assumed absolute power in Germany in 1933.
Smarting for years over the terms of the Treaty of Versailles, he
soon made it clear that he considered the Third Reich no longer
bound by the conditions of the armistice and Britain could do
nothing about it. Indeed, in a roundabout way, the government of
the day helped Hitler on his way. Realising that Hitler was intent
on expansion, the British government chose the course of
appeasement rather than confrontation when in June 1935 it

signed an Anglo-German naval accord allowing Germany to build up her naval power once again, effectively removing the controls on German naval rearmament included in the Treaty of Versailles once and for all.

Britain signed the accord after Hitler's Ambassador von Ribbentrop asked Britain to agree to relax the agreements and supposedly allow Germany to increase the size of the German fleet to 35 per cent of that of the Royal Navy. In theory, that limit seemed manageable but in reality it did not account for the potency of the pocket battleships and was in any event merely a beginning for a dramatic expansion. At the time, Germany possessed three pocket battleships, six light cruisers and 12 torpedo boats. The treaty gave Hitler British approval to build five battleships, two aircraft carriers, five heavy cruisers, 11 light cruisers and 65 destroyers. The official British line was that Britain and her Allies had quite sufficient ships to deal with any German threat. In reality, the Admiralty was far from happy, and its intelligence people were already predicting war 'by 1940'. The French were furious with the British move. A Paris newspaper remarked: 'Does London imagine that Hitler had renounced any of the projects indicated in his book *Mein Kampf*? If so, the illusion of our friends across the Channel is complete.'

Hitler was, by then, cutting all the bonds of Versailles, one by one. He had launched a massive rearmament programme across the board. He was building submarines which were expressly not permitted, he had tripled his aircraft production in two years and then reclaimed Rhineland. The following month, after doing a deal with France over their African interests, Mussolini went empire-building and attacked Abyssinia. France raised no objection, and after a brief sortie by the Royal Navy at Alexandria and in the Red Sea Mussolini was bombarded with no worse than words as he completed his objective. The League of Nations did nothing. The third element in the 1930s equivalent to the Axis of Evil – Japan – consolidated its own position in China and, in doing so, 'accidentally' fired on Royal Navy ships.

The scene was set for a return match, and that it was forestalled for a further three years while Hitler built up his forces and hardware gave the British a chance to at least repair some of the damage limitation by the Washington Treaty that it had stuck to rigidly while others had not. Only then did the new Conservative government under Baldwin begin to take heed of the Admiralty's assertion that a programme of shipbuilding had to be tackled without delay. As a result, two new 35,000-ton battleships, *King George V* and *Prince of Wales*, and two 23,000-ton aircraft carriers, *Illustrious* and *Victorious*, went into production. The battleships were armed with 14-inch guns to conform to the latest treaty but were heavily armoured, while the carriers incorporated a unique armoured hangar, to improve their resistance to battle damage. War was declared before they were completed, and therein lay another disaster area in British industry: the shipyards. During the lean years, many had closed or been curtailed to such an extent that they had lost skilled men. And when, in 1938, additional battleships and two more carriers were proposed, the British steel industry and armament builders were so overstretched that the Admiralty had to place orders for flight-deck armour with Czechoslovakia. Worse still, no new gun turrets could be delivered until 1944.

With some limited attention at last being paid to the deployment of carriers, the question of suitable aircraft also came under discussion. Once again, with the British plane-makers now heavily overloaded with orders from the RAF, the Admiralty would have to make do with the versatile and popular Swordfish, a biplane capable of just 140mph flat out, which doubled as a torpedo bomber and reconnaissance aircraft. But given that the RAF would be short of fighters and had no true daylight bomber until later in 1942, the Royal Navy would never get priority for its carrier fleet, as and when they eventually came into service. In fact, the war had commenced before any of the new warships were ready, and in the meantime old light cruisers and destroyers from the First World War were pulled out of the reserve fleet to be refitted. Several were re-equipped to become anti-aircraft ships, although still armed with weapons and shells that had been manufactured for the previous war. The battleship *Warspite*, one of the stars of Jutland, also went in for a major refit, as did *Queen Elizabeth* and *Valiant*, and both were months away from completion when war broke out. The 1917 battle cruisers *Repulse* and

*Renown* were also scheduled for modernisation and the installation of greater protective armour, but only the latter was completed in time to rejoin the fleet in 1939, *Respite* never making it into the shipyards before the fighting began.

In spite of the drawbacks, the dash for modernisation had at least helped the Royal Navy to overcome some of her weaknesses and, together with the ships of the Dominion navies, was able to put together a global complement of 379 warships by September 1939. This figure sounded much better than it was, given that the total ranged from 12 battleships down to a multitude of sloops, escort vessels, gunboats and patrol vessels of all shapes and sizes positioned in various parts of the world. Britain was well ahead on the battleship front but was already lagging behind Germany in the crucial area of submarines: Germany started the war with a dozen more submarines than Britain.

One great advantage for the Royal Navy, however, was announced on 3 September 1939 and was signalled to all ships: Winston's Back! Churchill had returned to the Admiralty as First Lord, which boosted morale no end.

# CHAPTER SEVEN

## The Guns Blaze Again

When war came, the atmosphere was not the gung-ho 'Let's go get 'em' response that abounded in recollections of seamen at the start of the First World War. There were too many fresh memories from the re-examination of stories of great heroism and much loss of life for such an attitude to prevail, and, of course, everyone knew that Britain was in reality in no shape for a long and hard war. The reaction to the news was one of nervous excitement, or in the words of John Gates, then just 18, 'a sort of disbelief, really'. He had joined the Royal Navy at the age of 16, and from his training ship had been posted to the six-inch-gun cruiser *Ajax*, commissioned in January 1938. It so happened that *Ajax* was destined to sink the first ship in the Second World War and, before long, would take a leading part in one of the most famous naval engagements of modern times, the Battle of the River Plate. As John Gates said:

*Ajax* was an excellent ship. I was one of a party of 60 boys who joined her then. We were commissioned as a completely new unit, and I think this helped to weld a happy ship's company together by all starting together. I have a most vivid recollection of the very moment war was declared. We were all falling in on the quarterdeck, and the Articles of War were to be read by the captain. And it was during this period that a ship appeared on the horizon. It turned out to be the *Orlinda*, a German tramp. The captain broke off and we closed on the steamer immediately, ordered the crew to abandon ship and at about half-past eleven we opened fire until she started to sink. The *Orlinda* was the first ship to be sunk in the Second World War. The crew was taken aboard and searched by the master of arms and then taken up to the recreation room. We eventually unloaded them to an oil tanker to land them into custody. The second day we found another German ship called the *Karl Frissen* and we sank her likewise, taking her crew aboard until we could pass them on to another ship to land them. While they were with us, they were put to work during normal working hours, general chores about the ship under supervision of a Royal Marine guard. Other than that they were just sailors, additional hands as far as we were concerned.

First blood to the Royal Navy, therefore, but the sinking of these two merchantmen was an insignificant act compared with the opening of the German's account against the British. Even as war was declared by British Prime Minister Neville Chamberlain, U-boats were fanning out around the British Isles and into the Atlantic, while the fleet stayed home, following almost identical tactics to those established in the First World War. The U-boat successes were immediate and spectacular. While the British had taken out a couple of merchantmen, a U-boat torpedoed and sank the Glasgow liner *Athenia* with the loss of 112 lives.

Two weeks later, the Royal Navy suffered its first major loss. One of her four aircraft carriers, *Courageous*, fell victim to the Germans' ability to intercept and decode Royal Navy radio messages, a facility they enjoyed until early 1943. At this stage of the war, very few British ships were equipped with radar, and submarines were difficult to spot on the surface, especially at night. *Courageous*, launched on 5 February 1916 and commissioned in January 1917 as a large light cruiser, was converted into a carrier and operated as such from May 1928. Fred Ball joined her as a boy, aged 15, in 1938:

Although she was only a small carrier compared with the ones that came later, I was simply in awe at the size of her. The boys' mess desk was very low down in the ship, almost in the bilges. We had to remain in our own mess decks; we weren't allowed to mix with an ordinary seaman or an able seaman, and that applied to all the navy ships at that time. You were only allowed off your own mess deck to do your work, whatever duties you were assigned. The rule was strictly enforced. If you got caught somewhere else in the ship, you were punished. I think the fear of homosexuality had a lot to do with the stringency with which this rule was applied.

As war approached, I don't think any of the boys really thought about war, but I think had I really known that it was a possibility I might have changed my mind about joining, but eventually I would have been called up anyway. On *Courageous*, the captain cleared the lower decks, getting everyone on the flight deck to tell us. We were all pretty stunned. We were at sea then, and I was the commander's messenger. We had quite a lot of reservists aboard, who were 40 or 50 years old, and we went out on patrol in the Atlantic.

On 17 September 1939 we were operating aircraft about 400 miles off the coast of Ireland, on reconnaissance, looking for submarines. I was in the signals distribution office on the bridge and my relief came up. He was about ten minutes early, fortunately for him. Then as we stood there, there was a terrific thud, and then another. I don't think anyone realised what had happened for quite a few minutes. In fact, they were landing aircraft at the time and the last one got on just as the ship started to keel over.

Kapitän-Leutnant Otto Schuhart in the U-boat *U-29* had fired three torpedoes at *Courageous* in the south-west approaches, 150 nautical miles off Mizen Head, Ireland. The carrier went down in only 20 minutes and 518 of her 1,200 crew went with her, including her commander, Captain W.T. Makeig-Jones. Fred Ball was among the lucky ones:

Everyone knew by then we had been torpedoed. None of the

127

aircraft had been strapped down by then, and you could hear them all smashing into one another. I went down from the bridge to the flight deck and ran aft towards the stern. I went over the side on a rope and I landed on a propeller shaft, which fortunately for me was stopped. I jumped into the water and swam away. I'm glad they taught me to swim, and I just kept going, remembering what they told us at naval school: always get away from the ship because of the suction when they go down. There were quite a few of them in the water. The lifeboats were all operated by electric motors, and because they had failed no boats were launched as far as I know. Nor did I see any Carley rafts, and there are stories that, with *Courageous* being so long in reserve, the Carley rafts had been painted so often they were stuck to the ship's side. Anyhow, I never saw a Carley raft in the water and there was no wreckage to cling to, nothing. I just kept swimming and I had been in the water for about two hours.

I was very, very cold and almost exhausted. There were times when I didn't think I could go on and I have to admit I was tempted to give up. I thought, 'Shall I just pack in and go under?' and then shook my head and said, 'No, keep going, keep going.' I kept repeating it and I kept thinking of my family, my mother and father and brothers and sisters. Even so, I couldn't have gone on much longer when an American merchant ship, *Collingwood*, came along and launched a boat looking for survivors. It was dark by then and we began shouting until they came towards us. Some of those in the water were singing 'Roll out the Barrel' and that sort of thing – I think to keep their spirits up. Later, Lord Louis Mountbatten came along in his destroyer, *Kelly*, and collected us. He gave us a talk and said it was the fortune of war, which didn't help much. We were taken back to Devonport, where we were kitted out and allowed to send a telegram free of charge.

My parents knew *Courageous* had been sunk. It was announced on 18 September but no relatives were informed of survivors for two days. I got two weeks' survivors' leave, and when we returned we were assigned to a holiday camp near Plymouth which the navy had taken over as reserve barracks for all the new people coming in, and about 20 of the boys from *Courageous* were employed in cleaning the place up. Not long afterwards, there was a public outcry about boys going to sea to fight a war whereas in the other forces they were not allowed to go to war until they were 17. The Admiralty sent a form to parents to give permission to go to sea before they were 17. My parents said no, and so I stayed ashore until 1940 when I joined *Dorsetshire* [in which, as we will see, Fred experienced his second traumatic sinking in the Far East].

Spotting U-boats was quite often more by luck than judgement, as in the case of U-boat *U-42*, which was preparing to launch an attack on the destroyers *Imogen* and *Ilex*, which were in company with the merchantman *Stonepool* on 13 October. By pure chance, a masthead lookout on the merchant ship spotted the U-boat on the surface. Signalling by light, *Stonepool* alerted the destroyers to the presence of the U-boat. Lieutenant Alastair Ewing, on *Imogen*, recalled:

*Ilex* suddenly altered course, increased speed and made to us by light 'submarine this way'. We followed at once. Almost immediately *Ilex* hoisted the 'submarine in sight' flag and opened fire. The U-boat dived, and as we came close both destroyers launched depth charges [whereupon] the U-boat suddenly came to the surface with a tremendous surge at about 20 degrees to the horizontal 1,000 yards away. It was a most exciting moment. The U-boat righted herself at once . . . Both ships opened fire with our 4.7 guns. The result: *Imogen* one hit, *Ilex* two [and the latter] went full ahead to ram. As she passed over, the torpedo gunner's mate fired the starboard depth charge thrower, but almost as soon as the *Ilex* had drawn clear the [U-boat's] conning tower opened and an officer appeared waving a piece of white paper [followed by] sailors with their hands up.

Only 17 of the crew of 38 were saved. The U-boats got their own back the following day, and at the same time scored their greatest triumph to date close to the burial ground of the German High

Seas Fleet in the last war – Scapa Flow. It was the most audacious, shocking and humiliating action against the Royal Navy because it took place within the confines of the supposedly impregnable naval harbour whose security had, in truth, been neglected during the difficult years of the 1930s and left a gap for an aspiring U-boat adventurer. In fact, only sheer good fortune prevented a major disaster befalling the navy's finest ships, which until 24 hours earlier had been *in situ* at Scapa Flow. A German reconnaissance aircraft had discovered the British Home Fleet at anchor and Kapitän-Leutnant Günther Prien set course for Scapa in *U-47*. But when he arrived, the fleet had already set sail, leaving only *Royal Oak* on guard duty. The old First World War battleship had been modernised, along with others of the *Revenge* class, and was still a fine capital ship with a new crew, including Howard Instance:

I was drafted to *Royal Oak* in June 1939 as a leading seaman with warrant officer qualifications. We commissioned her in the good old-fashioned way, probably the last one ever to do it. The whole draft – seamen, stokers, artificers, supply, cooks – we all mustered in the Royal Naval Barracks, Portsmouth. There were also 120 boys coming aboard, and I was to assist with their further education at sea. Our bags and hammocks were put into four or five lorries, and we lined up in fours and marched all the way from the Royal Naval Barracks to the farewell jetty in the dockyard behind a Royal Marine band, right down Queen Street with lots of Portsmouth people waving their hands. We got to the dockyard. We were halted alongside the ship and turned to face the ship. The commander came out on the sort of bandstand they had and told us what a fine ship she was and that she had the reputation of being the cleanest ship in the navy.

*Royal Oak* went north to join the fleet at Scapa Flow as flagship of the 2nd Battle Squadron. There were several alerts of German capital ships at sea but none ever appeared. The fleet commanders were, however, concerned about air attacks, and in mid-October decided to move the fleet to another anchorage around the coast of Scotland and out of range of German bombers. No one gave much thought to the threat from submarines at Scapa Flow but on this occasion it was fortunate indeed that the fleet was moved – all except, that is, *Royal Oak*, which had recently been slowed down by a mechanical fault. Her commander was instructed to remain in Scapa Flow to act as an anti-aircraft guard for Kirkwall, because the anti-aircraft defences around Scapa Flow had not been completed at that time. There was also another flaw in Scapa security, as Howard Instance explained:

Most sailors believed that when you've been out on patrol, once you got back through the boom of Scapa Flow you were home and dry. But in this case there was a gap, near the island of Hoy, where there were two block-ships that didn't completely block the entrance. The powers that be reckoned the water was too shallow for a submarine to get through submerged, although they were planning to send up some more block-ships but believed there was no hurry to do anything about it. Well, where this information came from to guide the German submarine nobody seemed to know. There was some talk about a [spy] in Kirkwall providing the information that there was enough room for a submarine to get between these two islands at high tides on the surface. High tide on 13 October, which was a Friday, was somewhere between 12 o'clock and half-past at night. Prien, in *U-47*, found a gap* and got into the Flow, actually on the surface. Once in the Flow, he submerged and went looking for the Home Fleet. According to his reconnaissance pictures, there should have been some major ships like *Renown, Hood, Ark Royal, Repulse* and numerous cruisers and destroyers.

He made straight for that anchorage but discovered there was nothing there. He then edged northwards up towards Kirkwall, and there in front of him, silhouetted against the curtain of light that you get in those high latitudes – aurora borealis – there was the dim outline of *Royal Oak*. So he got

---

*Between Orkney Mainland and Lamb Holm, according to his log.

into firing position and he fired his torpedoes. The explosion shook the ship from end to end [but no one at that time really knew what had caused it]. I immediately hopped out of my hammock and I went to the next bulkhead, which was the boys' mess, because I knew there was a clock there. It was four minutes past one. I shouted: 'Get out of your hammocks and get dressed until we find out what's going on.' Well, most of them sort of looked over their hammock and said: 'I'm going to stay where I am.' But being the leading hand of the mess I thought it was my duty to try to find out what had happened.

I saw the captain and the commander go through our mess decks forward. I suppose they were going to try and find out what it was all about. A submarine [attack] seemed out of the question, or so we believed. I wandered along the port battery, and just at the end of the port battery was a small heads [toilet], where there was a queue. I heard somebody say: 'I think it's one of the compressors has blown up in the forward refrigerator compartment.' But nobody knew. I personally thought a high-flying bomber had dropped its load somewhere near the ship. But then . . . there was another explosion, and about three or four seconds later another one much closer. About three or four seconds after that there was an enormous explosion right underneath where we were. I suppose a couple of seconds went by and then a huge sheet of orange flame came through the hatchway. It hit the chap in front of me and he went up like a match, just like striking a match.

It flung me right back inside the heads. The flame had gone straight up through the battery and would have incinerated anybody up there. All I could do was to huddle in the corner and cover my eyes and head and then I could feel the skin bubbling up . . . it went on for ten, fifteen seconds, something like that, maybe more. But all of a sudden it stopped and it was pitch dark. The ship was in complete darkness. I went unconscious for about five minutes and when I came round I tried to stand up and I couldn't. I thought: 'I don't know what's going on but I've got to get out.'

I crawled out of the toilet, across from the port side to the starboard side and I went down the starboard passage to where I knew the starboard screen door was leading under the quarterdeck. When I got to the door, I started to pull myself up and I suddenly realised then that I hadn't been crawling on the deck in the last 20 yards or so but on the bulkhead because she was over by about 60 degrees.

As I tried to get out, I fell and I split my head open, then slid down towards the guardrails. One rail caught me under the throat and the other one caught me on the stomach. I knew now she was going over . . . somehow I had to get out, although I was badly burned. A young midshipman was next to me hanging on the guardrails. He still had his telescope under his arm. I don't know who he thought I was in the dark but he said: 'Do you think we should abandon ship, sir?' Before I could answer him the guardrails went under and we floated off into the terribly cold water. This brought me round, sort of shook me out of my torpor. I laid on my back and I looked up and to my horror I saw the muzzles of two 15-inch guns slowly coming down on top of me. As the ship went over, the locking bolts of the turrets, which weighed about 300 tons, had sheered. I turned around and I swam the quickest 100 yards I've swum in my life until I was exhausted, and I knew then I was clear of the ship. I turned and looked back and against the night sky I could see the whole of the bottom of the ship as she was going over.

The noise . . . the noise was terrific. The only way I can describe it is to say it's like having a large biscuit tin full of nuts and bolts and you turn it upside down. One can only imagine what was happening inside the ship. All the six-inch ready-use shells were probably falling off their racks and thundering around the ship. All loose lockers must have been moving and falling everywhere. I could even hear the 15-inch shells, one-ton shells, coming out of their racks and – boom, boom, boom – bounding around the magazine, the shell room. It was awful to listen to. Then everything went quiet, although I could hear voices, people yelling and some screaming. And then gradually the hull began to disappear, surrounded by the foam from vents of air and water coming up, and it was gone.

I tried once again to get moving. I knew that about half a mile away we had a tender called *Daisy II*. She used to get our mail and take the liberty men ashore. She apparently had got back to the ship just before the explosions took place. When the ship started going over they had to cut the wires so she wouldn't go over with it. She backed off from the ship and Skipper Gatt was the man who saved over 200 men milling around in the water. But at that point I couldn't see many people, but I could hear them. It was very dark and I was beginning to feel the cold very badly.

Then a voice out of the darkness said: 'Who's that?' And I recognised my divisional officer, Lieutenant Hoare. I said: 'It's Leading Seaman Instance and I'm burned to buggery.' 'Oh,' he said, 'sorry, old man. Hang on to this lump of wood.' We had a plank between us and I recovered a bit then. He said: 'Look, that large light over there is the *Daisy*. Come on, let's swim to the *Daisy*.' Well, he was uninjured but we left the log and swam away. I could only make about 100 yards and then it was just a question of surviving, keeping myself afloat. But then came another hazard – the oil. Oh, it was about two inches thick, and I swam straight into it. It was like trying to swim in treacle. I thought: 'My God, I mustn't swallow any of this.' So I just dog-paddled around.

I could hear a few voices in the distance singing 'Down Mexico Way' of all things. I tried to sing 'Down Mexico Way' but I didn't know the words. I suppose I floated around for about half an hour or more. My sole motive was to keep afloat. Having got out of the ship, I was determined not to drown; that was my whole attitude. Then I heard a voice in the darkness, a young voice it was; in fact, it was one of the boys: 'There's one over here, sir.' Over came this little raft. It was no more than about four feet square. On it was this boy Lawrence and the commissioned shipwright officer. They had one paddle. I heard the shipwright officer say: 'Righto, pull him in.' Of course, this poor boy couldn't pull me in because he couldn't get hold of me. I was smothered in oil. So the shipwright officer said: 'Get hold of his hair and drag him in.' Well, I didn't have any hair; it was gone, burned off. So they tried to grab one of my hands. I screamed out because my hands were raw. And finally they got me under the armpits and sort of just slid me on.

I just laid on this thing and I remember thinking: 'They've only got one paddle so I'd better help them.' I remember paddling with my hand and then I went out and the next thing I remember was being hoisted up the gangway of *Pegasus* by two able seamen. We got to the top of the gangway and the officer of the watch was there. My trousers and jersey were charred and falling off. And I heard the officer of the watch say: 'Right, strip off all that charred stuff and undo that belt and sling it over the side.' My brain clicked because Friday, the day previously, we'd been paid and I had £5 in the belt pocket. So I said: 'No, no, I've got a fortnight's pay in there.'

He said: 'All right, put a blanket around him and put the belt around the outside of the blanket and then take him in the sickbay.' They half-carried me along the deck and past rows of bodies, men [who had] died of exposure, and into a small sickbay where they laid me on a bunk and poured Martini down my throat. The sickbay attendant put a cigarette in my mouth and I took a puff and when he took the cigarette away my lips came away with it. It so shocked me I went unconscious again. The next recollection I've got is being helped down the gangway.

I was taken down with about 20 other people who'd been burned on to another drifter. But this drifter wouldn't move from *Pegasus* to the hospital ship until daylight, and there we sat in this hold shivering, and the burns were beginning to really hurt. The hospital ship was about six miles away and we were hoisted in by cradle and crane and put into the big sickbay there where they had everything, nurses and orderlies, and they really looked after us. A shot of morphia puts you straight out. [When] I came to I couldn't see very well. I could only sort of see in front of me and I couldn't understand why. And I turned my head and looked at the chap next to me and he was bandaged all over with just two holes for his eyes and a hole for his nose. I said: 'Do I look like you?' He said: 'Yes.'

We spent two days on the hospital ship, and the next day German bombers came over. Well, the only target worth bombing, of course, was *Iron Duke*, the old battleship acting as a depot ship. They were laying their line of bombs down, trying to hit *Iron Duke*. And they were falling very, very close to the hospital ship. In fact, one string of bombs sort of lifted the hospital ship up and dropped her back in again. We all thought: 'Oh dear, we're not going to have to swim again, are we?'

Howard Instance's story was one of many such experiences among his colleagues on *Royal Oak*, and there were many examples of great heroism on the part of those who survived. In all, 833 men lost their lives, and of the 396 survivors many suffered severe burns and injuries. Howard, like a number of his colleagues, went through months of agonising skin grafts and treatment. When he was eventually discharged from hospital, he still couldn't wear a uniform and when he reported at the Royal Naval Barracks gates at Portsmouth in civvies, the regulating petty officer said: 'Yes, what do you want?'

'I'm a *Royal Oak* survivor,' said Howard.

The officer replied: 'Where's your uniform . . . Where's your identity card?'

'At the bottom of Scapa Flow.'

Although Howard suffered for many years from the effects of his burns, he returned to active service within six months, first taking a gunnery course and then spending much of his future service in destroyers attached to the Atlantic convoys, and again experienced many hair-raising scenarios among the U-boat wolf packs. He came perilously close to ending up in the water again when his ship was hit by a merchantman in thick fog. The destroyer began to sink with a gaping hope in her bow. Only fast action to close the watertight doors saved her from going down, and she limped back to Boston, Massachusetts, stern first.

In terms of the number of ships lost, Britain did not fare well in those early months of the war. On the other hand, the Royal Navy had played its part in successfully transferring troops and thousands of tons of guns, machinery and vehicles across the Channel to France in the first phase of landings by the British Expeditionary Force under Field Marshal Lord Gort, VC, to join their French Allies who were installed behind their so-called impregnable Maginot Line. Within a month, 160,000 men had been landed in France. The navy also brought grief to the German U-Boat Command in these first weeks, with 16 confirmed lost to mines, depth charges or torpedoes and another six suspected of being sunk in the first two months of the war alone.

However, the U-boats themselves were taking a hefty toll on British merchantmen, with 115 ships sunk by the year's end. Many of those, however, were down to the raiding operations of two of Germany's three pocket battleships, *Admiral Graf Spee* and *Deutschland*, which slipped out of Wilhelmshaven two weeks before the war began and headed first into the Indian Ocean and then on into the South Atlantic. It will be recalled that was exactly the route taken by German marauders in the First World War, culminating in the Battle of the Falklands in which the renowned Admiral Graf von Spee went down with his ship.

This time, the Graf Spee name, borne by the pocket battleship, would cause havoc again. That and *Deutschland* were given free rein to attack. They were fast and heavily armed, and easily a match for British cruisers. *Graf Spee*, under Captain Hans Langsdorff, carried six 11-inch guns and a secondary armament of eight six-inch guns. In ten weeks of operations, she sank no less than 50,000 tons of British merchantmen without loss of life to their crews, who were all picked up and taken prisoner. The latter fact was an important statistic to all sailors and the mark of an honourable captain. It was also true that when in battle – as she eventually was in the River Plate – captured crews on board at the time were eventually brought to safety unharmed. *Deutschland* was less successful and was subsequently called back to her home port to be renamed, Hitler realising the potential for embarrassment should she fall foul of British warships.

The roaming activities of *Graf Spee* continued to cause the British deep concerns, if for no other reason than she was tying up two key RN units: Force G, which patrolled the South Atlantic, and Force H, operating out of Cape Town. Finally, after another string of sinkings, Churchill instructed that *Graf Spee* should be hunted down and sunk with all due haste. The task fell to Commodore Henry Harwood, commanding Force G, who plotted the movements of the German ship from reports of the sunken ships. The final clue as to the German ship's movements came on 2 December, when Langsdorff sank the *SS Doric Star*, which managed to send out a distress call shortly before the crew evacuated, putting their position in the mid-South Atlantic. From that, Harwood surmised that the most likely route would at some point take the German ship to the River Plate, where on the northern flank stood the neutral port of Montevideo and on the southern side pro-German Buenos Aires.

He was right, and soon all the elements were in place for one of the most fascinating episodes in naval history: the Battle of the River Plate, a tale that went well beyond that of mighty ships hurling shells at each other. Harwood had four cruisers under his command, one of which, HMS *Cumberland*, was at Port Stanley for a refit. The remaining three were *Exeter*, under Captain Frederick Bell, Harwood's flagship *Ajax*, under Captain C.H.L. Woodhouse, and the New Zealand cruiser *Achilles*, under Captain Edward Parry. *Exeter* was an eight-inch-gun cruiser and the other two six-inch, all substantially outgunned by *Graf Spee*. John Napier, a young rating aboard *Exeter* at the beginning of his long career in the Royal Navy, remembered:

> We had been shadowing German ships when war broke out, although we had returned to the UK for a brief spell and given shore leave. But we were recalled after three days and went straight to sea again, on our way to South America. The captain was clearly expecting trouble. En route, we dumped all wood on the ship's decks, anything that would burn and thus add to any conflagration [that might occur in battle]. We refuelled at Rio and headed south towards the River Plate, where we were to link up with *Ajax* and *Achilles* on 12 December. We had been told by the ship's commander that there was a German pocket battleship in the area and we were out to get her. We knew we had only eight-inch guns against her 11-inch armament, and if there were a battle we would

have to win it by manoeuvrability and speed. We were under no illusions that she could do us very severe damage, as indeed was ultimately proved.

But there was a great deal more riding on this battle than the ability of the ships. The German people were deeply unsettled by Hitler's failure to open up peace negotiations with the British, and the Führer needed a strong morale-booster. The same applied in Britain, for different reasons. There was deep apprehension among a nation ill-prepared for war, and the PR spin from some good news would be a great fillip. Thus, on 13 December *Graf Spee*, now Hitler's pride and joy that he proclaimed would demonstrate once and for all that Britannia no longer ruled the waves, came into contact with Commodore Harwood's Force G off the coast of neutral Uruguay.

Harwood directed *Exeter* to steam west while the two light cruisers moved in the opposite direction for a pincer movement. John Napier on *Exeter*:

I had had a full night of action stations, and off shift I went to sleep. At around 6.15, the bugler sounded action stations at the double. I dashed to my station. I could see smoke [from *Graf Spee*] on the horizon dead ahead. We could feel the vibration of the engines as the ship picked up speed towards the enemy. I remember the fall of shot from the enemy on either side of us, and at the same time we had been ordered from the bridge to take cover. At that order, myself and a colleague took shelter under the bridge super-structure. We hadn't been there a few minutes before B turret had been hit, and the shell must have continued on straight through the bridge, killing most of the personnel except the captain and the commander. I was standing near the ladder that went up the commander's cabin at that time and a decapitated head came tumbling down the steps and we recognised the face. We were devastated by the sight, and it is something I have never spoken of. The experience of it coming towards me shook me so much that I didn't know what to do with myself. It was terrible. I was just turned 20 at the time, although some of the lads were 17 years old.

Langsdorff directed his 11-inch guns at *Exeter* for a full 25 minutes while shells from his 5.9-inch secondary armoury were sent towards *Ajax* and *Achilles* as they moved to their stations to open with their six-inch guns, which in fact did little damage and were unable to penetrate the German ship's protective metal, but at least their harrying distracted the full attention of Langsdorff's guns. The situation on *Exeter* was dire, as John Napier recalled:

We moved from the bridge knowing we could do nothing in that area and went down towards the torpedo tubes and discovered the starboard torpedo tubes had been hit by shrapnel from a near miss, killing most of the torpedo gun crew and wounding several others. I helped with the first-aid parties, doing the best we could with the wounded. At that point I had the experience of seeing an 11-inch shell tear through the port side of the ship and come aft into the four-inch magazine and burst just past the magazine. The draught and the force of the wind and the pressure coming up through the hatch was terrific, and at the same time the chief torpedo gunner's mate was blown up through the hatch. One of the damage-control people went in directly after the shell had passed through and recognised our blacksmith and went to help him, and as he did so he literally fell to pieces. He must have been burned to smithereens.

We were now on fire from the paint shop for'ard right to the bridge. We had jettisoned both aircraft but there was still a lot of aviation fuel about. People were busy up above washing down. We'd set a smoke screen and turned away to get Y turret bearing. When there was only one gun firing it was decided by the commodore to pull us out of the action. During this period, our decks were swimming with water. The hydrants had burst in places through the shrapnel damage. I heard someone calling for help in directing [verbal] steering orders from the after control position to the after steering position, and this I did until the ship drew out of the action and headed for the Falklands.

Before pulling away, *Exeter* had managed to land a direct hit that left a six-foot hole in the bows of *Graf Spee* before her own last turret was put out of action by another shell from the enemy. Meanwhile, *Ajax* and *Achilles* drew the Germans' fire with a fresh barrage of their own, and their shells, though not powerful enough to penetrate the main armour, were causing casualties and damaging the superstructure.

*Exeter* finally pulled out of the battle and headed off to the Falklands, shipping water and listing badly and with 62 of her crew killed and another 29 injured. *Ajax* and *Achilles* kept up the pressure, and Commodore Harwood ordered them to close *Graf Spee* and, although hit by two shells which put two of her turrets out of action, *Ajax* landed more shells on the battleship which started a serious fire. *Achilles* followed up with four torpedoes, which were avoided, but *Graf Spee* was already on the run, badly damaged and with 39 of her crew dead and more than 60 wounded. Remarkably, 62 captured British merchant seamen were safe and sound down below.

Captain Langsdorff pulled away, apparently having decided to seek shelter and repairs, a move which surprised Harwood, especially as he could easily have finished off *Exeter*. With his two remaining cruisers running short of ammunition, Harwood adopted the classic shadowing role, 15 miles from his prey. *Graf Spee* set course for Montevideo, where the neutral government granted the Germans' request for shelter but limited her stay to just three days – nowhere near sufficient to carry out repairs. Meanwhile, the two remaining British cruisers took station at the mouth of the River Plate, in case the pocket battleship should attempt to make a run for it. Whereas the Battle of the River Plate had made front pages around the world, the events that followed in its wake continued to enthral as a battle of wits opened up between diplomats and secret service agents.

Langsdorff cabled Berlin, explained his plight and cited the three options open to him: to remain in Montevideo and accept internment, to try to make a run for it through neutral waters and then try to fight his way to Buenos Aires or – the unthinkable – to scuttle the ship. According to evidence available after the war,

Hitler was incandescent with rage. Why had the captain not fought to the last, and if necessary gone down with his ship like a hero? Did the name Graf Spee mean nothing? Now, he had put the German navy at risk of humiliation and, worse, the possibility of dangerous consequences. Although supposedly neutral, Uruguay had a pro-British president and Montevideo was well known as a centre of intelligence intrigue, with the British representation well to the fore. The Germans now believed it was more than a possibility that if the battleship were interned, it would not be long before vital codes and other secrets found their way into hostile hands.

The British, meanwhile, took advantage of Captain Langsdorff's predicament by putting out rumours to the avid newspaper representation in Montevideo that a force of British ships, including the battle cruiser *Renown* and the aircraft carrier *Ark Royal*, were expected at any moment to join Harwood's two cruisers and ensure the destruction of *Graf Spee*. This was a total fabrication. The two ships were 1,000 miles away at the time. However, to cover the possibility of Langsdorff moving out of Montevideo to try to reach Buenos Aires, the British representative won some breathing space by pointing out that, under international law, a hostile ship was barred from leaving port within 24 hours of the departure of a merchant vessel belonging to the opposition. Coincidentally or not, a British merchantman had just sailed, thus ensuring that *Graf Spee* was trapped until at least 16 December 1939.

All of this toing and froing was being eagerly reported in the international press, and finally Captain Langsdorff sought a decision from Berlin: should he accept internment or scuttle the ship? Hitler himself made the decision: scuttle, and ensure that all security equipment and materials were destroyed beyond redemption. Thus, on 17 December 1939 all but a skeleton crew were taken off *Graf Spee* and transferred to the German tanker *Tacoma*, and shortly after 6 p.m. crowds lined the dockside as she weighed anchor for her last journey, surrounded by small boats carrying journalists, cameramen and radio reporters. Four miles out of the River Plate, Langsdorff gave the order: stop all engines, drop anchor. He and the skeleton crew were taken off by steamer, and soon afterwards there were six explosions aboard. *Graf Spee* blew up in a spectacular morass of flame and smoke.

Later that day, Langsdorff rejoined the rest of his crew in Buenos Aires on the other side of the River Plate estuary. Two days later, overcome by remorse and the indignity of return to Germany to face a tirade from Hitler, he wrote letters to his family and then shot himself in his hotel room. His body was found lying across the German naval flag, which did not carry the swastika, that he had carried from *Graf Spee*. His funeral in Buenos Aires was attended by Captain Pottinger of the British merchant vessel SS *Ashlea*, representing the British crews whose ships had been sunk by Langsdorff but whose personal safety he had ensured. These were the prisoners who were still on board *Graf Spee* when she docked in Montevideo. Almost another 300 were unaccounted for, and were in fact aboard the battleship's supply vessel, *Altmark*, which had sailed unnoticed from Montevideo and made a dash for Germany, having dismissed the opportunity to land her prisoners at a neutral port.

The alert went up, and in spite of the needle-in-a-haystack potential the Royal Navy picked up *Altmark*'s trail and she was spotted in the nick of time, in neutral Norwegian waters, and intercepted by destroyers. Captain P.L. Vian of HMS *Cossack* challenged the German skipper, who denied he had any British prisoners aboard. Unconvinced, Captain Vian pulled alongside and sent a boarding party scrambling on to *Altmark*, and after a brief but violent fight the men reached the hatches to the unlit hold and their leader shouted: 'Any British down there?'

They were greeted by a loud, roaring cheer from below, and the party leader shouted down: 'Well, come on up. The navy's here.' And out clambered 299 officers and men of sunken British merchantmen, starving hungry but otherwise safe and sound.

There was one further element to this story, and that concerned the eventual fate of *Exeter*, now an heroic ship in the eyes of the entire British public. John Napier concludes his account as the ship departed the encounter at the River Plate, almost a floating wreck:

On the journey down to the Falklands, there was a deathly quiet about the ship. We stopped twice to hold burial services. In Port Stanley, many of the wounded were taken ashore and put up in residents' homes because the ship was so badly damaged. We lost several other men from their wounds, and they were buried locally. We attempted to make repairs there as best we could. In fact, it was a remarkable effort. The hulk of ss *Great Britain* was lying there at the time, and we utilised some of the steel plates to make us watertight, and we worked for weeks cleaning up and making her habitable again, given all that had happened. That she was made good to get back to Britain under her own steam was nothing short of a miracle.

On the journey back, *Renown* and *Ark Royal* met us at Freetown and escorted us back to the western approaches, where we were met by eight or nine destroyers. At the same time as we were met by them, one of the Blue Star liners passed quite close to us and the men on board had waved and shouted to us as we passed. But – lo and beyond – just as she got over the horizon we heard a thump and then a terrific bang. She'd been torpedoed.

Lots of U-boats had been waiting for us but they'd missed *Exeter* and hit the liner instead. Coming into Plymouth Sound on that cold February morning, into the outer harbour by the fort, word got around that *Exeter* had arrived, and as we approached there were people lining the Plymouth Hoe as far as the eye could see, and as the ship proceeded up the harbour in Devonport all the dockyard mateys were cheering and the tugs sounding their sirens. It was a tumultuous welcome and when we reached our berth Winston Churchill came on board and gave a welcome speech. He said the people of the nation were very proud of us [this action, he said, will long be told in song and story]. We were allowed to go on leave wearing our cap badge and we were recognised everywhere we went. We saw Churchill again later when we took part in parades in London and attended a dinner at the Guildhall for the presentation of medals by George VI.

The arrival home of *Exeter* was indeed given particular attention. At that point in time, Britain was in desperate need of some good news.

# CHAPTER EIGHT

## The Narvik Tragedies

The action of HMS *Cossack* in rescuing the merchant seamen bound for German prisoner-of-war camps put the spotlight on Scandinavia, where Norway and Denmark were desperately trying not to upset Hitler and remained neutral while Finland had a battle of its own. Taking advantage of the conflict in Europe, Russia invaded Finland in October 1939. The Finns stood their ground and kept the Red Army at bay well into the New Year. The attack temporarily diverted the interest of the European contenders towards that region, and specifically to Kiruna in northern Sweden, which was Germany's main supplier of iron ore. In winter, the ore was shipped through the ice-free Norwegian port of Narvik on the western seaboard and then through neutral Norwegian waters to Germany. On the pretext of supporting Finland against the Red Army, the British had, with French acquiescence, worked out that on the way they could occupy Narvik and Kiruna, the two key centres for the shipping of iron and ore, and halt the flow of vital supplies into Germany.

The action would require the cooperation of both Norway and Sweden. Both nations refused, in the vain hope of maintaining their neutrality. By then, it was too late. Prevented by bad weather and adverse intelligence reports, the German High Command delayed its invasion of the Low Countries still further and instead

focused on the developing situation in Scandinavia. The upshot
was Hitler's approval of an incursion into Denmark and Norway
on 7 April 1940, the latter through eight ports from Narvik and on
down around the western and southern coastline to Oslo and, for
the first time ever, using airborne troops to secure inland sites. A
British Task Force, having laid their mines around Narvik, was at
that moment sailing home and actually passed the German ships
without seeing them, leaving the way clear for largely unopposed
landings on the morning of 9 April.

As German warships appeared off the Norwegian coast, the
airborne invasion began inland. Within 48 hours, the Germans
had landed seven divisions and captured all the main ports while
the airborne troops secured their position in Oslo and major
airports. The weather halted the planned parachute drops at Oslo
airport, and infantry troops were landed in a succession of Junker
52s to take possession. Five companies of parachute troops did,
however, drop at other key airports. The Germans established a
firm hold on the southern half of Norway.

Oslo was overrun by noon that day, yet the Norwegian
government decided to make a stand and moved to Elverum,
there to send word inviting the British and French to dispatch
troops immediately to their assistance. The terrain was rugged
and difficult, and with more than 200,000 troops already committed to the BEF to confront the German invasion that must
soon surely come, the British army agreed at last to the formation of 'guerrilla forces' backed up by a Royal Navy Task Force
and an RAF fighter force consisting of bombers, anti-aircraft
ships and fighters, the last to be included in a Fleet Air Arm
action involving both RAF and Royal Navy fliers, with the
carriers *Ark Royal* and *Glorious* in support, although the latter
was to end in great tragedy.

First, however, the Royal Navy Task Force moved in to harass
the Germans at the very time of their invasion of Norway,
knowing well that they could not stop the onslaught but that at the
very least they could throw some fireworks into the party. The
sorties became known as the First and Second Battles of Narvik,
on the 10 and 13 April respectively.

The first battle involved the 2nd Destroyer Flotilla, under

Captain B.K.W. Warburton-Lee, made up of five H-class ships, *Hardy*, the flagship, *Havoc, Hostile, Hotspur* and *Hunter*. In blizzards and fog, they moved into Westfjord and then on through Ofotfjord to enter Narvik Bay, where a far superior German destroyer force awaited them, along with a number of supply ships. In a sharp battle, the British sank six supply ships and two large German destroyers and damaged five for the loss of two of their own small destroyers. In his memoir record for the Imperial War Museum, Chief Petty Officer Fred Kemp, in *Havoc*, provides the commentary on what turned out to be a brilliant operation for such a meagre force:

The weather was absolutely vile. The blizzard was such that the ship ahead had to switch on the stern light so that we could follow. But in spite of the conditions, we were alive to every navigational order being passed from Warburton-Lee. In the TS [transmission station], we had a wireless telegraphy operator all ready in case we went into concentrated fire. I was the senior chief PO in charge of the whole fore part of the ship – that's the TS, the loading position, magazines and shell rooms – seeing that everything went right and, of course, our TGM [torpedo gunner's mate] used to switch on the secondary diesel arrangement in case our main electricity force faulted. The action began as soon as we entered Narvik harbour. We loomed up alongside a [German troop] transport. We were so close I saw an officer on the bridge of this ship pointing a gun at my captain. He was immediately cut down by a Royal Marine with a long burst from the twin Lewis gun. That wiped out their bridge personnel. But before we went on, we gave the transport a full salvo of 4.7 shells at point-blank range. Then we came across another transport. She also got the works. Meanwhile, *Hardy* and *Hunter*, which were leading the attack, had spotted German destroyers taking on oil. They sank both with torpedoes. In *Havoc*, we now observed a lone destroyer, which we took on in a gun battle and hit her twice in the stern. It seemed to set her after magazine on fire, whereupon the ship blew up and that was the end of that.

The other four ships had been similarly engaged and, said Kemp, there were German wrecks all around Narvik harbour. But the British destroyers also took a heavy pounding, especially *Hotspur* and *Hostile*:

They came limping out of the gloom, having had a battle with the shore batteries and suffered very badly internally. They had to retire to get patched up, tend to their wounded and bury their dead. *Hotspur*, especially, was in terrible trouble. She had been hit amidships, with major problems in the boiler room and engine room. They managed to shore up and get out of Narvik Bay into Ofotfjord while we guarded their stern. The next thing that came out of the mist was two large German destroyers of the 1,600-ton type, which took us on, and our senior officer, Lieutenant-Commander Rafe Courage, played the battle of his life. Fortunately for us, they had spent their torpedoes but we still had all of ours – eight in number. Commander Courage went straight for them. He carried out his first torpedo attack, having closed the range to somewhere in the region of 2,500 yards. The German destroyers were still conforming as a subdivision to concentrate firepower [believing they] would savage us. But it was to our advantage by virtue of the fact that, as a subdivision, we had one target. With our first attack, torpedoes ran excellently. They exploded at the end of their run [signifying a hit], which was a great thing. Directly he'd carried out his torpedo attack, Courage altered hard over and then went back to shield the two cripples, *Hotspur* and *Hostile*, to get them out of the bay, then he turned and made another attack. By that time the Germans had also turned around. They had also closed the range . . . close enough for them to spray our ship's side with their small guns. In doing that they brought about one casualty on the torpedo tube. They opened up a number of holes in our ship's side, but most important they set on fire our ready-use shell lockers at A gun. It was imperative, absolutely imperative, that we kept A gun working. Until then, because of this dashing forward and going straight at the enemy, Y gun, our after gun, had little or no prominence in the action because it could not bear. So immediately I ordered Y gun's crew to man A gun and assist. They galloped along the iron deck to give the assistance. Nearly everybody had gloves on so they were able to throw these burning cartridges over the side. We had plenty of troops supplying ammunition, so once again A gun was back and doing its stuff. So A and B guns and X gun were providing the fire power and we overcame all their gun power.

Now we went in for the final attack. We had three torpedoes left, and Commander Courage went to them, once again closing the range up to about 2,500 yards. He fired his last three torpedoes and they all exploded at the end of their run. We then turned away and made hell for leather, full speed. When we made our last run to get out of Narvik Bay, the old girl did over 40 knots. She was built for 36. We waited outside Narvik Bay. Nothing happened. The Germans didn't follow. They didn't know they had the advantage. If they had come directly after us they could have wiped out our total force. There was only us to overcome. I had fired two-thirds of my fire ammunition. We had no torpedoes left. We were low in oil. We were low in everything except morale.

Kemp's account, of course, relates only to his portion of the battle. Similar forays were played out by the remainder of the force, whose aggregate attack amounted to six German supply ships and two big destroyers sunk and five destroyers holed or set on fire. One of the supply ships discovered by *Havoc* contained 12,500 tons of ammunition, which, after evacuating the crew, Courage blew up with a salvo from *Havoc*, a mighty explosion that even damaged his own ship. Among the casualties of the overall battle was the Task Force leader, Captain Warburton-Lee. On 7 June 1940 the *London Gazette* announced the posthumous award of the Victoria Cross:

On being ordered to carry out an attack on Narvik he learned from Trannoy [lighthouse] that the enemy held the place in much greater force than had first been thought. He signalled to the Admiralty that the enemy were reported to be holding Narvik in force. Six destroyers and one submarine were there. That the channel might be mined. That he intended to attack at dawn, high water. The Admiralty replied that two Norwegian coastal defence ships might be in German hands, that he alone could judge whether to attack, that whatever decision he made would have full support.

Captain Warburton-Lee gave out the plan for his attack and led his flotilla of five destroyers up the fjord in a heavy snowstorm, arriving off Narvik just after daybreak. He took the enemy completely by surprise and made three successful attacks on warships and merchantmen in the harbour. The last attack was made only after anxious debate. On the flotilla withdrawing, five enemy destroyers of superior gun power were encountered and engaged, and the captain was mortally wounded by a shell which hit *Hardy*'s bridge. His last signal was: Continue to engage the enemy.

On 12 April the RAF joined in. Bomber Command launched its largest operation of the war so far, sending more than 80 aircraft to hit German positions around the Norwegian theatre in daylight raids. But with a network of anti-aircraft guns already in position, the Germans shot down nine precious bombers, and thereafter Bomber Command restricted the Norway raids to attacks on enemy airfields and minelaying operations.

The following day, the Second Battle of Narvik opened up when a larger Royal Navy force of nine destroyers in company with the battleship *Warspite* steamed towards Narvik harbour, where there remained eight German destroyers and seven supply ships. The British destroyers moved quickly ahead of *Warspite* to launch a surprise attack and opened fire as soon as they turned into Narvik Bay, scoring a number of direct hits. *Warspite*, meanwhile, began an incessant bombardment of the shore batteries, and anything else that came into view, with her 15-inch shells, which were causing the Germans much grief. The German destroyers attempted a rapid response. A running battle ensued for almost five hours and developed into a swirling mass of ships, changing course and speed, to which was added action from shore batteries.

One of the British destroyers, *Eskimo*, had her entire bows blown off, accompanied by a spectacular sheet of flame after being torpedoed by the German destroyer *Georg Thiele*. She managed to limp away to safety with the B gun's crew still firing away above the mangled metal where the bows used to be amid cheers from the crew of *Hero*, which happened to be passing at the time. Another kind of hero was *Cossack*, which encountered a badly damaged German destroyer, *Dieter van Roeder*, which, like *Eskimo*, was still exceedingly trigger-happy in spite of her wounds. The two ships came face to face and began firing ferociously with all guns that would bear. The German ship was finally silenced as, one by one, every gun crew ran out of ammunition, and at that point the order to abandon ship was given and time-fused explosives were left aboard to send the German ship to the bottom. *Cossack* had been hit seven times, twice with eight-inch shells from the shore batteries, which put her steering out of action. She quickly drifted on to the rocks. Some hasty running repairs were attempted while at the same time continuing the battle, this time against a field gun that had been a particular menace. Unsuccessful attempts were made to put her under tow, and then a remarkable incident occurred.

Two young Norwegian cousins, Torsten and Lief Hansen, skied down from a small village over the mountain to tell the British that the German troops had retreated into the hills. The two boys also rowed out to an abandoned German ship and removed her ensign, which they presented to *Cossack*; this was later placed on display at the Imperial War Museum in London. Meanwhile, *Cossack* managed to float off the rocks at high tide, although she could only travel astern because of the damage. She made slow time to the Lofoten Islands, where local residents joined the ship's engineers to salvage plate from wrecked ships to patch up her wounds. After three weeks, she was sufficiently mobile to cross the North Sea and back to base, although she had lost nine men killed and 21 wounded. But the Germans had been routed in the two Battles of Narvik and the backbone of her destroyers were themselves destroyed.

For the British, the battles were a preamble to the main event around Narvik, an Allied invasion of ground troops which was to be preceded by a number of smaller landings by British troops to the south, around Trondheim and Bergen. These involved the first Commando raids landed by the Royal Navy, independent companies manned mostly by volunteers from County Regiments and TA units, forerunners of the Army and Royal Marine Commando Brigades that Churchill instigated later in the year. The independent companies were supposed to operate behind German lines, attacking and harrying wherever they found the opportunity, but in fact they were poorly prepared, ill-equipped and without adequate clothing and once again had to rely on tourist maps. With German aircraft screaming overhead, they made little impact, in spite of cover from the navy's C-class anti-aircraft ships *Cairo, Curlew, Coventry* and *Calcutta*, which were to be extensively engaged – and damaged – around the whole of the western coastline during the Norwegian campaign from mid-April until early June.

They were joined on 22 April by regular army units and what should have been the first ship-borne air operation of the war when the aircraft carriers *Glorious* and *Ark Royal* carried the RAF's No. 263 Squadron equipped with Gloster Gladiators, the last biplane fighter in British service and no match for German equipment. They flew successfully from the ships to a makeshift landing strip on a frozen lake, of all things, which proved to be an almost impossible surface from which to scramble against incoming German aircraft. Two days after their arrival, ten of the Glosters were still on the ground when they were wiped out by Ju-88s and Heinkel 111s. The remaining five Glosters were flown to another airstrip 20 miles away, but in dire conditions and impossible visibility all were damaged or crash-landed. And so, without going into action, the air mission was knocked out and the pilots and ground crews withdrawn. The two carriers, meanwhile, returned to Scapa Flow amid talk of another mission, although none was to materialise until mid-May.

A larger invasion force was already being planned for Narvik, however, along with a massive bombardment by Royal Navy capital ships supported by an RAF fighter force – this time including Hurricanes – which was again to be brought up by the carriers *Glorious* and *Ark Royal* in conjunction with the landing of a combined force of 24,000 Allied troops, including Norwegian and British units as well as the French Foreign Legion and units of the French 27th Chasseurs Alpins. Among them was John Yeowell, an Englishman in the Legion:

We left Brest on two cargo ships for Glasgow, where we spent a couple of days. Then we embarked on the Canadian Pacific liner called *Monarch of Bermuda*, the first troops to sail in this magnificent ship. The staff were still in their white starched jackets as if they had never left the West Indies. Our ship travelled alone and unescorted in an area infested with U-boats. When we reached the fjords north of the Arctic Circle, my section was transferred to a Royal Navy mine-sweeper. It was an exhilarating experience to sail silently up these great inland seas at 1 o'clock in the morning. It was 24-hour-daylight and we were able to see in the distance these wonderful vistas of white mountains and tiny nestling villages with their timber houses and pastel-coloured roofs and walls. It looked idyllic.

Then, on the Sunday afternoon, there suddenly appeared off the coast the Allied fleet. It was an inspiring sight. My battalion boarded HMS *Effingham* and we were soon en route to another unknown destination. As usual they didn't tell us a bloody thing. Later, as I stood at the rails gazing idly at the passing scenery, one of the crew said: 'Look over there . . . that's Narvik. And they've got the bloody swastika flag flying – the cheeky bastards.' I had never heard of Narvik and couldn't see any flag, but I said: 'Yes, the cheeky bastards . . .'

Further along the coast was Bjervik. We formed up on deck, still without being told anything, although it was obvious we were going ashore. Before we could attack Narvik itself, the village of Bjervik had to be cleared and secured. The high ground behind it overlooked the strategic port. At

midnight on 13 May the massive guns of the British battleship *Resolution*, the cruisers *Effingham* and *Vindictive* and five
destroyers opened fire on the picturesque village and its
surroundings to send the Germans scuttling. Soon afterwards,
the troops hit the beaches in infantry and tank landing craft.
It was the first time in the war that such combined operations
took place in the face of enemy fire. As we stood on deck, we
heard the slight metallic sound of the battle flags, the Union
Jack and the Tricolour, as they went up the mast at great
speed. It was like the signal for the bombardment of Bjervik
to commence. The town's inhabitants had already gathered on
a hill at the side of the fjord so that they could be seen, and
there they stood watching their homes being shelled and
burned to the ground. It must have been desperate for them.
A little armoured car, German, was going down the front by
the shore firing a stupid little machine gun at the fleet until it
was blasted into kingdom come.

The bombardment of Bjervik went on for a quarter of an
hour, then we went ashore in what I suppose were ships'
boats. Some had motors, others simply had to be rowed by
men of the Royal Marines. One man in my company and one
in the company to our right were detailed as scouts. I was one,
and the other was my colleague Calthorpe. Funny, really, two
out of three English legionnaires in Norway being chosen for
this honour. That's what I thought then; in practical terms,
however, it meant we had to walk out in front. If we were
shot, then it would be unsafe for those behind us to go on.
Still, what the hell. You can only die once. We crossed the
narrow beach and went over the road and headed through the
blazing town. The place had been shot to pieces. Every garden
gate and every fallen telegraph pole I suspected of being
booby-trapped, and by God was it hot! We were quickly out
in open countryside, which was covered in snow. It was so
deep in places you would sink right up to your thighs. Then
we had our first meeting with the enemy. I had reached a
slight rise in the ground, and as I lay there looking around,
less than three yards in front of me was a man walking right
across my field of vision. All the enemy were scattered about

like this in isolated pockets. It was probably the only method of defence in such a complicated landscape. They didn't appear to know we had landed and seemed to be taking it easy for a bit. My grenade killed all three of them, poor buggers.

On board *Resolution* was seaman Frederick Hutchison, who had joined the navy in 1937. For the earlier part of the war, the ship had been engaged on 'the gold run', as it was known – carrying Britain's gold reserves from the Bank of England's vaults to safekeeping in Canada. Several trips were made, also using *Royal Sovereign*, so that all eggs were not placed in one sinkable basket. That task complete, *Resolution* joined the Task Force of Norway:

We were involved in helping the French troops to land, and we carried a considerable number of small two-man tanks. We watched them going ashore and charging up the beach to attack the Germans. We always had a good view, because there was never any darkness. On the other hand, we were also good targets and we were subjected to continuous and heavy bombing from German aircraft. It got so bad in the end that we ran out completely of four-inch anti-aircraft shells, firing at them. The ship remained at anchor at all times during those raids because the fjords were so narrow you just had to lie there and take whatever came. We became very, very efficient with our gun drill. At times we were not allowed to leave the gun. Our food was brought up, and we could only take snatches of sleep between raids. The captain was still trying to main a level of discipline and used to parade the Royal Marines band for the colours at eight every morning. And one particular morning the band was marching up and down the deck ready for colours and a German aircraft came over, catching the band unawares. There was a cacophony of noise as the band disappeared down below.

The bomb hit on the starboard quarter and did a considerable amount of damage, killing one man. That was our worst hit in Narvik, and fortunately the Germans were not as efficient at ships as they were on the land because the amount of bombs and air raids that we had it seemed impossible with the ship lying at anchor that she wasn't hit more often than she was. We, meantime, did a lot of heavy bombarding with our 15-inch guns on Narvik and other ports along the coast, but we never saw the targets or the results because we were firing from a range of up to 15 miles away, liaising with the army ashore. We used the four-inch guns to bombard targets we could see on the shore, such as army vehicles and troops.

*Resolution*, which had a large hospital bay, also received wounded from other ships and from troops on shore. We also had a German whose fighter we shot down. He was a very arrogant young man of about 19, and when he stepped on board he gave the Nazi salute, only to be completely disciplined by the Royal Marines who were accompanying him. One of them gave him a hefty slap with the butt of his rifle to bring him into line.

To the ground invasion at Narvik was added additional support from the Fleet Air Arm and the RAF, along with the C-class anti-aircraft ships that were kept on a round-the-clock mission to rout the incoming German air attacks. The Allies now brought up their own fighters, this time including 18 precious Hurricanes flown by the RAF's No. 46 Squadron, the obsolete Gloster Gladiators of No. 263 Squadron and the Fleet Air Arm's much-loved but dated squadron of Swordfish that really were no match for the Germans' vastly superior air power. Once again, aircraft were carrier-borne, which initially turned into something of a fiasco through no fault of the navy, as Sir Kenneth Cross, leading 46 Squadron explained:

We were told that we would be ferried to Norway by the aircraft carrier *Glorious*, but it wasn't possible to land on the carrier because tests which had been done at Farnborough indicated that the deck wasn't long enough for the Hurricanes to come to a stop. They had no hooks, as the Fleet Air Arm aircraft had. So we flew off 18-strong up to Abbotsinch near Glasgow and landed there. The next day we taxied the aeroplanes through fields to a jetty, put them on a lighter and went down the Clyde to where *Glorious* was anchored. We got all 18 aircraft hoisted aboard using cranes. The next day we went up to Scapa Flow with the other aircraft carrier, *Furious*, which now contained No. 263 Squadron with its Gladiators, then set forth for Norway. When we got into position there we received a signal to say that 46 Squadron was to go to an airstrip called Skaanland on a fjord near Narvik. We understood that 263 Squadron was to go to another airstrip further away at Bardufoss.

Bardufoss was ready, but Skaanland wasn't ready. After two or three days waiting it was necessary for us to return to Scapa Flow to refuel the aircraft carrier. Then we set out again for Norway. This meant that we were in this ship for something like ten days. Finally, we were ranged on deck in sixes. I, as the squadron commander, was the first to take off with a Hurricane, which had never been done before from a carrier. We didn't know whether the Hurricane would do it or fall over the edge. But in point of fact, with our variable-pitch airscrews and the full power of the Merlin engine, they leaped off the deck without any difficulty at all.

The air attack on Narvik began the next day, and during the ensuing 14-day campaign the two squadrons flew 638 sorties and claimed 37 enemy aircraft destroyed. In fact, the campaign centred on Narvik had gone well, and a victory of sorts seemed in sight until, on 28 May, Belgium and Holland surrendered to the Nazi blitzkrieg across Western Europe, France was on the brink of capitulation and the entire British Expeditionary Force was surrounded as the German force of 750,000 troops pressed onwards with Paris in their sights. The British war planners decided they had no other alternative than to end the Norwegian campaign immediately and evacuate all troops, as Sir Kenneth Cross explained:

We'd pushed the Germans right back to the Swedish border, and in another two weeks the whole of north Norway would have been ours. [But then] we listened to the news of the German advance into France, and it was a great disappointment to us when the following day the government decided to evacuate Allied forces from north Norway. We understood perfectly well that the amount of shipping required to sustain an expedition of this size would be substantial. So the entire British and French force was to be withdrawn immediately, and the air force were to cover the evacuation of the troops from the various fjords by destroyers.

But as soon as the Germans got wind of the British evacuation, they began a massive aerial bombardment and moved battleships, destroyers and U-boats to the North Sea to attack the departing British convoys. The results were to be catastrophic. At all points of evacuation down the north-western coastline of Norway, the movement of the British flotillas into the open sea came under heavy fire from land-based air attacks. The small group of remaining RAF fighters were last to leave and put up a brilliant effort but were hopelessly outclassed by wave after wave of the Luftwaffe's finest, and the Allied ships steamed out under murderous swooping fire. Lieutenant John Mosse, in the destroyer *Havelock*, said:

> We heard the scream of a dive-bomber as it roared out of the sky and dropped two bombs just astern of *Southampton*. Arriving in formations of 15 or 20 planes at a time, they bombed us incessantly for two hours. Everyone increased to full speed and manoeuvred independently within the narrow limits of the fjord. The valley reeked with the bitter stench of cordite fumes from the guns. Time and again the ships were hidden from one another by vast columns of water.

Able Seaman Charles Hutchinson, on the anti-aircraft cruiser *Carlisle*, covering the evacuation from Namos, saw five planes swoop down on the French destroyer *Bison*, and a bomb burst on the fo'c's'le. Soon she was a cloud of smoke: 'Three destroyers went to stand by her [to take off survivors]. *Afridi* was the last to leave her, when a fresh batch of planes came. I saw a huge explosion on *Afridi* and she heeled over, her bows dipping low into the water. We steamed slowly on, guarding the troopships. It wasn't long before *Afridi* went down. What a tragedy, after picking up the survivors of the French destroyer.'

Several ships in the convoys were sunk or seriously damaged before they managed to pull away into the open sea, but there in the vast expanse of water ahead lurked a greater danger. Germany's infamous new battle cruisers *Scharnhorst* and *Gneisenau* were, unknown to the Allies, out there somewhere with the cruiser *Admiral Hipper* and some destroyers waiting to pounce.

Sir Kenneth Cross and his RAF pilots, who were among the last to leave the Norwegian scene, said that the departure brought hair-raising possibilities, quite beyond the threat of enemy aircraft:

On that last day, eight Gladiators remained operational and were flown back to *Glorious* for the journey home. No Hurricanes had ever landed on an aircraft carrier and so No. 46 Squadron was ordered to destroy the remaining ten Hurricanes so that the Germans could not get their hands on them. When the evacuation was complete, we were told we would have to burn the aeroplanes as the last thing at Bardufoss. But the Hurricanes were valuable, much-needed aircraft and we were determined to get them home, and ten pilots stepped forward to make an attempt to land on *Glorious*. Farnborough figures said it was impossible; my pilots didn't believe it was, and we were damned well going to try. We had been flying for 24 hours solid when we flew to the ship. It was a very welcoming sight. We saw the blinking light which these carriers always carried on the horizon. Then it was time to land. It actually turned out to be a relatively simple operation. My Hurricane stopped a little over two-thirds up the deck. I was standing on the brakes pretty hard all the time. All remaining aeroplanes in the squadron followed me in, and when they were safely aboard we went below for some hot cocoa and some sleep.

However, the final and most appalling drama in the evacuation from Norway was yet to be played out. On 8 June, as the convoys cleared Norwegian waters, the captain of *Glorious* decided, against advice of his Fleet Air Arm colleagues, to press on ahead of the Allied ships in company with two destroyers to return to Scapa Flow. His reasons were unclear, but later inquiries revealed that he was hurrying back to Scapa to instigate a court martial against an air commander with whom he had had a violent row over the deployment of aircraft earlier in the campaign. Fleet Air Arm Lieutenant (and later Admiral) Donald Cameron Gibson, who had served on *Glorious* but had just been transferred to *Ark Royal*, recalled: 'There was a great deal of friction and unhappiness between the captain and his senior officers, and especially the commander (air) whom he had put ashore.'

Although he had six Swordfish of the Fleet Air Arm aboard, as well as the RAF aircraft, he had none on reconnaissance, nor even on deck, despite the fact that *Glorious* did not have radar. Nor were there any lookouts in the crow's-nest, and so he did not know that *Scharnhorst* and *Gneisenau* and the cruiser *Admiral Hipper* were on his tail until 20 minutes before their approach. Even when their smoke was eventually spotted on the horizon, almost 40 minutes passed before the German ships began firing, and even then only two aircraft had been brought on to the flight deck and neither was launched. The two accompanying destroyers, *Ardent* and *Acasta*, immediately turned to take on the approaching battle cruisers. *Ardent* was sunk almost immediately. *Acasta*, however, managed to fire two torpedoes, which hit *Scharnhorst* and put two of her three engine rooms out of action before *Acasta* herself was sunk.

*Glorious*, meanwhile, had also taken a severe hammering from the German ships and was sinking fast, with 1,474 of her own ship's company, as well as the RAF pilots and their badly needed Hurricanes, on board. James O'Neill, from the Isle of Man, had been serving on *Glorious* and recalled that under his first captain the ship's company had been a happy bunch who worked together despite the difficult circumstances in the previous two years which kept them at sea for long periods of time. O'Neill was critical of the new captain, an authoritarian and former submariner who had only recent experience of carriers. He confirmed that the captain was preoccupied with getting back to Scapa Flow to bring one of his commanders before a court martial.

All he wanted to do was get back and disgrace him. He was rushing to get back, but we were in trouble. We were on our own, hardly any protection at all, and we didn't even have any planes up to spot for us. We sent a signal that we were being attacked, and they reckoned they did not receive the signal – although the Germans did intercept it. It was *Admiral Hipper* that got *Glorious*, ten miles away from us. The first salvo ripped the flight deck up, and they just put shell after shell into her until she was no more. I was in the engine room and I could hear we were in action. Then, one of the boiler rooms got hit and they had to close it down. I then went on a fire-and-repair party, going round putting fires out all over the place. We never thought the ship was going to sink, but soon fires were breaking out all over the place. There wasn't a place on the ship that they weren't firing at; she was ablaze from stem to stern. It was frightening in one sense, but you don't really think about it because you have so much to do. In the middle of this [one of my superiors] said to me: 'I've left my gas mask and other possessions behind. Will you go and get them for me?' So I was running along the companionway and I thought: 'My God! What am I doing? I might never get back to him.'

I went on to the stokers' mess deck for his gear and it was just like a butcher's shop. There were bodies all over the place. The planes were on fire in the hangars; everything was just chaotic. The captain piped 'Abandon ship' but then, for some reason, he belayed the order. We didn't know what was going on. Then finally the pipe came again, and by this time there was a big list. And those of us who could make it were going to go over the side. *Glorious* was a big ship, well out of the water, and the lifeboats couldn't be lowered down. She was listing so much the boats were hitting the side of the ship and they couldn't get them down on to the water.

She had bulges on the side of her and I climbed down to one of those and then jumped into the water. Some were jumping in from the top deck. The marines tried to get things organised. They were cutting the Carley floats free and throwing them into the water and then telling the number of men they would carry to jump in after them. But eventually they were jumping all over the place. They had no alternative; you had to get away. She was burning furiously, although she was still moving and the propellers were still turning, and you had to get clear of those very quickly; some didn't make it. You had to swim away at right-angles to the ship, otherwise you got caught up in the wash and I would have been chewed up.

The sea was very cold but I couldn't think about that. I just wanted to swim away from it. But where to? We were 40 miles inside the Arctic Circle, and 200 miles from Norway. There was nowhere to swim to, miles from anywhere, and the Germans didn't hang about to pick us up; they just cleared off as our trio of ships went down. There were also so many bodies and fellows in the water, people dying with the cold. There were hundreds in the water, hundreds, shouting and crying and then dying. I was swimming and floating and paddling around for two hours. We just couldn't understand why no one was coming to search for us, or rescue us. The two destroyers which had turned to attack the German ships were blown out of the water in minutes, and those who survived were also in the sea.

About 7 o'clock, I saw this Carley float and I swam towards it. It was totally overloaded, about 60 men aboard, all standing up. I tried to get on, but some were shouting that it was full up. I shouted back: 'It's not a bloody bus service.' And I pushed myself on. The padre was on board, and he tried to keep our spirits up. He got us all singing and so on, but it didn't last. A number of the men became delirious, and even by the end of the first day a lot had died. As it went on, day after day, our hope of being rescued was fading and these chaps were dying by the hour so that on the fourth day there was only myself and another boy left. To begin with, we had to slide the bodies into the sea, but in the end we were too weak and when we were finally rescued there were eight bodies in the bottom of the Carley, and we just sat on the side.

We were picked up by a Norwegian trawlerman who was escaping from Norway to go to the Faeroes – this boy who was with me spotted the boat. But he then seemed to be turning away from us. Our hearts sank. I thought he hadn't seen us. Then we realised he was going round looking in all the Carley floats and picking up the survivors. In fact, there were only 36 still alive out of all the floats – 36 men out of almost 3,000 men in the action.

Why did we survive, and all the others didn't? It's something I will never know . . . the sea is a funny thing, mysterious . . .

The trawlerman satisfied himself there were no more survivors and went on to the Faeroes, where the islanders opened a big hall and laid out beds for the 36 survivors until they were picked up by a destroyer and taken to hospital, first in Edinburgh and then Aberdeen, to be treated, mostly for frostbite, which was so severe that several had to have amputations. Meanwhile, two other survivors from *Ardent* were spotted floating on a life raft and picked up by a German seaplane and were taken into captivity at Trondheim.

James O'Neill and his comrades were later interviewed by officers from the Admiralty:

They asked whose fault we thought it was. Quite a few of us were very angry. I said: 'Where do you come from?' They said: 'The Admiralty.' And I replied: 'Then it's your fault. You people didn't give us the protection we should have had. The captain should never have put us in that position. And then you lost or misinterpreted the signal that we were being attacked by three German battleships. You were told exactly where we were – and nobody came. It was criminal!'

We were there a few weeks, when the doctor asked me how long since I'd been home. I told him it was three years. So he said: 'Well, go home now.' And that was that.

165

The loss of *Glorious* and her two heroic destroyers added substantial tonnage to the Royal Navy's losses during the Norwegian campaign, which additionally included two cruisers, seven destroyers, one sloop and a submarine, plus six ships severely damaged and around 60 aircraft. The German losses were high: three cruisers, ten destroyers and six U-boats along with heavy damage to three battle cruisers, two cruisers and a number of smaller vessels. The crippling of a number of German ships was due in no small measure to this first major operation involving the Fleet Air Arm flying from *Glorious, Furious* and *Ark Royal*. Donald Gibson recalls that at the time on *Ark Royal*, 803 Squadron was flying the fighter dive-bomber Skua, which was not especially effective and hardly the right tool for the job:

Trouble with pointing yourself at the target is that you are re-enacting the Charge of the Light Brigade. Those on the ground can see you coming and you collect all the flak, as we often did. When the Germans towed the damaged *Scharnhorst* into Trondheim after the Allies had pulled out, we launched Operation Skua, which I must say was typical of the bad planning that prevailed at the time. It was an operation to finish off *Scharnhorst* with a heavy bombardment, planned by men who didn't know their job. We took off from *Ark Royal* soon after midnight, and it was planned that we should make landfall at a lighthouse 60 miles from Trondheim. To do that, of course, produced the absolute certainty that the Germans would know we were coming because the lighthouse keeper would ring up and say we were on our way, which doubtless he did because they were waiting for us.

Although this was carried out in the middle of the night, it was daylight. We knew this was going to be a nasty one and we were scared stiff. Two squadrons, 801 and 803, put up 15 aircraft between them, and on arrival at Trondheim there were many German fighters in the air as well as intense flak. We were being picked off as we went along. We eventually carried out a dive-bombing attack on the ship, but we didn't get a single hit, mainly because most of the experienced pilots had already been killed or taken prisoner and most of the pilots in the squadrons were people like myself, straight from flying school. When we got over *Scharnhorst*, I got rid of my bomb, I put up my flaps and went down into Trondheim itself, right flat on the deck to escape. In fact, I was flying so low as I followed a road out of Trondheim I was level with a horse on the bank. When we eventually got back to *Ark Royal*, the fleet commander had taken us into a fog bank, which meant it wasn't easy to get back on the ship. Only seven from the two squadrons made it back.

By then the Norwegian campaign had been abandoned to the status of inconsequence as one of the greatest dramas in modern military history was under way at Dunkirk.

# CHAPTER NINE

## The Greatest Escape

Even as the rapid and ignominious evacuation from the Norwegian campaign was under way, the Royal Navy was already under extreme pressure to cope with the demands of action on a number of critical fronts, including the Atlantic convoys, the Mediterranean and the Middle East. But one area in particular would test them like no other – that of the exodus from Dunkirk. As the German army continued its relentless march across Western Europe, the prospect of a great disaster befalling Lord Gort's British Expeditionary Force now seemed inevitable, prompting the immediate fear of an invasion of the British Isles. The Germans had outmanoeuvred the British, French and Belgian armies and had surrounded 400,000 Allied soldiers, who were being pushed back towards the coast and Dunkirk, the last Channel port still in Allied hands. It was literally their only way out – the alternative being the total humiliation of surrender and capture, which would heighten beyond measure the possibility of Britain under siege, and possible capitulation.

On 26 May Lord Gort ordered his British divisions, along with about a third of the French 1st Army, to abandon their forward positions on what was known as the Lille Pocket and to join the main body of troops forming a new front line around Dunkirk. The movement was carried out in the nick of time, for the very next day the Germans forced the surrender of Belgium. Gort now mounted a defensive perimeter around Dunkirk which was to hold the line until attempts were made to evacuate this enormous population of troops on to ships and across the English Channel to safety. Even Churchill feared that it would be his 'hard lot to announce the greatest military disaster' in British history, and his own estimate of the number that might be brought home was a mere 45,000.

However, he launched Operation Dynamo to perform the miracle that it became: the rescue of as many of the stranded troops as possible by a multitude of ships and boats of all shapes and sizes. The operation was headed by Vice-Admiral Bertram Ramsay, Royal Navy Flag Officer, Dover, who took over Dover Castle for the duration. He faced what seemed an impossible task of sailing into Dunkirk under the murderous, incessant onslaught of Luftwaffe air bombardment and artillery fire on the troops as they gathered in great hope on the beaches of Dunkirk. What followed is a story familiar to all, told and retold in film and media, but it is perhaps worthwhile to recall some of the facts and figures that made this operation so exceptional and heroic.

When Churchill made his gloomy estimate of the number that might be brought home, he reckoned without the incredible response from commercial organisations and civilians, who were to join every available vessel in the Royal Navy in this foray into the teeth of the German guns and bombs. Even so, during the first 24 hours or more of the expedition, it looked as if Churchill's prediction was not far wide of the mark. Oliver Anderson was aboard the minesweeper *Sutton*, having recently returned from Alexandria. She was an old First World War vessel which had been laid up for years, but along with several others had been brought out of mothballs at the beginning of 1939 and was now serving as part of the 4th Minesweeping Flotilla. She was capable of only 14 knots. As Oliver Anderson recalled:

There wasn't much news of what was happening [in France] and in fact we weren't even told we were going to Dunkirk, not until we were almost there. We really had no idea what was going on, or what we were expected to do when we got there. No one realised that virtually the whole of the BEF would be coming on the beaches, and it was such a haphazard operation at the beginning. Our flotilla was among the first to arrive. It was just about daylight. The weather was calm, the sea flat. We seemed to be approaching in a direct line, and away to our starboard was Dunkirk. The oil tanks were in flames, and as we approached we could see what looked like a queue of people on the beach, a large number, but nowhere near as many as later on. We lay in as close as we could, and dropped off our motorboat and whaler, which would be towed behind, and went towards the beaches to begin picking them up.

They had a fair way to go, then we had to get the soldiers aboard and bring them back, unload and return. One of our ships managed to get closer in and they were actually wading to her, with only their heads and helmets above the water. It was very slow, and I think by lunchtime we had only loaded about 300 or 400. Fortunately, there was very little action overhead, but that was to come later.

The difficulties facing the navy and their helpers were very apparent on that first day, 28 May 1940. Regardless of the number of ships, at that rate of loading it would take for ever to pick up the great surge of troops on their way to the Dunkirk beaches. The operation needed strong organisation on the beach, and a stiff disciplinary presence, to control any disorder after a large number of French soldiers and refugees tried to storm the ships while their British counterparts lined up as if, said one, 'we were queuing for fish and chips'.

The Navy put ashore a large number of beachmasters to try to bring order to the chaos that developed as the Germans began bombing the rescue mission. The attacks became especially heavy on 29 May and in the remaining five days of the operation, in spite of valiant efforts by the RAF, whose fighters had less than 30 minutes' flying time over the area before having to head back across the Channel. By then, however, the great armada of 'little ships' had joined the navy's own rescue fleet.

The figures were staggering in every respect: Bertram Ramsay managed to muster the anti-aircraft cruiser *Calcutta*, 38 destroyers, 38 minesweepers, 61 minesweeping craft, 18 anti-submarine trawlers, 6 corvettes and 80 other small naval craft, including gunboats, motor torpedo boats and drifters. The Merchant Navy contributed 39 passenger ferries, seven passenger ferries converted into hospital ships and 262 trawlers, barges, tugs and dredgers. Then came the motley assortment of civilian-owned boats of every conceivable type: yachts, powerboats, launches, motor cruisers and any other soft of craft that could withstand the crossing, along with some that couldn't. The French, Belgians and Dutch also joined in, providing 19 French destroyers, 65 French civilian craft and 43 Dutch skoots with RN crews. During the entire operation, 850 vessels took part in Operation Dynamo.

As the operation proceeded, orders were given that only the fit men and walking wounded were to be taken aboard the ships. It was a decision, made by the War Cabinet, that most upset Churchill. He explained later that the government 'found itself compelled to evacuate the fighting troops before the wounded, of which there were many thousands. It was only the dire circumstances of the war that made such an order necessary for the sake of the future: the able-bodied could be taken off in greater number than stretcher cases and numbers were vital for continuing the struggle.'

The hospital ships were, however, standing by, with markings clearly indicating their purpose. It was hoped that the Germans would allow them safe passage, but one was sunk on the second day and another so severely damaged that she never made it to Dunkirk. Most of the wounded were therefore left behind, those who survived going into captivity. When Operation Dynamo ended on the afternoon of 4 June, 338,226 soldiers, including 123,095 French, had been evacuated. The remaining 60,000 were either killed or went into captivity, and the BBC reported that the beaches of Dunkirk were littered with bodies and the debris of a shattered army that had retreated under the merciless hail of bombs and machine-gun fire and that in the surrounding roads and villages, all the way back to the original front line, thousands of vehicles and weapons had been discarded. Another statistic that is often overlooked was the fact that on the last line of defence, established by Lord Gort on the perimeter of Dunkirk, Allied troops fought a ferocious battle to keep the Germans at bay while the evacuation went ahead. To maintain their positions, they required 2,000 tons of ammunition delivered to them every day by parties from the destroyers coming in to pick up the troops.

When they eventually pulled out, the BEF left behind a staggering inventory of weapons and equipment: 475 tanks, 38,000 vehicles, 12,000 motorcycles, 8,000 telephones, 1,855 wireless sets, 7,000 tons of ammunition, 90,000 rifles, 1,000 heavy guns, 2,000 tractors, 8,000 Bren guns and 400 anti-tank guns. On 6 June the War Cabinet was informed that there were fewer than 600,000 rifles and 12,000 Bren guns left in the whole of the United Kingdom, and the losses would take up to nine months to replenish. It was truly a desperate situation that was kept well away from public view.

The tally of ships lost, though bad enough, was relatively low, given the ferocity of the German attacks: nine British and French destroyers and eight personnel ships sunk, and of the hundreds of civilian craft, 72 were sunk by enemy action, 163 were lost in collisions and 45 were damaged by bombs. The worst single disaster of the evacuation of France, however, occurred off St-Nazaire, one of the French ports to the west where smaller evacuations took place.

The liner *Lancastria* had successfully embarked 5,000 troops and set sail for home. The Royal Navy beach parties and remaining troops watched in horror as a German bomber swooped in low when she was three miles out. Two bombs hit her amidships, and within a very short space of time she rolled over – and then, an incredible sight. She remained on her side with the hull still visible above an otherwise calm sea, and there on top were hundreds of men sitting on it, singing loudly before they floated off as *Lancastria* slowly sank, taking with her to the bottom 2,000 soldiers still trapped inside. Many were undoubtedly killed by bomb damage, but others were simply unable to find their way out of the huge ship in the darkness below before she sank. The loss was to be the largest individual total for any ship in the Second World War.

Meanwhile, in the euphoria over the rescue of so many troops from Dunkirk, a stark fact was pushed to the back of minds: that had the entire BEF been captured, as at one time seemed a strong possibility, Britain may well have found it difficult to continue the war, and would have had to concentrate on battening down the hatches to prevent the invasion of the British Isles. That proposition was next on Hitler's list after his army marched into Paris on 14 June, leaving the French to sue for peace.

Just two weeks before, British soldiers had been dying in their thousands to try to save France, but even before the Germans arrived in Paris, relations between the two countries had soured. Churchill had long been anxious not to upset the French, hoping that if Germany offered them peace terms, they would remain neutral. In the middle of the Dunkirk crisis, the British Prime Minister and his entourage risked being shot down by the Germans and flew to Paris on the morning of 31 May for a meeting with the French. He gave them the assurance that the British troops would stand firm to allow equal numbers of French to escape the German onslaught. But then, even as Dunkirk was being evacuated, the French begged Churchill to send a fresh army to help their troops hold the line along the Somme.

It was already too late, and the Prime Minister pointed out that in any event huge and unsustainable losses had already been incurred: of the nine divisions that originally made up the BEF, fewer than five full divisions remained. The Regiment of the Guards, which had been deployed in Belgium, had taken the brunt of the German attack and lost half its men, while the two Rifle Brigade battalions had been cut to ribbons. Of the 3,000-strong force, only 30 soldiers had survived. There were now no forces left that could be sent from the United Kingdom without jeopardising the nation's ability to withstand a possible invasion attempt by Germany, and in any case the equipment lost in the evacuation could never be replaced in such a short space of time.

In addition, and against all advice from his air force commanders, Churchill said that of the 39 squadrons allocated to the defence of Great Britain, ten had been lent to France originally for a short time, but of them there were as of that day very few left. It was also well known that the RAF had been badly treated by the French, given the worst tasks and offered little in the way of gratitude. In some perverted way, senior people in the French administration seemed to blame Britain for their plight, which of course was nonsense and had more to do with the fact that the French had put rather too much faith in their ridiculous Maginot Line.

The arrival of Hitler's army in Paris was the beginning of the end for France, and within a week the new head of government, the weak and defeatist Marshal Philippe Pétain, described by Churchill as 'a very dangerous man', faced the final humiliation of signing away his country in the same railway coach, preserved for posterity, that the Germans had accepted armistice terms in 1918. It was also the beginning of the end of British contact with France, although there remained one major issue that Churchill wished to resolve: that of the destination of the substantial French fleet, then located at various points around Europe and North Africa.

Between the arrival of the Germans in Paris and the signing of the armistice with France on 23 June, a lull in the fighting provided Churchill with the opportunity to try to extract from the French a deal to keep the fleet out of German hands and thus prevent its being used against the Royal Navy. Secret meetings were arranged in Bordeaux, which was not in German hands, between British and French diplomats inviting Admiral J.L. Darlan, the commander-in-chief of the French navy, to instruct his entire fleet to sail to the West Indies, where the ships could remain under Royal Navy protection. Darlan, however, assured them that the fleet would go on fighting, and that position remained until details of Germany's demands on the French in the armistice agreement changed everything.

Article 8 of the Franco-German Armistice stated that the part of the fleet guarding French colonial interests would remain active but the rest would be delivered to ports to be specified and there demobilised and disarmed under German supervision. The British response was that the French were either incredibly naive or stupid to believe that Hitler would honour the agreement, as events soon proved. A flurry of diplomatic contact continued, and it now became clear that Darlan and others in the French hierarchy had become hostile to the British and made it clear they had no intention of delivering the fleet to a safe harbour or neutral port away from Europe.

At that point, Darlan and the rest of the French hierarchy broke off their secret contact with Britain, and the British War Cabinet was now faced with a dilemma. It either had to accept the situation or send the Royal Navy to sink those elements of the French fleet that it could reach, i.e. capital ships, destroyers and submarines then anchored off the North African coast, at Casablanca, Oran, Dakar and Alexandria.

Part of the problem could be immediately resolved. Elements of the fleet comprising two battleships, four light cruisers, five submarines, eight destroyers and a number of smaller craft were already lying in England, off Portsmouth and Plymouth. These were immediately impounded on the afternoon of 3 July, when negotiations with the French finally broke down. At the same time, in Alexandria, Admiral Sir Andrew Cunningham's Mediterranean Fleet swung their guns on their former Allies in Force X, consisting of one French battleship, four cruisers and some smaller ships, and achieved possession without firing a single shell.

It was a different story at Oran, in the French military port of Mers-el-Kebir, where were docked the French ships that represented the biggest threat to the Royal Navy if they were to fall under German or Italian control. They included the two finest battleships in the French fleet, *Dunkerque* and *Strasbourg*, two older capital ships, one carrier, two cruisers, nine destroyers, six submarines and many smaller craft. At Algiers there were also seven cruisers and an aircraft carrier, while at Dakar the brand-new *Richelieu* was undergoing final preparations for action and was moored with a number of other French ships. On Churchill's bidding, the British War Cabinet had already agreed that if the French refused to cooperate, the French ships would be sunk by the Royal Navy. First, however, Flag Officer, North Atlantic, Admiral Sir Dudley North would arrange to meet the French Admiral Gensoul in command at Oran to explain the British government's position in the hope of achieving an amicable solution. He travelled by fast destroyer and was subsequently and ceremoniously welcomed aboard the French admiral's flagship, ironically named *Dunkerque*. Sub-Lieutenant Geoffrey Brooke, who accompanied North, recalled his notes of the meeting:

> I could not forget some of *Dunkerque's* officers whom I had
> met at Rosyth during a French courtesy visit before the war.
> They had been so confident and proud of their ship. I could
> not but imagine them now, in the beautifully panelled ward-
> room with paintings by well-known artists, waiting for a
> future that could bring little beyond despair. Unless, of
> course, they joined with us, but somehow it didn't seem
> likely . . . the practical difficulties were immense. Questions of
> nationality, especially relatives at home, and many other
> points would be unsupportable to all but the most courageous
> and united crews. Admiral North returned after an hour, and
> a further conference was held in the captain's cabin. The
> French would not accede to the British proposals, and if
> attacked would fight their way out to a home port.

North returned gloomily to Gibraltar having achieved not a hint
of agreement and reported to Vice-Admiral Sir James Somerville,
commanding the Mediterranean-based Force H, which had just
been supplemented with the arrival, fresh from the Norwegian
campaign, of *Ark Royal* and *Resolution*. They were later joined by
the battleship *Warspite* along with a protective screen of two
flotillas of destroyers and set off for Oran to enforce the British
government's will. Somerville, in his flagship 'the mighty' *Hood*,
Britain's largest and most impressive battle cruiser, was to deliver
to Gensoul at Oran a final three-point ultimatum from the British
government: that the French fleet could (a) join with the Royal
Navy and fight the Axis forces, (b) sail with reduced crews under
British control to a port where they would be demilitarised, or
perhaps be entrusted to the United States, the crews being repatriated, or (c), as a final option, allow the French to scuttle their
ships within six hours. If none of those alternatives was acceptable, said Somerville, 'the British government require me to use
whatever force is necessary to immobilise your fleet'.

Theodore Arthur Joughlin was on board *Resolution* when
Operation Catapult, the codename for the action, was set in
motion and the British Force H arrived off the coast of Algeria: 'It

was beautiful weather, fine and calm, when we arrived and what happened? Well, we just cruised up and down outside Oran. We went up and down, up and down. We hadn't a clue what was going on.'

The reason for the delay soon became apparent. Cedric Holland, captain of *Ark Royal*, had been sent on ahead in one of the destroyers to act as a go-between, carrying Somerville's ultimatum. He had previously served as naval attaché to Paris and knew many of the senior French officers personally. But the French commanders were in no mood to talk and simply stalled for time. After an exchange of signals, Captain Holland was finally allowed to board Admiral Gensoul's flagship, *Dunkerque*, for talks. Back in Britain, the Admiralty was receiving decrypts of Gensoul's Top Secret signals as the negotiations proceeded, and it soon became apparent that all the French ships had received orders from Paris, apparently from Marshal Pétain, that if the British opened fire they were to respond in kind. This possibility moved a step closer when on 3 July Somerville signalled to Gensoul that the final deadline for acceptance of the British terms would expire at 5.30 that afternoon. The signal was received at 5.15 and was handed to Gensoul as he was having the final conversation with Captain Holland on the French flagship.

Gensoul shrugged his shoulders; there would be no deal. Holland signalled the answer by projector as he left the ship to return to *Hood* by motorboat. 'I do not believe he thought that fire would be opened,' Holland wrote in his report. 'We left *Dunkerque* at 17.25 and at the same time action stations were sounded off. Very little effort seemed to be made to go to action stations and, as we passed, large numbers of the crew were still on the upper decks of the battleship. The Officer of the Watch saluted smartly as we passed. We transferred to our motorboat at 17.35 and were clear of the net defences about one mile to seaward when fire was opened . . .'

Aircraft from *Ark Royal* were sent up for reconnaissance and range-spotting, and it would appear that some of the British seamen were hardly convinced that they would soon be called into action, as Theo Joughlin explained:

Everybody was closed up at action stations, in our white duck suits with anti-flash gear over your head, and just your eyes showing. I was on my action station, which was the high-angle anti-aircraft gun. But we sat playing the naval game of ludo, called ukkers. It's played with a big ludo board made of canvas that was about two feet square and you threw wooden dice from a bucket. 'What's that?' someone shouted. And on our port side as we were going in was a massive spume of water coloured blue and then another one landed with a yellow spume. The colours were indicators to show the shore batteries where the shells landed so they could fix their range and bring their guns to bear on the ships. 'Christ, they're firing at us,' someone shouted. And then our 15-inch guns, which had been trained into Oran harbour, opened fire.

The ludo board went up in the air because when those guns fire it shakes everything; it really rumbles. And the rest of the big ships fired. I think they destroyed nearly everything in the harbour. One French battleship got away, and *Warspite* chased her and fired at her as she went up on the beach. It was all over so quickly really for an action like that, and that brought an end of that particular part of the French fleet at that time.

Did it worry us that we were sinking our Allies? Well, Dunkirk had been a letdown, and there was a lot of talk about whether the French could have done better. I don't think they had a lot of time for French people, or French ships. But I believe that seamen all over the world are a special fraternity and I think they feel for each other. A lot of the chaps on the ship were young men and they wouldn't willingly have killed people; no one ever does that unless it's in the line of duty. The fact is that you were on the ship and it was either them or us. I think we all felt that it was a job that had to be done, but it was a sad job none the less.

Thus Force H demolished the main part of the French fleet with ruthless efficiency and at a cost of 1,250 French sailors killed. Of the capital ships, *Dunkerque* was damaged and run aground, *Bretagne* was blown up and *Provence* beached. One ship,

*Strasbourg*, did manage to escape, along with two destroyers, as a great cloud of dense smoke hung over the harbour. Swordfish aircraft gave chase and dropped torpedoes, but under the cover of darkness she managed to reach Toulon.

The French fleet in Alexandria having surrendered without a fight, Somerville now moved on to Dakar, the principal port in French Senegal, where another group of belligerent commanders awaited the arrival of the British, and they were in no mood to negotiate. Donald Cameron Gibson, the RNVR flier who had come down from action in Norway with *Ark Royal*, remembered:

> There was a strong element of hate. The French were in a very bad temper that we were destroying their fleet. *Ark Royal* was being fired at by shore batteries as soon as we arrived in Dakar. It was a complete shambles. Our job was to protect our ships from French fighters, which came out and tried to attack them with primitive bombs. There was a lot of action below, and then I and my observer were flying over *Resolution* when she was torpedoed. We saw the torpedoes running and tried to warn her, but the Morse code didn't get through. We saw the torpedo hit . . .

Theo Joughlin, on *Resolution*, takes up the story:

> *Resolution* and *Ark Royal* lay well off shore and we had with us a merchant liner with General de Gaulle and Free French soldiers who had arrived from England [apparently as added weight to the persuasion tactics, which failed]. Once again we steamed up and down outside while the ultimatums were given, and ignored. The prime target was *Richelieu*, the brand-new French battleship, but we were told that the target for our 15-inch guns would be a pile of peanut husks in the harbour that create a massive cloud of dust so that nothing could be seen in the harbour. The battleship *Barham* was to be the one that fired at *Richelieu* if the negotiations failed, which they did.
>
> The thing that struck me that day was the intense heat. I was on anti-aircraft guns, so we were up top. But the chaps in

the turret must have been losing pounds and pounds in sweat. We lost one lad who died through drinking cold water. He got stomach cramps, and they warned us not to drink cold water, but to drink tea or something warm. This lad from Gateshead was in one of the turrets. We buried him later at sea.

On the third morning we went in at 9 o'clock with *Barham* ahead of us, and we noticed that a buoy had been placed at a point where we turned into the bay. We realised, too late I suppose, that it was a marker to line us up for being torpedoed. And as we went in, so one of the French submarines fired six torpedoes at us. One hit us full on and the others are still going somewhere. It was a powerful strike and we heeled over. I thought we were going to turn turtle. But we didn't, although we remained at an acute angle, and we were badly damaged. The submarine surfaced and put up a white flag, but one of our destroyers rammed it and sank it. *Barham* had hit *Richelieu* with her 15-inch guns, striking her stern and sinking her along with a number of other smaller French ships.

We were in a bad way, and it was panic stations. We couldn't use our engines and we just sat there and the French sent a plane out from Dakar to bomb us. I saw the bomb coming out of the sky, a massive thing, but fortunately it missed the ship completely and caused no damage. There were other aircraft about and battles with our own planes from *Ark Royal*. We had to get away, but couldn't move until *Barham* took us in tow all the way to Freetown, where we were laid up for about four months.

The sinking of *Richelieu* was the final act in Operation Catapult and one that the Mediterranean commander, Vice-Admiral Andrew Cunningham, spoke of as 'a difficult situation for us all, but one that has to be cleared up so that we can get on with the war with the Italians'. The tasks ahead were enormous, and certainly no sideshow to a main event elsewhere. For much of the time that main event was the Mediterranean, and for the next three years massive and often desperate activity fell under Cunningham's command and all those who successively joined his battle, for such it became. At the outset, the Mediterranean was a vital lifeline to the British war effort. It was the major thoroughfare that had to be kept open for British shipping and the convoys of food and troops that passed through in their thousands from the East and the Antipodes. Initially, it was not the Germans who were his main foe but the well-equipped Italian navy, if somewhat erratic, and air force of Benito Mussolini, who made no secret of the fact that the Italians regarded the Mediterranean as 'mare nostrum' (our sea). On Italy's entry into the war, Cunningham's Alexandria force consisted of three battleships, *Warspite, Malaya* and *Royal Sovereign*, the carrier *Eagle*, five cruisers, 17 destroyers and just two submarines. It was totally inadequate to meet fierce and relentless action that began to unfold almost immediately, battles to protect merchant convoys, troopships and the huge areas of British influence at the eastern end of the Mediterranean as the war opened up in North Africa and Greece. But it was also a new kind of sea warfare in which the inter-dependence of air power in cohesion with big surface guns and submarine torpedoes of the opposing navies were brought to a previously unimagined extent. The merging of these two great strengths developed almost its own volition out of necessity.

The Mediterranean saw it all, every permutation of maritime warfare, that engaged the complete range of naval hardware from human torpedoes through to the battleships, and, in fact, on one famous occasion (see below) it was the David that put the Goliath out of action. As one of the participants described it, there 'was an air of manic desperation about the whole business', due in part to the knowledge that free passage of the Mediterranean was the key to Britain's success in North Africa and eventually the springboard for an invasion of Italy. Three key areas, which were under pretty constant attack, were vital to Britain in maintaining access to and free passage in the Mediterranean: the naval establishment at Gibraltar at the entry from the Atlantic, the island of Malta in the centre for its naval and air bases and Alexandria in Egypt at the far end. These positions serviced the very busy shipping route through the Suez Canal. The French had equally massive Mediterranean interests from her North African bases and direct access from the huge naval port of Toulon, or at least they had until Britain blew them up. Their demise left a huge security gap at the eastern end. Spurred on by the knowledge that the Royal Navy and the Royal Air Force had become fully committed to their own life-or-death struggle in the Battle of Britain, Mussolini sent his troops to invade Egypt. There, he opened up the infamous battleground in the Western Desert that would rage for nearly three years, long after his own armies had been defeated and replaced with a head-to-head between Rommel and Montgomery.

The very act of war in North Africa meant a massive increase in seaborne activity, and although the Italians weren't much of a match for the British Army on the Nile their navy included some of the newest and fastest warships in the world. They also had a strong submarine fleet and a host of other new and well-versed inventions, such as human torpedoes, magnetic anti-ship mines and exploding motorboats. At that time, British aircraft carriers did not carry fighters to help defend their fleet, only reconnaissance planes and torpedo bombers. In the first few months of confrontation there were a number of engagements between British and Italian forces, but none of great significance.

The first important clash came a month after Italy's entry into the war, on 9 July 1940, when a British submarine sighted a convoy bound for Libya, protected by two Italian battleships, *Confe di Cavour* and *Giulio Cesare*. Cunningham, with three battleships, an aircraft carrier, five cruisers and 17 destroyers, headed to intercept. The Italians saw them coming and launched a torpedo bombing attack which damaged the British cruiser *Gloucester*, but the Italian navy were clearly not disposed to a fight and retreated. As they went, Cunningham's *Warspite* found a bearing on *Giulio Cesare* and hit the Italian ship at a range of 15 miles, thereby establishing a record for long-range gunnery.

The Italian fleet did not venture out often thereafter and so in November Cunningham, widely regarded as one of the great commanders of the war, decided to take the fight to them by launching an attack on the base in Taranto. He sailed from Egypt with four battleships, two cruisers and seven destroyers. He also had plans to experiment with an airborne attack, sending out 21 torpedo bombers in two waves from the carrier *Illustrious*, and in due course the ancient Fairey Swordfish biplanes arrived over the

Italian fleet, bobbing along as if they were out for a Sunday afternoon pleasure flight. They were travelling at a 'loaded' top speed of around 140mph and, so the story goes, because they were so slow, the Italian gunners couldn't get a range on them and were aiming too far in front. The Swordfish sank the battleship *Littorio* and damaged the rest of the ships in harbour with the loss of only two aircraft.

Mussolini's delusions of grandeur were being turned at every point, and Hitler was forced to come to his aid, first by deploying Fleigercorps X to Italy at the beginning of 1941. Their first attack against Cunningham's fleet brought disabling damage to *Illustrious* on 10 January, and the following day the cruiser *Southampton* was sunk. Short on air cover at all points of his theatre of operations, Cunningham was under further pressure with the deployment of British troops to Greece beginning in March – a massive movement of Allied forces and machines. Germany instructed Italy to at least make some attempt to interrupt the British convoys, and the scene was set for the Battle of Matapan. Cunningham and the Italian fleet prepared to do business in the Ionian Sea between the Greek mainland and the island of Crete.

Italy's Eastern Fleet were given two objectives: to intercept British troop transports and supply ships heading for Greece and to attack the British naval base at Suda Bay in Crete. Cunningham, reinforced with the carrier *Formidable* with her Albacore aircraft, was one step ahead with reconnaissance and left Alexandria to meet the Italians head-on. Early on 28 March 1941, the cruiser *Orion*, scouting some miles ahead of Cunningham's force, came across the Italian battleship *Vittorio Veneto*, which promptly gave chase and was led straight towards the oncoming British battleships *Warspite, Valiant* and *Barham*.

At the same time, Cunningham ordered the carrier *Formidable* to prepare for attack in three waves, and over the course of the next several hours the Albacore torpedo bombers hit and damaged *Vittorio Veneto* and the cruiser *Pola*. Late that night, Cunningham brought his fleet towards the foundering *Pola* and two other Italian heavy cruisers and four destroyers that had returned to help her. While the destroyer *Greyhound* lit the scene with searchlights, *Warspite* and the British destroyers finished them off in the space of less than an hour. The British ships rescued 1,168 Italian seamen and took them in as prisoners and then signalled the Italians to give them the locations of the remaining survivors. Even so, Italian casualties exceeded 3,000. The British lost two aircraft, but not a single man aboard their warships.

It proved to be the last time the Italians brought out their fleet in such a manner, which was just as well because suddenly Cunningham was under great pressure to maintain his position. Although General Archibald Wavell led his Army on the Nile towards swift and decisive advances, capturing Tobruk and taking 100,000 Italian prisoners, the euphoria of the British successes was to be short-lived. In February 1941 Hitler sent General Erwin Rommel with the advance party of what would become the mighty Afrika Korps, which began landing at Tripoli to rescue Mussolini's army, and the real battles began. As this movement was going ahead, Hitler launched a devastating blitzkrieg against Yugoslavia and then onwards to Greece with a massive invasion force of ground troops supported by around 1,250 aircraft, including Stukas and the deadly Messerschmitt 109s.

Greece was as good as lost, and Cairo ordered the withdrawal of all British troops as the Greek army surrendered on 23 April. There followed a mini-Dunkirk operation in the evacuation of troops from Greece, but, as at Dunkirk, substantial amounts of vehicles, equipment, ammunition, fuel and heavy guns had to be abandoned along with a number of damaged, but repairable, fighters and bombers. Even so, some 43,000 troops and civilians were evacuated successfully. The heroics of the Royal Navy and the Royal Air Force, along with their Australian counterparts, in these operations could not mask this further setback: the immolation of much-needed troops and the loss of 189 aircraft during the Greek campaign.

Worse was to come. Enigma decrypts from Bletchley Park revealed that the Germans were planning a massive invasion of the strategically important island of Crete and the Royal Navy base at Suda Bay, which at that time had a mere 14 Hurricanes and seven Royal Navy aircraft available to defend the enemy onslaught. Churchill ordered Wavell to send reinforcements: more guns, more tanks, more everything. The commander wired back that he could spare only six tanks, 16 light tanks and 18 anti-aircraft guns, although the Allied manpower on the island was bolstered after the fall of Greece to around 30,000 Australian, New Zealand and British troops under the command of General Bernard Freyberg.

Churchill, having viewed the Germans' precise order of battle – courtesy of the Enigma decrypts – still had grave concerns that they had sufficient firepower to hold on. His worst fears were realised on the morning of 20 May when Stuka dive-bombers and artillery aircraft screamed out of the sky and began pummelling the Allied troop positions and Royal Navy ships. They were followed by wave after wave of stinging aircraft attacks and landings, including Ju-52s towing huge DFS 230 gliders packed with troops, vehicles and guns. Suddenly, the skies were filled with the greatest airborne invasion force ever mounted in the history of warfare.

By late afternoon, almost 5,000 men had been dropped or landed on the island, and one of the most costly battles of the war to date was under way as more German paras and mountain troops were delivered to the island hour after hour, eventually totalling 22,040. They met spirited Allied resistance whose strength had been hugely underestimated by German intelligence. Even so, it was a hopeless task for the Allies, even with the supporting bombardment from Cunningham's fleet. The Germans, meanwhile, had assembled a force of 650 combat aircraft, 700 transports and 80 gliders in Greece. For more than a week the Luftwaffe bombarded Crete and shot the few remaining British fighters out of the sky until, devoid of air cover, the British fleet was exposed to grave danger as it began the evacuation of Allied troops.

Three cruisers and six destroyers were sunk, and an aircraft carrier, six cruisers and eight destroyers were hit by varying degrees of damage, and many sailors were killed or drowned. The final toll showed the extent of the disaster: 4,600 Allied troops killed, 2,000 wounded and 11,000 taken prisoner. In North Africa, the picture was no less encouraging. After the rout of the Italians, Rommel had reinstated the Axis advance backed up by a hefty Luftwaffe force. He launched a full-scale land offensive in April, and the British Army on the Nile was put to flight, forced back towards Egypt, and in the process 9,000 Allied troops and three British generals were captured.

By the end of May the British were digging in for what would become a long, hot summer of attrition. It was in this period, too, that the attention of both the Axis and British turned towards the island of Malta, whose role in the oncoming Battle of the Mediterranean was to become crucial. In the spring of 1941 Cunningham re-established his submarine base at Valletta, until then it had operated on a shoestring. Six submarines had been transferred from the Far East, but within a month of arrival three were sunk by Italian torpedo bombers. Four new T-class submarines were transferred from convoy-protection duties and two of those were sunk en route. The new commander on the Malta station, Captain G.W.G. 'Shrimp' Simpson, was promised a prompt delivery of additional submarines to administer his priority directive: Stop all Axis supplies and troops from getting from Italy to Tripoli.

Since the major naval base at Alexandria was 1,000 miles along the coast, Malta became the key operational base for Britain's submarine force. Over the coming months, the submarine service in the Mediterranean went to great lengths to achieve the ambitions of the war planners in causing as much grief as possible to the Axis powers, and for that they needed the urgent and effective cooperation of the RAF, which was not always possible because resources were already overstretched. As Captain Ronald Mills, commander of *Tetrarch*, one of the first submarines to arrive at the base, recalled: 'From the moment we arrived, the Italians were bombing daily, and at one point we had just three aircraft on the island piloted by the governor's own staff. Then, when the Luftwaffe set up shop on nearby Sicily, it was a different ball game altogether. We were in real trouble.'

Then another great disaster struck, on 13 November 1941, when, virtually in sight of Gibraltar, the heroic carrier *Ark Royal* was hit amidships by a torpedo and the damage was clearly fatal. She remained afloat but out of control for almost 14 hours, which allowed the destroyers *Legion* and *Laforey* to ferry 1,487 officers and men ashore, leaving just a skeleton crew aboard until she finally capsized and disappeared. Remarkably, only one man was killed when the torpedo struck. Further trouble came later in the year as the Germans sent additional U-boats into the Mediterranean and *U-331* soon claimed the battleship *Barham*, with the loss of her captain and 861 of her crew; 450 were saved. Soon afterwards, the British fleet in the Mediterranean was reduced to two battleships when *Valiant* and *Queen Elizabeth* were put out of action from a totally unexpected source.

At the time, the two giant ships lay sheltered behind torpedo nets at Alexandria. At 0330 on 19 December, two Italian sailors were discovered clinging to the anchor buoy of *Valiant*. They surrendered immediately and were taken ashore for interrogation and then, to their dismay, back to *Valiant*, where they confessed that the battleship was about to blow up. There was, of course, considerable disbelief, but even so the crew was eventually mustered to deck and the watertight doors were closed. But shortly after 0600 the ship rocked and shuddered as the charge set by the Italians blasted a large hole in her stern.

Soon afterwards, *Queen Elizabeth* reared up from two explosions from charges attached below the water line and both ships were temporarily out of the war. It soon emerged that the explosions had been caused by charges carried by three piloted torpedoes, driven by a team of six men from the 10th Light Flotilla of the Italian navy, trained to remain underwater for miles wearing flexible rubber-suits, breathing gear and fins. Although slow and cumbersome, the piloted torpedoes were to do a great deal of damage to Allied shipping. In this instance, the torpedoes had been launched from Prince Julio Borghese's submarine *Scire* off Alexandria, with two men astride each of the three piloted torpedoes. The men travelled to the target ships, where the time-fused warheads from each one were disconnected and attached to the ships' hulls. They then made their exit on the remaining part of the torpedo and returned whence they came. The operations even drew praise from Churchill as an example of 'extraordinary courage and ingenuity'. Escapes were always planned in advance. But on this occasion the two Italians had to adopt the course of last resort – which was to surrender to the nearest safe haven.

# CHAPTER TEN

## Clash of the Titans

The Home Fleet, meanwhile, had to contend with Nazi control of a coastline running from north Norway to the Spanish border and maintained a round-the-clock alert to (a) blast the invasion barges out of the water, should even Hitler have tried to get across the 21 miles of choppy English Channel; (b) to ensure that the German big ships did not break out into the North Sea and Atlantic; and (c) to keep a permanent watch over Britain's lifeline, the supply convoys bringing essential food, raw materials, troops and war machinery into the United Kingdom, to which was now to be added supply convoys onwards to Russia, in an attempt to keep Stalin in the war. The last task alone was hazardous enough, given the shortage of ships and the fact that German U-boat production had doubled, then trebled, since 1939 and the boats were coming out in swarms.

It was from this standpoint that what became known as the Battle of the Atlantic blew up almost from the beginning of the war and continued at a worrying rate for three years when sheer brute force, aided by some magnificent technological advances, helped the Royal Navy to get the upper hand. It was a period in which thousands of ships from Britain and her dominions travelled millions of miles and could virtually guarantee that somewhere along the line they would run into trouble. Again repeating the tactics of the First World War, Hitler – having failed to invade – hoped to subdue the British by starving the nation of food and fresh equipment. Germany's main naval weapon in these attacks was the U-boat, and control of the Biscay ports provided the Germans with bases from which they could go out into the Atlantic without having to pass either through the Channel or around the north of the British Isles at the end of every patrol. There were also two new battleships entering the fray, the massive *Tirpitz* and *Bismarck*, which were about to come into service. And although the Royal Navy had more ships by far, these two totally outclassed anything on the British list. Apart from the fact that they were crammed with the most up-to-date technology, they were also bigger and faster by far. Unlike Britain, Hitler had totally ignored the international convention limiting the size of ships to 35,000 tons. These two topped 50,000 tons.

At the start of the war, the British Merchant Navy possessed 3,000 deep-seagoing ships and tankers and 1,000 coasters, amounting to more than one million tons. Under normal circumstances, there were perhaps close on 2,000 ships at sea on any given day, which took a very great deal of protection. Furthermore, the journey times from far-off colonial ports were lengthened by having to avoid normal shipping routes. The closure of the Suez Canal when Italy invaded North Africa, for example, meant a long detour, increasing the distance to Bombay from 6,000 to 11,000 miles. The Atlantic crossing, however, became the focus of German attacks, as Winston Churchill warned in April 1941:

> In order to win this war, Hitler must either conquer this island by invasion or he must cut the ocean lifeline which joins us to the United States. Wonderful exertions have been made by our navy, and our air force . . . by the men who build and repair our immense fleet of merchant ships, by the men who load and unload them, and, need I say, by the officers and men of the Merchant Navy, who go out in all weathers and in the teeth of all dangers to fight for love of their native land and for a cause they comprehend and serve.

As the war progressed, convoys of between 40 and 60 ships became the norm. They would steam in columns with two miles between each column and a third of a mile between each ship. A 12-column convoy would extend five and a half nautical miles in length and almost two miles deep. The escorts of surface ships, submarines and aircraft would accompany convoys at various stages en route. The benefits to the merchantmen of sailing in convoy could be seen almost immediately. In the first full two years of the war, 12,057 ships arrived at British ports in 900 convoys. Only 291 ships in those convoys had been lost to enemy action, just under two per cent of the total. But there was a chink in the lifeline, and it became known as the Atlantic Gap.

In the early months, naval escorts for outgoing convoys from the British Isles could go only 300 miles out to sea before having to turn back to escort incoming convoys. Escort destroyers could stay out safely for only seven days without refuelling, which meant three and a half days' cover for a convoy and three and a half days back. This was increased to 400 miles by October 1940 and to halfway across the Atlantic by April 1941. Since air cover for shipping could also be provided from the British Isles, from Canada and from Iceland, the Atlantic space left open to the U-boats was reduced by May 1941 to a width of around 300 miles.

Even so, it was a yawning chasm, and in any event it did not stop German submarines exploiting their targets wherever they might find them. Under the guidance of Admiral Karl Dönitz, the U-boats gradually built their devastating coordinated attacks on British and neutral shipping, with the Nazis once again playing the 'unrestricted warfare' card, which meant they would hit anything and everything that came within their sights. This was amply demonstrated by the 1941 sinking of *Andora Star*, an independent ship of 15,000 tons carrying German and Italian refugees from Liverpool to Halifax, Nova Scotia. In August the Germans hit the Dutch liner *Volendam*, which was carrying 320 refugee children, off Malin Head, and only good fortune and an excellent rescue operation saved them. A month later, 200 adults and children on *City of Benares*, sunk by a U-boat attack, were not so lucky.

The mounting convoy losses in the Atlantic were causing grave concern. There was a great apprehension about the possibility that

191

the new German battleships would come out and cause havoc among the convoys, in addition to the U-boat threat, which was substantial. *Admiral Scheer* was roaming the seas for four months in the winter of 1940–41 and sank 100,000 tons of shipping along with the armed merchant cruiser *Jervis Bay*. Meanwhile, the names of Germany's big two, the brand-new *Bismarck* and *Tirpitz*, became as well known to the British public as their own famous ships even before they had fired a shell, and the Royal Navy declared that it would hunt them down.

The battle cruisers *Scharnhorst* and *Gneisenau*, along with the cruiser *Admiral Hipper*, also broke out into the North Sea early in 1941, under the command of Admiral Lütjens, and sank over 100,000 tons of shipping in a very short space of time. The level of fear that these ships raised among the Admiralty hierarchy – perhaps to some extent fired by Churchill's obsession to have them destroyed – can be gauged by the number of attempts to dispose of the 'S and G' problem. No fewer than 127 aircraft were lost in attacks on these two ships, and around those efforts were incredible stories of heroic crews flying a storm of flak. Eventually, the RAF put them temporarily out of action when they were bombed in Brest harbour. Among the many acts of bravery over that place, one was recognised with a posthumously awarded Victoria Cross for a young pilot, Flying Officer Kenneth Campbell, who flew a Bristol Beaufort of RAF No. 22 Squadron on one of the raids on Brest, on 6 April 1941. He went in low, flying just 50 feet above the protective mole of the inner harbour to release a torpedo that struck *Gneisenau* below the water line. Every flak gun now turned on him, and he, his plane and crew were shot to pieces. The action came to light only weeks later from a report through the French Resistance. *Gneisenau* was out of operation for four months.

Admiral Lütjens, meanwhile, had been appointed to command Hitler's next major naval adventure, flying his flag in *Bismarck*, under Captain Lindemann, which came out for the first time in the company of the cruiser *Prinz Eugen* initially in a campaign in which they were to link up with *Scharnhorst* and *Gneisenau*, which was temporarily shelved after the attacks at Brest, where the two ships were kept bottled up by a constant Royal Navy patrol.

*Bismarck* and *Prinz Eugen* moved into the Baltic, and to reach the North Sea they had to pass through the narrow passages of Kattegat and Skagerrak, which the British had mined with submarine minelayers months earlier. As they proceeded through these hazardous waters, they were spotted by a Swedish vessel, whose information was in turn relayed to the British naval attaché in Stockholm, who just happened to be Henry Denham, whose recollections of his service in the First World War, especially in the Dardanelles campaign, are recorded in earlier chapters. RAF Coastal Command was alerted and sent out torpedo bombers to launch an attack off the Norwegian coast, without success.

British Home Fleet commander-in-chief, Admiral Sir John Tovey, was certain that *Bismarck* was preparing to make an attacking sortie into the North Atlantic and alerted his eight-inch-gun cruisers *Norfolk* and *Suffolk*, which were already patrolling, and in addition immediately sent one of the great stars of the British fleet in an era when names of ships were very familiar to the general public, the battle cruiser *Hood* – almost 20 years old and just refitted – together with the brand-new battleship *Prince of Wales*, to join the patrol and engage *Bismarck* immediately she was sighted. With them went half a dozen destroyers for additional support.

The choice of *Prince of Wales* for this mission raised a few eyebrows among officers of the fleet. She was fresh out of the dockyards with an inexperienced crew and known to have teething problems with the most important aspect of her build: the guns. She had been commissioned from Birkenhead amid great fanfare and a visit from King George VI and Queen Elizabeth, the latest in the *King George V* class, but although publicly the ship was seen as one of Britain's fine new assets, there were problems resulting from altering the designs of the gun mounts, so that when she sailed into action against *Bismarck* engineers from the shipbuilders Vickers were still on board. Gunnery Officer Colin McMullen explained:

When the *King George V*-class ships were designed, there was a limit on the size of ship under the international convention, and we originally had 12 14-inch guns in three four-gun

193

turrets. Then, with the air threat, they reckoned they wanted much more deck armour, which made her heavier, so the ships were redesigned again, with ten 14-inch guns. Both *King George V* and *Prince of Wales* suffered teething troubles in their turrets because it was an untried, very complicated mass of machinery. Anyway, with Vickers' people still on board, we put to sea that evening in company with *Hood* with Admiral Holland in command of this squadron. There were problems with *Hood*, too. Few were aware that *Hood* was very lacking in deck armour, so she was definitely a battle cruiser as opposed to being a battleship. Although she was a marvellous ship, marvellous to look at and so on, she in fact was very vulnerable to plunging fire. We didn't know this then, of course, and although there were plenty of butterflies in tummies when we went into action we felt confident and safe being astern of the mighty *Hood*, as she was universally known in the navy.

We proceeded at high speed and then had this sighting report from the two cruisers that were in the Denmark straits, and suddenly realised this was it. We were really going to go into action. I found it hard to realise that this was going to be me versus *Bismarck*'s gunnery officer on the other side. Finally, we were all closed up and circuits had been tested. From the sighting reports, we knew roughly the direction from which we could expect the enemy. Sure enough, a smudge of smoke appeared on the horizon and the captain had sent a boy up to the crow's-nest as a lookout. We heard him shouting, 'Enemy in sight bearing green 40,' which is 40 degrees on the bow.

Up over the horizon came the masts and fighting tops of these two ships. [Then, an unexpected incident . . .] Our padre had asked permission to say a prayer over the loudspeaker before going into action, but for some reason he'd been delayed and just as we sighted the enemy every loudspeaker throughout the ship suddenly started praying when I was giving my orders for the first procedure for engaging the enemy. I remember being extremely angry at the time, but it was just one of those things. He was a splendid bloke, and when we were sunk [later, in the Far East] he was last seen tending the wounded.

Anyway, the prayer before action was completed, and it had been decided that *Hood* and *Prince of Wales* would concentrate on *Bismarck*. *Hood* made the 'Open fire' signal, 'Engage the left-hand ship'. Over the horizon came these two ships, one leading the other, exactly the same silhouette: four turrets, one funnel. I turned to the spotting officer and commented that the leading ship was not *Bismarck* and immediately realised that *Hood* had made a mistake in identification. She was going for the wrong ship, which was quite understandable because the silhouettes were so exactly alike. So we opened fire on *Bismarck*, but we never saw any of *Hood*'s fall of shot. I'm afraid she only fired I think two or three salvoes. Suddenly, the whole of the inside of our spotting top [took on the appearance] of a sudden sunset. This was when our great ship *Hood* blew up. I didn't see her blow up because I was looking at the enemy, but the buzz went through our ship just like that, the mighty *Hood* had gone, in minutes she had disappeared.

So there we were. At one moment we were full of confidence and the next as a new, untried ship we were facing *Bismarck* and *Prinz Eugen*, both of which then concentrated on us. We suffered various damage. I can't remember the exact number of hits. I know *Prinz Eugen* hit us three times. I think *Bismarck* hit us five times. One of the hits on us went through the bridge and killed everyone on the bridge except the captain, the chief yeoman and the navigator, who was very seriously wounded. The captain, realising the state of our turrets, quite rightly went hard aport and circled round, making smoke. At the time I was conducting the shoot. Although we were well over at the start, we quickly straddled and the shoot was going very well, which was borne out later, of course, by the fact that we did hit her.

When I realised the captain had gone hard aport, that we were breaking off the action, like any gunnery officer whose shoot has been interfered with, I was furious. To my boy messenger I said: 'Go and tell the captain everything's going fine.' What I didn't know was that when the captain went hard aport at full speed, Y turret had jammed and was out of action for an hour or so. But in fact the boy messenger was so horrified at the mess of wounded and decimated corpses that this poor boy came back and said he couldn't find the captain.

While Vickers' civilian engineers found themselves attempting to bring the broken turret back into operation, *Prince of Wales* slowed from the action. But in spite of her difficulties, she had hit *Bismarck* with two 14-inch shells, one of which holed the forward fuel tank, leaving a trail of oil slick, at which point Admiral Lütjens turned from the engagement and set course for the safety of the French coast, leaving *Prinz Eugen* to continue the original mission of attacking convoys.

With *Hood* lost, Rear-Admiral Frederick Wake-Walker, commander of the 1st Cruiser Squadron in *Suffolk*, was now the senior officer among the remaining ships. In view of the severe damage to *Prince of Wales* and the fact that one of her four-gun turrets was out of action, he decided not to re-engage *Bismarck* but to maintain a shadowing operation. Meanwhile, the Admiralty began what amounted to an all-points alert to all Royal Navy ships within 500 miles of *Bismarck* and by the early evening of 24 May a pincer movement was under way to trap and finally sink the star of the German fleet, an operation that ultimately involved four battleships, two battle cruisers, two aircraft carriers, 12 cruisers and ten destroyers, all detached from existing duties and heading towards a likely point of interception. This massive force included ships from the Home Fleet under Admiral Sir John Tovey, heading south, and Admiral Somerville's Force H heading north from Gibraltar, as well as the battleship *Rodney* and other ships pulled out of convoy-protection duties.

The carrier *Victorious* went on ahead of Tovey's ships with an escort of four cruisers of the 2nd Cruiser Squadron and was still more than 100 miles from *Bismarck* when nine Swordfish aircraft carrying torpedoes and four reconnaissance aircraft were dispatched from the windswept deck of the carrier. As they made contact with their prey, they were met by horrendous fire from *Bismarck*'s flak guns. Although several planes were hit, all

managed to pull out and return to the carrier after dropping
their load, leaving the German ship swerving violently to dodge
the torpedoes as they dropped one after the other from the
bellies of the flimsy aircraft. Only one hit the target, but the
damage was insufficient to halt *Bismarck* and during the night
contact with the ship was lost.

No further attempts were made against the German ship until
the morning of 26 May, when ten Swordfish from *Ark Royal*,
heading north with Somerville's Force H, were sent from a deck
heaving under appalling weather and with waves so large that the
deck was constantly awash. But Lütjens had for the time being
given them the slip, and they returned without making contact.
Later that morning, however, a Catalina flying boat from Coastal
Command finally picked up the trail again and reported *Bismarck*
700 miles from the French coast, apparently heading for the safe
haven of Brest and the prospect of German air cover as she came
closer. Somerville's force was now less than 50 miles away, and
once again the Swordfish from *Ark Royal* went out under difficult
conditions, with the deck swept by 50mph winds and rising more
than 50 feet on the swell.

Although they approached *Bismarck* in cloud, they were hit by
radar-controlled anti-aircraft flak as they came within range,
although again none was shot down, despite a number of holes in
the fuselage and airmen's bodies and then, after the first wave of
the attack, *Bismarck* began firing her big guns on a flat trajectory,
sending up massive plumes of water. Once again, *Bismarck* was
swerving violently to avoid the torpedoes unleashed from the
aircraft. One gave her a glancing blow and exploded on her bow,
but another, from the aircraft of Leading Airman K. Pimlott, the
last to attack, made a significant explosion aft, damaging her
rudders.

By then, the ships from all points were edging closer, and
Captain Philip Vian, in *Cossack*, and four others from the 4th
Destroyer Flotilla virtually had *Bismarck* surrounded and began
random torpedo attacks until the cavalry arrived in the shape of
the battleship *Rodney*, soon to be joined by *King George V*, *Norfolk*
and *Dorsetshire*.

Captain Roger Lewis was at the time torpedo officer on *Rodney*, which had been escorting small and very fast troop-carrying convoys across the Atlantic.

In point of fact, on this trip we were also going over to do a refit at Boston, and had on board 500 civilian passengers, a whole mass of refit stores, and 2,000 tons of armour plating, which was going to be fitted in the ship, around the A and B turrets. So the whole of the upper deck was littered with stuff, and none of our six 4.7 anti-aircraft guns were capable of being fired.

We were detached from the liners we were escorting to proceed on the *Bismarck* chase and were eventually joined up with *King George V*. We had to leave our escorting destroyers, so that, when we opened fire on *Bismarck* that morning, we were completely denuded of any anti-submarine escort. We were within 700 miles of Brest and enemy U-boats were known to be about. *Rodney* was fitted with sixteen 24.5-inch torpedoes – as was *Nelson*, the only capital ships then in the navy with torpedoes. One of *Bismarck's* first shells damaged the starboard bow door, so that I had to fire, and did fire, all 16 of my torpedoes from the port tube only. This wasn't a very sensible thing to do, but the opportunity of hitting an enemy capital ship with a torpedo from a British capital ship was never likely to arise again. Admiral Tovey gave us full permission to fire them when and how we could.

After scoring a hit or two, we decided to go in with our 16-inch guns to point-blank range. We fired at ranges of about 3,000 yards in what was known in gunnery circles as deliberate broadsides. We could see all nine shells going through the air, and all of them entering *Bismarck*. It was a disgusting sight. We could see the crew diving into the sea to escape. It was frightful. In point of fact our captain said: 'We've done enough! This is a holocaust!' Even so, we were exhilarated by what we'd done because it was a terrific success.

The shelling and torpedo fire from *Rodney* was matched by a similar onslaught from *King George V*. But *Bismarck* refused to go down, and Rear-Admiral Wake-Walker now called on the latest arrival, *Dorsetshire*. Fred Ball, one of the survivors of the sinking of *Courageous*, was in the main armament spotting tower:

> We arrived early in the morning of 27 May and *Bismarck* was still firing when we drew close. She opened fire at us and one of her 15-inch shells came over the top of the funnel. If it had hit, a lot of people would have been killed on the upper deck. We were told to open fire. I believe we fired 240 eight-inch projectiles and the three torpedoes that finally sent her down. I looked out and saw her going down. We stopped to pick up survivors, but not for long because we had been told there was a U-boat in the area. So we had to leave those still in the water. I got to know one of the prisoners we took on board, one of them in particular: Hans Zimmerman. Another, who was ill, stayed in England after the war and married the nurse who had looked after him.

Now, the great German ship rolled over and remained so for a few minutes, with the remaining survivors standing on her side pleading to be rescued, before the mighty ship disappeared beneath the waves. Of the 2,200 ship's company, only 110 survived. Admiral Lütjens was not among them.

There was one final postscript to the story. *Prinz Eugen* later suffered mechanical failure and managed to reach Brest without being discovered, where she joined *Scharnhorst* and *Gneisenau* for repairs. Hitler now ordered them back to their home port, and under an operation supported by 100 aircraft in the air at any one time the three managed to evade a joint RAF and Royal Navy search when their move from Brest was discovered. Churchill was furious that they had escaped, and the newspapers of the day roundly criticised what was claimed to be a grave tactical error. Worse: that the most powerful of all Germany's new ships, *Tirpitz*, was still out there somewhere, lurking in the Norwegian fjords waiting to pounce, and that fact alone gave convoy participants nightmares.

By the end of 1941 total losses of Allied shipping since the start of the war amounted to more than 10 million tons, more than half of which were sunk by U-boats. A more vital statistic, however, was that in the last half of that year U-boat strength was doubled to more than 230. By then, U-boats were roaming around in packs. They were called wolf packs, known to the Germans as Rudeltaktik, and were created by Dönitz specifically to operate against the Allied convoys. With a pack of heavily armed submarines, he reckoned a 30- or 40-ship convoy would be a duck shoot, with sufficient distance between them for the U-boats to retreat quickly before they could be attacked by the escorts. He finally had enough U-boats and handy coastal bases to try his idea, and initially it was exceedingly costly to Britain and the Allies. The packs began to work to a distinct pattern, with the Atlantic carved into prearranged grids and using patrol lines to scout for convoys. Once the convoy was located, a single U-boat would shadow it to report direction and speed.

In the early stages, Dönitz directed many of the operations himself. He had all reports relayed back to his own command and would give his instructions for the deployment of the remaining boats in the pack attack on a convoy. Sometimes he would go for the strategy of picking off the stragglers, of whom there were always several. On other occasions he might surround a particular section of the convoy, and the packs would attack more or less in unison, usually at night and on the surface. Almost 140 wolf packs would be formed during their most active period, between 1941 and 1943, operating together for around two or three weeks. The smallest group would consist of three or four boats, although larger groups – even as many as 20 in one pack – were not uncommon. But even as these problems became more pressing to the Home Fleet, developments in the Far East now presented further demands on the Royal Navy's men and increasingly over-stretched equipment.

# CHAPTER ELEVEN

## Massacre in the East

The war in Europe, combined with the massive deployment of ships in the Atlantic, while at the same time forming a protective screen around the British Isles against a possible invasion, was bad enough, but a simultaneous war in the Far East was the stuff of nightmares for the Admiralty planners. In fact, conflict in the East had been secretly pronounced an unwinnable enterprise by some of the more realistic among Churchill's advisers. To say so was defeatist talk, but it was nothing short of the truth, and the reality had to be faced when intelligence reports showed great activity among the Japanese military machine, which had taken advantage of France's predicament and occupied French Indo-China (later known as Vietnam).

Their further ambitions were the subject of intense discussion between Britain and America, resulting in President Roosevelt demanding that the Japanese withdraw at once, which they did not. The possibility of the Japanese now pressing on with their acquisitive ways across the whole of the British and Dutch interests in the Far East, such as Singapore, Malaya, the Dutch East Indies, Thailand, Burma and perhaps even India, kept the midnight oil burning at the Admiralty in the dread fear that they at last might have to provide ships for another major front. The only hope was that if the Japanese refused to pull back, the Americans might enter the war, but at that time there was still a firm body of opinion in the United States which said they should stay out of it.

Even so, in the late summer, Australian Prime Minister Robert Menzies, in fear of invasion by the Japanese himself, proposed that some kind of British naval presence should be moved immediately to Singapore, which was virtually unprotected by any seagoing force of any consequence and only lightly manned by the RAF and the military. Menzies pleaded for five capital ships to be sent immediately east of Suez as a first step to building up naval reinforcements to that region. Having witnessed the fear that emanated from the escapades of *Bismarck* and *Tirpitz* against the Atlantic convoys, Churchill was convinced, as he wrote to First Sea Lord Sir Dudley Pound, that a minimum force of two battleships and an aircraft carrier would 'exert a paralysing effect upon Japanese naval action'.

It was a forlorn hope. Pound wrote back to say that the *King George V*-class battleships could not be sent out because '60 per cent of the crews consisted of men under 21 who have never been to sea before'. He also stated that no aircraft carriers were available because *Illustrious* and *Formidable* were undergoing repairs from damage in action and *Furious* and *Ark Royal* were undergoing urgently needed refits. As the Japanese threat heightened over the coming weeks, Churchill wrote to the new Australian Prime Minister, John Curtin: 'In order to deter Japan, we are sending forthwith our newest battleship *Prince of Wales* to join *Repulse* in the Indian Ocean.' This meagre force, accompanied by just four old and tired destroyers, under the command of Admiral Tom Phillips, was supposed to deter the might of a Japanese military machine whose prowess in both ships and aircraft had been amply demonstrated in their war on China and lately in taking Indo-China.

It was also well known to the hierarchy that *Repulse* suffered the same armour weakness of *Hood* and that *Prince of Wales* was one of those ships with a new, young crew. Those at the sharp end of this mini-Task Force fully realised that they were in for a rough time. Commander Richard Poole was at the time a young officer on *Repulse*, which he had joined in 1937:

I would have preferred to have gone to a smaller ship, where life wasn't quite so formal. There were over 100 officers and that's very different from the 20 or so in a light cruiser or the ten in a destroyer. But one soon settled into it. She was the oldest ship, from the point of view of anti-aircraft armoury, in the Royal Navy and was due for a major modernisation but the war had scuppered that. One of the reasons that we didn't get into some of the hotter spots was our lack of anti-aircraft guns. We had speed so we were employed in fleet duties and in the cover force for the sweeps patrolling for the German ships. Rumour had it that we were going to escort convoys possibly via the Far East and ending up in San Francisco, but we didn't really know where we were going. We escorted a convoy out to Durban in company with the cruiser *Sheffield* and then we travelled on to the Indian Ocean, where there was a scare over a German raider. Using Mombasa as base, we did the next four weeks with the carrier *Hermes*, searching. It was a pleasant interlude, the calm before the storm, you might say. We left Mombasa and once we were at sea were told we were going to Colombo.

Curiously, I heard the paymaster commander say to another officer: 'Well, I'm sure we are going much further east than Colombo, and I wonder whether we shall ever come back.' And, indeed, after a visit to Colombo, where we did a demonstration of firing for the C-in-C, we were told that in fact we were to rendezvous the next morning with *Prince of Wales* and then go on to Singapore. This was 30 November 1941 and in very rough seas. It was a marvellous sight as she came ploughing up with her four destroyers with great seas breaking over the top of her, and off we went, passing through the Malacca Strait, where we had our first sight of the East, with Chinese junks going, very hot, and we arrived in Singapore on 3 December.

Things were hotting up in the Far East, of course. We weren't thinking in terms of war against Japan, although we had silhouettes of various ships posted so that we could recognise them if they appeared on the horizon. Arriving in Singapore was a great moment. We received a terrific welcome and a lot of media attention, in spite of the fact that the new Far East Fleet was a little short in numbers – one new battleship, one old battle cruiser in need of a refit and four destroyers, two of whom were in need of repairs. There were other ships meant to come in but they weren't yet visible. There was a cruiser in dock and a damaged destroyer from the Mediterranean being repaired. We had no idea what would confront us. Indeed, we were rather scathing about war preparations in Singapore.

On the second day, however, we were sailed for Darwin, in northern Australia, where there was a lot of unrest, and the idea was that we would go down to show the flag and help sort things out. We set off for Darwin but got about halfway, then on the afternoon of 6 December we were suddenly turned around and headed back to Singapore at full speed . . .

Intelligence tracking Japanese fleet movements had raised the alert in the US, although the Americans were unable to predict the arrival of war to its own territories. In the Far East, meanwhile, Japan launched simultaneous offensives on three fronts to coincide with their devastating attack on Pearl Harbor on 7 December 1941. On that day, a massive Japanese offensive was launched towards Hong Kong and then, as the month progressed, to the Philippines, Malaya and on towards Burma in the north and, going south, Singapore and Sumatra. In the parallel actions, the Japanese landed substantial forces at Kota Baharu, on the east coast of Malaya, just short of the border with Siam (now Thailand), and while the thinly spread RAF defenders were drawn to cover that area the main Japanese invasion was occurring a hundred miles north at Singora to begin their lightning thrust north towards Burma and south to the British jewel of Singapore. At the same time, the only defence of Singapore city rested with just two RAF squadrons, Nos 36 and 100, flying Vickers Vildebeests, an old biplane of late-1920s specification originally intended for patrolling home waters as torpedo bombers. There were also two squadrons flying 1935 Short Singapore flying boats, to which would now be added the modest Far East Fleet, somewhat hopefully called Force Z, which was hastily making its way back to Singapore, as Richard Poole recalls:

We arrived back on 7 December and immediately had oilers alongside to fuel. There was a lot of conjecture, subdued excitement, and then there was a rumour that some Japanese transport had been spotted in the Gulf of Siam. On the morning of the eighth, air-raid warnings were given and the city's lights went off everywhere. We rushed up to our repel-aircraft positions and there was a complete hush all over the ship with just the odd command coming from the captains of the guns and the noise of shells being unloaded from the ready-use lockers and thumping on the deck.

The next thing, we saw searchlights fingering about the sky and revealing ten or 12 aircraft, very high and flying dead over the top of us. We all opened up, spectacularly, with masses of flame from the muzzles of the guns of *Prince of Wales*. They flew on, no bombs were dropped on us, but they had already dropped them on Singapore. Then there was a broadcast by the commander to say that the Japanese navy had attacked Pearl Harbor and as of that moment we were at war with Japan. Next day, the captain went to several meetings and then at midday gave orders to prepare to go to sea. At 5 o'clock that night, *Prince of Wales* left her berth and passed us and we all fell in astern. Everyone was very keyed up and excited.

The captain had indicated that we were off to look for the Japanese and expressed the opinion that this was going to be a fairly dodgy operation and fully expected that one of the ships would not come back. He also said that there was little use staying in harbour because we would undoubtedly be bombed. So we were off, with four destroyers with us, which included two very old First World War destroyers, that couldn't really go the whole way because they didn't have the endurance. Once at sea, we were told that the army was very hard pressed in the north and that there were Japanese transports lying off the coast. We were going to try a high-speed raid on those ships and sink them all if we could to stop the troops going ashore and generally do what we could to help the army in what was a pretty desperate situation.

We were also told we might be running into the Japanese battle cruiser *Kongo*, and the admiral said in his message that, whatever action we ran into, he hoped to finish quickly and try to avoid air attacks. The weather was monsoon, low visibility, very rough and very hot, and we clamped down at action stations. We were steaming quite fast towards the South China Sea heading straight for the south tip of Indo-China, hoping to get to a position where we could run in to Kota Baharu, where there was very fierce fighting and already the two forward airfields had been lost. They were having a very rough time.

Morale was so high that what we wanted was action. We were sure we would equip ourselves well. It was a tremendous disappointment on the afternoon of the ninth when right on the horizon at about six we saw two or three seaplanes, and everyone knew then we had been seen. The full implications didn't really dawn on the more junior officers and ship's company, and subsequently the admiral made another signal saying that since we had been spotted by enemy air reconnaissance, he was going to continue on course until after dark and then reverse course and head back to Singapore.

At about that time we received a signal from Singapore that there had been an enemy landing at Kuantan, on the east coast of Malaya, which was directly on our way home. The admiral decided that since we weren't going to be where the Japanese expected us to be, we should at least go in and have a look, and arrived there at breakfast time.

In fact, the location to which the ships had been directed showed no signs of an invasion force and the ships turned south and resumed course towards Singapore. One of the destroyers, *Tenedos*, had been detached the night before because she was short of fuel and now made a report that she was being heavily attacked by Japanese aircraft. The message was relayed to Singapore air base, requesting cover for the incoming ships, but for some reason it was never received. Soon after 11 a.m., Japanese aircraft were spotted coming in from the south-west at about 12,000 feet in a flat V-formation. The bombers were about to demonstrate with clinical accuracy how greatly the British had underestimated the quality and capability of the Japanese air force, in range, equipment and tactics. Richard Poole:

*Prince of Wales* opened up with her 525 high-angle guns and we could see the shell bursts all around the formation, but this did not deter them at all and we had the impression this was as good as anything we had seen. When you are in that sort of situation, with an enormous number of guns firing, there is the most tremendous racket, the whole ship is shaking and great clouds of yellow cordite smoke are coming back at you. It is terribly exciting and impressive and a great deal to think about. The bombers passed right over us, and we then heard the scream of the bombs and one momentarily shuts one's eyes, wondering what the hell's going to happen – is this going to be my last moment, so to speak.

Two bombs hit the ship, one of them 30 feet from where I was standing at the time. I went over to look into the hole where it went through, and smoke and steam were coming up from it as the senior engineer officer moved in with the fire-and-repair parties. The message came up that one bomb had killed quite a large number of marines under the armoured deck. It had gone right through and exploded inside. The one close to my area had fractured a steam pipe, but the damage was under control.

We were steaming at about 26 knots, and everyone was concentrating on where and when there would be a target for one's own guns. On the horizon I saw another formation of bombers dropping down to sea-level, and it seemed to us that it must be a torpedo attack. It was difficult to assess which ship they were going for, but as they came in they released their torpedoes immediately, a range most beyond anything we had expected. In that very first attack, one torpedo hit *Prince of Wales* and I have a vivid memory of her just heeling over as she was hit and an enormous column of dirty, grey water shot up close to her stern and a lot of cordite smoke drifting with it. Very shortly after that, we saw aircraft coming in looking as if they were coming for us and we prepared to open fire, and at that time tactics for torpedo bomber attacks were to fire a fixed barrage with shells fused to explode at the range. The idea was to put up a screen through which they had to fly. But it was soon evident that they had dropped their torpedoes outside the range of our barrage and could then evade our fire.

Once again there was this hideous din of battle, and the ship was turning, manoeuvring very well to avoid the torpedoes, and I think five or six individual attacks were made on *Repulse* and each time the captain had avoided them. But finally we were caught, and from my position I could see the torpedo in the water coming towards us. It's quite a frightening thing to see this enormous thing, with 1,000 pounds of TNT in the head, coming straight at you and you don't know it's going to hit you. It hit the ship abreast the mainmast, and there was a tremendous shuddering explosion and the mainmast, all 150 feet of it, sort of whipped, and the ship staggered, but she picked up and carried on. I think most of us who saw this on the upper deck had a very good idea that we couldn't stand much more of this, and unbeknown to us then *Prince of Wales* was already hit and crippled.

John Gaynor, a gunnery rating on *Prince of Wales*, saw *Repulse* under fire:

... and the reason we had time to look around was that the torpedoes had already hit us in the screws. The propellers were like a car's fan belt: when they turned they drove the motors which supplied the electricity for the entire ship. The *PoW*, being modern, was all electric; there was nothing hydraulic, no messy mechanics. So when the electricity went, everything ceased. We couldn't control a gun electronically. So now, all the concentration of this modern technology was thrown out of sync. We were hit by two torpedoes in the bows and one in the stern and, give the Japanese pilots their due, they were pressing home their attack in wonderful aircraft.

By then, she began to take a list to port, which meant the starboard side was coming up out of the water, and as with all battleships she had a 12-inch armoured belt stretching along where a shell is liable to strike, but below that is the vulnerable underbelly that shows when the ship lists. So the Japanese pilots went around again, and now they came in on the exposed portion of the ship and in come the torpedoes, because she could no longer fire back at them. One minute she was looking as if she was going over to port, now she's rocked back to starboard. I looked over . . . the torpedoes, the wreckage and people hanging all over the place, lots of bodies floating around. It was carnage. Anyhow, this was the time for the survivors, of which I was going to be one . . .

The captain of *Repulse* saw that *Prince of Wales* was in trouble and, despite his own torpedo damage, went to offer assistance. Richard Poole:

Our captain turned back when he saw *PoW* flying the nautical signal for being not under control, which was two black balls. Our captain signalled to the admiral, 'Can we help?' and received no reply at all, and it was at that time that another wave of bombers came over, and then another wave followed, randomly, in fours, sixes and ones. They were being very clever: get the ship to turn one way, while another aircraft came in from the other side and fired. There was no formal tactical arrangement. *Repulse* was hit three times in fairly rapid succession – making five hits altogether – and suddenly I realised that our guns wouldn't elevate enough. It then dawned on me that it wouldn't elevate because it was already at full elevation because the ship had a tremendous heel to the port side.

At that point, the gunnery officer was shouting over the back of the bridge relaying the order to abandon ship. It had been broadcast as well, but no one had heard it because of the noise. It was only the fact that the captain, having realised the ship was going to sink and there was nothing more to do, that if 1,300 men were going to get away, they had to go and go now – and he gave the order only just in time.

We had to scramble up the deck and it was a bit slippery because unfortunately several men had been killed by cannon fire because one of the characteristics of the Japanese attacks was that, having dropped their torpedoes, a lot of them came straight on in firing their cannon at us. They were quite fearless, flying through our barrage. I climbed down the decks, walking more or less vertically on the ship's side, which was horizontal, still going through the water at five or six knots. I wasn't quite sure what I was going to do. There were a lot of people jumping off. I had time to think of a very famous picture of the German First World War battleship *Blücher* [see first picture section] lying on her side with the ship's company walking down the side and jumping into the sea. And I thought: 'Here we are, the very same thing.' I was also very aware of the propellers still going around. I finally took a gigantic jump into the water and swam as hard as I could to get clear of the suction, and then I got into a panic and took my clothes off, which was a stupid thing to do because I got horribly sunburned. I swam away and turned to look back in time to see the bows of the ship rear out of the water and seeing it shining in the sun and slide away down below. I started to swim slowly that way, encouraging people to follow me. Some people were hanging on to bits of wreckage. In the distance, I saw one of the destroyers coming towards us . . .

A similar fate had befallen the pride of the British fleet, *Prince of Wales*, but there were to be many more survivors. Because the ship had been out of control some time before she was mortally damaged, one of the destroyers managed to get alongside and rescue a large percentage of the ship's company (see first picture section). Even so, some were still on board when the destroyer had to pull away for her own safety as the ship began to lurch in its final death throes. John Gaynor was among them:

So I got on to the foredeck of the ship, round by A turret, and with an officer, I think, familiarised myself with the various life-saving apparatus, knowing that we were about to take to the water. I also began to release as much gear as would float. So, therefore, we went round and released Carley life rafts and anything wooden that would float. But much to my amazement, while I was busy doing this, the deck on which I'm standing is now assuming alarming proportions. And where normally I would sort of stand and look straight ahead, now looking to my left, I'm looking down into the water, looking to my right, the ship is beginning to tower up above me . . . we were going down, but one could not instantly recognise that fact. Remembering tales I'd heard about ships sucking people with them when they go, I thought: 'It's about time I left.'

So as the ship gradually turned, I hung on to a ventilator as the ship turned turtle. I'm for ever climbing upwards now, and then I walk down the ship's side, which is now horizontal, and suddenly find myself going over a lovely curve, and now I'm on the bottom of the ship as she rolled completely over. I sat between the two great twin keels of the ship, and I looked towards the stern, where I see four enormous propellers still idly turning, though the ship is upside down, and as I look down I see that the water now is gradually coming up towards me, like the tide coming in. So I slid down on my behind and bang, bang, bang over the bottom of the ship and into the water, and when I came up it was like swimming in black custard, and it burned your eyes and mouth. I looked around, and there were heaps of wreckage, but it was just like a bed sheet with all lumps underneath it, and all these lumps were bits of debris, pieces of ship floating, and bodies. And as I was striking out towards a raft, one of these lumps suddenly lifted itself up and tried to grab me. It was a fellow who said: 'Help me, I can't swim.' And here am I in the China Sea, faced with the dilemma of someone who looked like a Kentucky minstrel telling me he can't swim.

There's no good having a discussion on the joys of learning to swim at this point. He'd had the opportunity and lost it. So I said to him: 'Right, here you are, mate, you hang on to this, and then follow me.' I pushed him over something that was floating. It was impossible to keep track of him. I had been in the water near enough two hours when a boat from the ship came along and they hauled me in, and then we went around among all this debris to see if we could see anybody else. On board the destroyer there were so many survivors that they were stacking those who had been killed like firewood, five one way, five another. And I will always remember gazing into the eyes of a fellow who was a messmate of mine. He was dead, but didn't seem to have a mark on him, and I almost felt like saying: 'What are you doing there?'

Remarkably, 1,285 out of the ship's company of 1,618 on *Prince of Wales* were rescued. The crew of *Repulse* was far less fortunate: only 796 out of 1,306 survived, among them Richard Poole:

After an hour I arrived at the destroyer. They had rope ladders and scrambling nets over the side and people were lining the rails pulling them up. The trouble was we were all covered in oil, and eventually I got on board and in turn helped others aboard. The impression I got on board the destroyer was that the upper deck was boiling hot, covered in bodies, oil fuel and gun crews, and at that moment we received another alarm of enemy aircraft, and through all this the destroyer had to close up for action stations. However, we weren't attacked and we then backed up towards the main body of survivors until we picked up all those we could find before setting off very gingerly for Singapore. The destroyer *Electra** was absolutely crammed. There was not a space anywhere, with an extra 500 on board. We just sat down and some time in the early hours of the morning we got back to the naval base.

As we unloaded, there was an ominous line of bodies of men who had died from their wounds or oil poisoning. All the officers went to *Exeter*, which had just arrived to join Force Z, and they had laid on a buffet meal and lots of whisky as we arrived, rather like a peacetime cocktail party. We ate and

---

* The same destroyer that rescued three survivors from *Hood*.

talked until about three in the morning, when we were taken to the officers' club, where they laid out mattresses all over the floor space, and we had a shower and solvent to get the oil off, and all the immediate necessities. The next morning everyone had to write a report describing every single aspect of the operation as they saw it. The rest of the day was spent sending telegrams home and getting kitted up with uniforms and generally recovering.

The one thing that we did realise was the tremendous effect on morale of the people in Singapore at the loss of the two big ships, which they believed had come to save the day. I think the full impact of the disaster then hit us, because there was no doubt about it that on top of the disastrous news from the north, the fact that the invincible navy had been sunk as well was just about the last straw.

Then the controversy raged as to whether we should have gone out at all, but most of us didn't know enough of what went on. Certainly, on reflection, there were mistakes. The first one probably was the idea of sending us out there in the first place. It was done against the naval staff's advice; Dudley Pound fought against it. I think Churchill didn't really understand naval warfare, as it had changed. He rather believed that we could go out there and exercise the same malign influence that *Tirpitz* had done in home waters. But we had none of the backup and the only friendly aircraft we saw came when we were on the destroyer on our way back, when a flight of [ancient] Buffaloes arrived. One of their officers later wrote how impressed he was with the naval spirit, all waving and cheering. In fact, they weren't cheering; they were waving their fists. The spirit was much the same as Dunkirk, when the men were critical of air cover.

There was also criticism of Admiral Tom Phillips [commander of Force Z, who did not survive the sinking], which I personally didn't feel was justified. He had no option. It was impossible. The right thing to do was to get the hell out of it. But having had this enormous and purposeful build-up to try to deter the Japanese, it would have been even worse to have sailed away with our reputation ruined and to upset interservice relationships, which weren't all that hot anyway. One knows now that in the light of the intelligence situation, he had no option. The Malayan campaign was a shambles.

John Gaynor, the rating from *Prince of Wales*, was less than understanding about their plight:

So this is the part for sour grapes, I suppose. As far as they [the expat community of Singapore] were concerned, the war hadn't been on until now. The Japs had only just started to bomb them, because they were now driving along the Malay peninsula. And all the staff had been sitting the war out since 1939, mowing their lawns and going to the club for drinks and governor's balls and knitting a few socks for the sailors and soldiers, when all of a sudden the war caught up with them, and people's lawns were being destroyed by Japanese bombs. It was so terrible for the British Empire. This permeated into naval people, who were what the army would call basewallahs. Now all of us bedraggled shipwrecked mariners appear on their doorsteps, our ship had gone, our mates dead, no clothes, destitute. They had to feed us and look after us, and this was now like a trade union – it was outside their office hours, sort of thing.

Luckily, some of the people, like the petty officers' mess, were very good. Someone would give you a pair of shorts, someone else gave you a shirt, a pair of sandals or sandshoes. So now you begin to get dressed, you feel like you belong to the human race again. The only other group that helped us was the Australian Red Cross, which I thought was admirable. Everybody who came off the ships was supplied with two blankets, a pair of underpants, a vest, toothbrush, shaving brush and I think a razor. The naval base, we were told, simply did not possess surplus stores for that number of survivors. So everyone knew we were the survivors from the way we were dressed – chaps with green sports shirts and white trousers and wearing sandals – a motley crew without a doubt.

The very next day we are called on to the parade ground

and every single one of us is to be questioned. A typical service reaction: they all know what happened. They were there. And now they're asking me, or they're asking some bloke who was turning the wheel down in the engine room. All he ever saw was the end of his spanner. But they're asking him 'What happened?' or 'Why did we get sunk?' or 'What were you doing?' They're asking a cook who was making sandwiches or opening tins of corned beef, 'What did you do?' And I always remember the officer said to me, 'Where were you when we got attacked?' There I am, like a parrot, having to tell this bloke everything. 'I was in the starboard HA [high-angle gun] director.' 'What were you doing there?' What was I doing there? Well, I wasn't going up there to lay an egg!

Then after that we all line up in the days that follow . . . each morning it's parade ground muster . . . must keep up the old routine . . . you 15, clean the hut . . . you 15, wash the windows . . . you five, get a pair of scissors and cut the lawn.

Most of the officers of the two ships were assigned to other ships, while the seamen were given an assortment of tasks, some of them acting as drivers and guards on trains carrying troops towards the front when the locals ran away. Some, however, were still in Singapore helping with the evacuation of British nationals aboard two liners when the British were forced to surrender to the Japanese onslaught on 15 February 1942 and went into captivity. The members of the two Royal Marine detachments who survived the sinkings were attached to the British army units in the last stand against Japanese forces swarming into Malaya and Singapore. Many were killed in the process, and the rest also became prisoners of war, where more than half died, as did a number of ratings from the two ships who found themselves abandoned in Singapore, eventually to be captured.

Nor were the reversals over yet in the Royal Navy's ill-starred and undermanned expedition to the Far East. There was to be one further attempt to slow down the Japanese advance, which threatened the territories of Britain, America, Holland, Australia and New Zealand. The Americans were already under pressure in the

Pacific. The Dutch East Indies was about to be invaded, and Australia and New Zealand feared they would be next. In an attempt to halt the Japanese landings on Java, the allies formed the ABDA fleet (so called from the initials of American, British, Dutch and Australian). It was hastily pulled together from available ships of those countries within range, and the Royal Navy sent the repaired battle cruiser *Exeter*, the name famous from her crew's heroics at the Battle of the River Plate, along with three destroyers: the ever-present *Electra, Encounter* and *Jupiter*. The most powerful ship in the fleet was the USS *Houston*, a heavy cruiser built in the early 1930s but – like *Hood* – conforming to the Washington Treaty limiting the thickness of the armour plating on the ship. She had no radar and was already damaged after a month on patrol and numerous actions. One of her main gun turrets had been knocked out, and before setting off for the ABDA task the crew held a service to bury their dead from previous encounters with the Japanese. The rest of the fleet comprised two Dutch cruisers, *De Ruyter* and *Java*, and the Australian cruiser HMAS *Perth*, along with four American and two Dutch destroyers.

The expedition hit trouble from the start when the four nations argued over command, which was first placed with the Americans and then handed to the Dutch, who argued that they were attempting to halt the invasion of Java, which was their territory. That was all very well, but the project went ahead at such a pace that the Dutch admiral commander omitted to prepare a battle plan, if should an eventuality arise. It did, and the ABDA fleet was at an immediate disadvantage, quite apart from the fact that the admirals were arguing among themselves as to the best course of action.

They were following intelligence reports that the Japanese invasion force of almost 60 ships, protected by two heavy cruisers, two light cruisers and 12 large destroyers, was already at sea. Although in terms of the major ships, the two fleets appeared to be fairly even, it was far from the case. The majority of the ABDA force was obsolete, while the Japanese ships – some of which had been built in British yards – were fast, heavily armoured and bristling with guns. There were also communications difficulties, given that all commands from the Dutch flagship had to be translated to the non-Dutch commanders of the rest of the fleet, with inherent problems, especially under fire. Furthermore, in advance of the invasion the Japanese air force was on hand to soften up the enemy.

What became known as the Battle of Java, therefore, was already weighted heavily in favour of the Japanese. The moment came on 27 February 1942 after three days of poor intelligence and wild-goose chases. Having just returned from another fruitless search, a positive sighting of Japanese ships was reported and the ABDA fleet set sail again, with the British destroyer *Electra* sent on ahead to scout. At 1612 that afternoon, she confirmed contact with the enemy force steaming ahead in three columns. Unknown then was that the 56 ships of the invasion force were coming up behind.

Battle was joined at 1625, and with the benefit of better range the Japanese went straight for *Houston* and *Exeter*. Japanese fire was remarkably accurate, but even so the Allied force met and replied to the Japanese shells for a full 30 minutes of heavy exchanges in which ships on both sides took serious damage. Then the Japanese fleet commander ordered his destroyers to detach and move in to a distance of less than 16,000 yards from the Allied force and, in the face of heavy fire from the Allied ships, let go with their torpedoes – a barrage of 40 were on the way. Incredibly, the attack failed to damage one of the Allied ships. Then smoke from the Japanese invasion fleet appeared on the horizon and the Japanese came in with another attack, this time closing to 7,000 yards and firing no fewer than 64 torpedoes followed by heavy shelling.

Alfred Warner, a gunner on *Exeter*, recalled: 'We had a shell which killed the right-hand gun crew and went down into the engine room and killed most of the men down there. We actually passed one of the destroyers, which was turned over and the crew was standing on the bottom of the ship. But we couldn't stop to pick them up because we were in the line of fire.'

Two British destroyers in the company of *Exeter* took heavy shelling, which left *Electra* badly holed and sinking fast. One of the Dutch destroyers was also hit and split in two. Bow and stern halves rose and then disappeared, and in the midst of the firing the sea was swarming with survivors. The battle raged for almost two and a half hours before the Japanese pulled back to regroup and attend to the advancing invasion fleet, at which point the Allied fleet commander decided to take a new position close to the coast of Java and from there to attack the troop transports as they came through. As they completed that manoeuvre, the British destroyer *Jupiter* steamed straight into a newly laid minefield and blew up, with only 78 survivors in the sea, who were picked up by the last British destroyer, *Encounter*. She also happened upon 113 survivors from the sunken Dutch destroyer and was ordered to detach and land them all at the Javan port of Surabaya, which for the time being was still in Dutch hands.

*Exeter*, meanwhile, although damaged, was still capable of somewhat limited action but had run out of ammunition for her eight-inch guns, and so the ship went into Surabaya with *Encounter* and the American destroyer USS *Pope* to reload. The cruisers *Houston, Perth, De Ruyter* and *Java* remained to fight on, a fact that a Japanese reconnaissance aircraft soon discovered. At 2300 on 27 February, the Japanese battle fleet returned for what would be the *coup de grâce* and opened fire as soon as they were in range. *Java* was hit with the first attack, broke in two and sank, taking 512 crew to the bottom of the Java Sea. Just one minute later, the Dutch cruiser *De Ruyter*, which was also the ABDA flagship, suffered a similar fate, struck by one of these torpedoes. The fleet commander, Admiral Doorman, went down with his ship, along with 376 of his crew. Before he lost contact, he ordered the remaining two cruisers, *Houston* and *Perth*, to withdraw immediately and not wait to pick up survivors.

They had already been badly damaged themselves – 'falling apart' was the description of one eventual survivor – and in due course headed for the Sunda Strait, a narrow water passage between the islands of Java and Sumatra, leading to the Indian Ocean. Intelligence reports indicated that it was clear of Japanese ships. Somehow, reconnaissance flights missed a whole invasion convoy unloading troops and supplies on to the northern coast of Java. While the troops were being landed, the escort fleet set up patrol zones. They alerted the protection fleet to the oncoming cruisers, and by the time *Houston* and *Perth* reached the point of no return an ambush of 20 Japanese ships was waiting for them. The Japanese set upon *Houston* and *Perth* like ferocious guard dogs, and in an hour-long battle the Japanese are known to have fired more than 1,000 shells and 90 torpedoes. Dead tired and virtually out of ammunition, the last two members of the ABDA fleet put up a spirited fight until all that was left was practice shells, and they fired those, too. *Perth* was slowed by three torpedo hits and, unable to take avoiding action, she was pounded by enemy shells. Abandon ship!

The full concentration of fire now centred on *Houston*. She was hit by a shell that wiped out all the personnel in the after engine room. Then a torpedo hit the forward starboard side and wrecked the main battery control station. *Houston* remained under continuous and heavy fire until, at 0025 on the morning of 1 March, the crew was ordered to take to the water. As they did so, a Japanese destroyer came in to machine-gun the crew, and more shells were landing all over the place, killing even more men. It was assumed to be punishment for landing a shell on their own fleet commander's flagship and making him jump into the water for safety. *Houston* went down quickly. Out of 1,064 officers and men aboard, approximately 365 survived the sinking and the swim to shore. POW camps claimed the lives of more than a hundred, and only 266 men eventually got back to America. Those from *Houston* who went into prison camps were among those who built the bridge over the River Kwai.

Of the 682 crew of *Perth*, 353 were killed or missing in the sinking, while another 100 died as prisoners of war. Only 229 survived to return to Australia.

Of the ABDA fleet, there remained one major warship afloat – *Exeter* – which, it will be recalled, left the scene of the battle to go into Surabaya to take on fresh supplies and ammunition, accompanied by the British destroyer *Encounter* and USS *Pope*. Alfred Warner recalled:

When we arrived at the base, the captain discovered to his horror that they had no eight-inch shells left, and all we could take on were ack-ack shells, which were pretty useless against Japanese warships. So now it was decided that because we had no ammunition, we should try to make our way up into the Indian Ocean and on to Ceylon, as it was then, because we were totally useless without ammo and in any event we were damaged down below. We hadn't travelled far out to sea when we spotted a reconnaissance aircraft from one of the Japanese cruisers, which meant they now knew where we were. We were looking forward to our tot time at 11.30 and also that they had a load of fresh chickens (picked up in Surabaya) in the oven for our meal. At about 11 o'clock the Japanese navy opened fire on us from extreme range – we could barely see the red flash on the horizon. We fired the few shells we had left and sank one of their cruisers.

Then we took another shell, which burst in the other engine room and took all the power out of the propellers. We were effectively out of action. After a while the captain ordered 'Abandon ship!' and set time-fused charges to scuttle her when we had evacuated. Actually, we need not have bothered because the Japanese just blasted her out of the water. We went to the port side because the ship was heeling over to the starboard side. In the controlled act of abandoning ship, you took your shoes off and I remember we all lined them up neatly against the bulkhead. You never went over the side with footwear on. Once in the water, it's every man for himself, and luckily enough I came across a yellow raft which belonged to our Walrus aircraft until we lost it earlier on. I climbed aboard and some others climbed in. The Japanese navy was still firing and by then most of the survivors were in rafts.

After the ship had gone down, we saw two Jap destroyers coming along picking up some of the lads. I and a lot more were left floating about the water for about 24 hours in shark-infested waters. We were just left there. The sharks were swimming round and round and everyone had to make sure there were no feet dangling in the water. Then some more destroyers arrived the following morning and picked us up. They stripped us of any rings and watches and made us sit on the fore part of the ship. They gave us water and hard biscuits. They didn't beat us. That came later in the prison camps. We

220

lost 62 in the sinking, although many more died later in the Japanese prison camps, and after the war our captain dedicated a plaque to their memory in Exeter Cathedral. I finished the war as a prisoner in a coal mine close to Nagasaki, which I saw before the atom bomb and the devastation afterwards.

The final act in the battle of the Java Sea then centred on the destroyer *Encounter* and USS *Pope*. They were also intercepted and sunk as they made their way towards the Indian Ocean. So ended the Royal Navy's first major encounter with the Japanese, and Admiral Somerville was sent from Force H to form a new Eastern Fleet, following the death of Tom Phillips, with the principal aim of defending Colombo. By the early summer of 1942, he managed to bring together a fleet including *Warspite* and four other 25-year-old battleships, on which conditions in this climate were appalling, three carriers, six cruisers and two destroyers. Within a month, two of the County-class cruisers, *Cornwall* and *Dorsetshire*, had been sunk in an attack by 50 Japanese dive-bombers, followed soon afterwards by the carrier *Hermes*. Fred Ball, who survived the *Courageous* sinking and the battle of the *Bismarck*, was on *Dorsetshire* and among the survivors of that sinking, too. He subsequently transferred to *Valiant* and, as we will see, was in the Mediterranean in time for the invasion of Italy, where subsequently his new ship was to be attacked by brand-new German weapons: guided missiles.

# CHAPTER TWELVE

## Chasing the Ogre

While the supposed 'paralysis of fear' that Churchill had hoped (but probably never expected) would result from sending *Prince of Wales* and *Repulse* to South-East Asia failed to materialise as far as the Japanese were concerned, there was certainly something very close to it in Britain in relation to Germany's battleships, and especially the brand-new *Tirpitz*, sister of the late *Bismarck*. As the New Year dawned, this latest addition to the Nazi fleet was given the final clearance for action after six months of trials and was ready to join *Scharnhorst, Gneisenau, Prinz Eugen* and the rest of the big guns in preparing sorties to attack the Atlantic and Arctic convoys delivering crucial supplies to both Britain and Russia.

German policy was clearly aimed at the absolute devastation of the supply lines into Britain and then Russia. Hitler believed his prized fleet of technically advanced ships was the model of modern maritime warfare, although in reality it was Dönitz who held the pistol to Churchill's head by creating by far the greater mayhem with his U-boats. In this, the German navy was ably assisted by the unique dive-bombing and torpedoing skills of the Luftwaffe, who also possessed the finest aircraft for that purpose – now matched only by the Japanese – and it was well into 1942 before the Allies came close to matching the quality and efficiency of the Axis equipment. These had been no better demonstrated to

Allied warships and merchantmen ships braving the obstacle course – or bomb alley – down the east coast of Britain, where ships travelling that route were lucky to escape aerial bombardment or the attentions of U-boats.

The arrival of *Tirpitz* into service at the beginning of 1942 added a further worrying dimension to the scenario, but particularly in regard to the safety of the convoys. In spite of Britain's greater naval force in terms of numbers, there is no doubt that the Nazi warships represented a fear that, as already noted, became something of an obsession with Churchill, and with good reason. The tonnage of shipping lost to German attacks was already averaging 650,000 tons a month, and indeed the total for that year alone reached 7,790,000 tons, which translated into 1,664 ships sunk. Over the course of the months ahead, the Royal Navy surface fleet, the submarine service, the RAF and newly formed Commando units would all find themselves engaged in grandiose schemes to sink the stars of the German fleet, with *Tirpitz* at the head of the list.

She had originally been assigned to the Baltic Fleet, to support the German action in Russia. The latter event had, of course, brought benefits to Britain, in that Hitler postponed his planned invasion of the United Kingdom when the RAF won the Battle of Britain and never did try again, even though he had positioned invasion barges all along the Channel ports of France in readiness. However, after studying German intelligence reports suggesting that the Allies were planning an invasion of Norway, Hitler ordered a 'cautious' deployment of *Tirpitz* in the Norwegian fjords as soon as she became operational, and thereafter to begin sorties into the Atlantic. In fact, the 'invasion' of Norway was in part true – but only as a series of harassing 'hit-and-run' raids by Commandos, backed up by naval bombardment.

Indeed, it was a boarding party from the destroyer *Onslow* that captured code books and ciphers from a beached German escort ship – along with a curious-looking machine that turned out to be one of the first Enigma machines to fall into British hands. The Task Force made two landings during December as part of assaults against the enemy under the auspices of the Combined Operations group. This all-embracing arm, under the command of the First World War Zeebrugge hero Sir Roger Keyes,* was inspired by Churchill's call for storm troops and special forces from all the three services to attack enemy-held coastline over the coming months, by means of full-frontal assaults, sabotage and indeed any kind of activity that caused the enemy grief. The December 1941 raids on Vaagso fjords, in which the Royal Navy joined with Commandos and RAF bombers, prompted Hitler to issue a directive in which he stated: 'Norway is the zone of activity in this war. I demand unconditional obedience to my orders and directives concerning the defence of the area.'

He sent a personal representative on a tour to make a thorough assessment of the invasion possibility, and on his recommendation three more divisional commands were sent, and defensive hardware strengthened to cover all entrances to fjords and harbours. But as Lord Lovat, leader of one of the Commando raids, told the author: 'These assaults forced German High Command, bowing before Hitler's directive, to heavily reinforce the northern coastlines, but as it happened the Allies never returned to Scandinavia until towards the end of the war, whereas on the Allies' D-day invasion of mainland Europe the Nazis still had 300,000 men in the Norwegian garrisons. They would have made a hell of a difference if they'd been on the beaches of Normandy.

One other direct result of the Combined Operations raids on the Norwegian coastline was Hitler's insistence that *Tirpitz* should remain in the Norwegian fjords and should not stray too far into the Atlantic. That arena was already well covered by the U-boat force, increasing every single week throughout 1942, from 95 operational boats at the beginning of the year to a massive 312 by the end of it. Similarly, however, the U-boat losses were rising proportionately, and in that year as a whole 85 were sunk by the Allies – mostly at the hands of the Royal Navy – of which 59 went down without a single survivor.

The much-feared *Tirpitz* would be a harder nut to crack. She was finally cleared for operations on 14 January 1942 and in the

---

* Sir Roger Keyes' son Geoffrey led one of the operations, an ambitious plan to assassinate Rommel with an assault on his North African headquarters in November 1942. The attack went disastrously wrong, and Geoffrey Keyes was among those killed. He was posthumously awarded the Victoria Cross.

company of four destroyers sailed from Wilhelmshaven, Germany, to Trondheim, Norway, to be anchored in the well-protected Fættenfjord two days later. The sheer psychological impact of positioning *Tirpitz* in this attacking position laid heavily on the Royal Navy commanders, and on Churchill himself, and was in turn responsible for keeping a greater number of British warships on hand to meet this potential threat, which could well have been used to strengthen the Royal Navy's positions in the Mediterranean, the Indian Ocean and the Pacific.

There is no doubt that the addition of *Tirpitz* was seen as substantially raising the stakes, and the convoys would need to be afforded even greater protection by British warships while at the same time a host of tactical operations would need to be devised in an ongoing attempt to minimise risks and ultimately to dispose of the best of the German fleet. Churchill did not underestimate the effect a disruption of supplies to Russia could have on the alliance. He wrote at the time: 'The Russians are fighting for their lives and are dependent on us for the very large supplies which we have most painfully gathered, and which we shall faithfully deliver.'

With *Tirpitz* strategically positioned to disrupt those supplies, the first attempt to sink her was made as early as 30 January 1942 when an RAF force of seven Stirling bombers and nine Halifaxes took off from Lossiemouth with the new ship as sole target. The attack failed, partly through appalling weather conditions and partly because of the anchorage. She was carefully lodged beneath high-sided terrain that made it difficult for aircraft to approach and deliver while at the same time recovering their flight path to escape. The scientist Dr Barnes Neville Wallis, later more famous for his creation of the bouncing bomb dropped in the Dambusters' Raid, was called on to come up with a solution to the problem and would in due course produce a bomb specifically designed for the *Tirpitz* situation.

In the meantime, other plans were afoot. The British Home Fleet had a reasonable intelligence network and a surveillance operation to monitor *Tirpitz* should she move from her mooring. In fact, she did not venture out of her protected anchorage until the beginning of March, and it was believed that her first target would be convoy PQ-12, which sailed from Reykjavik, Iceland, escorted by the battle cruiser *Renown*, the battleship *Duke of York*, the cruiser *Kenya* and six destroyers under the command of Vice-Admiral Curteis.

A further enticement to *Tirpitz* was the prospect of a returning convoy, PQ-8, leaving Murmansk at around the same time, and they could be expected to pass each other around 7 March. Given the prospect of a scrap, the battleship *King George V*, the aircraft carrier *Victorious*, the cruiser *Berwick* and six destroyers were detached from the Home Fleet at Scapa Flow on 6 March to give PQ-12 added protection. *Tirpitz* sailed on the same day, clearly intending to cause trouble. The opposing forces were on course for battle some time on 9 March, and at dawn that day six Albacore aircraft were sent out to look for *Tirpitz* from *Victorious*, followed an hour later by a dozen Albacores carrying torpedoes under the command of Lieutenant-Commander W.J. Lucas. But in thick fog the German ships eluded the strike force and, now aware of the approaching additional protection for the convoys, *Tirpitz* made her way back to safety; on this occasion the two convoys were untroubled.

But her very presence in the Norwegian fjord was sufficient for the British to launch another massive air attack, on 31 March 1942, this time by no fewer than 34 Halifax bombers. But once again her secluded position, along with camouflage nets and a dense, artificial fog that was released on the alert of enemy aircraft approaching, made the attack virtually impossible. Only one aircraft managed to sight the target, but its massive bomb load dropped without causing damage, although five aircraft were lost.

By the end of April the special mines prepared by Barnes Wallis were ready for use and yet another air attack was planned, this time to send an incredible 43 aircraft to bomb the ogre of the German fleet. The force included high-level Lancaster bombers with a massive conventional payload of 4,000-pound bombs and brand-new, low-flying Halifax bombers carrying the adapted mines, although only 32 aircraft made it to the target. Squadron Leader Don Bennett, at the head of the Halifaxes of RAF No. 10 Squadron, explained:

The Royal Navy intelligence boffins dreamed up this scheme

227

to roll spherical mines created by Barnes Wallis down a mountainside and under the soft belly of *Tirpitz* to burst the hull from below. Each of my squadron carried five of these things, which weighed 1,500 pounds each. The ship was moored very close to the shore, and all we had to do was drop these mines and they would go down and do their stuff while the Lancasters bombed from height – that was the story. We know now that nothing would touch the soft belly of *Tirpitz* but, anyhow, we set off to make the attack. I led the raid in at low level in bright moonlight, over what turned out to be the worst possible planning route you could ever have – over heavily defended islands and coastal defences and close to supporting ships.

It was to be an exact stopwatch run, exact speed, height and timing, and then we would drop our load. It would have been perfect but for the fact that when we arrived there was man-made fog filling the whole of the fjord. It was a very clever thing. They sprayed chemical on the water and it produced a fog about 200 feet thick. You couldn't see a damned thing. The drop wasn't very accurate, and guns were opening up all around us. It was pretty hopeless. Anyway, the result was that the ship was undamaged. Naval intelligence had done it again . . . letting us go into an area where they knew there was going to be this fog without telling us. We lost five aircraft, hacked down by the flak guns and defending ships – myself included. It took me three days and nights to get across country and into Sweden, dodging the Germans out with dogs looking for us.

There was a further attack the following night and that, too, hit the same problems. *Tirpitz* thus remained undamaged by the succession of aerial attacks, which had, in total, involved more than 100 aircraft, of which 12 did not return. Throughout these operations, the Admiralty was receiving intelligence on any possible movements of the German ships, and to some extent these attacks were coordinated by Combined Operations, which was itself under new management and already looking at another *Tirpitz*-related operation.

The new man at the top was Lord Louis Mountbatten, appointed personally by Churchill to begin a meteoric rise to the top of the pile, eventually to the position formerly held by his father, Prince Louis of Battenberg before he was forced to resign over his Germanic connections at the outbreak of the First World War. Churchill, it will be recalled, was then First Lord of the Admiralty and the reluctant recipient of Prince Louis' resignation. It has been suggested that this, more than any other factor, was behind Churchill's move to set the prince's son on the road to stardom. It was certainly a surprising choice. Although evidently a popular figure among his men, Mountbatten had many detractors. He had never commanded anything larger than a destroyer – and had the unfortunate experience of having had his ship, HMS *Kelly*, in dock on three occasions with substantial damage before she was finally sunk after overturning on a sharp avoidance manoeuvre during the Crete evacuation in 1941. Two of the incidents could only be described as resulting from unforced errors, which even his biographer, Philip Ziegler, admitted made his ship 'the laughing stock of the navy'.

The First Sea Lord, Sir Dudley Pound, was so concerned as to the wisdom of this appointment that he wrote to Churchill to express his concerns that it might be seen that (a) it was being done on his advice, which it wasn't, and he could 'not shoulder the responsibility for it'; (b) it was made contrary to his advice, which would give the impression that the Prime Minister had overridden his views; or (c) the appointment was made because Mountbatten was royalty, which would do him harm in the service. In any event, said Pound, the Royal Navy would not understand 'a junior captain in a shore appointment being given three steps in rank'.

The protests were ignored, and Mountbatten swept into the Richmond Terrace headquarters of Combined Operations. In the spring of 1942 Churchill let it be known that he would be promoted to Acting Vice-Admiral, his title would be changed to that of Chief of Combined Operations – and was then known to all in the department as The Chief – and as such he would be given 'full and equal membership of the Chief of Staffs Committee', which was something of a slap in the face for his opponents.

Mountbatten made it clear from the outset that he encouraged ideas and would usually give a hearing to schemes that others would have simply chucked out of the window. He would listen to them all and, according to Ziegler, 'the more outrageous the methods, the more he relished them'. Others, with the benefit of hindsight, have recorded a harsher assessment of Mountbatten's early projects as being rash, ill-considered and carrying risks far beyond the call of duty for his men. Certainly, the casualty figures support that notion, when set against the benefits achieved.

The first major operation of its kind was a strong case in point. There was an intelligence belief – totally unsupported by firm evidence – that the Germans intended to establish a haven for *Tirpitz* on the Atlantic coastline of France, where deep-water ports and safe estuary docks were giving sustenance to enemy shipping of every description. There were five U-boat bases alone. Several were large enough to service German battleships and destroyers attacking the Atlantic convoys.

The port targeted by Mountbatten's new improved Combined Ops was St-Nazaire, at the mouth of the River Loire. It had been suggested that the place should be put out of action, and the idea came forward to use exploding motorboats – fast launches packed with explosives of a kind used by the Italians in the Mediterranean. The exploding motorboat appealed to Mountbatten, who immediately ordered a British prototype to be built – but not for the St-Nazaire project. The vision of an exploding vessel suddenly grew into something far grander than a motorboat. Why not a bigger vessel? A motor torpedo boat, perhaps? And then Mountbatten said: 'Why not a ship . . . a big ship? An old destroyer, for example?'

Hence Operation Chariot was born. It did indeed look, on the face of it, to be an outrageous idea, but slowly it developed into a firm proposal that was to be staffed by a joint force recruited from the army Commando units and the Royal Navy. They would sail a ship packed with explosives and crash it into the hugely fortified dock at St-Nazaire. The Commandos would follow on behind the ship in a flotilla of 16 small craft, dodging the flak and defensive gunfire, then scramble ashore and set a dozen other massive explosive charges. Their task was to ensure that the dry dock at St-Nazaire was blown apart by the ship, and that various installations, such as the pump-house used to empty the dry dock, the power station and fuel supply lines, were damaged beyond repair. Additionally, two torpedoes with delayed timing mechanisms would be fired from two of the boats into the locks and set to explode at around the same time as the ship.

That was the plan and Mountbatten thought it was wonderful. The hunt was now on for a ship to be used as the exploding Trojan horse: Mountbatten called for suggestions from the Royal Navy and was presented with an old destroyer, HMS *Campbeltown*, formerly an American vessel known as the USS *Buchanan*. Its funnels were cut down to disguise it as a German torpedo boat.

The joint force would be made up of 240 Commandos and a similar number of navy personnel to sail the exploding ship and the 16 Fairmile motor launches, known as Eurekas, which would carry the troops into attack. The MLs were hardly the right sort of craft for the job. They were built of timber and had to have extra fuel tanks fitted on the deck, which were identified as an immediate hazard in the event of attack. The reason they were being used, it was explained, was that they were not uncommon in that area, being used on anti-submarine sweeping operations, and it was hoped that if they were seen no one would become suspicious.

The flotilla of MLs, along with one motor gunboat and one motor torpedo boat under the overall naval command of Commander R.E.D. Ryder, RN, were to follow in a particular formation in front of and behind *Campbeltown*, which was under the command of Lieutenant-Commander S.H. Beattie, RN. The ship carried six tons of explosives, which had been cemented into her bows. Two groups of the assault force and five demolition parties also travelled in the destroyer and would jump over her bows or clamber down scaling ladders on to the dock at St-Nazaire after she had rammed it. The rest of the assault and demolition teams in the motor launches would come ashore at given locations.

The night of 27 March was very calm, and the convoy had a remarkably uneventful journey across the English Channel into the Bay of Biscay. The flotilla travelled four miles along the Loire when, suddenly, from the St-Nazaire bank, searchlights panned the river followed by a short burst of fire. *Campbeltown* answered this with signals that she carried a German force who had encountered action in the Bay of Biscay and that she was making her way into St-Nazaire to repair damage with casualties on board, and could they please meet the ship at the quay with ambulances. This seemed to pacify the Germans for a time, and the ship made progress up the river without problems for about another quarter of an hour. Ernie Chappell, in one of the motor launches, recalled:

At that time we were again challenged from the shore. *Campbeltown* came under heavy fire, and we saw her German flag come down and the White Ensign go up. We were glad when that happened; we wanted to fight under our own flag. Heavy fire immediately opened up from both banks and from various ships in the harbour. We were being fired on from all directions, the stuff coming at us was . . . like all the colours in the world – a wall of metal. You had to be frightened. *Campbeltown* sailed on, making her way up towards the caisson, which she had to ram. According to our plan, it was timed for 1.30 a.m. and we arrived only two minutes late. Commander Beattie stood on deck and piloted the ship without flinching, straight up into the caisson, and all this time under terribly heavy fire, really heavy fire.

Our MLs were coming up in two columns astern of the destroyer. We were under the same fire. We were firing back. We were in the rear, and by the time we reached our landing area several of our boats were on fire and were burning in the river, their petrol tanks having been hit.

This made it virtually impossible for us to reach our designated position. When we got to the Old Mole there was a motor launch there, well alight. The sea was ablaze with burning petrol. One of the most pitiful sights was to see fellows swimming in the burning water and having to pass them by. They were screaming for help. We shouted at them: 'We'll pick you up on the way back.' We knew damned well we couldn't do that. We didn't like it but we had to press on. Several of the MLs took heavy casualties.

A ferocious battle was now raging at the point where *Campbeltown* had struck the entrance to the dry dock. Coastal batteries of six-inch guns opened up as the demolition parties and the assault force tried to scramble ashore. Not least in everyone's mind was that somehow the cemented-in explosives – whose timers had been set to blow at midday – would go up while they were all still in the vicinity. The ship took two direct hits on her bows, one of which blew off her 12-inch gun, killing the crew. Many of the Commandos were also killed or badly wounded before they could even get off the ship. Many of those who got ashore went straight into captivity or died from their wounds. Fighting went on for an hour or more while the Commandos placed explosives in other preselected installations, and by the time they were ready to make their exit the original force had been decimated and those who managed to get to their motor launches were well on the way out of the Loire as the minutes ticked by for the big event.

*Campbeltown* was well and truly lodged in the gates to the dry dock. That morning, the Germans, unaware of its lethal six-ton cargo of dynamite hidden in her bows, were crowding around the dry dock wondering what to do when fuses activated and the ship blew apart with an almighty explosion that rocked the port, completely demolishing the dock and killing 400 people, including many officials who had come to inspect the damage. In mid-afternoon there were two more explosions – from the delayed-action torpedoes fired by the first MLs and which had lain silently embedded beneath the surface in the harbour structure. The damage was greater than even the planners had anticipated, and the dock remained out of action for almost ten years.

For that reason, the raid was considered a great success. The human cost, however, had been high. Only five of the 16 motor launches that set out on the mission and the motor gunboat made it back to Falmouth. Of the 242 Commandos engaged in the operation, 59 were killed and 112 captured, many badly wounded. The Royal Navy suffered even worse casualties among the motor launch crews and those aboard *Campbeltown*. They lost 85 killed or missing, 106 captured and, again, a large number wounded. Those who were capable of walking were taken to a compound exclusively for St-Nazaire captives and were later put in a prison camp, still all together, which was unusual, and were eventually joined by others recovering from their injuries. Some of the more badly injured were repatriated in 1943.

Back in London, Mountbatten was jubilant at the 'great success' of the first major raid originating under his command of Combined Operations and organised great publicity for his heroes. They were also recognised by an unprecedented number of medals, considering the size of the force: 83 awards in all, including five Victoria Crosses given to the Royal Navy commanders Beattie and Ryder and to the Commando commander Lieutenant-Colonel Newman, who all survived, and posthumously to Sergeant Tom Durrant and Able Seaman Savage, both for manning guns on board the MLs until they dropped, virtually cut to pieces. If the Germans had planned to use St-Nazaire for *Tirpitz* – and it was never a firm proposal – the prospect was now firmly demolished along with the superstructure. Yet even as the raid was being carried out, the German naval commanders had already earmarked her for another project, back on the convoy trail.

Since the successful passage of PQ-12 in March, the British government had continued to send convoys of supplies to Russia and 70 had been successfully delivered to Murmansk, with the 'acceptable' loss of only 16 merchantmen, one cruiser and a destroyer. The actor Douglas Fairbanks Jnr, a close friend of Mountbatten, who was eventually seconded for special duties with the Royal Navy, was at the time an officer on one of the American ships engaged in convoy protection. He recalled in his memoir for the Imperial War Museum:

> It was very hard work running between Iceland [where incoming convoy ships assembled for the onward journey to Russia] and Murmansk, and I suppose the worst part was the winter when the entire ship was laden with ice, and the physical discomfort, of bashing back and forth in huge seas, and no sleep, day or night, just tossing and turning and twisting and shipping water in terrible storms. It all made for a lively time, especially for the destroyers. But equally we dreaded summer, because in good weather we'd be in battle virtually the full 24-hours, night and day, with the midnight sun of the Arctic,

warding off the incessant air raids and keeping our eyes peeled for U-boats and torpedo trails.

As the summer approached, the Germans began to step up the pressure, and the likelihood of *Tirpitz* being brought back into play was evident from developments in mid-June 1942. Two battle groups joined together for the launch of Operation Knight's Move, Group I under the fleet commander, Admiral Schniewind aboard *Tirpitz*, and Group II under Vice-Admiral Kummetz on board the heavy cruiser *Lützow*, and together forming an attacking force of more than 20 ships, including such well-known names as *Admiral Scheer* and *Admiral Hipper*.

The target was the eastbound convoy PQ-17, which was gathering in the Icelandic port of Hvalfjord in late June 1942 and eventually had a procession of 33 merchant ships carrying much-needed supplies to Russia, including 480 tanks, 210 aircraft and thousands of tons of ammunition bound for the Red Army on the Eastern Front, and politically sensitive to bolster the Anglo-American-Soviet alliance. They were to be escorted by a screen of British and American ships, including six destroyers, two anti-aircraft cruisers, two submarines, four corvettes and 13 other vessels.

Standing off from the main body of the convoy was a joint British and American force amounting to a total of 26 ships, including two battleships, an aircraft carrier, four heavy cruisers and more destroyers. Although they were there to offer a measure of protection, in truth this massive show of strength was spoiling for a fight with *Tirpitz* and her consorts. This prospect seemed likely when RAF reconnaissance aircraft discovered that *Tirpitz* had left her safe haven, although her exact location could not be established. In London, the Admiralty assumed that she would be heading for the convoy. This was the beginning of a chain reaction of errors on both sides that led eventually to disaster for PQ-17. The Germans misread the air activity as indicating the presence of a carrier, and with a carrier there was likely to be a battleship or at the very least a large destroyer force, and after several days of cat-and-mouse tactics *Tirpitz* was ordered to withdraw and sail north – for safety, not for action. The Germans pulled away without a ship's gun being fired, but in London confusion still reigned over her whereabouts. The First Sea Lord, Sir Dudley Pound, therefore ordered the convoy to scatter, splitting into small groups, and make their own way to a Russian port. But as Douglas Fairbanks recalled:

> It turned out to be a very bad misjudgement of what was happening at the time. And the U-boats and bombers were waiting to pounce, and were able to pick off the ships one at a time: torpedoed by the wolf packs or sunk by the continuous air bombardment that followed, night and day, because we had the midnight sun. So it went on for several days. When we came back, a lot of ill will developed. Top-ranking officers of both navies blamed the Admiralty and possibly also the US navy department to a lesser degree for this decision to scatter, because up to that moment we thought we had the thing pretty well under control and we could have made Murmansk. Actually, the Russians were supposed to come up and join us and help us to get in, but when the trouble started they just stayed in port.
>
> Of course, it was a disaster, and many sailors went down with their ships. Even at that time of year, survivors would not last long in the cold sea. The only ones who could survive were those who made the lifeboats or rafts. We could see some survivors from a distance. We could have gone to pick them up had we been allowed to, but it would have put in danger an enormous cruiser, a very modern ship, with 1,500 others on board to pick up maybe two or three survivors. It was absolutely awful. Morale was very, very low as a result, with everybody blaming everybody else. The ultimate blame rested with the Admiralty in London, who made a false assessment on the basis of intelligence that was in error.

*Tirpitz* scared the Admiralty so much that she could now destroy a convoy without even being there. When the merchant ships scattered, and as the warships took off to regroup, the U-boats moved in for the kill, followed soon after by wave after wave of German bombers. Only 10 of the original merchant convoy of 33 ships reached Russia. Almost 100,000 tons of cargo were lost and 153 seamen died. It was, said Churchill, one of the most melancholy naval episodes in the whole of the war.

Even more dramatic and despicably spectacular, however, was the convoy that was gathered to end the siege of Malta the following month, in August 1942. For months, the island had been under constant bombardment from Axis aircraft based on the Italian mainland along with a large contingent of Stuka dive-bombers on the island of Sicily. On 16 April the island was famously awarded the George Cross, the civilian equivalent of the Victoria Cross, for withstanding almost two years of continuous air attacks but specifically for the 2,000 air raids or alerts suffered in the first four months of 1942 alone, at a time when British could supply less than adequate forces or aircraft to defend the island.

The RAF, unable to spare more than a couple of squadrons at a time, did a good job of chasing the Italians away, but the arrival of 400 German aircraft on Sicily was more than they could effectively cope with. The Mediterranean had been necessarily neglected and the Royal Navy had also been forced to withdraw its submarines from the base on Malta because of the constant air raids, and for ten weeks operated from the eastern end of the Mediterranean, from Alexandria and the Lebanon.

Even so, the submarine flotilla went on to record some acts of great heroics* in underwater warfare, especially with the new T-class boats, which proved to be a magnificent addition to the fleet, as indeed did the smaller U-class that followed in their wake. VCs were won in both. And now, as the Allies glimpsed the beginning of the great fight back that was to emerge in the months ahead, there was a task that needed urgent attention if the war was to be won in the Mediterranean, and undoubtedly Operation Pedestal, formed to relieve Malta's suffering, will remain in history as one of the epic events of the war – and one of the most important.

It was organised, in a nutshell, to send a convoy of 64 warships

---

* Fully documented in *The Silent Service*.

surrounding 13 freighters and one tanker carrying food, ammunition and fuel to the starving island, pursued and attacked relentlessly throughout the journey by bombers and U-boats and at the same time dodging minefields and torpedoes. Hitler was convinced that control of Malta would not only hurt the British because of its historical connections with the island but, more important, would give the Axis forces control of the Mediterranean at the very time that Rommel's push in the deserts of North Africa had been halted by Montgomery's Allied forces at El Alamein.

Thus, the outcome of both – Malta's survival and the desert war – would in turn affect the outcome of the war in southern Europe, but it was now quite plain to all that Malta would be simply forced to surrender if fuel, grain and ammunition did not get through before the end of August. And so the world watched as this convoy of 14 vessels, including the giant fuel tanker USS *Ohio*, guarded by no fewer than 64 warships at various stages en route from the Clyde, began their run to Malta on 3 August knowing full well that the massed German and Italian air forces and submarines were waiting to give the convoy one of the most intensive bombardments in the history of maritime warfare. For the last stage of the journey, the convoy had an escort of two battleships, three fleet aircraft carriers, seven cruisers and 20 destroyers, for 14 cargo ships. Relentless attacks began virtually from the moment they passed through the Strait of Gibraltar on 10 August and onwards, day and night, running the gauntlet to Malta. It was a journey of sheer hell, beginning with an immediate disaster when the aircraft carrier *Eagle* was hit by U-boat torpedoes and sank in six minutes, taking 184 members of crew and 14 aircraft with her. Over the next four days, wave after wave of German and Italian torpedo bombers and Stuka dive-bombers joined a marauding band of U-boats and Italian submarines in attack after attack. They had clear instructions to target the merchantmen first and indeed succeeded in sinking nine of the merchant ships, with a loss of 154 crew members. Few of the escort ships escaped without damage, some severely and with considerable loss of life. The most heroic struggle was, famously, the tanker *Ohio*'s, whose cargo of 11,000 tons of petrol was the key to the whole operation. Without her, the defending aircraft on

Malta could not fly and the island would have been lost. She took dozens of hits en route, was listing badly and was at one time on fire. Two destroyers, *Penn* and *Ledbury*, moved alongside literally to help prop her up and keep her afloat. That she made it through the incredible barrage of heavy metal was due to the sheer determination and seamanship of those involved. She was literally dragged into Valletta Grand Harbour amid scenes of wild jubilation on the medieval battlements around the capital. Malta had been saved, but, more important, Hitler was denied the key to the door of the Mediterranean, which in turn could well have led him to control the Suez Canal and indeed hold back the Allied invasions of North Africa and Sicily which were soon to follow.

# CHAPTER THIRTEEN

## The Great Fight Back

The build-up was under way for the reclamation of North Africa, and supposedly the raid on Dieppe, organised by Mountbatten under the auspices of his Combined Operations command, was to test some of the skills or otherwise that would be required of the Allied invasion forces in the months to come. Apart from giving the enemy a bloody nose, it would save lives in the future by running a real-time examination of all the possibilities and pitfalls that might arise as the Allied commanders led their troops into the coastal assault in Oran, and later in Sicily, Salerno and Anzio. If indeed that was the motive behind Mountbatten's grand plan for Dieppe, then it was an exceedingly costly exercise which left thousands dead or captured and did not give the Germans much of a nosebleed, either.

There were, however, some definite positives to come out of the operation, particularly in relation to giving a trial run for the newly formed Royal Navy Commandos and beachmasters who were to play such an important role in all major invasion plans for the future, and many other operations besides. The RN Commandos were a little-known group formed in the spring of 1942 from general-service and hostilities-only volunteers. They were assigned to 'beach party' units, each one commanded by two Royal Navy officers, with the minimum rank of lieutenant-commander or commander, plus a petty officer and 17 ratings. Later, as their expertise grew and their contribution appreciated, units were expanded to a minimum of ten officers and 65 other ranks divided into three parties of 25 men each, and their tasks would relate to a specific section of a beach under invasion. Their first trial run came in August 1942 when members of the Royal Navy Commandos were included in Mountbatten's plans for Dieppe.

The attack on the French port was launched in the early hours of 19 August 1942. It was described as a 'raid, not an invasion' – in other words, a surprise attack to be firmly struck, followed by an equally swift withdrawal. The operation involved 6,100 troops, of whom almost 5,000 were Canadians, along with British army and Royal Marine Commandos and 50 American Rangers. The troop carriers were screened by eight British destroyers, which also provided gunnery support at the point of attack, and their arrival was timed to coincide with air operations involving 74 RAF squadrons and 12 from the Royal Canadian Air Force. The plan called for assaults on five different points on a front of roughly 12 miles, but at almost every stage the raiding troops hit problems that had not been anticipated or forewarned by intelligence.

In parts, the beaches were extremely narrow and overlooked by lofty cliffs where German artillery were well dug in, at some points with guns on rails, sited in caves, which they rolled out to the cliff's edge at a suitable point in time. Success depended on surprise and darkness and neither of those vital aspects was maintained. Fierce defensive activity was ready and waiting, and in the growing light the raiders met violent machine-gun and heavy artillery fire, cutting down the soldiers as they landed. On each of the designated assault areas, attempts to breach the German defences were beaten back, and even the British tanks were halted, bogged down in the shingle beaches. The raid was aborted soon after lunchtime, when the survivors retreated to their landing craft for the getaway, leaving behind a huge number of casualties. Of the 4,963 Canadians who embarked on this misadventure, only 2,210 returned to England. Of the remainder, 907 had been killed and 1,946 made prisoners of war. Overall, it was a far greater toll when the statistics from other groups involved – fielding around 3,000 support personnel – were added in. The Royal Navy crews manning the ships, motor launches, boats and landing craft suffered heavily, and the first operation of the RN Commandos saw virtually the entire force either killed or captured. The extent of the air battle over Dieppe was also evident from the losses suffered by the Allies: 106 planes shot down, with only 30 pilots surviving, against Luftwaffe losses of 96 aircraft. Other hardware lost by the Allies included 300 landing craft and launches, 28 tanks destroyed or abandoned and one destroyer gutted.

The recriminations began on the homeward journey, but the PR machine in London was already spinning a tale of success. Mountbatten's communiqué spoke of great lessons learned for the future, meaning the eventual invasion of mainland Europe, and accentuated the positive by pointing out that two-thirds of the attacking force had returned home. Lessons were undoubtedly learned – or relearned, because they had been learned before, at Gallipoli – but whether it was worth the cost was quite another matter, about which opinions were deeply divided. The debate would go on for years, with particular bitterness aroused in Canada, quite naturally, whenever the topic of Dieppe arose.

None of the leading personalities involved would ever admit to failure or defeat, but each of them must have felt some guilt, even shame, for what had happened. As for the Royal Navy Commandos, it was a baptism of fire. Up to that point their training had more or less been confined to that of becoming beachmasters, going ashore to organise the incoming landings. A beach party was assigned to each of the landing zones to guide in the troops and secure the beach perimeters, but many of the personnel were unable to reach their positions through the hail of gunfire or when their landing craft were turned back or sunk. The Dieppe experience pointed up the need for RN Commandos but in a much wider sphere of operations, and a specialised training depot was established at Ardentinny, Scotland, with up to 600 men going through the course at any one time.

One unusual feature, given the strict social code in the Royal Navy, was that officers and ratings were mixed in together. They all went through intensive specialised training at Loch Long in amphibious landing drills, reconnaissance, weapons usage, rock climbing and assault courses along with using landing craft of all types under battle conditions. They then took army Commando training to Green Beret standard at the Achnacarry training school, and around 25 per cent of recruits at each intake went on for even higher-grade training in SAS and SBS specialities, such as parachuting or covert swimming into enemy-held territory.

In fact, the number of tasks for which they trained merely pointed up the skills required to manage the major troop landings that were pencilled in for the coming months: going in ahead of the first wave to clear the beaches, to mark the limits of and secure the beachhead, keeping landings on the move, quickly and safely, helping moor landing craft correctly, removing mines and underwater obstructions, taping the safe passage routes on and off the beaches for the wounded, setting up ammunition and supply dumps, supervising the control of enemy prisoners of war, and finally – on the basis of first in, last out – maintaining rearguard action during any withdrawals. Later, as will be seen, associated RN groups were formed to conduct preliminary surveys of landing areas, even before the RN beachmasters went in – to avoid such traps of selecting a landing area which had unseen deep or shallow approaches or had impossible terrain behind it, such as steep cliffs and poor departure access for vehicles.

All these disciplines were soon to come into play in the Middle East as Montgomery turned the tide and the church bells were ordered to be rung across England after his famous success at the Battle of Alamein on 30 October 1942. Seven days later the Allies launched their first invasion of the war with Operation Torch, which put 65,000 Allied troops on to the North African coastlines, landing around Casablanca, Morocco, and Oran, Algeria.

The landings in November 1942 provided the first major test for the RN Commandos, and they supplied almost 500 men in beach party units to aid the first major Anglo-American amphibious operation of the war. They landed with the first assault elements and immediately secured the beaches, eliminating snipers and then digging trenches. They set up Lewis guns for use against low-flying enemy aircraft to give cover for the first troops ashore, and in fact the whole operation ran without hitch, with the initial landing of almost 30,000 troops brought ashore along with 2,400 vehicles and 14,000 tons of supplies on three different beaches. The bulk of the troops were provided by the United States, but the Royal Navy provided the main naval support with suitable bombardment from the Mediterranean Fleet. They were followed by three battalions of British paratroops, two coming in by ship from the UK and the rest by air. Although progress on land was to be slower than anticipated, with some rough battles ahead for the troops, the war planners were already preparing the counter-offensive: Operation Husky, the invasion of Sicily, in July 1943. And, following the débâcle of Dieppe, another brand-new Combined Operations unit was formed under the Royal Navy banner, linked to both the RN Commandos and the Special Boat Service but under the general command of officers of the Royal Navy. This was principally designed to obtain advance warning of likely dangers that were not evident from reconnaissance photographs to ensure a smooth landing for the invading forces.

It was to be achieved by conducting clandestine underwater surveys of the approaches to all invasion beaches, and then to go ashore and check the soundness of the landing areas, plus all potential hazards such as defensive positions, pillboxes and, crucially, that all invasion points had an adequate exit for the masses of men and machinery coming ashore. It was undoubtedly one of the most dangerous of all the pre-invasion tasks, inasmuch as all potential invasion beaches were invariably under heavy guard and often had 24-hour maritime patrols.

The inventor and pioneer of modern beach reconnaissance was Lieutenant-Commander Nigel Clogstoun Willmott, a veteran of the Narvik campaign and a close friend of Blondie Hasler, RN, creator and leader of the Cockleshell Heroes' raid on Axis ships in the Gironde in December 1942. In North Africa, Willmott had also worked with Roger Courtney, founder of the Special Boat Service, in beach reconnaissance in 1941. The task required many hours of underwater swimming and sorties ashore for a complete survey. Willmott's proposals eventually wound up on the desk of Mountbatten, who recognised their value instantly.

He took the proposals direct to Winston Churchill, at a private meeting, given that it would have to be a top-secret organisation with knowledge of Allied invasion plans ahead of their launch. The result was that the group was formed under the spoof title of Combined Operations Pilotage Parties (COPPs) and was strictly operated within the terms of the Official Secrets Act in that their existence was never referred to in any newspaper or in BBC broadcasts or internal services communications that did not bear the stamp MOST SECRET.

They were given a cover story that they were supposedly checking boom defences, and few Allied commanders below the rank of commander-in-chief knew of their true role. If COPPs officers were challenged by a higher rank, which was not an uncommon occurrence, they were to make no statement but were to refer the enquirer direct to Mountbatten's office. If they were captured, or faced capture, cyanide pills were standard issue, although one or two in difficult situations were said to have drowned themselves. The secrecy surrounding COPPs was maintained after the war, even though they were disbanded, because of their hand-me-down connections with modern warfare which was taken over by the Special Boat Service. But, in the event, their wartime existence was not publicly acknowledged by the Ministry of Defence until 1959, and documents relating to COPPs activities were not released into the Public Records Office until the 30 years' secrecy period had expired. Those involved remained remarkably tight-lipped among the wartime memoir-writers.

Willmott and SBS men tested the water, going in ahead of the Torch landings, and COPPs came into being with barely enough time to train parties to plot the course for the invasion of Sicily, given that it would entail an Allied force totalling 478,000 soldiers, sailors and airmen, including amphibious divisions of some 160,000 soldiers, 4,000 aircraft and 2,590 vessels in the invasion. The whole assault area would be examined in detail: gradients of underwater approaches, obstacles, sand bars, rocks, beach consistency, land surfaces, mined areas, beach defences, beach exits, natural hazards such as cliffs and hills, lockouts, sentry posts, gun emplacements and finally, enemy positions – all to be mapped and charted ready for the invasion troops.

Ronnie Williamson, later to be a close friend of the founder (he was best man at Willmott's second wedding in 1982), recalled:

Nigel convinced Mountbatten and Mountbatten convinced the war planners that it would be impossible to win the war unless they could land thousands of men safely on exactly the right beaches that would stand up to the heavyweight backup of tanks, artillery shells, transport – the whole mass of an army such as Montgomery's landing in Sicily, brought ashore in good order. The beaches had to be thoroughly surveyed, the forces guided in and onwards speedily and perhaps under enemy fire. To have them bogged down in shifting sands, to have vehicles or men drowned, or to be unaware of underwater obstacles or mines, or lacking in detailed intelligence of hazards unseen from aerial reconnaissance photographs – those were the nightmare scenarios that COPPs had to overcome. From my own standpoint, it shook one as a virtual youth to discover that you were part of something as internationally important as this; it was viewed by all of us, I know, as just a sheer honour to be part of it. You had to pinch yourself to believe it was true. Hitler would have paid millions of pounds to know what we knew. Mountbatten realised quickly that Nigel's job would be utterly impossible unless he was granted Top Priority of the War.

As the Allied armies slowly began to push the Axis forces into the sea, the invasion of Sicily loomed ever closer and initial preparations were secretly under way soon after the start of the New Year. COPPs teams began clandestinely surveying the Sicilian beaches in late February. The party, formed only a matter of weeks earlier, badly needed rehearsals but barely had time for them because their reports were required by mid-March. The weather was wintry cold, and the suits used for lengthy swimming missions were ill-fitting and often leaked. The men were taken aboard three submarines from Malta and set off for the Sicilian coast, 75 miles away, for night-time operations. The submarines would surface two miles off the coast after periscope surveillance.

If all was clear, the Coppists would set off in pairs in canoes to their designated beaches to a point 180 metres from the beach. The paddler would remain in the canoe, suitably camouflaged, and attempt to maintain a stable position, unnoticed, while the reconnaissance officer would slip into the water. He would be wearing a hefty suit of rubberised fabric, which was supposed to give him buoyancy and protect him from the cold. The suit had a built-in life-jacket that could be inflated by mouth and had pockets laden with equipment, including a .38 pistol, a fighting knife, an oil-immersed prismatic compass, sounding lead and line, beach gradient reel, an underwater writing-tablet with Chinagraph pencil, 24-hour emergency rations in case of separation, and two torches to home in on the canoe for the return.

The survey would take several hours, after which the swimmer would return to the canoe, and then they would rendezvous with the submarine. The Sicilian recce ran into trouble from the beginning. All the beaches were heavily guarded with sentries posted at around every hundred yards. First, the leader of the COPPs expedition, Lieutenant-Commander Norman Teacher, RN, failed to return to his canoe and was presumed dead or captured. The former proved to be the case. His paddler, Lieutenant Noel Cooper, an experienced canoeist who had been on Operation Torch as a beachmaster, returned to the submarine rendezvous completely exhausted after a long search.

In spite of that, Cooper went out again with Captain G.W. Burbridge on 2 March. They did not return and were never seen again. On 3 March Lieutenant Bob Smith and Lieutenant D. Brand failed to return to their submarine in rough weather. They were feared dead, but in fact they had been thrown off course and, unable to locate their mother sub, simply set a course for Malta and kept on paddling – 75 miles back to base. They completed the journey in just over two days and landed in the Grand Harbour in Valletta, exhausted. Meanwhile, the reconnaissance mission around Sicily was still in trouble.

On 6 March Lieutenant A. Hart and Sub-Lieutenant E. Folder, also from the Middle East section, did not come back. On 7 March Lieutenant P. De Kock and Sub-Lieutenant A. Crossley failed to meet their connection, and the following night Lieutenant Davies went to look for them and did not return either. Others also went missing. Of the 16 who joined the original mission, only four returned. Five – Teacher, Cooper, Burbridge, De Kock and Crossley – were never heard of again, presumed drowned. The remainder had been captured.

The three lost officers of COPPs – Teacher, Cooper and Burbridge – were believed by some to have hit trouble and had taken the ultimate precaution against capture and torture by drowning themselves, thus not giving the Germans the chance to discover the purpose of their top-secret mission. Others disagreed and thought they had simply drowned or perhaps been captured or shot and their bodies buried. In spite of the losses, however, the beach surveys went ahead with COPPs reinforcements brought out to Egypt. Reconnaissance missions were finally completed successfully and would indeed prove their worth. Clogstoun Willmott, meanwhile, had to get his force rapidly trained to cut the number of casualties on future tasks. This he did, and COPPs went on to provide this vital service for the rest of the war, later adding to their versatility by using midget submarines.

Operation Husky proved to be an entirely successful venture for the Allies, opening a Western Front against the Germans and reopening the sea lanes to the eastern Mediterranean and establishing a springboard for the invasion of mainland Italy, which began at the end of August 1943. Italy surrendered and the warships now moved on to Salerno, where they stood by to support the invasion forces with a substantial bombardment – only to discover themselves under attack with a completely new type of German bomb.

On 10 September intelligence officers intercepted and decoded radio messages from Berlin instructing its German pilots which ships to attack the following day. A total of 58 bombers were sent to Salerno to attack the Allied maritime force, which was locked up for action stations well in time for the attack. Allied fighters were also on hand to take on the approaching German force, and in the middle of the aerial battle the crew of the American cruiser *Savannah* spotted an incoming Dornier aircraft at about 18,700 feet, out of gunnery range, and then what the gun crews thought was a second aircraft diving very fast, then making a severe correction at about 400 feet above the starboard side of the main deck before it slammed into the ship at the number-three gun turret. In fact, *Savannah* had become the first Allied ship to be hit by Germany's secret weapon – a primitive guided missile, based on the early technology that produced the V-1 and V-2 rockets that were soon to hit London. There were two types identified, the HS293, the low-level glider bomb, and the HX90, which was a high-level guided dive-bomb.

The missile hit with such force that it pierced 36 inches of steel at the base of the gun turret before exploding, killing 204 sailors, five chief petty officers and nine officers. The British flagship *Warspite* and the cruiser *Uganda* were both hit and severely damaged. In the case of *Uganda*, the missile penetrated seven decks and exploded underneath the ship. Both ships had to be taken under tow to Malta for repairs along with *Savannah*. Between them, the three ships had taken more than a hundred hits, but the killer blows came from the new guided dive-bombs.

By the time the Allies moved up to begin Operation Shingle, the invasion through Anzio, they anticipated the deployment of radio-guided missiles. Roger Lewis, a mine and bomb disposal specialist whom we last met on *Rodney* chasing *Bismarck*, remembered:

We were very worried about protecting the Anzio landing area from attacks by guided missiles, and to protect the anchorage we collected seven LSTs – landing ships (tanks) – that were damaged and were not fully fit for service. We drove on board lorry-borne RAF radar sets, through the bow doors, hoisted them on to the upper deck, and anchored these seven LSTs as an outer ring of radar cover for the anchorage, and a whole lot of scientists from London, who were researching the V-weapons problem, came out for the Anzio landing and listened in and did all sorts of funny things. I think they were trying to find out the frequencies used for the guidance systems. The fleet signal officer and myself actually got hold of a very high-speed dental drill from a dentist in Bizerte and converted that to jam the signals. It worked quite well. Even so, these weapons were used, and they hit the brand-new cruiser *Spartan* and several other targets. And some of my former RN mine and bomb disposal team from the UK were sent over to Sardinia, where a specimen of the HS293 had crashed and collected it for analysis.

The Allied specialists soon developed a counter-measure to the missiles, and the US Naval Command placed an army fighter direction team aboard two ships to monitor all Luftwaffe radio frequencies and intercept and jam any radio signals sent from a bomber to a guided missile in the hope of forcing a miss produced by a lost signal. Although very much in its early stages, the German missiles and the strategy developed to counteract them for the Anzio landings started a new trend in aerial aviation.

Operation Shingle was a tough nut to crack. The Germans, with heavy reinforcements sent in after the collapse of Mussolini's Fascist state, were fighting a hard land battle, and the Allies' advance was reduced to a crawl. Although they had been sent back home by the invasion commanders earlier, some of the Royal Navy's big guns were recalled in January 1944 to deliver a further heavy bombardment to get the invasion force moving again.

However, the cruiser *Spartan*, which was anchored close to shore when hit by the high-level missile, capsized almost immediately and, thankfully, was the last major loss of the Royal Navy in the Second World War. The Mediterranean was by then under Allied control, with now only a few U-boats remaining in the maritime war to cause concern. Indeed, by the turn of the New Year something of a finalising focus was already under way in the Battle of the Atlantic. By the end of 1943 the battle was as good as won, with the merchant losses halved since the beginning of the year, down to a more acceptable 280,000 tons.

Hitler wanted to know why, and Admiral Dönitz persuaded the Führer to allow him to bring *Scharnhorst* and *Tirpitz* back into the attack at the head of a new force to hit the convoys from Britain to Russia. The RAF had been long keeping watch for *Tirpitz*, and in June 1943 reconnaissance pilot John Dixon, flying alone in his long-range Spitfire with a camera in the nose, spotted the German ship in Altenfjord, and from that point in time a regular check was made on her location because the Royal Navy was engaged in yet another plan to sink her. That summer, the first six mini-submarines known as X-craft began coming off the production lines. A daring scheme had been worked up whereby the six mini-subs would be towed to within range by six conventional submarines and then, under their own power, head for Altenfjord and lay substantial explosive charges beneath the ship. One added complication was that *Tirpitz* was surrounded by anti-submarine nets. The six mini-subs began their journey on 20 September 1943. One disconnected from the towing submarine and was never heard of again, and another had to pull up and abandon the mission because of damage to her buoyancy chambers. Another was lost close to *Tirpitz* for reasons that were never discovered, and the fourth had to lay up for three days to repair leaks. The attack by the other two had taken place by the time the submarine drew close, the target area was swarming with activity, and thus they gave up and returned home. Out of the six X-craft, the remaining two under the command of Lieutenants Basil Place and Donald Cameron reached *Tirpitz*, and the citation for the Victoria Cross they received provides a summary of the action:

> . . . a most daring and successful attack on the German battleship *Tirpitz*, moored in the protected anchorage of Kaa fjord. To reach the anchorage necessitated the penetration of an enemy minefield and a passage of 50 miles up the fjord, known to be vigilantly patrolled by the enemy and to be guarded by nets, gun defences and listening posts, this after a passage of at least a thousand miles from base. Having successfully eluded all these hazards and entered the fleet anchorage, Lieutenants Place and Cameron, with complete disregard for danger, worked their small craft past the close anti-submarine and torpedo nets surrounding *Tirpitz*, and from a position inside these nets carried out a cool and determined attack. Whilst they were still inside the nets a fierce enemy counter-attack by guns and depth charges developed which made their withdrawal impossible. Lieutenants Place and Cameron therefore scuttled their craft to prevent them falling into the hands of the enemy. Before doing so they took every measure to ensure the safety of their crews, the majority of whom, together with themselves, were taken prisoner. In the course of the operation these small craft pressed home their attack to the full, in doing so accepting all the dangers inherent in such vessels and facing every possible hazard which ingenuity could have devised for the protection

in harbour of vitally important capital ships. The courage and utter contempt for danger in the immediate face of the enemy shown by Lieutenants Place and Cameron during their determined and successful attack were supreme.

Four explosions from the X-craft charges had in fact inflicted crippling damage, and one of them, from Place's X-7, went off exactly below the battleship's engine rooms, severely damaging both her main turbine and fire-control system. *Tirpitz* was put out of action but was repairable.* For months, the RAF and Fleet Air Arm kept watch for *Tirpitz*, but in fact it was *Scharnhorst* on which attention next focused, at Christmas 1943. A signal had been intercepted on Christmas Eve from Dönitz instructing her captain to join the action against a 40-ship convoy heading for Murmansk. Also involved in the German side were *Admiral Hipper* and the pocket battleship *Lützow*, but now anticipating trouble the Royal Navy commanders had time to spring a trap, with two convoys providing the bait. Shadowing the westbound convoy, and forming the anvil for the attack, the 1st Cruiser Squadron, consisting of *Belfast, Norfolk* and *Sheffield*, was on its way from north Russia, while the battleship *Duke of York*, the cruiser *Jamaica* and four destroyers were approaching from Scapa Flow.

Jack Stead, telegraphist on the destroyer *Onslow*, which was in the convoy escort, recalled:

No one aboard gave *Duke of York* a snowball in hell's chance of getting anywhere near us before *Scharnhorst* had blown us to kingdom come. So we assumed that we would be left with the impossible task of keeping *Scharnhorst* away from the

---

* Meanwhile, the X-craft were used for other attacks. *X-24*, under the command of Lieutenant Ian Fraser, went to Bergen harbour on 13 April to attack a large floating dock and sank a 7,800-ton ship, leaving the port's loading facility badly damaged. Two others, *X-20* and *X-23*, were used in conjunction with the Coppists for preliminary surveys and to mark invasion beaches for the D-day landings. With their usefulness in Europe now virtually at an end, the midget submarines were moved to the Far East to begin operations against Japanese shipping.

convoy until our ships arrived. What a Christmas present! The ship was cleared for action and we waited for the first contact, which we guessed would be in about 24 hours. Christmas Day passed, and we could hardly believe our luck. *Scharnhorst* had failed to find the convoy. Our hopes were growing with each passing hour. By early Boxing Day there was still no sign, and I had taken over watch on fleet wave, a channel reserved for inter-ship communications during action and due to the imposition of strict radio silence. But then I received a message that was passed immediately to the bridge. The British cruisers had made contact with *Scharnhorst* on their port quarter, range 14 miles. The cruisers opened fire and *Scharnhorst* responded . . . and from then on, progress of the battle that afternoon was relayed to us over the ship's loudspeaker system and inside the ship it was like a Wembley Cup Final . . . groans when anything went wrong and cheers when we scored a hit.

*Scharnhorst* was completely unaware that the British cruisers were approaching from the east and she took a direct hit from *Norfolk*, destroying her radar; in reply, the County-class cruiser also took shell damage. Given that she had orders not to take on heavy forces, *Scharnhorst* now withdrew and attempted to make a fast passage to the safety of her Norwegian anchorage, leaving her slower destroyer escort to make their own way back.

Less than an hour into the journey, however, a ten-gun broadside from *Duke of York* revealed the oncoming force from Scapa Flow, and *Scharnhorst* was now trapped amid 13 British warships. Although she attempted to make a run for it, *Scharnhorst* was slowed by a direct hit to one of her boiler rooms, and the British intercepts picked up a signal: 'To the Führer. We shall fight to the last shell.'

She did indeed keep on firing, and the British destroyer *Saumarez* took a severe hit that killed 11 of her crew. Force Commander Admiral Fraser now called his ships to encircle *Scharnhorst* to prepare for a combined attack in which more than 2,000 shells and 55 torpedoes were fired. It was the cruiser *Belfast*, attempting to deliver a second torpedo attack, that signalled: '*Scharnhorst* sunk.' Of the total crew of 1,968 men, only 36 survived.

There remained, however, the continued possibility of *Tirpitz* returning to the fray, and reconnaissance aircraft continued to keep observation to watch for signs of her re-emergence. When that appeared imminent, a new attack was ordered. On 3 April 1944 the Fleet Air Arm sent bombers and fighters from *Victorious, Formidable* and three other aircraft carriers to make a fresh assault on the ship in her Norwegian anchorage. Two waves of aircraft, consisting in total of 42 Fairey Barracuda torpedo bombers and 80 American-built Grumman Wildcat and Hellcat fighters, had to dodge 68 anti-aircraft guns now surrounding *Tirpitz* but managed to score a number of direct hits which put her out of action again.

Four more attacks were launched by the Fleet Air Arm in July and August and then, finally, 28 Lancaster bombers dropped another load on their way to England from Russia. Dönitz finally conceded that the pride of the German fleet was done for and had her towed to Tromsofjord to act as a coastal defence battery. Even that plan was thwarted when the RAF made one more run and bombed her. This time she blew up when her own ammunition store exploded, and fewer than 90 of her trapped crew of 1,000 survived.

Effectively, the German navy's heavy ships fleet had been taken out of the equation before Operation Overlord for the liberation of Europe was launched, although there were still a multitude of U-boats and light surface vessels. The Royal Navy's substantial contribution to the invasion was codenamed Operation Neptune, and on 6 June 1944, across the unusually stormy English countryside, the greatest movement of men and machines ever known was under way, with 156,000 men and thousands of tons of heavy metal going ashore in the first 12 hours, followed in the coming weeks by an army of more than two million, a movement that involved some 7,000 seagoing vessels of varying shapes and sizes. Overhead, as the D-day landings progressed, were some 11,590 Allied aircraft, of which 5,510 were from the Royal Air Force, plus a large contingent of air-sea rescue aircraft from Coastal Command and 406 British and 1,200 American transport aircraft used to drop paratroops and tow the gliders of the airborne units.

A key element of the Royal Navy was to form a blockade at both ends of the English Channel so that the initial invasion armada of over 4,000 landing ships could move without fear of attack. Meanwhile, the warships were ranged along the coast to provide a continual bombardment of German positions at the same time as troops were landing on the beaches. To do justice to this operation is impossible in the space available, but for the atmosphere let us join the cruiser *Ajax*, of River Plate fame and still going strong. Harold Edgar Siggins was on board:

As we approached Normandy there was a feeling of stillness about the ship and, unlike the weather of the previous 24 hours, it was relatively calm. Because of the enormity of the force going across, there was a great feeling of wellbeing about it. Everywhere you looked there were ships – battle-ships, merchant ships, landing craft of all descriptions – hundreds and hundreds of ships, not to mention the follow-ers, such as seagoing tugs, trawlers, motor launches – a veritable armada, the like of which would probably never be seen again. The sight that greeted the Germans as they looked out from their beach emplacements must have been absolutely overwhelming, and overhead, of course, the great waves of bombers, fighters, transport and gliders.

When we got to our zone, I took up my position in the main gunnery transmitting station right down in the bowels of the ship, the area that controls the firing of the guns. We had grid map references and as soon as it was possible we would be receiving specific targets from spotting planes, and my job was to mark the grid reference number given by the spotting plane, hand this to the gunnery officer and transmit it to the plot, the gunnery table, and the gunnery officer would then decide what kind of shell he was going to fire; the ranges would be set and the 'gun ready' signals would light up in red. Preparing to fire and the shouts would come in: 'A turret ready, sir, A turret ready, sir, X turret ready, sir, Y turret ready, sir.' Up go the lights and the firing gongs – gong, gong, gong, gong – and off the guns would go and the shells sent on their way. The same was happening with the ships all around us, firing at their targets.

Then contact is made with the spotting plane and, after a ranging salvo is fired, he came back: 'You're too high, too high.' Back 50. We fired another salvo and another turret fired: 'That's it,' he shouted. 'That's it. Give 'em all. Give 'em the lot.' And all four turrets, eight six-inch guns, belched out. The spotter came back: 'Marvellous. They're running. They're running. Keep firing.' Up ten. Up 20 . . . and so on, then moving on to fresh targets, which included enemy tanks, enemy positions, enemy troop movements. Anything that we could hit and hurt the enemy capability. It was extraordinary, that here we were seven or eight miles off the shore, picking off these individual targets, as indeed were all the others lined up with us.

There was no incoming fire to the ships or enemy aircraft action against us, but of course the troops on the beaches were taking the fire. But I cannot conjure up in words too greatly the tremendous force that was going in that day. I don't think that whatever the Germans might have done by way of counter-attack they would ever have broken the power of that impregnable armada.

There was a long, hard struggle ahead for the Allied ground forces, and indeed still a good deal of maritime action around the European coastlines before the end came for Germany, but by then the focus for the Royal Navy, at least, had already switched to the Far East. There, Mountbatten had been running a tough South-East Asia Command, although he had operated on a wing and a prayer in terms of ships but with a strong contribution from the submarine service, COPPs, RN Commandos and lots of men in small boats. These included a particular operation by the midget submarine operators to perform a task similar to the raid on *Tirpitz*, this time against the Japanese battle cruiser *Takao*, anchored at Singapore. Once again, VCs were awarded, this time to Lieutenant Ian Fraser and his diver, Leading Seaman James Magennis, for completing their task with aplomb, placing charges under the ship after negotiating 80 miles of minefields and a host of other anti-submarine devices – and back again.

Since the surrender of Singapore, there had been no eastern fleet as such, simply because Britain did not have the resources to match the Japanese.

The battles in that regard had been left to the Americans, but in order to place the Union Jack back *in situ* on all the lost colonial territory when the fight came back, a naval build-up began progressively, if slowly, from the spring of 1944 when the carriers *Illustrious, Begum* and *Shah*, along with the capital ships *Queen Elizabeth, Renown* and *Valiant*, joined a US Task Force, led by the USS *Saratoga*, in raids on Japanese positions at Sabang and Soerabaya, in north-west Sumatra.

Carriers and their aircraft were the principal implements here in the maritime war, with Sir Bruce Fraser, commander of the British Pacific Fleet, eventually leading the creation of Task Force 57, with around 80 ships, including troop carriers, tankers and support vessels. His principal fighting ships, however, were the carriers *Indomitable, Victorious* and *Indefatigable* joining *Illustrious*, and the new arrivals included *King George V, Howe* and *Duke of York* supported by five cruisers and 14 destroyers. They were all in position by March 1945 and were joined soon afterwards by two more carriers, *Formidable* and *Implacable*.

In these final months of the conflict, the British Pacific Fleet joined the vast American force and saw considerable action, especially during the Okinawa campaign, where the British invention of armoured hangar carriers proved a godsend under attacks by the Japanese kamikaze suicide pilots. Fleet Air Arm fliers, finally equipped with some decent aircraft after spending much of the war forced to make do with outdated machines, came into their own. Even so, the Americans wanted to be the kingpins in this arena, and of course they had the equipment to do the business, except in one area where they showed a particular weakness, as Peter Macdonald Scott, flying from *Indomitable*, recalled:

We were going in on strikes on the various islands, the Ishigaki-Miyako chain of islands which went between north of Manila and Okinawa, in fact a chain of islands really going right up to the Japanese mainland. This was part of the systematic invasion getting progressively closer to mainland

Japan. But this particular operation which was taking place at the time was all in relation to the landings on Okinawa and Iwo Jima, so our responsibility was primarily to stop the movement of all aircraft from Manila through to Japan, via this chain of small islands, all of which had either two or three airstrips. So the idea was to keep the airstrips unusable and to destroy any aircraft that we saw.

So we had a lot of ground attack work to do, with dive-bombing as before as well as rocketing, and a lot of ground strafing work. We also did some bombardment spotting for the two battleships who decided that they would like to have a crack at putting the aerodrome on Ishigaki out of commission. A very impressive sight, I might say, these big ships using their main armaments. There was very little opposing air activity for us, because at that stage of the war the stuffing had really been knocked out of the Japanese air force. But there was still a continuous danger from kamikazes, whose aim was a simple one – to make a suicide dive straight into the target – and the fleet suffered this on a number of occasions.

I think all the carriers were hit at different times, never very seriously because we had armour-plated decks, whereas the Americans did not and they suffered very greatly from the kamikaze attacks, usually resulting in major fires on board and considerable damage even to the extent of putting the carrier out of operation. Quite a number of American carriers had to leave the battle area altogether and were sent home. They took enormous damage. On the other hand, these kamikazes just bounced off our decks. *Victorious* was hit one morning, and she was landing her own aircraft back on again shortly after lunch.

The aircraft came in quite low, and many of the pilots were just kids, ill-trained, just being churned out to operate as kamikazes. It wasn't worth training anyone to a sophisticated extent for that purpose, and few of them had more than 25 hours' flying time. We had no admiration for them, and certainly no sympathy. We just wanted to get rid of them. The type of radar available today would have picked them up all right, but radar in those days was just about capable of picking something to the visible horizon, but that is no distance in relation to an aircraft travelling at 200 to 300 miles an hour at very low level. But when they were spotted, you had the problem of the air patrols over the fleet being guided on to them, and at the same time the fleet wanting to protect itself with its own gunfire. So it was a pretty dangerous situation for all concerned because the amount of fire from the ships was enormous, and our own aircraft getting mixed up in the middle, trying to find these other chaps, there was no means of stopping the ships firing; they were going to do that anyway. So it was quite a risky business chasing kamikazes into the fleet.

The battleship bombardments among the islands proved to be the last action in which the British capital ships fired their guns in anger during the Second World War. In the Indian Ocean, the seaborne assault on Rangoon was made after the Japanese had withdrawn and the long-awaited amphibious landings in Malaya did not take place until after Hiroshima. On 2 September 1945 Admiral Sir Bruce Fraser signed the Japanese surrender on behalf of the United Kingdom in Tokyo Bay. The next day, Royal Marines from HMS *London* reclaimed Penang, on the fifth the destroyer *Rotherham* sailed into Singapore to fly the Union Flag once more over the naval base and on the ninth Malaya once again came under British control. Even so, keen though Churchill and the colonialists were to regain their possessions, the days of Empire were well and truly done for.

# CHAPTER FOURTEEN

## The Yangtze Incident

The cost had been high in every respect. A total of 1,525 Royal Navy vessels, amounting to over two millions tons, had been sunk during the war, of which 224 were major ships and 74 were submarines. More than 50,000 personnel lost their lives, including many from the Royal Naval Reserve and Royal Naval Volunteer Reserve. From a pre-war strength of 129,000, the total number of personnel employed peaked towards the end of the war at 863,500, of whom more than 70,000 were members of the Women's Royal Naval Service who were, by then, indispensable in many shore technical and general administration establishments. The majority were, of course, employed on the thousands of vessels of all types in commission at the end of the war but, quite apart from the expansion of personnel required at sea, a significant and very necessary expansion had occurred in shore-based activity, ranging through training and support facilities, intelligence, logistics and the considerable growth in technology and research. The land-based operations had quadrupled, not least in the area of managing the new divisions, such as the vast landing craft operations, the substantial increase in aircraft carriers and the development of the Fleet Air Arm, which was not even in existence 18 months before war broke out.

The incredible rate of technical progress that changed the face of maritime warfare in the Second World War was handled in the main with efficiency and skill, given that for much of those straitened times there were desperate shortages of virtually every commodity required to effect these changes while at the same time the organisation was fully engaged in every theatre of war. The Admiralty grew itself into a massive organisation, absorbing almost a tenfold increase in its manpower and twice that in terms of ships and hardware, the extent of which was no better demonstrated at the end of hostilities when the Royal Navy had in commission 9,136 vessels of varying shapes and sizes – and, indeed, another 727 under construction. These latter additions to the fleet were all cancelled immediately, and those that did not make it to the sea included three massive new aircraft carriers of 53,000 tons apiece, *Malta*, *Gibraltar* and *New Zealand*.

Ironically, the completion of these three ships would have enabled Britain to maintain its fixed-wing Air Arm capability for the rest of the twentieth century, just as America did with similar ships, which were retained in service for the ensuing 40 years. At the time, however, they were luxuries Britain could not afford, with the nation once again deeply in debt to America and entering a phase of severe austerity in terms of military spending that would last for almost two decades. Those three ships alone would have made a major contribution to the Royal Navy's ability to meet the challenges of the future, many unimagined at the time the war's end brought at least the hope that peace and security would this time last longer than the 20 years that had elapsed after the First World War.

It was, of course, a forlorn hope, and the evidence of the potential for future strife was not long in emerging. In the immediate future, however, the Royal Navy, along with the army and RAF, faced the logistical nightmare of bringing home men and machines, as well as the thousands of prisoners of war, especially those in the Far East, tormented and starved in Japanese camps. There was also an immediate reduction in manpower to be arranged, as tens of thousands of 'hostilities-only' personnel sought a prompt release from service to return to their families just as soon as it was physically possible. For many, that hope would take many months to achieve and for the signed-on crews there would be no let-up. Trouble-spots were emerging that would require the navy's continued presence in a number of volatile areas in the Mediterranean and the Far East. The partition of Palestine, leading eventually to the creation of the state of Israel, saw the beginnings of a massive influx of Jewish refugees into that country and the start of the ongoing conflict between Palestinians and Jews that remained unresolved 60 years later. Apart from the ground forces engaged in these troubles, the Royal Navy deployed its destroyer forces to police the Mediterranean in an attempt to stem the flow of immigration, the 'exodus' of Jews from Europe and beyond. It was a task that required the utmost patience as Royal Navy boarding parties were required to stop and search the incoming tide of ships laden with immigrants.

Civil war in Greece, tension with its old enemy Turkey, the Communist takeover in Yugoslavia and Albania and rising nationalistic fervour in Egypt all added to the unease, and any spark threatened a major conflagration. It was thus with some restraint that the British reacted to having its patrol vessels shelled by Albania in 1946, and in October the same year two destroyers, *Saumarez* and *Volage*, were both severely damaged by mines in the Corfu Channel, resulting in the deaths of 44 sailors. The Albanians denied responsibility, but Britain took the issue to the International Court in the Hague, which ruled that although the mines were of German make, they had only been laid recently. The court ordered compensation of £800,000, which the Albanians refused to pay, and the British, in turn, held on to £5 million in Albanian gold in London. The losers were the families of the sailors killed, who received no compensation.

Elsewhere, the stirrings of other troubles that would plague successive British governments for years hence were evident. In the Far East, Indonesia was threatening war against the Dutch to gain possession of the Dutch East Indies along with British-held territory on Borneo, nationalism was stirring in Malaya and the Communist forces of Mao Zedong resumed their civil war in China against the nationalist regime of General Chiang Kai-shek soon after the Japanese pulled out. It was in this region that the first major diplomatic flashpoint occurred, which attracted the focus of the world to an obscure British gunboat, the frigate HMS

*Amethyst*, one of the Hong Kong-based British fleet that had resumed patrols of the Yangtze river, a fast-flowing natural phenomenon that rose in Tibet and stretched 3,400 miles to north of Shanghai, varying in width from one to 20 miles, and along which there remained some vestiges of British interest. The Nationalists, led by Chiang Kai-shek, were still nominally in power, and their forces were massed around the capital, Nanking, where the Yangtze river was, in effect, the front line of battle with the Communists and *Amethyst* became trapped in no man's land.

Among those aboard was 19-year-old Don Redman, who had just signed on for 12 years in the Royal Navy, much to the chagrin of his brother when he came home from the war in 1945, having served as a hostilities-only sailor. He'd had a rough time, and when Don told him he'd joined up his brother cuffed him around the ear and said: 'You must be crazy. Joining this mob? You're an idiot.' His first draft was to *Illustrious* at Portsmouth, where he specialised in radar, before being posted to *Amethyst* in the Far East Fleet, taking up duties as the navigator's yeoman.

Initially, we were in Hong Kong and then came the order which we thought was routine: patrolling up the Yangtze River to Nanking. Before we left, we took a draft of eight to ten boy seamen. We experienced a typhoon all the way from Hong Kong to Shanghai and the boys were very seasick. It was a really bad trip, but worse was in store. None of us were made aware of what we might expect, and in fact an Australian frigate was due to do the run but the Australian government thought it inappropriate that a frigate should be sent at that time, given the current situation between the Communists and the Nationalists. So we went instead and were warned not to walk about the upper deck because we might become target practice. Off we went, quite unprepared for what was about to happen.

The mist on the first evening set in and, because the river is poor for navigation, we anchored in a bay alongside some Chinese Nationalist ships. Next day, a bright sunny day, we set off again, and I was on the open bridge standing next to the skipper, Lieutenant-Commander Skinner, the navigator, two signalmen and a Chinese pilot. Everyone was chatting and at ease. Suddenly, about 200 yards for'ard of our bow, there was a huge splash in the water and the skipper said in a typically English manner: 'I do believe someone's firing at us.' And he called: 'Action stations'.

We drew closer to the battery that had fired that shell, and there was one almighty explosion and the for'ard gun was hit, and there were several other explosions on the stern. The skipper had by this time ordered the battle ensign to be hoisted and then: 'Open fire!' We started responding and just as he gave the last command there was a huge explosion on the bridge where we were all standing. A shell exploded on the centre of the bridge, and the skipper, who was two feet away from me, was mortally wounded, and Lieutenant Berger, the navigator, also caught the blast and had most of his clothes blown off him, leaving just his underpants in shreds, although he wasn't seriously injured. It was an amazing scene.

The Chinese pilot, standing two feet behind me, had the back of his head blown off and we were all splattered on the deck when Lieutenant Weston came up on the bridge to get order because the ship's helm was heading for a mud bank and everyone was wondering why the order for full astern hadn't been given. The reason was that the telegraphs were out of order and the helm, which was in the chart house below the bridge, was stuck, and the ship was heading towards the mud bank. We did indeed hit the mud, and stuck firm. The engines were stopped and the firing continued. Weston attended the skipper, who was just minutes away from dying, and before he did so he passed command to Weston. I myself had been knocked unconscious, and as I came to I saw all the carnage of the bodies, arms and bits of body hanging around, and blood everywhere.

I was helped from the bridge and had large lumps of shrapnel sticking out of me. I was patched up by a shipmate because the sick berth attendant who had been patching people up had just been killed, and after they did a few temporary repairs on me I was able to stand up but I was still bleeding heavily. One of the men said we needed someone to find the doctor. I volunteered and got up on deck to discover there was still firing going on, with a lot of shrapnel flying around. I ran along the deck and found the doctor, who was dead, his body in a terrible state. So I automatically turned around to go back to where I had come from, and as I was passing the galley I was shot in the elbow by a bullet, and a bit further on I was hit again by shrapnel but managed to get below and give them the news.

I was helped down on to the deck, and was leaned against the bulkhead. They put a shipmate alongside me who was in a very bad state, his stomach ripped open, and I put my arm around him and held his stomach best I could and he died in my arms about 30 minutes later. The firing continued for a while and then there was a lull and we were briefly able to try to bring some order to the ship.

At this point, 37 dead or wounded still lay on the deck, with 20 more wounded, and as the crew attempted to cope with the injuries, help seemingly arrived in the shape of the destroyer HMS *Consort*, which was based further up the river at Nanking, acting as guard ship for the British expatriates there. *Amethyst* was due to replace her in that role, but having read *Amethyst*'s signals reporting that she was under fire, *Consort* hurried downriver in the hope of getting the frigate out of trouble. But she, too, came under heavy fire as she steamed towards the stricken vessel. Don Redman:

As soon as she turned up, all hell broke loose. They started firing again and then . . . one of the bravest things I saw in the Yangtze river. *Consort* passed us by after one attempt to rescue us. But this time there had been several killed on her, too. She went about and returned to the scene and tried to help us, but the shellfire started up again and *Consort* sustained several more hits. She made one more attempt under very heavy fire in such a narrow river with all the Chinese artillery firing at her. She finally signalled to us, 'Sorry can't help. Best of luck', and steamed off towards Shanghai.

On her way downriver, *Consort* met the cruiser HMS *London*, which had been visiting Shanghai when a signal was received to go to *Amethyst*'s assistance. *London* set sail into the Yangtze in company with the frigate *Black Swan*, both with Union Flags and a red cross draped around the upper decks, and met *Consort* coming in the opposite direction. She also had a number of casualties, who were treated in *London*'s better-equipped sickbay, and all but one were returned to their ship, which continued downriver to Shanghai. The next morning, the passage towards *Amethyst* continued, with action stations in force, and barely had the two ships set off before they came under fire from shore-based artillery, steaming as fast as possible but confronting one battery after another, seemingly all lined up and ready to open fire. *London* returned fire but the eight-inch armament was not designed for such short-range combat, and there was little room for the ship to manoeuvre. Soon, *London* and *Black Swan* were taking heavy damage, and before *Amethyst* could be reached the captain decided to call a halt. After consultation with his officers, he decided that it would be suicidal to go further and gave the order to go about and return to Shanghai, again running the gauntlet of shore batteries. In the three days of action, *London* and *Black Swan* sustained heavy casualties, with 25 killed and many wounded. *Amethyst*, meanwhile, remained trapped, and the crew decided that they had to get help for the wounded, as Don Redman explained:

There was another lull in the firing, and by this time we were in desperate need of medical attention. I myself was still bleeding heavily, and a group of able-bodied men got into a boat and took us across the shore to the friendly bank, which was held by the Nationalist Chinese, while the men on board were signalling to the RAF base in Shanghai to see if they could fly a doctor up in a Sunderland flying boat, which we knew they had there. Anyhow, as we got to the other bank, the firing started again and you could hear the whine of shells going overhead. We went inland about 100 yards when we were stopped by a young Chinese officer accompanied by eight soldiers with fixed bayonets. They must have thought we were mercenaries or something, because the young officer thrust a revolver rather painfully in my face, shouting and screaming until I managed to draw an outline of the ship with a Union Jack and a red cross, indicating we needed help.

He realised then we were British and needed a doctor. He indicated for us to follow him and we walked for about a mile – and I only had one shoe on – and finally we did manage to receive first aid. In the meantime, the Sunderland aircraft from No. 88 Squadron had taken off, but when it arrived they made a couple of passes but found it so difficult that they couldn't land the very large flying boat on such a narrow river. Yet these brave guys weren't about to give up and finally they landed this huge aircraft right under the noses of the Chinese. The door opened and out popped Dr Fernley, an RAF medic, who jumped into a sampan. The firing had stopped now, and we could only think it was because the Chinese were awestruck at the sight of this aircraft landing right in front of their guns. But when they realised what was happening, they opened fire again and the Sunderland had to take off and several of the crew were injured.

Eventually, someone turned up carrying instructions from the British embassy at Nanking that all the injured should be mustered in a position about 12 to 15 miles from where we were, and due to bandits from the Communist army who had already infiltrated, we were to walk and only after the hours of darkness. Well, that was an absolute nightmare. We marched through the night and had several stops through exhaustion and pain, and eventually ended up in a rural Chinese hospital, where there was just one very young doctor and some nurses who clearly didn't know how to handle the situation confronting them. Several of us had serious injuries; some were on stretchers. We rested there for a while and the next part is a bit of a blur to me because we were all still suffering from shock, but it now became apparent that someone had, in fact, taken charge of organising our extraction. But in any event we were eventually taken by lorry to a large hospital in Shanghai, where we were operated on, and eventually transferred to Hong Kong, where I was in hospital for two months, receiving further treatment for five bullet and shrapnel wounds.

The crucial point in Redman's story was the moment he realised that, at the time he was falling in and out of consciousness through loss of blood, he had the feeling that somewhere in the background, something was moving, that someone, somewhere was actually getting help. It turned out to be the man who would ultimately become the hero of this story, Lieutenant-Commander John Kerans, who was at the time assistant naval attaché to the British embassy in Nanking. He had kept in touch with the plight of *Amethyst* since reading her signals on the first night of the attack. But the instructions from London were: 'Play it cool. Do not exacerbate the situation, and above all do not let the Chinese think we are especially concerned.' This was not merely the Admiralty speaking but Prime Minister Clement Attlee who (a) wanted to avoid any kind of escalating confrontation and (b) did not want to upset the Chinese Communists who, it was judged in all quarters, might soon be knocking on the door of Hong Kong.

In fact, to demonstrate just how unconcerned the British were, Captain Vernon Donaldson, the naval attaché, insisted that Kerans should not set out on his mission to help *Amethyst* that night but should continue with a prior engagement, attending a banquet for local dignitaries, while the men of *Amethyst* lay wounded and dying. This was typical of the bowler-hatted civil servants in London and the pink-gin snobbery of diplomatic circles abroad in that era, to whom the needs of the men at the sharp end of the action were of secondary importance. However, after a meeting between naval officials and the British ambassador, Kerans set off the following day to investigate the position, if possible make contact with the ship and report back. Although the Admiralty in London may have looked at Kerans' record and bemoaned having to have such a man to undertake this delicate diplomatic task, as things turned out there was probably no one better.

Kerans had what might be termed 'a history' that in recent times had developed into something of an aversion to authority, which is why, having once had command of his own ship, he now found

269

himself buried away in a desk job, far away from his wife and family in England, and anticipating no further promotion. Of Irish extract, a public school education and graduation from the Royal Naval College at Dartmouth, he at one time seemed on the fast track to high rank. At the start of the war, he was appointed to naval intelligence in Singapore but requested a transfer to join the action, and he was drafted to the cruiser *Naiad*, mostly engaged on convoy duties. The ship did, however, take part in the evacuation of Crete in May 1941 and with her sister ship *Orion* took severe damage from German dive-bombers, killing 300 soldiers. Back at Alexandria, Kerans was among those assigned the task of clearing the dismembered bodies from the ship, and like many others he was traumatised by the experience. Later, his own ship was sunk and he was in the water for several hours before he was picked up. Just before D-day, he was given command of a destroyer, *Blackmore*, which had one or two scrapes which his superiors felt could have been avoided, and which his brother officers put down to his increasing tendency towards heavy drinking, for which he was subsequently awarded 'their lordships' displeasure'. A further career mishap occurred in Malta in 1947, when guests at the fleet admiral's cocktail party witnessed a number of officers urinating over the side of Kerans' ship after a boozy night out, and thereafter they proceeded to strip naked and dive into the sea. At a subsequent court martial, he was found to be negligent in his duty, stripped of his command and posted to Nanking. It was a move that was to prove fortuitous to the stranded crew of *Amethyst* as the days, then months began to tick by while they, like the crew of a sailing ship becalmed in the ocean, sat it out on the hot and humid Yangtze river, bored to tears and half-starved in a rat-infested ship that threatened disease, and wondered if they would ever get home.

On 22 April 1949, after a tortuous journey not without its dangers, Kerans reached *Amethyst*, where he took up residence, appointed himself commander and, on the instructions of the ambassador in Nanking, tentatively opened negotiations with the Chinese to get the ship released. He was expressly forbidden to make any dramatic moves, such as attempting to run the gauntlet. The ship was to stay put, and he was to attempt to resolve the crisis by negotiation. It was still not generally known that these orders came from the Prime Minister's office in London and, not unnaturally, questions began to be asked in the House of Commons: was it not beyond the wit of the Royal Navy, fresh from so many heroic escapades and daring in the Second World War, to at least rescue the trapped sailors?

Apparently, they were not allowed to try, and for the next 13 weeks Kerans became involved in long and meaningless negotiations with Chinese officials who were looking for a face-saving excuse to let the boat go free. At every one of his meetings with the Communist officials, they would demand he signed an admission that the British ship had fired first, which he refused to do because it was patently untrue. At each meeting, he demanded to be allowed free passage to the open sea through the Yangtze, universally recognised as an international waterway. The Communists said: 'Not any more it isn't.' And so it went on, day after day, week after week, while the 72 men on board were becoming severely affected by their imprisonment in the stifling humidity, with only themselves and the rats for company.

The British government was making little headway either. How do you negotiate with a moving army? And the situation took an even grimmer note on 26 May when Mao Zedong's Communists captured Shanghai after a month-long siege: fearful that the same fate might soon befall Hong Kong, the Labour government of Prime Minister Attlee was not prepared to get involved in a war with the Chinese. Frank Goldsworthy, who was in Hong Kong to report on the *Amethyst* drama for the *Daily Express*, recalled in his memoir for the Imperial War Museum: 'At the time, I had an invitation through the Royal Navy to go out with a group of Harbour Defence Motor Launches who were taking with them a number of local businessmen to give them experience of handling small craft in case the colony had to be evacuated and there was going to be a need to ferry people out to ships.'

Kerans, from his meeting with the Chinese, could see that they were quite prepared to sit it out for as long as it took. That was the nature of the people, and the British government seemed altogether unsure how to handle the situation, which by now was receiving a daily media commentary around the world. Nor were there to be any attempted heroics. The Admiralty, whose hands were tied by the politicians, had ordered Kerans not to try anything stupid – like making a run for it. It was, after all, a 140-mile journey under the guns of the Communists to reach the open sea.

As another month passed, however, Kerans found his thoughts turning increasingly to that very possibility, of making a dash for freedom. He and his crew had talked about it often enough, and towards the end of July they were talking in positive terms of running the gauntlet at night down the Yangtze. 'They'd had enough, and bugger what the British government wanted, and bugger the Chinese too,' said Frank Goldsworthy, who talked to them all later. It would be a risky operation at best, but they were far from at best, sailing in the dark with only half a crew in a badly damaged ship over a difficult waterway, without charts or a pilot and under the noses of a well-armed enemy. The odds were stacked against them.

However, the alternatives were desperately unappealing: possibly weeks remaining on board in increasingly foul conditions, not to mention the lack of food and drinkable water. So Kerans consulted his chiefs and petty officers and the people who would be running things in the boiler rooms. They were all agreed that they should make a dash for it, or at least get as far as they could. The distance to the open sea was 140 miles, and they would be travelling at 20 knots – slower at some of the difficult points along the river, negotiating mud banks and booms in the darkness. They calculated it would take around seven hours, and by the end of July Kerans' mind was made up. They began preparing the ship for the journey, planning their departure for the night of 31 July and calculating that they would have to set off before 10 p.m. in order to get past the main dangerous points before daylight. As dusk closed in, Kerans summoned his 17 chiefs and petty officers to his cabin for final instructions. The anchor cables had already been covered in bandages from greased torn bedding, and as darkness fell some other crucial tasks were dealt with, such as blackening all areas of white paint and gleaming brass work, which had been polished throughout as a matter of course. They next rigged up layers of black canvas to change the profile of the ship, so as to create as near as possible a silhouette that, in the darkness, would resemble some of the Chinese ships that used the river.

Just before setting off, Kerans signalled the commander-in-chief of the Far East Station in Hong Kong, Admiral Sir Patrick Brind, who was at the time on the brandy and cigars after hosting a dinner aboard HMS *Belfast*, moored in the harbour. It was a cryptic message indicating his intentions, which was in due course read by the Admiralty in London. The Admiralty made a signal in return expressly prohibiting the attempt, but Hong Kong claimed the message was garbled and could not be passed on. Could London please send it again? By then it was too late. The engines were running, positively purring, and, as he prepared to cast off, Kerans had his first piece of good luck: a merchant ship, the *Kiang Ling Liberation*, came around the bend heading downriver. Kerans moved swiftly to fall in behind, so that not only could *Amethyst* use the ship as a pilot but the merchantman would lead the way through the points where there were most likely to be Chinese observation posts. All went well for the first 40 minutes, when at one of the observation posts shots were fired across the bows of the merchant ship. She replied with a signal from her siren and altered course a little to starboard, and Kerans followed, although he noticed another small vessel on his port bow which turned out to be a Communist landing craft. A flare went up, followed by gunfire from the Chinese craft, which appeared to be challenging *Amethyst* to halt. In fact, the gunfire was aimed at a shore battery on the other side, which retaliated, and *Amethyst*, caught midstream as heavy fire developed between the opposing forces on both banks, was hit below the starboard water line.

The ship shuddered and water poured in, but the hole was plugged and, as the pumps began to operate, *Amethyst* righted herself and Kerans ordered full ahead, making smoke. At the same time, he gave the command for B gun to open fire. With *Kiang Ling Liberation* now dead ahead, Kerans overtook her with just inches to spare and pushed on past the merchantman and headed on downriver, past the shore batteries but now well aware that the Communists would be fully alerted to the oncoming British ship.

Twice more she came under fire but just kept on going flat out, with the crew under severe pressure, especially in the boiler room, where several men literally fainted with the heat and dehydration. At 2.40 a.m., having completed a hundred sea miles of his passage, he sent a signal to Hong Kong: 'Hundred up.' Admiral Brind replied: 'A magnificent century!' And it was at this point that the British government decided to reveal to the world that *Amethyst* was running the gauntlet. Earlier in the evening, Prime Minister Attlee had been told of Kerans' actions, in complete disregard to orders. But with the situation now diplomatically tense with regard to the possible invasion of Hong Kong itself, Attlee was persuaded to agree to release the news when it was pointed out that as a public relations exercise the British couldn't lose. If *Amethyst* were halted again by shelling, it would draw considerable criticism of the Chinese from the world's media, and if Kerans completed his bid for freedom the coverage would be immense. 'And so,' explained Frank Goldsworthy, 'we British journalists were informed of the hundred-up message and the Reuters news agency correspondent was raised from his bed to flash the message around the world. But the ship still had to pass the big guns at Woo Sung, so at that point it was never really sure she was going to make the open sea.'

In fact, the two fortified emplacements at Woo Sung, armed with six-inch guns, was the last great hurdle, and one that represented a very real threat to *Amethyst*: one lucky hit could send her to the bottom. As the ship approached, the searchlights swung towards her and lit her in full for a few seconds and then swung away. If the Communists knew by then that this was the fleeing British ship, they made no further attempt to halt her. The guns stayed silent, and *Amethyst* made it to the open sea with her crew cheering and hugging each other with a mixture of sheer elation and tears of relief.

The destroyer *Concord* came to meet her, joined by the cruiser *Jamaica* that had been sent up from Hong Kong, rendezvousing off the coast of Formosa. Frank Goldsworthy had managed to get on board:

When we met *Amethyst*, I was up on the signal platform. The *Jamaica*'s entire crew were lining the rails cheering and waving, and I took a photograph over their heads of

*Amethyst* which was printed around the world. The crew of *Amethyst* were absolutely shedding tears of sheer joy, and their arrival in Hong Kong was a great emotional experience for everyone concerned, including myself. I had the privilege of going aboard *Amethyst* for the run up the harbour. It was incredible. Every ship was hooting, there were fire floats with their hoses, great jets of water, the crews of two cruisers were lining the rails to cheer, Spitfires were flying overhead, the army was out lining the hilltops and all along you could see the silhouettes of soldiers.

The governor of Hong Kong was there with a guard of honour. It was just something that you had to experience to appreciate, because the atmosphere was almost beyond description. It was such a terrific moment for these men, who had been isolated for 101 days. There was a great deal of indignation everywhere over the way the Chinese had played this game of cat-and-mouse with these lads, who were under their noses and had no real prospect of being released. They would now be the subject of news stories all over the world – that they had put up two fingers to the Communists and got out, despite all the risks of the 140-mile dash down the river. It was something that lifted the hearts of the whole British nation, who were in those days facing such austere and miserable times.

In the euphoria, the key question was overlooked: what was the navy or the government doing, allowing a moderately armed gunboat to sail on an inland waterway on the banks of which opposing forces were intermittently blasting away at each other – and anyone else who got in the way – ad infinitum? The skipper who brought them out, Lieutenant-Commander John Kerans, was awarded an immediate Distinguished Service Order, and the navy quickly realised the propaganda value in their wayward hero whose past misdemeanours were hastily covered up, and he was fêted everywhere and, with all other members of the crew, given a great welcome. After repairs, the ship sailed home to England, stopping at all the naval bases en route, where further celebrations were staged. The ship arrived back at Devonport early on

1 November 1949 to a further welcome by thousands of well-wishers lining the quayside, including Kerans' wife Stephanie and daughter Charmian. He became the hero of the hour and, indeed, the following decade. He received hundreds of invitations to speak, there were naval and civil celebratory receptions, a book and a film, entitled *The Yangtze Incident*, in which Kerans was played by one of the leading British actors of the day, Richard Todd. Later, he became a Conservative MP and was involved in a number of business ventures that eventually faded, along with his notoriety.

And, as with many such stories, it was only the name of the ship that remained in the public psyche.

# CHAPTER FIFTEEN

## Korea and New Horizons

Barely had the hero ship *Amethyst* been patched up and made good from the Yangtze experience than she was on her way back into action. She was to take her place as part of a large contingent of British ships to be deployed with a Commonwealth and American force off the coast of Korea, where the threat of a new major conflict arose at a time when the Royal Navy's Far East Fleet was in a pretty parlous state. There were 22 British warships in Far Eastern waters, but many were old, battered and bruised from Second World War service. The fleet had widespread commitments quite apart from the defence of Hong Kong, including the Malayan and Singapore patrols and, still, in the Yangtze estuary, where British trading interests continued to flourish.

With tense situations emerging in both the Mediterranean and the Far East, the available ships were to be thinly spread, and quite a few men who were about to retire were asked to remain in service. Even so, when the eyes of the world suddenly turned to the new flashpoint of Korea, the Royal Navy managed to contribute a significant contingent to what was to be the first-ever Allied operation under the auspices of the United Nations and, indeed, the first conflict in which the United Nations had sponsored the use of military force against an aggressor. Although the operation was largely driven by the Americans, who also supplied 90 per cent of the troops, hardware and equipment, the Royal Navy's contribution over the period of the war amounted to five fleet aircraft carriers, six cruisers, eight destroyers, 14 frigates/sloops, a depot ship, a hospital ship, four supply ships, 14 tankers, 14 squadrons of the Fleet Air Arm and a specially created 41st Independent Company, Royal Marines.

In fact, such a conflict was the last thing that hard-up Britain needed, and the causes were linked once again to colonialism. Japan had ruled Korea since 1910, but, when the Russians and the Americans kicked them out in 1945, Soviet troops occupied Korea north of the thirty-eighth parallel, while American troops controlled the country south of this line. In 1947 the UN General Assembly declared that elections should be held throughout Korea to choose one government for the entire country. The Soviet Union refused to sanction elections in the north, but on 10 May 1948 the people of South Korea elected a national assembly. North Korea responded by forming the Democratic People's Republic of Korea. Both claimed the entire country, and the Communists made their move and invaded South Korea on 25 June 1950.

When UN demands for withdrawal were ignored, member nations were asked to provide military aid to South Korea. Sixteen UN countries, including the United Kingdom, sent troops to help the South Koreans, and 41 countries sent military equipment, food and other supplies. The North Koreans, meanwhile, had the backing of the Soviets for equipment and advisers and the Chinese for additional manpower, of which they had a vast reservoir. Apart from being one of the most brutal and dehumanising conflicts in modern history, the war was unique for a number of reasons, not least that it was a forerunner of Vietnam and thus its horrors soon became somewhat overshadowed by even greater controversies. Issues beyond the battle lines included the brainwashing techniques used by the North Koreans and Chinese Communists on prisoners of war as well as other atrocities, and allegations that germ warfare was used by the Americans, which was never substantiated but is not beyond belief, given what happened later in Vietnam.

The ground forces of the UN nations, along with the South

Koreans, came under the command of the US 8th Army, led by General MacArthur. US troops were the first to land, followed soon afterwards by British Commandos, and initially the war went very badly for the UN force. The North Koreans dashed south and quickly captured the southern capital of Seoul and pushed the defenders into the south-eastern corner. With a massive injection of UN reinforcements, MacArthur launched a surprise amphibious invasion in September, well behind enemy lines at the city of Inchon on South Korea's west coast, about 25 miles west of Seoul.

Among the first British ships to arrive on the scene was the cruiser *Jamaica*, and in the ship's company was Fred Ball, whose experiences in the Second World War have been recounted in earlier chapters, including the sinking of his first ship, the carrier *Courageous*, the *Bismarck* chase and the sinking of his second ship, *Dorsetshire*. That summer, *Jamaica* had been assigned a month-long cruise around British bases on the Japanese islands, and a party of NCOs from the Middlesex Regiment and the Royal Artillery had been invited on board for the trip to Japan for a recreational break from their duties in the New Territories, where the Bamboo Curtain separated Hong Kong from Communist China. They sailed from Hong Kong in early June, heading for Japan, and it was while on that passage that they received a signal to stand by, following the North Korean attack on South Korea. With the two most powerful Communist states backing the North, America feared the domino effect across the Far East and moved immediately to counter the threat. Fred Ball on *Jamaica*:

We were informed we were heading into possible conflict with North Korea under the banner of the United Nations, and the army NCOs were asked if they wanted to stay on board or to be put ashore and most of them opted to remain. We went up straight to the east coast of Korea, to be joined by the frigate *Black Swan* and USS *Juneau*. This took us right up to, and I believe beyond, the thirty-eighth parallel. As we travelled on, we saw evidence of the appalling slaughter that had been taking place, when in a calm, flat sea we found large numbers of floating corpses bound up in pairs. It was a terrible sight. Once in our designated area, we began bombarding coastal targets such as shore batteries, troop convoys, railways, bridges, anything that would hinder the Communists' invasion. As always on ships of the Royal Navy, we were at action stations at dawn – which is standard procedure as it is supposedly the most likely time for an attack. At dawn on 2 July, the ship was at action stations, and I was in the bridge plot room. That day, one of the boy-sailor lookouts shouted: 'Some small boats approaching, sir.' The officers took a look and identified six motor torpedo boats.

With the gun crews already at action stations, we were quickly able to deal with that threat. This was the first action by any of the United Nations ships; in fact, *Jamaica* had a reputation for being first at everything: first there, first into action and then first to take a hit. [On 8 July] we were bombarding targets on the coast with *Juneau* when *Jamaica* took a direct hit near the base of the mainmast. Unfortunately, [six men] were killed, five of whom were soldiers who volunteered to act as ammunition numbers at various gun mountings when required. Five others were wounded. The dead were all buried at sea. Later on, after switching operations to the west coast and the landings at Inchon, *Jamaica* became the first British ship to shoot down an enemy aircraft that had strafed the decks, fatally wounding a boy seaman.

The flagship of the British force on the Korean mission was the cruiser *Belfast*, and on board was Frederick Hutchison, veteran of so many wartime operations, such as Narvik, the attack on the French fleet, the Pedestal Convoy and the D-day landings on *Warspite*. Now he was the ship's diver on *Belfast*, his last appointment in the navy:

I had a team of six divers, and the action station I was given was director-trainer for the six-inch main armament. We were mainly operating on the west coast and occasionally around to the east to support the Americans. We mainly carried out bombardments. The diving operations included one to rescue a Canadian destroyer which was carrying out a

*Above:* The pock-marked *Amethyst* arrives in Hong Kong after the dramatic escape from China in what became known as the Yangtze incident

*Above insert:* Lieutenant Commander Kearns, the replacement captain who led the dash to freedom and won international fame

*Below:* The aircraft carrier *Ocean*, part of the considerable Royal Navy force involved in the Korean war in the early 1950s, pictured here at Sasebo, Korea

Going south: images of the Falklands War in 1982 with (*above*) a remarkable picture of the inside of the carrier *Hermes*, crammed with soldiers and Harrier jump jets, on the journey down. And (*below*) one of the victims of the conflict, the Type 21 frigate, *Ardent*, bombed in Falkland Sound

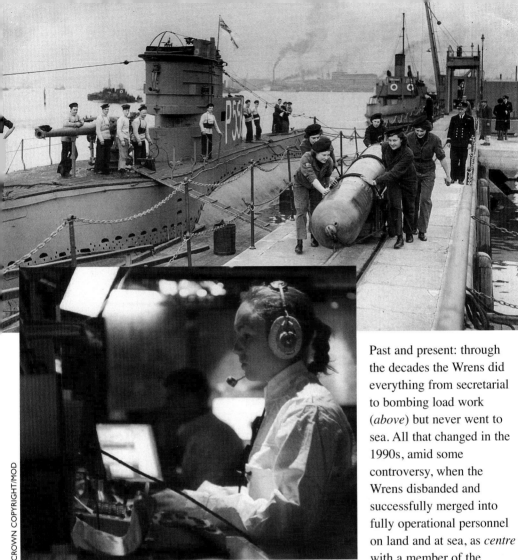

Past and present: through the decades the Wrens did everything from secretarial to bombing load work (*above*) but never went to sea. All that changed in the 1990s, amid some controversy, when the Wrens disbanded and successfully merged into fully operational personnel on land and at sea, as *centre* with a member of the communications staff on duty in the Gulf in 2003. But some things never change: (*left*) young trainees still have to learn to tie knots!

*Above:* A less-publicised area of Royal Navy operations is humanitarian aid after conflict or natural disasters. Here an RN surgeon tends a sick child in the aftermath of the Afghanistan war against the Taliban

*Below:* Little and large: America continued with giant fleet carriers, a policy that Britain abandoned in the 1970s. The difference in size is amply indicated here in 1998 during Allied patrols which were to culminate in the war on Saddam Hussein five years later. On the left is the USS *John C. Stennis* alongside the British carrier *Illustrious* during Operation Southern Watch

CROWN COPYRIGHT/MOD

CROWN COPYRIGHT/MOD

Royal Marines on patrol in support of the British moves to secure Basra during the second Gulf War and (*below*) the Royal Navy's hovercraft teams prepare for action at Umm Qsar on the az-Zubayr river

*Above:* Constantly in action, the flight deck of *Ark Royal*

*Below:* Trouble-spotters: the Force Protection teams on the carrier

CROWN COPYRIGHT/MOD

CROWN COPYRIGHT/MOD

*Below:* Operator maintainers loading a general purpose gun on the bridge of *Ark Royal*

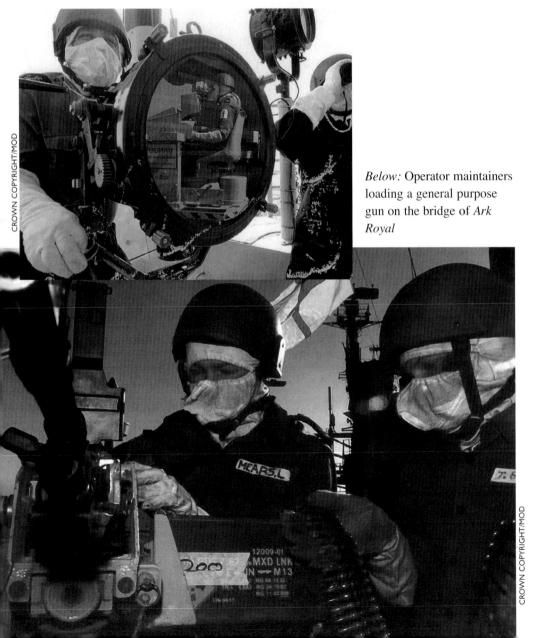

CROWN COPYRIGHT/MOD

*Above:* Coming up: a Sea
Harrier is brought to the
carrier's flight decks

*Right:* Ground transport for
the Commandos is loaded
into a helicopter on the flight
deck of HMS *Ocean*

*Top:* A vision of the future: computer image (*above*) of what will be the largest ship ever built by the Royal Navy – one of the new breed of carriers costing £1.4 billion each, weighing 60,000 tons, capable of accommodating 50 aircraft and due to enter service between 2012 and 2015. The aircraft will probably be the Lockheed Martin X-35

The windowless Type 45 Air Defence Destroyer, the largest and most powerful air defence destroyers ever operated by the Royal Navy which will begin arriving into service in 2007 night bombardment several miles above the thirty-eighth parallel. They had dropped some marker buoys and just before daylight, when they went to recover them, they accidentally wrapped the wires of one of the buoys around a propeller and were unable to move. So it was a sitting-duck situation when I was rushed up to help the diving team on board because the water was so cold, 26 degrees, and we had to work all the next night to clear the propeller. I was Mentioned in Dispatches for that.

*Belfast* was also hit by a howitzer shell and, ironically enough, we had on board Chinese laundry people and Chinese stewards, and the shell hit the Chinese mess deck and killed one of the Chinese stewards. The damage was on the starboard side, and anyone visiting *Belfast* at its moorings on the Thames will see the plate on the starboard that was welded over where the shell hit, just underneath A turret.

That apart, it was really a walkover for *Belfast*. During the whole time we were there, we carried out many bombardment operations and troop support manoeuvres, but we had no problems with either aircraft or enemy ships. In fact, our worst experience probably came from a hurricane that turned into a typhoon. I have a vivid memory of it – worst weather I had ever experienced in all my years in the Royal Navy. The damage it caused on *Belfast*: huge steel doors were bent, boats ripped to pieces, mess decks flooded inches deep in water.

The British contingent was also joined by ships from Australia, New Zealand and other Commonwealth countries to make up what was termed the Commonwealth Task Force, the largest Allied naval force assembled since the war. The naval base at the tiny port of Sasebo in Japan was used as the main logistical base, although for repairs and refits the ships had to return to Hong Kong. By the end of October, advance units of the UN force were fighting the Chinese as well as North Koreans. After initial success by MacArthur's troops, the Chinese returned to the attack, this time fielding huge numbers of soldiers and heavy armoury, and in the bitter Korean winter they soon had the UN force in retreat.

The Communists advanced back into the south, and it took a massive counter-attack by the entire UN command, codenamed Operation Killer, on 21 February 1951 to hold them. Under pressure of superior firepower, the Chinese slowly withdrew northwards. Heavy fighting continued, however, month on month on the ground and in the air. The UN now had more than 300,000 troops in Korea in addition to 340,000 of the South Korean army. The Communist forces were put at close on 900,000, which included two Chinese armoured divisions and one mechanised division with 520 tanks. Air power played a key and spectacular role in the war as the first-ever war with dogfighting jets. The Chinese had developed into a major air power. Half of their 1,400 aircraft were Soviet-built MiG-15s, operating from bases in Manchuria. The UN virtually lost its air supremacy over what was known as MiG Alley in north-west Korea until President Truman ordered the urgent supply of new F-86 Sabres. Large-scale air battles and dogfights resulted, and this was also reflected in the maritime action.

Throughout the war, the Commonwealth Task Force kept at least one carrier on station around Korean coastal waters, while another would be close at hand being resupplied. Intermittently during the campaign, carriers off patrol were frequently called in to assist with air cover for British troops moving into the Malayan peninsula to quell what was termed the Malayan Emergency. Ching Peng, a Chinese Communist leader who was awarded an MBE for his services to the Allies during the Second World War, had now turned against the British and had amassed an army of 5,000 men dedicated to ridding Malaya of British rule. The 'Emergency', which was never referred to as a war, began in June 1948 and was confidently predicted by military analysts to be 'over by Christmas'. In fact, it turned into a monotonous game of hide-and-seek in the dense jungles of Malaya that engaged some of Britain's best troops, as well as RAF and Fleet Air Arm squadrons, for almost 12 years.

Back at the main event of Korea, however, although principally a land-based war, the maritime effort had a considerable impact and, with a strong carrier presence within the United Nations force, full use was made of the potential for hit-and-run air attacks launched from the sea against North Korean troop movements and positions, as well as acting as bombardment spotters for the navy guns. The result was the emergence of a very efficient air-to-air and air-to-ground representation. It also saw the innovative use of ship-borne helicopters for the first time in any conflict. They were utilised in a number of roles, including search and rescue for downed pilots and close-quarter reconnaissance for minefields in the absence – certainly in the early part of the war – of an effective minesweeping operation. Curiously enough, minesweepers were not included in the Task Force sent by the Royal Navy.

The carriers were also extensively used alongside the bombardment campaign and later to enforce a rigid blockade of the North Korean ports after exceedingly successful operations against Wonsan, Hungnam and Songin from early in 1951 to the cessation of the conflict, thereby tying up large numbers of North Korean troops and armoury. Pilots new to the scenario, including the first RNVR pilots arriving in Korea from No. 832 Squadron, were given lectures and briefings on the peculiarities of the Korean theatre, of which there were many. Not least among them were the escape-and-evasion tactics if they were brought down. They were also provided with an escape kit comprising a 0.38-calibre revolver with 24 rounds, a Sten gun, stowed in the cockpit, cloth escape maps, ground recognition panels, a commando knife, two-star red flares, a barter kit of watch, fountain pen and compass, emergency rations, a fishing kit, mosquito net, medical kit, marching compass and spare socks.

Operations for pilots, and for the carrier crews as a whole, were lively and demanding, given that the aircraft were carrying two 1,000-pound bombs and had overloaded fuel tanks which challenged the talents of all concerned in takeoff. There were some hair-raising moments, and some unusual results on shore. In a log of the various tours of HMS *Ocean*,* there is mention of Lieutenant-Commander Dick's luck when he attacked a bridge from low level: 'His bomb went into a field, bounced and followed the rail line for half a mile, before disappearing into a tunnel and

* Can be viewed in full at www.britains-smallwars.com/carriers/ocean.html.

exploding. This developed into the chancy ploy of skip-bombing; some pilots' aircraft being hit by debris from their own bombs in skip-bomb attacks, and having to pull up smartly, to avoid the mountains.'

During her fifth patrol, *Ocean* was operating well to the north of her usual position and sent her planes over North Korea, where the pilots became the first British airmen flying piston-engined aircraft to encounter MiG jet fighters, bad weather having grounded all the USAF jets. Airmen from No. 825 Squadron were attacked by four MiGs north of Chinnampo. Later, Lieutenant Peter 'Hoagy' Carmichael won the very rare distinction of being the pilot of one of a few piston-engined aircraft to shoot down a jet-engined aircraft.

Nor were the MiGs far away as the next significant action came into view. For many months the Mediterranean Fleet had been keeping a watching brief on developments in Egypt after President Nasser signed a trade pact with the Russians. He began urging the British to depart his country and to give him back the Suez Canal, in which the British had bought a controlling interest in 1888 and in which the Royal Navy, not to mention every major commercial maritime company, had a particular interest as their gateway to the East. In 1954 Nasser agreed not to press the matter further if the British on their part agreed to a gradual withdrawal of all remaining forces of what once formed a 70,000-strong British Army on the Nile. This arrangement seemed to calm the heightening tension between Nasser and the West, but it didn't last.

By early 1955 more Russian MiG fighters and copious amounts of other hardware from the Soviet bloc arrived in Egypt on a £200 million buy-now-pay-later arrangement for which Nasser mortgaged his entire cotton for the next five years. The West responded by withdrawing from negotiations to finance Nasser's dream project, the Aswan High Dam, which he was desperate to build to improve the nation's irrigation, and therefore crop production, as well as to generate hydroelectric power. Backed into a corner, the then toughest operator in the Middle East came out punching, and on 26 July, a month after the last of the British troops had been pulled out under the 1954 agreement, Nasser announced he was nationalising the Suez Canal without compensation to the imperialists, and that night there was dancing in the streets of Cairo. What is generally referred to as the Suez Fiasco now began to unfold. Charles Piercy Mills, who had been commander of HMS *Concord* during the Korean War and a veteran of planning for the Torch and D-day landings, now found himself at the sharp end of the Suez crisis:

I was Chief of Staff in 1956 to the admiral, second in command of the Mediterranean Fleet, and in June 1956 we were visiting Alexandria. That night, I went ashore to meet friends for dinner, and on the way out I passed through the square where President Nasser was going to make a speech that very evening. There were flags all out and the microphones set up, and people were already gathering. Anyway, I went on my way to meet friends, and towards the end of the evening we were told that in his speech Nasser announced that he had nationalised the Suez Canal. Back aboard ship the following morning, we were told to sail immediately and proceed to Cyprus. We felt rather sad because there were 30 or 40 of the British community waving us goodbye and it looked as if we were deserting them in their time of crisis. However, we sailed on to Cyprus and were then told the admiral and operational officers were required to fly to London at once and to start planning for an operation. The next morning we had an interview with Admiral Mountbatten, the First Sea Lord, who told us that the previous evening he had been sent for by the Prime Minister, Anthony Eden, along with other Chiefs of Staff, and they had been told to prepare an operation to land and capture the Suez Canal.

We went immediately to an annexe of the War Office, where we started planning with the army and the air force for the landing. Our original plan was to land at Alexandria, but that was changed to Port Said. For the next two months we made more plans, which had to be altered for various reasons, some political and some military. But in September 1956 we were told to put the operation on ice but to remain on hand at short notice. There were apparently many problems, and all sorts of people came and went, including the Australian Prime Minister, Foster Dulles and then members of the Canal Users' Association, who all had a view.

By then, it was clear that the international community, and America in particular – currently in the throes of re-electing Eisenhower for a second term – would not support any heavy-handedness, given that the Soviets were hovering in the background. Notwithstanding this lack of support, British Prime Minister Anthony Eden and his French counterpart pressed on, and secretly accepted the offer of some side-action from one of their few supporters in this venture, Israel. In spite of Eisenhower's pleadings not to endanger peace in the volatile region, Israeli Prime Minister David Ben-Gurion gave the order for his troops to invade Egypt on 29 October, and thus provide the Anglo-French forces with a carefully prearranged excuse to zip across the Mediterranean and take possession of the Canal Zone. A joint British and French ultimatum called on the Egyptians and the Israelis to pull back from the Canal Zone within 12 hours. Israel agreed on condition that Egypt did the same, but Nasser naturally rejected the call.

The invasion of Suez thus moved towards its finale. The British contribution to the assault was a Task Force led by 20 ships of the Royal Navy, including two aircraft carriers, 18 squadrons of Canberra and Valiant bombers, to be flown out of Malta and Cyprus, the 16th Parachute Brigade and a contingent of seaborne Royal Marines. Originally, the entire parachute brigade of three battalions and a headquarters unit was to be dropped on strategic targets, but the RAF had only enough transport aircraft available to carry 668 men. This meant that 1 and 2 Para would now have to go in by sea along with the Royal Marine Commandos.

On the afternoon of 29 October Israeli paratroops were duly dropped 30 miles east of Suez and their forward advance was supported by drops of arms and food from French aircraft. As this diversion took hold, Eden pressed the button for the British attack to begin. It entailed a two-phase air assault to bomb all Egyptian airfields, using Canberras of Nos 10 and 12 Squadrons and Valiants of No. 148 Squadron. They took off from Cyprus in the afternoon of 31 October and arrived over Egypt as dusk was closing in. Flares dropped by pathfinders marked the targets, which were hit relentlessly with 500- and 1,000-pound HE bombs as the RAF pilots dodged anti-aircraft fire, but they saw little opposition from Egyptian MiGs.

The second part of the assault was by courtesy of the Royal Navy force, which assembled off Cyprus carrying troops and light artillery. The ships were so heavily loaded that they were unable to carry sufficient troop-carrying vehicles. These had to be acquired 'fair means or foul' on arrival. For the first time in any amphibious assault, the Royal Marines were flown in by helicopter from the carriers and did so, incidentally, into the teeth of heavy machine-gun fire. However, there was sufficient firepower to ensure that the invasion force quickly achieved their pre-set goals and were moving rapidly towards their objectives. Charles Piercy Mills, on board the depot ship HMS *Tyne* with the invasion commanders, recalled:

Word came that Port Said was ready to capitulate, and the three commanders of the land, naval and air forces took to a boat and went ashore. As they reached the harbour and the Egyptians opened fire on them, the commander, navy, apparently turned to the commander, army, and said: 'I don't think they're quite ready for us yet, general, do you?' And the boat turned around and came back to *Tyne*. Eventually, we moved in and were alongside at Port Said that first evening. But at dinner in the admiral's cabin, we received a signal from the marine commando general ashore which said: 'I have just heard on the BBC that we are to cease fire at midnight. Request instruction.'

This was the first we had heard of this, and General Stockwell, the army commander, got up from the table like a flash and sent his Chief of Staff to make a signal to his troops ashore to advance as far as they could up to midnight. This, of course, was caused by Eisenhower on the telephone to Eden, furious that the invasion had gone ahead without telling him and threatening to withdraw American support for the pound, and so on. So were sat there in Port Said after dinner, waiting and wondering what was going to happen. Eventually, we were told to withdraw our forces and do nothing until finally the United Nations people arrived in the middle of December. Then we sailed away, leaving them in control and they had to clear the block-ships in Suez which we had been told not to do. We sailed back to Malta, and that was the end of it as far as we were concerned. There had been great frustration over the way it was handled. While in Port Said, on the same day we had been told once to advance and then to withdraw, so there was great frustration about what was going on and we had to treat it almost as a joke, because there was so much order and counter-order, but by this time, I think, we were resolved to almost anything.

Even when the planning was being done, the military objective was very uncertain because of the changing political input. Eden's declared intention was to topple Nasser, whatever that meant, and there is no doubt that we could have captured the canal had we been allowed to go on. It was virtually done. But what then? That was the unanswered question . . .

The cease-fire, which had been declared in London and told to the BBC before being relayed to troops on the spot, followed a United Nations Security Council meeting in New York which had received a US-sponsored resolution calling for a cessation of force in Egypt and 'to refrain from giving aid to Israel'. Eisenhower was piling on the pressure. Sterling was in free fall more or less directly as a result of the Americans' actions, and the British government faced a crisis of monumental proportions which, as history records, cost Anthony Eden his job and saw the British troops pulled out ignominiously, to be replaced by a 6,000-strong United Nations peacekeeping force. All of this, of course, was long forgotten when the representatives of the Blair and Bush campaign to declare war on Saddam Hussein attempted to railroad the UN Security Council into backing them in March 2003. Thereafter, British military power, and particularly the strength of the Royal Navy, declined more or less in tandem with the fading elements of Empire.

Following the success of the carrier operations at Suez, *Bulwark* and her sister ship *Albion* were both converted to assault carriers with helicopters for Commando landings, and there was plenty of action to keep them occupied. The tensions in the Middle East followed on from President Nasser's personally proclaimed victory in Egypt against the imperialist forces of the West. In the aftermath, a group of young military officers in Iraq murdered the young King Feisal and his uncle, Crown Prince Abdullah, while the Prime Minister, Nuri el-Said, was kicked to death by a mob as he pleaded for calm. The coup immediately put pressure on Jordan, Iraq's partner in the Arab Union, and British political and economic influence over a string of sheikhdoms, sultanates, monarchies and protectorates became the focus of bitter reaction among Arab republicans.

At various points along the way, the Royal Navy was called on to land troops and evacuate expatriates, and in 1961, when the new ruler of Iraq, Colonel Kassem, threatened to annex Kuwait, the Royal Navy sailed in with a timely show of strength. In an incredibly short time frame, the navy spearheaded a Task Force comprising all three service elements. *Bulwark* put 750 men of 42 Commando, Royal Marines, ashore as the leading element, while the carrier *Victorious* sailed in to provide air cover. Within a week, 5,700 British troops had been landed, by which time Colonel Kassem had had second thoughts and the issue was resolved – for the time being, at least.

The one remaining vestige of colonial power east of Suez was Aden, which Britain had ruled for 128 years but where her control hung tenuously in the balance. The last strategic base there was a fortress at the mouth of the Red Sea through which southern access was gained to the Suez Canal. This piece of British-controlled turf and waterway sat uneasily among a string of tribal sheikhdoms, spread around the southern Arabian coastline along the Gulf of Aden, which formed the South Arabian Federation. The vast and mountainous lands that stretched far into the distance towards Saudi Arabia became the location of a war between the Soviet-funded People's Republic of South Yemen and the Federation backed by Britain. By 1960 Aden was surrounded by hostility, and in a chain reaction of events the Royal Navy had to ship in 45 Commando to begin the longest stint in the history of the Commandos with regular attendance by the navy carriers. The operations, notably in the Radfan, which included some spectacular involvement by the SAS, continued until this piece of Empire was also finally given up and evacuated in 1967, for which the forces who had served there in appalling conditions of heat and awfulness said prayers of thanks.

As this long saga in the Middle East began, the continuing fallout from the Malayan Emergency also drew the Royal Navy's presence, both in terms of the old-style gunboat threat as well as the modern addition of air and ground assault forces. Although the Malayan issue had finally been resolved, related issues sparked another long-running action on the island of Borneo, where Britain was responsible for the defence of the Sultanate of Brunei and the former colonies of North Borneo (later Sabah) and Sarawak, which shared a border with Kalimantan, the Indonesian region of Borneo. President Sukarno of Indonesia had ambitions to take over the entire island, and in 1962 the Royal Navy's assault ships landed further units of 3 Commando Brigade and the Gurkhas to begin what was politely termed the 'Borneo Confrontation' – never officially a war, but one that soon drew in 28,000 Allied forces from Britain, Australia and New Zealand as well as strong contingents of Special Forces.

The Royal Navy's part in this was to demonstrate the assault and striking power of the carriers and to supply disembarked helicopters to assist troops operating in the jungle, either by firepower, the quick insertion or extraction of troops and in supplying units engaged in long patrols. It proved an entirely effective partnership from which many lessons were learned for future operations, particularly in relation to Special Forces' operations. The extent of the navy's contribution to the land-based operations can be judged by the 3,500 sorties flown from carriers in the first six months of the operation. The navy also patrolled the Malacca Strait and thwarted many attempted landings and remained in action there until the Indonesians pulled back and the threat dissolved in 1965.

At that point, another long-running saga brought HMS *Eagle* to the east coast of Africa when the white government of Ian Smith declared unilateral independence in Rhodesia. Harold Wilson's Labour government immediately applied sanctions and, with United Nations backing, ordered the blocking of all oil supplies to the country. The Royal Navy was to be on hand to enforce these sanctions, initially through a strategically positioned carrier, *Eagle*, supported by ships of the Royal Fleet Auxiliary. As the dispute dragged on – monotonously for the Royal Navy crews – the patrols remained in force until Zimbabwe was created under the regime of Robert Mugabe in 1980.

Apart from the gradually declining attention to these smaller wars and incidents of naval police work through the 1960s and 1970s, a much more fundamental issue had taken hold in Britain with regard to the size, efficiency and capability of the three arms of its military establishment. The army was still driving Bedford trucks from the Second World War, the RAF had what might be described as a somewhat eccentric entry into the jet age, curtailed by lack of funds for decent fighters and yet charged with commissioning the largest and most costly defence ingredient in years – the V-Bomber Force was the principal carrier of Britain's nuclear capability. Meanwhile, the Royal Navy, resting somewhat on the laurels of an heroic past, was being cut and curtailed at every turn by successive governments, while America and the Soviet Union were dashing ahead with massive spending sprees that Britain could not hope to match.

This was, truly, the dawning of the age of realisation that Britain no longer ruled the waves and that every year from 1957, when the navy had 820 ships, onwards British naval power in terms of her surface fleet showed decline on decline, so that when the Queen celebrated her 25 years on the throne in 1977, the navy paraded just 101 ships for the Spithead Review, drawn in from all foreign stations. But, of course, that was not the end of it by any means. So what had happened, apart from repeated cutbacks in the navy's ability to re-equip with new ships? The Soviet Union also poured massive development effort into conventional submarine production, which, disturbingly for the British, not only mirrored the latest technology but also the Second World War production levels of Germany. As the first signs of the Cold War set in, Stalin set in motion a fast-track production programme designed to provide the Soviets with an instant and highly capable submarine force of 500 boats. He died before the target was achieved, but even so almost 270 boats, labelled Whiskey and Zulu class by NATO observers, were completed between 1950 and 1958. Taking the comparison further, the Soviets built more submarines than all the world's other navies combined between 1945 and 1970, with a production total of 560 new vessels extending through their complete range of conventional and nuclear boats. This was alongside an equally impressive build of major ships that matched and then overtook Britain substantially.

In America, there was also a great emphasis on the development of submarines as capital ships, after the US Pacific Fleet suffered heavy surface casualties. US designers now focused on developing a missile-carrying submarine, and at a stroke introduced an entirely new role into submarine warfare, which would be taken further by a small group of scientists working on theories of nuclear-fuelled, missile-firing submarines. The Soviets swiftly followed suit, and a new maritime arms race was under way that Britain could not possibly compete with. The Ministry of Defence, for years, simply had to put their hands to the sky and say: 'What can we do?' In fact, quite a lot, and doing something became necessary through Britain's defence commitment to the North Atlantic Treaty Organisation (NATO), formed after the war, with the US to become the buffer that the Soviet Union would meet across Europe if the Cold War ever turned hot.

After the Suez débâcle, Eisenhower's sulk lasted a couple of years, until February 1958, when the Americans agreed to sell Britain the works for a nuclear-powered submarine, which was laid down by the Duke of Edinburgh on 12 June 1959. It was, after all, his uncle, Lord Mountbatten, who had smoothed the path for Britain to possess this powerful addition to her fleet and who was convinced that without it the country would be at the mercy of Soviet Russia. The Americans were by then well on their way towards the launch of Polaris, the submarine-launched ballistic-missile system, and Mountbatten dreamed of the day when Britain's nuclear deterrent would depend not on land-based missiles or the RAF's bombers but on the efforts of the Royal Navy. He had the statistics: that 70 per cent of the surface of the globe was sea, 50 per cent of the world's population lived within 50 miles of the sea, 40 of the 55 cities with more than a million inhabitants were seaports – it was obvious that the future deterrent must come from under water. He argued that 'if the British can put their share of the deterrent into submarines, there would be no call for the Russians to attack our missile sites and bomber fields as an act of self-preservation if they feared a possible attack'.

Based on that rationale, Britain eventually went along with the idea of her nuclear deterrent being carried by the Royal Navy's submarine fleet, and made a start by building the nation's first nuclear-powered submarine, christened *Dreadnought*, the ninth ship in naval history to carry that most famous name. In a subliminal way, this perhaps demonstrated that the Admiralty had finally acknowledged that the submarine had graduated to capital ship since it was Jackie Fisher's *Dreadnought* that led the naval revolution at the start of the century. And there was another clue . . . she was launched by the Queen at Barrow-in-Furness on Trafalgar Day, 21 October 1960, by which time, incidentally, America had already built 15 nuclear-powered boats and had another 14 under construction.

Thus, Britain's first conventionally armed nuclear-powered submarine was commissioned in April 1963, four years in building and costing £18.5 million. Life on board a British submarine would never be the same again. Submerged endurance would soon be counted in months rather than days and the ship was capable of a diving depth of 1,000 feet. *Dreadnought* was quickly overtaken by advancing technology but served for 20 years before being laid up in 1983, when her nuclear fuel was removed and her equipment stripped out. She was towed to the Rosyth naval dockyard to remain in storage until hundreds of tons of radioactive material inside the steel hull has decayed. She will eventually be broken up or sunk deep in the Atlantic, although the disposal of all nuclear boats remain to be resolved.

*Dreadnought* was followed by the *Valiant* class, forerunner of the *Churchill*, *Swiftsure* and *Trafalgar* classes. *Valiant* led the way as the first all-British nuclear boat based on *Dreadnought* but slightly larger. Successively built between 1963 and 1993, 18 boats that made up these classes were classified as fleet submarines, or more commonly known as hunter-killers. Their role was to protect the nation's squadron of nuclear-armed submarines (see below), to undertake surveillance and the monitoring of manoeuvres of hostile nations, but specifically tracking the submarines and shipping of the Soviet Union throughout the Cold War, and to participate in both anti-submarine warfare and attacks on surface ships and terrain should the need arise. Only two of the 18 boats would ever fire in anger in the twentieth century: *Conqueror* sinking *General Belgrano* in the Falklands War and *Splendid* sending cruise missiles hurtling into Belgrade during the Kosovo crisis.

The beginning of the strategic submarine era with the first British nuclear-armed squadron of Polaris-carrying submarines began with the *Resolution* class, whose sole task was to roam the seas to provide round-the-clock cover so that a British second-strike deterrent remained totally credible at all times. *Resolution* was the first of the four (the others were *Repulse*, *Revenge* and *Renown*) to be commissioned, in 1967, and all four were to fulfil their mission until the early 1990s, when they were progressively taken out of service to be replaced by the *Vanguard* class.

This represented a major change of naval policy in the 1960s. Almost immediately, plans for new aircraft carriers did not even get to the estimating stage, and a major review was ordered by the Wilson government into the true requirements of a scaled-down British naval force. There was a good deal of thought given at the time to the need for a surface fleet of any major proportions when such power was being bandied around under the sea. The Empire was dead and buried, colonial interests were collapsing or being challenged at every turn and the day of gunboat diplomacy, at least in its traditional form, had gone with the wind of change, famously promised by Prime Minister Harold Macmillan. What was emerging, at least in Europe, was a multi-national surface fleet under NATO, although Britain's nuclear capability was held separately under strict guidelines laid down by the suppliers of the Polaris power pack, the United States.

The idea of strategic submarines had been around for a long time but became truly effective only with the arrival of nuclear propulsion, which allowed them to operate continuously submerged without having to surface or reveal their whereabouts. What was the point, it was argued, of having huge battleships sailing the world whose location could be plotted in a control room half a world away and then have them blown out of the water by a missile whose launch pad was in some other distant location? And the destructive force of the V-bombers, spectacular and brilliant aircraft though they were, could similarly be plotted and destroyed before they even came close to their target.

Quite apart from taking prime responsibility for the second-strike capability, the Royal Navy thus moved to the very front line of the Allies' intelligence war, and for the rest of the twentieth century remained at the forefront of a watching brief against Russia, to which the latter reciprocated in fulsome manner. A special nuclear-bomb-proof bunker was built at Northwood, Middlesex, in the 1970s to house the navy's command and control centre, and the awesome size and capability of the *Resolution*-class boats at least gave the Royal Navy fresh impetus after years of depressingly predictable annual cuts in their general defence budget.

Most awesome of all, of course, was the missile compartment in each boat, housing the 16 Polaris missiles, which was nicknamed Sherwood Forest, each missile being 9.5 metres in length, 1.4 metres in diameter and weighing 1,270 kilogrammes. Fired from a submerged submarine, the missiles would soar into the stratosphere and devastate a target 2,500 nautical miles away. The boats, which came on stream progressively between 1964 and 1968, were each assigned two crews of 143 men, turn and turn about, so that at any given time there was at least one, and hopefully two, boats on patrol. The average length of the patrols was generally two months, though in practice often longer, and the most significant feature illustrated the submarines' power and potential: one Polaris submarine carried more destructive capability than the total amount of explosives expended by all sides in the Second World War – including the atomic bombs dropped on Japan.

This, of course, could not be taken in isolation in terms of Britain's whole military and defensive package. In post-war Britain, the Royal Navy had been allowed to invest quite heavily in carriers, which was justified by their ability to support aircraft and, later, helicopters. The huge, majestic, conventional aircraft carriers like *Ark Royal* appeared in the early 1950s and in effect became the new battleships – until the nuclear submarines came on the scene. Coinciding almost exactly with approval for the new breed of submarines, the Defence Review of 1964 cancelled plans for a new generation of carriers that would have emerged in the late 1960s and served for another 25 years or so. And so, eventually, there were only two true carriers left, *Ark Royal* and *Eagle*. The latter was decommissioned in January 1972 and later that year she was towed to Devonport, where she remained until October 1978, when she was towed to the breakers' yard. By then, *Ark Royal* was destined for redundancy.

Three cruisers were converted to act as assault ships, capable of carrying a small number of helicopters and troops, and the whole defence strategy, which had been built around a central core of giant carriers, was in disarray. *Ark Royal* remained in service until 1978, and by then the first of the *Invincible* carriers, almost half the size and designed to accommodate vertical-takeoff Harrier aircraft and helicopters, had arrived in service. The decision to retire *Ark Royal* caused something of a furore among senior ranks at the Admiralty and among the public. The ship was a national hero, not because of any memorable action, but for just being there – and because the nation was taking leave of a whole era of naval warfare that bore so many memories. It was truly the end of an era when the towering carrier, with its great deck, its catapult launchings and its precarious landing encounters with the arrester wire, was finally declared redundant.

In less than a lifetime, the whole complex machine came and went. Wartime veterans, especially, took it to heart that the great Royal Navy fleet of carriers and a Fleet Air Arm of thousands of planes had been decimated and that the last carrier was being demobbed and the wings of the fleet trimmed to 250 or so machines. The third ship to bear the name *Ark Royal*, at 43,000 tons, was near to being the biggest warship ever built for the Royal Navy. She served out her 23 years as a peacetime fighting ship, training, exercising and showing the flag. An accidental bump from a shadowing Soviet destroyer in the Mediterranean was the closest she ever came to a brush with an enemy. But her equipment covered all the accumulated arts of operating warplanes at sea, including three ingenious British developments: the mighty steam catapult, the angled deck and the inventive mirror landing aid.

The new *Invincible*, the class leader in the navy's new breed of smaller carriers, was the one carrier then in operation, and it was fortuitous indeed that the Commando carrier *Hermes* had undergone a second conversion, this time to a ski-ramp carrier during a £30 million refit in 1981. She was now capable of operating the new Sea Harrier aircraft that was soon to prove so vital in the outcome of the Falklands War. But even the future of the brand-new *Invincible* was already in doubt.

The new thinking among the mandarins was that the Royal Navy should no longer be dominated by warships built to operate 'out of area', meaning out of the European theatre of operations. It had been argued since the decision to abandon the huge strike carriers that with Britain's diminishing role as a world policeman and its vanishing commitments to colonial interests, the fleet should be designed specifically to fit the NATO area requirements.

There was considerable pressure among the politicians in the late 1970s to prune even that commitment still further, thereby reducing the surface fleet's anti-submarine warfare capability and placing it almost entirely in the hands of the submarine fleet. But as one very senior Admiralty figure said at the time: 'There's a whole world beyond NATO.' He had barely finished the sentence when rumblings of trouble in distant but familiar waters emerged.

# CHAPTER SIXTEEN

## The Battle for the Falklands

The last time the Royal Navy fought a battle off the coast of Argentina was against the *Graf Spee*, and the navy got the worst of it from the pocket battleship although they won the day. In 1982 things were different in every respect: a battle on land, sea and in the air after the Argentine invasion of the Falkland Islands, but the result was the same. The era of the giant battleship was long past, but just as the Battle of the River Plate was observed for its own significance – pocket battleship against battle cruiser at the very start of the Second World War – so this confrontation would capture the attention of the world, and especially the interest of military analysts. It was unique in that it became the first battle in which the arsenals of the electronic age could be tried and tested. Once again, initially, the Royal Navy took some bad hits but came off victors in the end.

It was a conflict that remains one of the most analysed and studied of all the actions involving maritime operations in the second half of the twentieth century. Quite apart from the interest in dispatching a massive, hurriedly assembled armada 8,000 miles across the globe to fight, it was important in one other significant fact for the analysts. The Falklands adventure demonstrated, in the early stages at least, that the British military had indeed taken its eye off the ball in recent years, and political pressure and financial constraints had produced a Royal Navy, and indeed an entire military philosophy, almost exclusively geared to fighting the Cold War. In company with her Allies in NATO, Britain's fighting arms had become somewhat institutionalised by the procedures and rigidity of aligning their troops, air forces and ships to the overall East versus West battle scenario.

The remorseless growth in the size and sophistication of the Soviet armed forces through the 1960s and 1970s, matched and, where possible, beaten by the vast resources of America, left lesser nations – a category in which Britain now found herself irrefutably anchored – no choice but to accept a very secondary role. If it ever came to the crunch, it would be the Soviets versus the United States, with the rest of the NATO alliance tagging along behind. Progressive cutbacks, switched on and off since the end of the First World War by successive governments of all political persuasions, had ensured the decline and fall of British military power, and more pointedly the demise of the Royal Navy as a world-beating force.

At the time of the Falklands War – and possibly a trigger to it – a further cutback was in the offing. Margaret Thatcher's Defence Secretary John Nott was in the throes of making more swingeing reductions, under which even the newest aircraft carrier *Invincible* might be sold off. In a plan for the future with the unoriginal title of *The Way Forward*, the thinking was once again reductive and primarily focused on Europe, where Britain and her NATO Allies faced a great concentration of Warsaw Pact forces.

There were four points highlighted: to provide an independent element of nuclear forces committed to the NATO Alliance; defending the United Kingdom homeland; a major land and air contribution on the European mainland; and deploying a major maritime capability in the eastern Atlantic and the Channel. This was a crucial statement that vividly came to be questioned when the Falklands conflict arose. Since the late 1960s, when the last of the colonial troubles faded, there had been a steady reduction in the capability of the three services to support large deployments outside the NATO area. All the demands of the Falklands Task Force – as it was soon to be known – were met, but only by giving it first call on resources and by using some stocks earmarked for

NATO operations. By the beginning of the 1980s, there was already considerable difficulty in terms of equipment and manpower in meeting the challenges of 'out-of-area' operations, a fact that the Ministry of Defence later admitted having had the benefit of the Falklands War to discover this shortfall in capability. Even so, what now began to unfold made the operation to meet Margaret Thatcher's demands for an immediate recapture of the Falklands all the more remarkable. The campaign, which was to test the British military like nothing else had in years, was launched after the sudden invasion of the Falkland Islands by Argentine forces on 2 April 1982. The next day they invaded South Georgia. Three days after the invasion, HMS *Hermes* and HMS *Invincible* left the United Kingdom to head what was to become the largest Task Force in recent history. Eventually, over 110 ships made the long journey to the Falklands, which, on the other hand, were only 400 miles off the coast of Argentina. They included 44 warships; 22 ships from the Royal Fleet Auxiliary (RFA) and 45 merchant ships, whose civilian crews were all volunteers. Ralf J. S. Wykes Sneyd on *Invincible*:

> I was in command of 820 Squadron Sea King MIV, a new marque of aircraft, a rather sophisticated passive warfare primary helicopter. I had been in command since June the previous year, and at the time we were alongside at Portsmouth having just returned from Norway, where we participated in an Arctic exercise. I was at home when I got the message. We were aware that there was trouble in the South Atlantic, but the speed of developments was surprising. Our job was anti-submarine warfare, but the aircraft we had was primarily orientated against nuclear submarines and, of course, ASW against a conventional threat was rather different from that which we had been practising. Our main task, therefore, was to prepare for ASW and surface surveillance and try to help provide the picture for the command of the fleet. There were also secondary roles, such as replenishment and delivery. There were 200 personnel and nine aircraft in the squadron, augmented by an additional two at the time of sailing. It was fortuitous that we were already in

Portsmouth for a short period of three weeks, and I had decided that, rather than disembark down to our parent station in Cornwall, we would keep the aircraft on board and take leave from the ship. So when the recall happened, we were ready to go quite quickly, whereas other squadrons had to embark themselves and get their people and aircraft together. I think by and large there were very few people on the ship who had had any experience of combat – probably only the captain, who had served in Korea. So I viewed it with a certain amount of apprehension.

After embarking, we had to wait for *Hermes*, which was not worked up and needed a good deal more preparation than ourselves. There was a very large sendoff, a rather momentous occasion, and I think that perhaps impressed on us the gravity of the situation, and the importance of it. It was a striking occasion. We sailed on to Ascension Island, where the fleet was assembling, and there we observed and participated in the tremendous logistics operation. The RAF had been flying out VC10s and C130s full of ammunition and all sorts of stores, and we sat on Ascension for three days taking on all these stores, which was done almost entirely by helicopters, bringing out these tons and tons of stores.

The sheer enormity of the project now began to unfold. The Task Force was to be dispatched in two phases, and engaged the joint logistical skills of the three services as well as the Merchant Navy, the Royal Dockyards, commercial ports and many firms in private industry who rallied to the call for specialist material. The Task Force had to be stocked and provisioned for at least three months at sea. Many of the merchant ships, including luxury liners such as the *QE2* and *Canberra* and such utility vessels as North Sea car ferries, required extensive modification to prepare them for their new role before setting off. The Task Force needed to be self-sufficient in food, water, fuel, ammunition and all the other military equipment it might require. The ships of the Royal Fleet Auxiliary and the Merchant Navy and the Royal Air Force's transport aircraft were to be the Task Force's lifeline. Merchant shipping alone transported 9,000 personnel, 100,000 tons of freight and 95 aircraft to the South Atlantic. The supply chain carried 400,000 tons of fuel. RFA support ships transferred ammunition, dry cargo and fuel on some 1,200 occasions, in addition to more than 300 helicopter transfers.

The British forces established a joint forward operating base at Ascension Island. The Royal Air Force moved over 5,800 people and 6,600 tons of stores through Ascension Island in more than 600 sorties by Hercules and VC10 aircraft. As the ships reached the Falklands, Hercules aircraft also made some 40 supply drops to the Task Force, which entailed mid-air refuelling in round trips lasting, in many cases, over 25 hours. Through these various means, 28,000 men and over 100 ships were assembled to take on a sizeable army and combat aircraft that outnumbered their own by more than six to one. While the ships of the main force were still gathering at Ascension, on 12 April the British government announced a maritime exclusion zone of 200 miles around the Falklands against Argentine naval ships and later warned that any approach by Argentine forces which could amount to a threat to interfere with the mission of the British forces in the South Atlantic would be dealt with 'appropriately'. Meanwhile, the tension was building for the oncoming Task Force. Wykes Sneyd:

We knew we would be facing a different sort of enemy than in the Cold War scenario and we really had to adjust our skills quite considerably. This demanded a great deal of work, because we would be facing weapon systems that were quite different from those we had envisaged as opposition in an East–West conflict. Among them was the Exocet missile, which was one of those we hadn't addressed as opposition. We also had to start thinking about surviving against fighter aircraft attacks, which was something, in our particular specialisation, we hadn't considered as an enormous threat, because we had trained for operations on the high seas. But we had the time to devote to develop and practise the techniques required.

We knew a certain amount about their ships and aircraft. Their two main submarines were small and going to be a formidable opponent, difficult to detect. We were using active sonar, which was not the principal method of detection we had been used to. So, generally, the journey down was also about progressively adjusting people's minds to what was to come and preparing them for it. We had to make sure, for example, that people were as fit as they might be. We'd been flying throughout the journey to Ascension and then we steadied down, providing a continuous screen around the force as we went down as well as conducting surface surveillance. We had one or two contacts, but there was some doubt as to whether they were submarines. There was a tremendous amount of marine life in the South Atlantic, more than we had been used to in ASW operations in the past. It therefore took quite a long time for people to settle down and get used to the type of environment they were operating in.

That continued on until we reached the exclusion zone, and by this stage people were pretty keen to get on with it, and get the job done. That weekend, we heard that we were going into the zone and one was constantly aware of morale, and despite the jingoism in the newspapers at the time of our departure, people were concerned as to what was going to happen. I had 200 people in my squadron, and it was clearly going to be a big operation, and you had to start thinking about people in a slightly different way.

In my case, of course, I had in my squadron a member of the royal family [Prince Andrew] and that was quite interesting because there was no doubt that there were people who were thinking it wasn't such a good thing for him to be participating. In my mind, it was absolutely crucial to the rest of my organisation that he should participate, from the point of view of morale. As far as I was concerned, I was his commanding officer, he was there to be a pilot, and that he should come, and he felt that too. But like everyone else, he was apprehensive about it. I may have laid it on a bit thick, but I also told him that when we reached the stage where it all becomes rather real, that if things got too exciting there was always a way that we could get him out if that was the thing that needed to be done. I'm not too sure I necessarily believed that myself, but as time went by he was as committed as anyone else and his role became no different from any other sub-lieutenant pilot. By and large he did what any junior pilot did and was not given any particularly difficult missions above the norm, because those missions were given to people who I might describe as my first 11. But he did his bit in the way I would expect an officer of his seniority to do. But his presence gave one a bit more to think about.

Meanwhile, the advance party of Royal Marines, SAS and SBS, which had assembled at Ascension, sailed ahead in the Royal Fleet Auxiliary tanker *Tidespring* under the protection of the destroyer *Antrim* and the ageing frigate *Plymouth*. Two nuclear submarines, *Conqueror* and *Splendid*, shadowed the group, which reached the island of South Georgia on 21 April, 800 miles north-east of the Falklands and not actually part of them. It had a small Argentine garrison but also possessed the most inhospitable landscape, with whirlwinds whipping up driving snow across treacherous glaciers. The SAS were first ashore, landing reconnaissance patrols on the hazardous Fortuna glacier. Within 12 hours they called for helicopters to evacuate them immediately because of the appalling conditions and impossible terrain. Two Wessex Mk 5 helicopters from *Tidespring* were sent to extract them but both crashed on the glacier when the pilots became disorientated and lost the horizon, which merged with the sky in white-out conditions. An ancient single-engine Wessex 3 from *Antrim* piloted by Lieutenant-Commander Stanley in suicidal conditions brought the SAS team and the crashed helicopter crews back to the ship, leaving the force's only two troop-lift helicopters destroyed on the glacier.

Then *Tidespring*, with the main body of M Company on board, set out to sea after reports on an enemy submarine prowling in the area. The Argentine submarine *Santa Fe* was sighted on the surface five miles out from Grytiken by Lieutenant-Commander Stanley. He attacked her with machine-gun fire and depth charges, which stopped her from diving until two British missile-carrying helicopters arrived to deliver a more devastating blow. The submarine was left badly damaged and later beached off the Falklands. The marines' landing on South Georgia now went ahead with the backing of guns from *Antrim*, and before long the Argentinians ran up the white flag. The garrison consisted of 137 men who, on 26 April, became the first prisoners of war. Back in London, Mrs Thatcher dashed out of the front door of No. 10 Downing Street and in front of television cameras shouted: 'Rejoice, rejoice. South Georgia has been recaptured.'

Meanwhile, as the Task Force was heading south, SAS and SBS patrols prepared to go ashore on the Falklands proper. They were inserted on 1 May to carry out reconnaissance of enemy positions. With them were two Naval Gunnery Control parties who were to survey and eventually direct naval gunfire on Argentine positions. Some of those units spent up to three weeks ashore, roaming across the windswept landscape gleaning intelligence.

On 1 May an RAF Vulcan bomber, flown from Britain with the help of air-to-air refuelling tankers, followed by Sea Harriers, carried out the first attacks on the Falklands, and the first Argentine aircraft were shot down. On the same day, the carrier group of *Invincible* and *Hermes* simulated an amphibious landing off Port Stanley to draw the Argentinians and reveal their defensive positions. The following day, one of the most controversial attacks of the war occurred when the submarine *Conqueror* detected the Argentine cruiser *General Belgrano*, accompanied by two destroyers, sailing towards the exclusion zone. Other Argentine ships were also thought to be probing defences to the north of the zone. *Belgrano* and her escorts, armed with Exocet missiles, were judged at Northwood command and control centre to be a clear threat to the ships of the Task Force. With the approval of Margaret Thatcher, she was sunk by torpedoes fired from *Conqueror* with the loss of 362 lives, although more than 800 survivors were picked up by accompanying ships. Thereafter, major Argentine warships remained within 12 miles of the Argentine coast and took no further part in the campaign, although Argentine submarines continued to pose a serious threat.

An even greater threat came from the Exocet missiles launched from Argentine Super Etendard aircraft, and on 4 May the Task Force suffered its first major setback when the 4,100-ton destroyer *Sheffield*, just five years old and costing £37 million, was hit while on forward radar picket duty. The missile struck fuel tanks amidships, killing 24 members of crew and wounding another 63. Serious fires filled the entire central section of the ship with acrid smoke, and after the crew struggled to quell the flames for almost five hours it became apparent that they were fighting a losing battle. Captain James Salt gave orders to abandon ship:

> We could feel the heat of the deck through our shoes. The superstructure was steaming. Paint on the ship's side was peeling off, and the area where the missile penetrated was white-hot. The whole working area of the ship was a roaring mass of flames, and we could see right down into the engine room. It was my decision to abandon ship, and I felt awful about it, but there was no alternative.

By mid-May the Task Force had accomplished two of its main objectives: the movement of the troops safely to the South Atlantic and the establishment of control of the seas around the islands. The role of the carriers *Hermes* and *Invincible* was crucial at this and subsequent stages in providing air defence and the means of attacking enemy ships and ground positions, while their helicopters provided constant anti-submarine protection. There were, however, shortcomings in the airborne early-warning capability, and other methods of attempting to abort the Exocet attacks were tried, as Wykes Sneyd pointed out:

> When *Sheffield* was hit, it was a moment of major significance and it had a very sobering effect. Here was a modern destroyer taken out by something we had no experience of. Initially, it was thought it was a torpedo, and it wasn't until some time after she was hit that it was realised that it was an Exocet. Also, it was a salutary lesson in just how sharp we'd got to be. It was in a way the price to pay to get the fleet into top gear and be really alert, because maybe there were those having difficulty in coming to terms with the fact that this was hundred per cent real and it really did affect them.
>
> It began to focus people's attention as to who were the pawns and who were the kings and queens of the chessboard.

Undoubtedly, we found that the expectation was that there would be a lot more pawns going down and that the king and the queen, to use a rather poor analogy for the two aircraft carriers, were absolutely vital. Without them, any thought of being able to retake those islands vanished. I think that initial period of finding oneself quite a long way from the islands quite surprising. But the philosophy was that we were wearing away at the problem, but making sure that we didn't expose ourselves to more risks than we really needed to. We wouldn't have been able to land on the islands without that essential air cover.

Interestingly, missions were faced that contained more risks than one thought about in the past. We knew jolly well that if we lost an aircraft, we were not going to get another one for eight weeks or so. And if you lost a crew with your aircraft, it was even more expensive, and the whole idea was to get the mission done with the minimum of risk. We stayed very much within peacetime rules in the way we flew our aircraft and to the limits in which we flew, and still completed the mission. I took the view that all these rules for aircraft clearances and deck limits had been tried and tested and there was no point in risking losses by going beyond them. Throughout May and the entire conflict, we were working from *Invincible*. Our squadron was looking after the carriers, in ASW and surface surveillance, and we were the last people to be tasked to do the other tasks, in general. We kept up this screen day and night through the conflict.

The prime threat was perceived to be the Exocet, and a good deal of work was done in studying the missiles and how we best dealt with them. You either try to knock them out of the sky – but we didn't have the capability – or you try to decoy them by throwing out lots of chaff [strips of metallic foil released to deflect radar signals and prevent detection]. But it became apparent that we were going to get through a great deal of this very quickly, and we needed to find an alternative decoy. What we did was make a radar reflector which we strapped on to a Sea King, and flew the aircraft on the side of a ship during an Exocet raid. We knew more or less where it would come in, the idea being that the missile would pick up this radar contact and be deflected towards it. It was quite safe, because the helicopter would hover just above the height at which the Exocet would fly through. With that experience we began to get confidence in dealing with the Exocet, and indeed with other things, such as the torpedo threat. It was always present, and the conditions of the water made it more difficult to detect submarines. Also, towards the end, the Argentinians started air raids with modern aiming methods, which was much more worrying. And always, of course, at the back of our minds was the possibility of submarines whose detection was our prime task.

These air defences were again crucial when the Task Force began its first large-scale amphibious landings under fire since the Second World War as a first step to repossess the islands. San Carlos was chosen as the site of the amphibious landings because it offered a good anchorage, which could be protected against submarine attack, and was an area known to be lightly defended by the enemy. Low hills surrounding the inlet provided good protection against the risk of Exocet attack, and detachments from the SAS and the SBS had already spent many days reconnoitring the area. Utilising the intelligence they had gained, and supported by a substantial navy bombardment, the SAS carried out a daring night raid on Pebble Island on 15 May. They destroyed 11 Argentine aircraft on the ground.

On 20 May the main amphibious force moved towards San Carlos Water, taking advantage of an overcast sky and poor visibility, and keeping strict radio silence. Meanwhile, the Special Forces mounted a series of diversionary raids at various points around East Falkland. Again with supporting naval gunfire, men of the 3rd Commando Brigade, RM, including the 2nd and 3rd Battalions, the Parachute Regiment, embarked their landing craft and headed for the shore. The landing was made over four beaches. Helicopters operated continuously, moving stores and helping to establish the beachhead. The operation achieved complete tactical surprise. Five thousand men were safely landed, and what little opposition there was quickly collapsed. British losses in this phase were two helicopters and their crews.

The next morning brought clear blue skies, but the landing force had won a vital few hours to establish defensive positions and to set up Rapier land-based missile units. At midday the Argentine air force began a series of fierce attacks against the beachhead and the ships supporting it. Sea Harriers on combat air patrol provided the outer layer of defence. The second layer was provided by a pair of ships known as the 'missile trap', positioned off the northern entrance to Falkland Sound. Destroyers and frigates armed with Sea Dart and Sea Wolf missiles provided the next layer of defence, and finally, in what became known as the 'gunline', a group of four ships was positioned inside the entrance to the Sound using every gun and missile system they possessed to fight off the incoming waves of attacking aircraft. Within the anchorage itself – nicknamed 'bomb alley' and where up to eight troop or stores ships unloaded at any one time – there were small-calibre guns and Sea Cat missiles being fired from the assault ships *Intrepid* and *Fearless*, together with Blowpipe missiles, machine guns and the Rapier fire units on shore.

The Argentine pilots continued their attacks, and ships of the Task Force suffered severe loss and damage during the first few days after the landing. On the 'gunline', the frigate *Ardent* was sunk on 21 May and her replacement, *Antelope*, was sunk on 23 May with the loss of 24 men killed and 52 others wounded on the two ships. Six other ships were damaged between 21 and 24 May, although 43 aircraft were shot down in the barrage of return fire from the defensive screen described above. Further heavy aircraft attacks were expected on 25 May, Argentina's National Day, and the worst fears of the British battle commanders were realised. The enemy jets once again came swooping in. The destroyer *Coventry*, which had not long entered the 'missile trap' to the north-west, had success-fully shot down three aircraft herself before she was singled out for a low-level attack by waves of Skyhawk aircraft and was hit by three bombs, which penetrated deep into her hull before exploding, killing 19 of her crew.

She capsized quickly, and survivors were rescued by *Broadsword* and helicopters. This setback apart, the attacks became less frequent and the British forces were safely established ashore. The battle of San Carlos had been won, providing an important confirmation, and a lesson for the future, of the successful use of the assault ships *Fearless* and *Intrepid* to launch and support amphibious operations. Helicopters deployed with the landing force also played an invaluable part and, of course, these were operations that, in the past, had only ever occurred as exercises and few of those under such conditions.

The first landings were thus secure, but the threat to the main body of the Task Force remained as strong as ever, and on 25 May the merchant ship *Atlantic Conveyor*, which had delivered Harriers to the Task Force and was also carrying much-needed supplies, including helicopters, was north-east of the Falklands when she was attacked by a flight of Super Etendard aircraft and was hit by two Exocet missiles. The explosion caused a major fire that spread rapidly and the ship had to be abandoned, with the loss of 12 lives and a dozen other casualties. It was a tragic loss and robbed the British of much-needed helicopters, which were to have been used to move the ground forces across the Falklands.

With the establishment of a firm bridgehead, the advance on Port Stanley became the next objective. One threat to the flank of any attack on Port Stanley lay in the significant Argentine garrison and airfield at Darwin and Goose Green. The task of removing those dangers was given to 2 Para and, seeking an early victory, overnight on 26–27 May one company of 2 Para secured Camilia Creek House. After a 12-mile night approach march, the rest of the battalion joined them. An artillery troop of three 105-millimetre light guns was flown into position to assist in the impending assault, which started at 0200 hours on 28 May.

Supported by naval gunfire, 2 Para began by attacking Darwin. The settlement was secured by mid-afternoon, but the battalion was then faced with an advance on Goose Green, where the enemy were dug in to strong defensive positions which had to be approached across the open ground of a narrow isthmus. Harrier aircraft were called in to attack the Argentine positions. The battalion was attacked by Pucara light aircraft from Goose Green, one of which was shot down by a Blowpipe missile. The battalion eventually overcame stiff resistance and pushed the enemy back into the settlement. A timely strike by the Harriers helped the progress of the paratroopers, and the next day the Argentine commander surrendered. British dead totalled 17.

Meanwhile, after a march of 50 miles over difficult terrain in inhospitable conditions, 45 Commando and 3 Para secured Douglas settlement and Teal Inlet on 30 May, while the SAS established a patrol base forward on Mount Kent. Making best use of the helicopter lift available, 42 Commando leapfrogged forward to secure Mount Kent and Mount Challenger, the western approaches to Port Stanley. The 5th Infantry Brigade came ashore on 1 June and the land force commanders now pressed on towards Port Stanley. When it was discovered that the Argentinians had evacuated Fitzroy settlement, 2 Para moved forward rapidly to secure the area, which was an important point in the advance on Port Stanley. The 1st Battalion, 7th Duke of Edinburgh's Own Gurkha Rifles, and the rest of 2 Para advanced by sea and by air while the 2nd Battalion, Scots Guards, the 1st Battalion, Welsh Guards, and logistical support units were transported to Fitzroy by sea.

On the nights 5–6 and 6–7 June the Scots Guards and elements of the Welsh Guards were successfully moved by *Intrepid* and *Fearless*. The deployment of the balance of the Welsh Guards was halted by appalling weather, and the following night they were carried forward by the landing ships *Sir Galahad* and *Sir Tristram* when a strong air attack came in. Three bombs hit *Sir Galahad*, which was completely burned out. *Sir Tristram* was also hit and severely damaged, but the attack brought the worst casualties of the invasion: 57 soldiers and crew killed and 46 injured, many of them severely. Courageous efforts of helicopter pilots and naval rescue crews saved many more, taking their craft into the flames again and again.

By 11 June, however, the first phase of the battle for Port Stanley was under way, with targets bombarded by naval vessels ahead of the move by 3 Commando Brigade to Mount Harriet and Two Sisters while 3 Para took Mount Longdon. They were all hard-fought battles, with British casualties put at 22 killed and 44 wounded. That night, the destroyer *Glamorgan* was withdrawing from a bombardment of shore positions around Port Stanley when she was hit by a shore-launched Exocet missile, killing 13 of her crew and wounding 18 others. Her company extinguished severe fires and the ship continued to be available for action. It was the last direct attack on a British ship in the campaign. The final land battles were in progress, with 2 Para's night attack on Wireless Ridge and the Scots Guards taking Tumbledown Mountain from a regular Argentine marine battalion whose heavily defended machine-gun emplacements put up fierce resistance for a number of hours. Once the Guards had secured their objectives, the Gurkhas moved through to take Mount William to the south-east. In this final phase, 20 men were killed, and thankfully they were the last casualties. Soon afterwards, white flags were reported over Port Stanley and the Argentinians surrendered.

This had been a unique operation in terms of securing an amphibious landing within range of enemy aircraft and without the assistance of airborne early-warning aircraft or land-based all-weather fighters for protection. Ships were inevitably at risk, and though the casualties were bad enough they were well within the range of expectation, and a good deal less than worst-case scenarios. In addition to the four warships, one RFA and one merchant ship were lost; eight other warships and two RFAs suffered varying degrees of damage. In all but three cases, the damaged ships were patched up sufficiently well by their own crews, or with the help of specialist teams, to continue in operations. As in the Second World War, important information was gleaned about the performance of ships under fire in relation to materials and reactions to smoke and fire, which in some cases spread far more rapidly than might have been expected and, again, in some situations smoke was a particular problem, especially that derived from cabling on older ships which had never been previously exposed to such intense heat. A good deal of study and experimentation followed, recommendations coming forward for improved fire zones; changes to the design of watertight doors and hatches; the provision of more escape hatches; resiting fuel tanks; and reducing the amount of inflammable materials.

As to the performance of carrier-based aircraft, the case for reducing the size of the Fleet Air Arm, which had been regularly cut back in successive defence spending reviews, was proved to be a total misnomer. The record was one of brilliant performance:

313

*Fixed-wing aircraft*: 28 Sea Harriers flew 1,960 combat air patrol missions and 90 offensive support operations, while 14 RAF Harrier GR3s flew 125 ground attack and tactical reconnaissance sorties. Sea Harriers, which were intended largely for air defence, were also employed in ground attack and reconnaissance roles: the Harrier GR3s, primarily ground air attack, were converted within a week to use Sidewinder AIM 9L air-to-air missiles in the air defence role. Six Sea Harriers were destroyed, of which two were lost to enemy fire – one to small-arms fire and one to a surface-to-air missile. Three GR3s were also lost to enemy fire, all to ground gunfire. Most aircraft engaged in offensive support survived damage, which usually resulted from intense Argentine anti-aircraft gunfire.

*Helicopters*: Almost 200 helicopters of seven different types (Sea King, Wessex, Lynx, Gazelle, Wasp, Scout and Chinook) were deployed and many were in the air virtually non-stop. After the loss of three Chinooks and six Wessex in *Atlantic Conveyor*, there was a shortage of helicopters to support the ground forces even though a squadron of Sea King ASW helicopters was converted to the support role. A single Chinook that survived the sinking of *Atlantic Conveyor* was one of the stars – with spares and ground support it flew 109 hours in combat conditions, carrying up to 80 armed troops in a single lift. In addition, helicopters were also heavily committed in the ASW or anti-surface vessel warfare (ASVW) role, logistics, search and rescue, casualty evacuation and reconnaissance or support roles.

The final tally showed that the naval aircraft operated at over three times peacetime rates as they faced an efficient land-based force of over 200 front-line aircraft, with virtually no fighter aircraft to respond. Consequently, the Task Force had to rely on a mix of systems for air defence, some of them invented on the spot. The result was that 72 enemy aircraft were shot down and a further 14 listed as probable kills. By the time of the final assault on Port Stanley, the Argentine air force had been effectively neutralised as a fighting force.

The post-war analysis also highlighted another vital aspect, and it arose out of the much-criticised sinking of *General Belgrano*. Quite apart from the debate as to whether she was inside or outside the required 200-mile exclusion zone when torpedoed, it was very clear that the Royal Navy established immediate 'strategic dominance' through its nuclear submarines by the sinking of the cruiser, which meant that the Argentine fleet kept well out of the way. The greatest threat of all, the aircraft carrier *25th of May*, never materialised. Had that situation been any different, casualties would undoubtedly have been far higher on the British side, and the task would have been so much more difficult to fulfil.

There was one other significant contribution that would be retained, examined and expanded for the future, and especially in the Gulf War and later in Kosovo, and that was in the use of civilian resources. Around 45 commercial ships were hired in and converted for appropriate action, ranging from the most luxurious of all passenger liners to humble trawlers. All the ships were manned by volunteer, civilian crews, supplemented by small naval or RFA parties. Some of the conversions were major works, completed in astoundingly swift time, including the fitting of temporary flight decks, which were designed and constructed in a matter of days and subsequently stood up to extremes of weather, and fully equipped hospitals, which allowed the medics of the three services to deal with all casualties who needed surgery within six hours or less, resulting in a 90 per cent survival rate.

These were all aspects that tend to be overlooked in the public examination and recounting of modern naval history but which the analysts paw over with great regard. In the case of the Falklands, apart from being a classic and courageous example of amphibious warfare under difficult and in some cases make-do-and-mend conditions, it threw up many scenarios that, once corrected, would save lives in the future.

# CHAPTER SEVENTEEN

## A Clash of Values

The return of the Task Force from the Falklands renewed the British public's fascination by and pride for the rare sight of the big ships sailing home, especially *QE2* and carriers like the old warhorse *Hermes* and the almost-new *Invincible*, which returned battle weary but relatively unscathed to a magnificent welcome home. Crowds, tearful and cheering, lined every inch of available dockside at Portsmouth waving Union Flags in scenes reminiscent of the arrival of conquering heroes of the Second World War. Prime Minister Margaret Thatcher was there to see *Hermes* sail in and then, a little later, the Queen and Prince Philip arrived to give *Invincible* a royal reception, and, of course, to be reunited with their son, Prince Andrew, who famously ran up and down the dockside with a red rose between his teeth.

Behind these scenes of jubilation, however, were some serious matters that would require the attention of both the politicians and the Ministry of Defence. Under the cuts proposed by the then Defence Secretary, John Nott, prior to the invasion of the Falklands, *Invincible* was to be sold off to Australia, although only four years old. That decision had been taken at a time when major investment had been earmarked for the submarine fleet, thus extending the reliance on submarines in the role of capital ships. First, at the turn of the new decade of the 1980s, plans were approved to replace the Polaris squadron with the much-vaunted Trident nuclear fleet. The Tridents were scheduled for completion in 1994, when Polaris would be almost 20 years old. The cost would be enormous: £14 billion, plus £200 million a year running costs. In addition, the new *Trafalgar* class of hunter-killer nuclear-powered fleet submarines was scheduled for progressive production through to 1993. Further, the new *Upholder* class of diesel-powered submarine was also approved and the first boats scheduled for completion by the end of the decade. With tremendous advances in conventional technology, the ships were heralded as great additions to the British fleet, but in the event never saw service. Only four were built, and they were immediately mothballed before being sold to Canada.

All these decisions, and the commitment to very substantial costs, were taken at a time when the future of the Royal Navy's surface fleet was being reviewed. The budgetary increases for the navy as a whole were seen by the Treasury as unsustainable, and it had been decided that only two carriers were to remain in service: *Illustrious*, completed soon after the Falklands War in 1982, and *Ark Royal*, which was scheduled for completion in 1985. Third in the *Invincible* class and the fifth ship of the Royal Navy to bear the name, *Ark Royal* was larger than her two sisters, at 683 feet long. She has a maximum beam of 117 feet and a displacement of 20,000 tons. She has Olympus gas-turbine engines that give a maximum speed in excess of 30 knots, and a steeper ski jump than in the other ships of this class is fitted at the forward end of the flight deck. *Ark Royal* was built to remain in service until at least 2012, when the next generation of aircraft carriers will enter service.

However, after the experience of the Falklands, when the apparent shortcomings in anti-submarine warfare and airborne early-warning capabilities were apparent in 'out-of-area' situations, it was immediately decided to abandon plans to sell *Invincible* to enable the Royal Navy to have at least two carriers at sea at any one time, given that refits and servicing would keep one of them out of service for long periods. The ancient *Hermes* was already out of the equation, destined to be sold to India. And so all three of the *Invincible*-class carriers remained on the Royal Navy's inventory and would do so well into the twenty-first century.

Cuts were to be enforced elsewhere, however, and that would become apparent purely from manpower figures of the coming decade. The Royal Navy, already having difficulty in manning all its ships, had 72,000 staff and 70 destroyers and frigates after the Falklands War. Ten years later, that figure was down to 55,000 staff and 40 such ships – and falling, although by then the effects of the end of the Cold War were also being felt. By 2003 the number of destroyers and frigates was down to 32. But a percentage of the reduction in manpower and general cost cutting also came from the gradual arrival of major changes in the way the navy was run.

Many of its shore-based establishments, such as the training school HMS *Ganges*, had already been closed down. Dockyards and other navy-run service units were being shut in favour of contracting out. New systems of accounting, man management, private contracting of support ships and even the leasing of warships were all to be employed to trim down the navy's cost base, much to the despair of many of the traditionalists, and some apprehension among the modernists who thought the whole process would result in the decimation of the Royal Navy to a point where it was no longer capable of meeting the challenges of the future.

All of this was carried out against a background of the continuing pressure of the Cold War and commitments to NATO's requirements to provide an effective and ongoing deterrent to possible engagements with Soviet-bloc forces at a time when the collapse of that threat and the dissolution of the USSR were nowhere in sight. Throughout most of the 1970s and 1980s, the Royal Navy provided core elements in intelligence and defensive activities against the navies of the USSR and the rest of the Communist bloc, both through the activities of the surface fleet and the submarines. At the same time, patrols at home called for a major commitment against arms shipments off the coasts of Ireland at the height of the IRA bombing campaigns, while overseas there was still intermittent activity around former colonies, especially in Africa and the Middle East, which required a naval presence in policing arms shipments, drug runners and even slave traders.

These were nervous and difficult times, passing through great troughs of international tension when the cut and thrust of East–West maritime operations led opposing ships to come close to blows on many occasions. The extent of the pressure on those involved – officers and ratings – during those years was seldom publicly acknowledged, simply because the bumps and bangs between opposing ships passing in the night or observing each other's exercises were never revealed because quite often they were supposedly top secret, although both sides generally knew what the other was up to. For the nuclear-loaded ballistic submarines, the pressures were even greater. Captain Geoffrey Jacques became one of the first Polaris commanders on *Revenge*:

The most significant factor of all was that we had a true submersible and one that was virtually silent in every respect when under way. Instead of having submarines which generally moved about on the surface, and had a limited period for endurance dived, suddenly there was a submarine that could stay dived, travelling as fast as it could for as long as was necessary, limited only by human nature. Initially, the average patrol lasted six to eight weeks, although there was no specific pattern because others might recognise it. Indeed, our first challenge was to get out of the Clyde and into deep water without being detected by the Russian ships, which were waiting for just that purpose. They were surveillance boats, converted fishing vessels, which were run by Soviet naval intelligence.

There was always one on station off Malin Head, and there were others about. One of their primary roles was to try to detect you coming out and ideally pass you over to a Russian nuclear submarine that would then stay on your trail. So the whole essence was one of cloak-and-dagger and cat-and-mouse. You'd never go out at set times or set dates. All sorts of measures were taken to avoid being pinpointed by the Soviets, and the whole point of the exercise was to get out there into the ocean undetected by anybody. Safe cruising depths were about 100 feet, so that any ship passing over the top would not cause a problem. Then you would choose your depth according to water conditions and what exactly you are trying to do, such as hiding, or you may take the view that you want to be able to hear and pick up someone else. So you have lots of priorities to weigh up in accordance with intelligence on who else might be in your area. You also have to balance this with communications.

The Polaris boats never spoke to anyone but were always constantly listening. We were given very large areas for our patrols, and no one would know where you were in that area so that everything was done to make sure you could remain undetected, and one of the best ways of achieving that was the freedom to operate in a large area and go where you liked.

The ship's navigational management people and senior officers were the only ones who knew where we were. North Norwegian Sea, right round the western Atlantic, the Mediterranean . . . if one assumes we were looking towards Russia, you just take your compass and take the range of the missiles and choose where you want to put people. Northwood headquarters gave you your water in which to operate and made it as large as possible, so you had complete freedom. You would have intelligence and knowledge of national, European and NATO naval activities because you would want to avoid getting involved in those areas, and we were fed as much intelligence on the movement of other people as they had available, so that you could keep out of everybody's way. In a sense, everyone else was the enemy, because the object of the patrols was to remain undetected. As far as I am aware, none of the patrols was ever compromised.

In regard to the missiles, target information came in sealed tapes. They were loaded into the computer that had various verification functions which said it had accepted the tape and recognised it, but the coordinates of possible targets were never displayed anywhere. There was a procedure to follow if that had happened. The missiles themselves were connected to the inertial navigator, so that they knew where they were starting from. The missiles were given the target coordinates and, when you fired them, on-board computers did the rest. It was a wonderful system, and whenever we had to fire the missiles on the test range in the USA the system always worked. Of all the gunnery systems one has had throughout one's time in the service, there were good days and bad days, but in my experience this one never had bad days. It was an incredible piece of engineering. It was a solid-fuel rocket, no nasty gases or liquids to handle, a very impressive system.

We were at the absolute sharp end of the Cold War, although it was never set up as a first-strike weapon, and we were all made aware of that. It was always there as a deterrent. As to our own feelings about being the deliverer of such a powerful force, one always felt that in the scenario that you might have to press this button, there would be so much chaos and mayhem going on, everything you'd ever stood and lived for was probably in smithereens, and you would have wanted to hit the button anyway. The scenario would have been filled with such doom and gloom that I don't think you'd have a problem if you received the signal to go, to get on with it. Also, I always had the feeling that it was a deterrent, and it was going to work, and because we had got it and because it was so awful, we were most unlikely ever to be faced with the problem. The system itself seemed to be so good, you felt confident that you had a system that was going to work and was recognised as such worldwide.

If you are going to have an effective deterrent, (a) you must be able to deliver a system to the other side that does work, (b) they have to know it is going to work, and (c) that you'll certainly use it. I really do believe that deterrents work, and it really did work. It was capable of enormous damage and therefore, providing you had a sane adversary who would not want this inflicted on him, then you did have a very nice big system. I don't think any of the COs had any hang-ups about what on earth we would do if we got a firing signal. I certainly didn't. I think in advance we would have already heard of how things were deteriorating, that there had been exchanges and that nuclear weapons had already fallen on London, Birmingham and the like. The firing signals, as far as we were concerned, had all kinds of built-in checks and balances, which started in 10 Downing Street and ended up in the CO's cabin. There were keys involved, and there was a set of procedures that had to be gone through in stages, with two people checking each stage and each other. It was a very elaborate system, and if it had ever come about there would have been no misunderstanding; you would be absolutely confident that you had the right instructions.

The surface fleet was also fully committed to Cold War operations, especially on the old routes of the Second World War convoys. Like the Soviets, many ships were engaged in surveillance and reconnaissance, along with major deployments on exercises arranged under the auspices of NATO, constantly updating training, intelligence procedures and battle plans should ever an East–West conflict arise. The surface fleet in these years, along with the fleet submarines of the *Valiant*, *Churchill* and *Swiftsure* classes, also had the role of upholding the defence against the 'alternative' scenario to a holocaust – that although the Soviets might not wish to begin throwing nuclear ballistics around, it was always possible that they would engage in a conventional encounter. In 1988 NATO staged its now-famous exercise, Teamwork 88, a massive demonstration of its maritime capability and strategy in which the Royal Navy contributed substantially. Less than a year later, the Cold War was all over.

The great Communist monolith finally crumbled and that, for the Royal Navy and all British military units, meant further scrutiny by the Treasury to discover what further reductions in cost could now be achieved. This study was under way by the early 1990s, when Malcolm Rifkind became Defence Secretary, and although he was considered a friend of the navy it was apparent that a further diminution was on the cards, although 'out-of-area' events once again took a hand to steady the tiller, if only temporarily.

Ten years earlier, the outbreak of the Iran–Iraq War brought a period of uncertainty and disruption to the Gulf that was to last for the rest of the century and beyond, threatening oil supplies. The ongoing instability was all too evident as these words were being prepared in 2003. At the time, Operation Armilla was launched to protect British shipping and commercial interests passing through the Gulf area, but the operation, which became known as the Armilla Patrol, was still in place 23 years later, at the time of the second Gulf War. It was maintained to ensure a Royal Navy presence to provide reassurance to friendly Gulf States and to 'act as a tangible demonstration of UK engagement in the region'. It was subsequently given an additional mandate to enforce a United Nations trade embargo against Iraq following the 1991 Gulf War, to halt illegal smuggling of oil by the Iraqi regime. The operation became an established tour of duty for a small Task Force, accompanied by a detachment of Royal Marines who were given UN authority to stop and search any suspect vessels attempting to leave Iraqi waters, as well as assisting in general surveillance operations against Saddam Hussein's regime with other coalition navies. The extent of the operation at the time before and immediately after the Gulf War was extensive, and even by April 1991 the Royal Navy alone had carried out 3,171 challenges and had sent boarding parties on to 36 ships, and thereafter the patrol continued through the following decade and beyond.

But the history of British involvement in the Gulf was to take another turn at the beginning of 1990 when intelligence, in part gleaned from the Armilla Patrol, suggested that the unstable Saddam was planning a major event following a disagreement with other Arab states over oil prices. As in earlier troubles in Iraq, Kuwait was once again in danger of invasion, of being 'repossessed' by the Iraqis. As early as 10 January 1990, *Ark Royal* was dispatched to the Mediterranean at the head of a Task Group comprising *Sheffield*, *Olmeda* and *Regent*, later joined by *Exeter* and *Manchester*, to join American and other Allied vessels to provide reassurance to Egypt, Turkey and the oil states. This show of force did nothing to deter Saddam's ambitions, and on 2 August his forces invaded the tiny Gulf state and the Western world went to panic stations. For years, Saddam had been courted and fêted by nations in the West, anxious for his oil and trade.

He was routinely supplied by principal nations, such as Britain, America, Germany and France, with arms, tanks, aircraft and materials that were quite obviously intended for the production of weapons of mass destruction. Only a mentally deficient could have believed otherwise. The evidence was already available, stark and horrific. He had been allowed to get away with murder, literally, having used mustard gas against enemy troops in the war with Iran and then killed 4,500 innocent men, women and children and injured hundreds of others in an attack on a Kurdish village during his experiments with chemical and biological warfare in 1987, which the world's powers had conveniently ignored.

In the words of Senator Donald W. Reigle, who chaired a 1994 Senate Committee investigating pre-Gulf War exports to Iraq from the US, panic gripped those nations that had kept up their trade with Saddam Hussein virtually to the day of the invasion of Kuwait. As Reigle recalled: 'Suddenly it dawned on people that we were going to have a real problem facing off against weapons that we had helped create . . . because he [Saddam Hussein] had not been on the bad-guy list at the time.'

By then, anyway, it was too late. Ill-judged assessments that Saddam would never go against his trading partners in the West, that he would not invade Kuwait, or, if he did, that it would be a temporary incursion, proved disastrously wrong. Pentagon military planners produced a stark assessment of what confronted them. William Webster, director of the CIA, said: 'The Iraqis are within eight-tenths of a mile of the Saudi border. If Saddam stays where he is, he'll own 20 per cent of the world's oil reserves, and he's within a few miles of seizing another 20 per cent. Jordan and Yemen will probably tilt towards him. We can expect Arab states to start cutting deals. Iran will be at Iraq's feet. Israel will be threatened.'

By mid-August 1990, Britain and America began the build-up of ships and aircraft in the Gulf region. A flotilla of mine-sweepers, along with naval support and supply vessels, headed for the Gulf, along with a Primary Casualty Reception Vessel unit complete with a hundred-bed air-conditioned hospital built in one of her hangars together with 20 doctors and 40 nurses, and equipped with four Sea King Mk4 helicopters from 846 Naval Air Squadron for the evacuation of casualties.

Meanwhile, Saddam had devastated Kuwait City, taken hundreds of prisoners back to Baghdad, never to be seen again, and in a scenario to be replayed a dozen years later, the United Nations

Security Council burned the midnight oil, huffed and puffed and finally passed a resolution demanding Iraq's withdrawal by 15 January 1991, by which time the damage to Kuwait was enormous, and gave the Iraqi troops sufficient time to set the oil wells ablaze before they departed. Along with the general military build-up, the Royal Navy had progressively deployed more war-ships and support ships to the region, including a large contingent from the ever-present Royal Fleet Auxiliary. Two *Oberon*-class submarines, *Otis* and *Opossum*, also went in early to land SBS and SAS patrols to reconnoitre selected zones for an amphibious landing should it become necessary.

The Task Force began preparing for combat and, although Saddam's navy was of little consequence, the Royal Navy contributed substantially by disposing of those ships that were threatening and providing additional combat and reconnaissance aircraft. These notably entailed the deployment of six Lynx helicopters armed with Sea Skua air-to-sea missiles from 829 Naval Air Squadron from four Royal Navy frigates. Over the three weeks before and during the Gulf War, the squadron sank 15 Iraqi ships, five of them by a single helicopter, Lynx 335, flying from *Cardiff*. Meanwhile, six Sea King Mk4 helicopters from 845 Naval Air Squadron and six from 848 Squadron were used independently of the fleet, giving air support for the 1st Armoured Division.

The Royal Navy's force also played a major role in mine-sweeping and anti-missile operations, a crucial element given that, apart from the British warships, the Allied fleet included eight American aircraft carriers. In one of the few dangerous moments for the fleet, the Iraqis launched a shore-based Silkworm missile attack on the 57,000-ton American battleship *Missouri* and her sister ship *Wisconsin*, which had been employed from the outset bombarding shore positions with their 16-inch guns. The Iraqi missiles were shot out of the sky by Sea Dart missiles fired from the destroyer *Gloucester*, with seconds to spare before they hit the American ships. Meanwhile, old and new minefields laid by the Iraqis were cleared by a flotilla of eight RN minesweepers, which between them accumulated and destroyed more than a thousand mines. Among them was Falklands veteran *Bicester*, which took the honours for clearing more mines than any minesweeper since the Second World War. They also sailed with the American naval strike force, clearing mines ahead of the action, and after the cease-fire *Cattistock* became the first ship to enter Kuwait, sweeping the way for US command ship *LaSalle*. This vital contribution of Royal Navy minesweepers was eventually recognised with the award of a General Service Medal with a Gulf Clasp for all their crews.

Ironically, the US warship *Tripoli*, command ship for the anti-mine operations, was one of only two ships to be hit by mines. She was patched up at sea by the RFA repair vessel *Diligence* and casualties were treated on RFA *Argus*. RFA support and supply vessels were deployed throughout the Gulf and the Mediterranean, and names made famous at the Falklands, such as *Sir Galahad* and *Sir Tristram*, along with *Sir Percivale* and *Sir Bedivere*, delivered the tanks and heavy equipment and then followed up in their traditional role of fleet supplies and replenishment vessels.

The Gulf War was notable for one other famously controversial aspect, an event that would change the face of the male-dominated world of the Royal Navy for ever. In February 1990 the then Armed Forces Minister, Archie Hamilton, announced that for the first time members of the Women's Royal Naval Service would be allowed to go to sea. He told a jovial, if apprehensive, House of Commons that the decision had been taken for two reasons: a severe lack of male recruits, resulting in manning problems, and the evolution of 'social domestic trends'. Less than a year later, Wrens were not only at sea but in a war zone, on board escort and patrol vessels in the Gulf.

This marked the beginning of the end for the Wrens. After a trial period which put 60 female officers and 600 ratings on board 25 Royal Navy ships, the organisation was dissolved and the 4,535 personnel became fully fledged sailors. With the move came the opportunity of training for most of the previously well-guarded male preserves, such as aircrews, pilots, divers, instructors and engineering and supply officers.

The Wrens had been born in 1917 at a time when the military had lost a generation of servicemen on the battlefields and the call went out for women to take on the more menial tasks of war.

Under the leadership of Dame Catherine Furs, 5,000 volunteers, with the motto 'Never at Sea', became secretaries, cooks, cleaners and drivers as well as boat crews and wireless operators. When the First World War ended, the Wrens disbanded but were re-formed for the Second World War. By 1944, 75,000 women had answered the recruiting posters' cry of 'Join the Wrens and free a man to join the fleet'. They fearlessly took on many of the onshore male roles, including ship repair work as bombs exploded around them, rode on dispatch missions in the blackout and worked as deciphers at the top-security Bletchley Park listening post. Although their work brought exceptional praise and regard, the barriers that prevented women from going to sea, and indeed kept them from any front-line military position, remained as firm, even through the years of women's lib. In 1990, however, female officers were allowed to adopt Royal Navy rank titles, women were allowed to go to sea on warships and the rule that forced pregnant women to retire or face a compulsory discharge was ended. But there was no doubting that when women first joined the ships it was a terrible culture shock for all concerned, not least for the wives and girlfriends of sailors. At one time, Royal Navy wives went on the march through the streets of Plymouth, demanding that 'these women' were kept away from their husbands, and the tabloids fuelled their fears with a spate of stories that unsurprisingly were to follow in the vein of 'Sex at sea', 'Naval war over two-timing Wren' and 'Jacuzzi Wren's morning-after pill'. This sea change in life at sea clearly presented problems that would not easily be swept aside. Young, virile men and women, together in such a confined space, were hardly likely to ignore each other. For some it was too much. Among those who quit, Candida Brook told the *Daily Mail* that she was disillusioned and embittered that 'lewd and leering sailors' surrounded her on deck each morning, loudly and with relish discussing the most intimate parts of her body. She claimed that one of them pushed forward and told her: 'Look, love, we know what Wrens are like. I reckon at least half a dozen of us will bed you before the end of this posting.'

Such occurrences were to be expected, and the sensational headlines that the experiment produced gradually drifted away as the novelty wore off as women took their too-long-denied place in the Royal Navy, and indeed across the spectrum of service life, with rewarding and interesting careers.

It was, in fact, an exceedingly opportune time for the merging of the Wrens into mainstream naval life because, as in virtually all areas of the armed forces, the Royal Navy was struggling to meet its annual recruitment targets. Ahead, too, lay an exceedingly busy decade, which would be exacerbated by the decommissioning of the carrier flagship *Ark Royal* prior to going into dry dock for a massive refit and modernisation. She would be out of operation for more than seven years until the refit was completed to keep the ship in good stead for at least another ten years, until the new massive 60,000-ton carriers came into service (see Chapter Eighteen). In the meantime, through the 1990s the carriers remained the core of British naval strength.

Although the Cold War was over, Britain's commitment to NATO continued to represent the major part of the defence budget. As far as naval operations were concerned, the base was much broader, with expanding responsibilities that now included criminal as well as political miscreants, such as patrols against drug runners in the Caribbean and the Mediterranean. In many ways, however, the situation that confronted the Royal Navy was similar to times past – although not on the same scale – whereby military forces, over land and sea, had to be capable of flexible and fast deployment to confront major regional crises anywhere in the world. These would arrive in abundance, along with peace support operations, which called for equally vital flexibility and mobility, as well as an ever-expanding array of skills both in relation to the technology of modern warfare and in undertaking the humanitarian roles required in the aftermath of conflict and local wars.

Notwithstanding the speed and power of the fleet submarines, however, British naval Task Forces for these operations were principally built around aircraft carriers, which were capable of delivering a potent air-assault capability as well as a swift and versatile deployment of troops and Commandos, the latter usually for covert operations and the former often dispatched in a blaze of publicity to an area where, as the navy itself puts it, 'we can then poise for extended periods on the high seas and in allied territorial waters anywhere in the world; it can be held over the horizon, or be visible inshore, in support of political objectives'. Numerous eventualities were arising that could be ticked off on the calendar throughout the 1990s – Bosnia and the Balkan conflicts, various African states' troubles (notably Sierra Leone), Kosovo, Albania, Afghanistan, the Gulf and so on – where the assertive talents of the submariners, sailors, the Royal Marines and Commandos, combined with air personnel, all brought together under the auspices of the Royal Navy, demonstrated both their immense versatility and very considerable firepower.

In fact, in many ways it was a demonstration of the navy's chameleon act, shaking off the shackles of the Cold War to emerge leaner but more diverse and interesting, ready for the challenge of this array of new tasks. It was also from these experiences that the shape of the future Royal Navy would be determined, and, surprisingly to many, contemplation about the navy's future shape and equipment would see a reversion to the policy of giant aircraft carriers of the size of the 1950s *Ark Royal*. That huge ship was subsequently sold off in the 1970s along with the remaining vestiges that made Britain a global naval power. The Royal Navy, over this period, was cut to ribbons by continued defence spending cuts amid political declarations that Britain (a) simply could not afford ships of that size and (b) that modern warfare as it was then perceived – i.e. East versus West – was based on the nuclear deterrent. And although the possibility of conventional war was, of course, a key element in NATO's defence planning, as the years passed there was increasing apathy in Britain, as with other European nations, towards funding the navy for such an event, relying more on the overall NATO defence commitment to which America had committed its substantial resources and indeed had maintained its own giant fleet aircraft carriers.

Apart from the expense, the politicians – rather than naval strategists – decided that with the diminishing possibility of great naval battles, ships of this nature were simply not needed and, as already discussed, the new giants of the sea were to be the nuclear submarines. This underestimation of the need for Britain's own naval strength as a national, rather than a NATO, resource remained a key issue for many years. Successive governments followed the strategy of Harold Wilson's first Labour government in 1964 in continually paring naval expenditure to the point where the Royal Navy was in danger of performing a dramatic vanishing act. The greatest folly was that at the hands of Margaret Thatcher's Defence Secretary, John Nott, who announced draconian defence spending cuts that would have axed the remaining *Invincible*-class carrier programme and would have sold off *Invincible* herself. The Falklands conflict famously put a stop to that!

However, in spite of some remaining influential opinion to the contrary in political circles, the need for a strong maritime air force as an integral part of the fleet's fighting capability in all warfare disciplines was soon to be amply demonstrated in the 1990s, ultimately contributing to the decision to build vast new aircraft carriers for the twenty-first century, the largest ships ever to be built by the Royal Navy. In addition, the necessity for air cover by the 1990s extended to every frigate and destroyer, by which time the ships' helicopters had become an essential part of the vessels' weapons and sensor system.

The key area of flexibility in aircraft carrier operations was amply shown in the ability to counteract restrictions on armed overflight imposed by some nations when, even within NATO, a number of states had on various occasions refused to allow Allied air forces to operate from their airfields or in certain circumstances fly over their territory on missions – such as the US bombing of Libya or, indeed, the second Gulf War in 2003. Nor are maritime air operations generally constrained in this by the weather, and throughout the 1990s the succession of high-profile operations mentioned above demonstrated in spectacular fashion the ability of a sea-based 'airfield' to move at high speed into an area and commence operations almost immediately.

The composition of the air units within a Royal Navy Task Force could also be 'mixed and matched' to meet the specific requirements of the mission. While the Sea Harrier FA2 continued to be rated as one of Europe's most potent air-defence aircraft, there were many opportunities for the successful integration of the specialist ground-attack RAF Harrier GR7. Equally important was the ability to launch a substantial and multi-tasking helicopter force, and this key contribution of aircraft carriers in a modern scenario became of paramount importance in the type of conflicts emerging in those years, especially in the Balkans, first during the Bosnian crisis and later in the NATO bombing operations against the former Yugoslavia to halt the Milošević regime's ethnic cleansing of Kosovo.

For the Bosnian conflict, it took just ten days to put a British aircraft carrier into the Adriatic, fully operational and able to put aircraft over Bosnia. Once on station, the aircraft carriers were able to provide almost continuous cover, operating back to back for over three years with FA2s, which flew many thousands of air-defence and ground-attack sorties without failure to meet their task.

It is in these areas that some of the most famous Fleet Air Arm and naval air service operations of the past are remembered, and it is perhaps fitting at this juncture to recall some of the heritage of naval air units which figure so strongly in today's Royal Navy aerial warfare capability. At the beginning of the twenty-first century the navy had 18 air squadrons, many with strong historical links. Among them, 800 Squadron claims to be the oldest, formed on 2 May 1933 from 402 and 404 Fleet Fighter Units. The squadron has since flown 15 different aircraft types, a number of notable 'firsts' among them including the Supermarine Attacker, the first navy-based jet. During the Second World War, 800 Squadron famously sank *Königsberg* by 65-degree dive-bombing with Skuas, was involved in the bombing of *Scharnhorst*, and its Hellcats flew to suppress flak guns during the raid on *Tirpitz*.

The squadron was involved in most of the major post-war operations, including the Korean War, the Suez Crisis and covering the British withdrawal from Aden. In 1980, 800 Squadron became the first Sea Harrier Squadron and operated from *Invincible*. With the formation of the second Sea Harrier Squadron, 800 moved to *Hermes*, and during the Falklands conflict flew a variety of missions, including Combat Air Patrol, reconnaissance, high- and low-level bombing, long-range probe and strafing. In the months of May and June 1982, aircraft of the *Hermes* group destroyed 13 Argentine aircraft in the air, bringing the squadron's total kills since formation to 50 – the highest of any naval air squadron.

During the early 1990s, 800 Squadron was also engaged in a series of deployments to the Adriatic in rotation with its sister Squadron 801. These were mostly in support of the United Nations peacekeeping effort, Operation Deny Flight, against the Republic of Yugoslavia. The squadron was re-equipped with the new Sea Harrier FA2 in April 1995, which coincided with the arrival of the AIM 120 Advanced Medium-Range Air-to-Air Missile (AMRAAM), thus making it the most effective air-defence fighter in the United Kingdom's order of battle. The squadron was redeployed to the Adriatic in *Invincible*, taking a major part in Operation Deliberate Force as part of the Allied air force whose bombing campaign was recognised as being instrumental in bringing about the Dayton Peace Accord that finally brought a halt to those years of appalling conflict in the ravaged land of Bosnia and facilitated the arrival of the NATO Implementation Force (IFOR) to aid the transition to peace.

The squadron was called back to the Adriatic aboard *Invincible* to join Operation Deliberate Guard, flying reconnaissance missions over Bosnia before being transferred to the Gulf in January 1998 to fly air-defence missions over Iraq to patrol the Southern No-Fly Zone as part of a joint naval force consisting of UK and US carriers. It was also to that unhappy place in April 1999 that *Invincible* returned in order to allow 800 Squadron to take part in Operation Allied Force during the Kosovo crisis, an event in which the nuclear submarine *Splendid* became the first ship in the Royal Navy to fire Tomahawk cruise missiles in anger.

Another of the squadrons with historical links is 820 Naval Air Squadron, also founded in 1933, which became established as one of NATO's principal anti-submarine air squadrons, flying Sea King HAS Mk 6 helicopters. The squadron normally operated from the anti-submarine carrier *Illustrious*, but was equally capable of being deployed to any carrier and certain ships of the Royal Fleet Auxiliary. When not embarked at sea, the squadron is based at Royal Naval Air Station Culdrose in Cornwall. The Sea King was especially flexible, capable of day and night operations under all weather conditions, and was soon recognised as one of the most effective and useful maritime helicopters in service anywhere in the world. It carries two pilots, an observer and a crewman in a multitude of roles, including anti-submarine warfare, search and rescue, passenger transport, heavy load-lifting, surface surveillance and stores delivery. It is equipped with Stingray torpedoes and depth charges.

Indeed, the squadron is a far cry from its more humble beginning when the flimsy Fairey IIIF aircraft of 450 Flight Royal Air Force were transferred to the Fleet Air Arm. Back then, the squadron was attached to the carrier *Courageous* for reconnaissance duties. Shortly after the beginning of the Second World War, it became clear that the carriers were too vulnerable to operate their aircraft solely in the anti-submarine role, so the squadron was re-tasked to undertake the roles of surface search and torpedo attack. It will be recalled from earlier chapters that the then *Ark Royal*, with 820 Squadron aboard, spent the first half of 1940 in the Atlantic on convoy-protection duties before going north in support of the Narvik campaign and subsequently helped trap and sink the German battleship *Bismarck*. Disbanded and reformed twice, 820 successfully flew over 4,700 hours in a variety of roles during the Falklands conflict from *Invincible*, which spent 166 days at sea, a world record for continuous carrier operations.

At the end of 1985 the squadron ended its connection with *Invincible* and formed part of the Air Group on board *Ark Royal* and subsequently took delivery of the much-improved Sea King Mk 6. In January 1993 the squadron was recalled from leave and sent at short notice to support the British contingent of UN forces in Bosnia for Operation Grapple, in the role of logistical support, ferrying men and supplies around the Adriatic. During the deployment, the squadron's aircraft carried out in excess of 1,400 deck landings and flew over 1,900 hours in support of the task. In 1994 the squadron continued operations in the Adriatic, embarked on *Ark Royal* before transferring to *Illustrious* the following year when the flagship carrier was decommissioned prior to a refit.

Many of the remaining naval air squadrons have similar links with the past and are still at the forefront of modern maritime-based warfare. These operations were typical of the navy's air capability, and that particularly busy era experienced in the 1990s continued without let-up into the twenty-first century. By then, the squadrons were operating from two principal naval air stations:

HMS *Heron* at Yeovilton in Somerset, which supported the Sea Harrier FA2, the Sea King Mk 4 helicopters and provided base support for all the Lynx helicopters; and HMS *Seahawk* at Culdrose in Cornwall, the base for the new Merlin anti-submarine helicopters, the Sea King Mk 6 Fleet, the Sea King AEW Fleet and 771 Search and Rescue Squadron. A secondary base for search and rescue operations remained at Prestwick, Ayrshire. These in turn support the four 'floating' airfields provided by the *Invincible*-class aircraft carriers, which operate Sea Harrier, Sea King and Merlin aircraft. The Commando helicopter carrier *Ocean* operates Sea King, Lynx and Gazelle helicopters.

Overall, the Fleet Air Arm provides the Royal Navy with a multi-role aviation combat capability able to operate autonomously at short notice worldwide in all environments, day and night, over the sea and land. To facilitate this wide-ranging commitment, the Fleet Air Arm employed some 6,200 personnel at the time of writing (2003), which represented 11.5 per cent of the total Royal Navy strength, operating some 200 combat aircraft and more than 50 support/training aircraft. Additionally, there are a small number of Lynx attack helicopters and the Gazelle reconnaissance/training aircraft, which work with 3 Commando Brigade.

There was considerable pressure on all these areas of the Royal Navy's operational units around the turn of the new millennium, culminating in their participation in Operation Veritas following the American-led invasion of Afghanistan in the wake of the Al Qaeda attack on New York on 11 September 2001. In the initial bombing raids to depose the Taliban regime, three Royal Navy nuclear-powered fleet submarines, *Superb*, *Trafalgar* and *Triumph*, were in the Indian Ocean but well in range of the land-locked country. The latter pair were equipped with the highly effective and very precise T-LAMs (Tomahawk Land-Attack Cruise Missiles), first introduced to the British submarine fleet in November 1998 and used operationally for the first time during the Kosovo campaign in 1999. Royal Navy T-LAMs were fired on the first night of operations on 7–8 October 2001 and again on 13 October.

A substantial Royal Navy Task Force, led by the carrier *Illustrious* and the Commando assault ship *Fearless* with 40 Commando, assembled in the area, supported by a large presence from the Royal Fleet Auxiliary. Earlier in 2002, the Commando helicopter carrier *Ocean* arrived carrying Royal Marines from 45 Commando, and subsequently formed the core of the British battle group deployed into Afghanistan itself. The battle group included a wide range of elements drawn from all three services to produce a fully self-contained force totalling 1,700 personnel.

It was to prove something of a dress rehearsal for events taking shape elsewhere.

# CHAPTER EIGHTEEN

## 'We Kicked the Door Open'

Somewhere under the oceans of the globe, one of Britain's nuclear-powered submarines, HMS *Turbulent*, whose locations are never made public, had already been at sea without a break for more than six months when, at Christmas 2002, her commander was placed on formal alert for possible action against the regime of Saddam Hussein. No one was sure when it would come, or even if it would, but alarm bells were ringing loudly in spite of a somewhat upbeat report to the United Nations from Hans Blix, the chief inspector of the team searching Iraq for weapons of mass destruction. British Prime Minister Tony Blair had already staked his political future on throwing his hand in with George W. Bush, who seemed determined to go to war come what may, and who was growing ever more impatient with the political manoeuvres at the United Nations.

And so *Turbulent*, in her secret lair, prepared to head off towards the Gulf, laden with the cruise missiles that were her speciality, otherwise known as T-LAMs, soon to feature strongly in the Coalition's 'shock and awe' bombing campaign over Baghdad. Before she was done, the *Trafalgar*-class submarine would have travelled 50,000 miles during a single deployment lasting ten months, with a route map that took her halfway around the world and back, and had included a supporting role in the

Afghanistan conflict. Many parents, wives, partners, girlfriends and children were beginning to get rather agitated.

At around the same time, ships, planes and troops were either on their way to the Gulf or preparing to go, and on 12 January Britain's largest warship, *Ark Royal*, set sail from Portsmouth amid cheers and tears and a mass of Union flags and banners as thousands lined the quayside to wish her farewell and a safe return. The steel-grey aircraft carrier, pristine after her long lay-off and a two-year refit costing £147 million, was the flagship of what would become the largest maritime deployment launched from Britain since the Falklands War. She would be leading a 15-strong battle group of destroyers, frigates and support ships that had been assembled, coincidentally, to take part in a long-planned exercise in the Far East, a journey originally destined to take them through the Mediterranean and Suez. But events had overtaken these arrangements, and now *Ark Royal* and her mini-fleet – soon to be joined by 18 other assorted vessels – were destined for the Gulf, and the war on Iraq.

At the time, of course, there was great public disquiet about this prospect, and few, save for Tony Blair and George W. Bush, could be sure of conflagration but, just in case, *Ark Royal* had disembarked all her fixed-wing aircraft in favour of troop-carrying helicopters and four Sea King airborne surveillance and control helicopters from 849 Squadron at RNAS Culdrose in Cornwall. The carrier also made a detour to Scotland after leaving Portsmouth to take on vast quantities of supplies and armaments before setting off for what was literally a journey into the unknown, a ship crammed with personnel and technological wizardry, and not a small measure of apprehension. The Royal Navy's flagship carrier is the fifth vessel to bear the distinguished name *Ark Royal*. (The first, a 38-gun ship built for Sir Walter Raleigh, saw action against the Spanish Armada in 1588.) Able to operate the navy's latest Merlin helicopters as well as Harrier jump jets, the ship can cruise at more than 30 knots. A central part of the navy's operational strength, *Ark Royal* is both a mobile airfield and a command and control base, with a total ship's crew of 1,051. At 683 feet long, *Ark Royal* is larger than her sister ships *Illustrious* and *Invincible* but less than half the size of the 1950s *Ark Royal* and a third of the size of the new breed of British carriers (one of which will almost certainly continue the name), planned for launch in 2010.

Commanding Officer Alan Massey said he was confident that the crew were prepared for the uncertainty of sailing without knowing whether they would go to war but that history rather pointed towards it: 'No carrier in the past ten years has ever completed a scheduled deployment. There is always something, whether Kosovo, Sierra Leone, Afghanistan. So why should it be any different this time?' And, of course, he was right, and it did not need a fortune-teller to confirm it. The sheer volume of men and machines from America already massing in the deserts of the friendly Arabian nations were not there for a suntan, and now they were to be progressively joined by 45,000 men from Britain, although at that point the UN Security Council was still arguing the toss, with France leading the doubting Thomases and ensuring a heap of vitriol from the Americans, which will take many years to subside.

From January onwards, the Royal Navy began the deployment of a substantial force of ships and Royal Fleet Auxiliary vessels, led by *Ark Royal* and the helicopter carrier *Ocean*. The main contingent included three Type 42 destroyers, *Liverpool*, *Edinburgh* and *York*; two Type 23 frigates, *Marlborough* and *Richmond* (as well as *Chatham*, already in the Gulf on patrol duties); mine-hunters *Grimsby* and *Ledbury*; and the RFA vessels *Argus* (hospital ship), *Sir Tristram*, *Sir Galahad*, *Sir Percivale*, *Fort Victoria*, *Fort Rosalie*, *Fort Austin* and *Orangeleaf*. They were later joined by 15 other Royal Navy and RFA vessels, including two additional minehunters, *Brocklesby* and *Blyth*. The amphibious force of more than 4,000 personnel also included 3 Commando Brigade, Royal Marines (HQ 3 Commando, 40 Commando and 42 Commando), and helicopter air groups. They were joined later by an Australian contingent consisting of HMAS *Darwin*, *Anzac* and *Kanibala*.

The British land force was led by Headquarters 1 (UK) Armoured Division and included 16 Air Assault Brigade, 7 Armoured Brigade and 102 Logistics Brigade, along with Royal Air Force contingents and 100 fixed-wing aircraft. In all, the

British contribution to the Coalition numbered 45,000 men and women, approximately a quarter of the total Coalition service personnel in the Gulf. A large deployment from the SAS, SBS and naval covert diving teams, surveying maritime invasion points, went in ahead of the main force, joining American Special Forces and CIA operatives gathering intelligence and target coordinates across the whole of Iraq long before the final countdown to war began as it became clear that Bush and Blair would not get a resolution from the UN Security Council authorising the invasion. In the face of worldwide anti-war protests, the American-led Coalition to depose the Iraqi regime edged closer with the air of unstoppable inevitability that had long ago settled over the whole scenario. Come what may, America was going in, with or without the support of France, Russia, Germany – or even Britain.

The onslaught began on the night of 20 March with an opening bombardment that was to be a dress rehearsal for the 'shock and awe' bombing that was to follow 24 hours later. A massive aerial attack on key sites was the prelude to a dramatic storming of southern Iraq, with British maritime forces in the vanguard. As cruise missiles fired by American ships and Royal Navy submarines in the Gulf and the Red Sea slammed into Baghdad, RAF Tornado GR4s took off from the Ali al-Salim air base in Kuwait to join the assault with US air force F15 Strike Eagle and US navy FA18 Hornet ground-attack aircraft.

Then British troops spearheaded the invasion as hundreds of Royal Marine Commandos stormed ashore in an amphibious assault on the Al-Faw peninsula, while British and American tanks roared across the frontier from Kuwait. Artillery including the 32 AS90 155-millimetre self-propelled guns of the 3rd Regiment, Royal Horse Artillery, blasted Iraqi front-line positions while Royal Navy ships *Marlborough*, *Chatham* and *Richmond* and the Australian frigate *Anzac* provided heavy bombardment cover for the Marines, hitting targets coordinated by Special Forces and Royal Artillery spotters. The navy began firing when an Iraqi bunker complex was pinpointed for *Marlborough*, and from six miles away on the Al-Faw peninsula her shells reached the target 25 seconds later. The first rounds were fired short to give the troops the chance to surrender, and then, after ten rounds had been fired and the white-hot shrapnel burst into the bunkers, an onshore spotter radioed back: 'Possible white flags being raised.'

As Jamie Wilson, sending dispatches for the *Guardian* from on board *Marlborough*, wrote:

Going to war with the Royal Navy is a very gentlemanly affair. There was no great bravado or bloodthirstiness – 'Poor bastards' was the comment I heard used most about the Iraqis. The enemy is a long way off, and there is a sense of dislocation from the battlefield. The job of the ship I was on was to offer naval gunfire support to the Royal Marines invading the Faw peninsula. The crew might not have been bloodthirsty, but they were fiercely competitive. There were four ships on the naval gun-line, and the crew desperately wanted both to be the first Royal Navy vessel to fire a shot in anger, and to fire the most shells. It's hard to believe now, but on that first morning of the war there was still a belief that all the Iraqi forces would throw up their hands and surrender at the first sight of a Coalition soldier. The gunnery officer was expecting to fire a couple of shells at most and perhaps none at all. It was only after the third or fourth fire mission, when the excitement of the gun booming on the front deck had subsided, that I realised that there were almost certainly lives being snuffed out underneath the explosive barrage. It was a sobering moment.

Meanwhile, US navy Seals and a company of Royal Marines moved towards their first major objective, to secure the vital Kwahr al-Amaya and Mina al-Bakr oil terminals as reinforcements were airlifted in by helicopter troop carriers containing the three companies of 40 Commando, Royal Marines, from their base in Kuwait, and other units were deploying from *Ocean* and *Ark Royal*, which had steamed in to the waters of the northern Gulf.

With memories of 1991, when Saddam ordered the destruction of the Kuwait oil industry by setting fire to 730 wells that took five months to put out, this was their first objective. With 1,000 wellheads in the southern oilfields, the potential for destruction was enormous, as Chief of Defence Staff, Admiral Sir Michael Boyce, confirmed in London that afternoon:

> The primary aim of the operation has been to secure the oil infrastructure in that part of the country before the Iraqis themselves can sabotage it. The enemy believes that sabotaging oil wells, that the thick black smoke such action might produce, can degrade our ability on the battlefield. The environmental repercussions of such action, especially with regard to oil being poured into the Gulf, are enormously damaging and, at the heart of our military planning in this operation as a whole, we are trying to make sure that the economic infrastructure of Iraq is left as intact as possible to benefit the Iraqi people after the campaign. As Royal Marines launched an amphibious and air-delivered assault on the Al-Faw peninsula to secure the oil infrastructure, a United States Marine Corps battalion launched its own attacks on the port of Umm Qasr, and that port will be available to us as soon as our British minesweepers are able to clear the waterway up there to allow shipping to move in safety.

While the marines dealt with that objective, US regimental combat teams began pushing forward towards the strategically important city of Basra, and their exposed flank was covered by two battle groups of Britain's 7th Armoured Brigade, including the Desert Rats, the Black Watch and the 1st Battalion of the Royal Regiment of Fusiliers. They moved quickly towards the outskirts of Basra itself, a movement supported logistically by helicopters flying from *Ocean* and *Ark Royal* and carried out under air cover provided by the US air force and by the Royal Air Force, whose Tornado GR4 aircraft attacked enemy artillery in the area with precision weapons, along with other military installations as far north as Al-Kut.

The early stages of the campaign were marred by accidental losses to British troops. Eight Royal Marines and four US crew members were killed when a veteran American Sea Knight CH-46 helicopter crashed. The following day, there was further tragedy when two British Sea King Mk 7 helicopters collided, killing all seven crew. Both were operating from *Ark Royal*, one taking off and the other coming in to land.

There was indeed a massive amount of air traffic from both ships and land bases, and in the first three days of operations more than 3,000 sorties were flown as the bombing campaign on targets in Baghdad now dominated the nightly action followed by devastation. In addition, on the second night of the war the massive 'shock and awe' air bombardment of Baghdad saw the release of more than 300 cruise missiles from American ships and Royal Navy submarines as well as more than 1,000 precision guided weapons launched from layer after layer of aircraft led by the giant B-52 bombers flying from RAF Fairford in Gloucestershire. Quite apart from the precisely targeted air raids, there was a mass of overhead activity in the southern skies with helicopters and aircraft lining up for landing and takeoff from ships and ground bases, a scene resembling the M25 on an English bank holiday. There were scores of operations of the American tank-busting aircraft and British helicopters on support missions as well as logistical duties, ferrying men, machines, transport, supplies and vast quantities of ammunition from ship to shore and then on to forward positions.

By 23 March the 7th Armoured Brigade (the Desert Rats) had moved to the west of Basra while the 16th Air Assault Brigade took up position at Ar Rmaylah, where they came under fire from Iraqi artillery from the 6th Division. The Coalition forces called in counter battery fire and close air support along with further and extensive bombardment from *Marlborough* and other naval guns, still covering ongoing operations on the Al-Faw peninsula. Within hours, the Iraqi 6th Division started to surrender, but the task of securing the southern area was certainly no walkover and some strong resistance was met.

In the early hours of 23 March, Iraqi forces, including tanks and personnel, moved south-east from Basra towards 3 Commando Brigade on the Al-Faw peninsula. The Commandos did not have their own tanks but coordinated and deployed a combination of Milan anti-tank missiles and hand-held anti-tank weapons to engage the enemy forces and managed to stop a number of the tanks. It soon became apparent, however, that the threat was more significant than at first thought, and so they requested assistance from Coalition aircraft, which provided close air support for our forces on the ground. Nineteen Iraqi T55 tanks were destroyed in the engagement. As Coalition air attacks continued against Iraqi troop formations, British forces completed operations to secure Umm Qasr while US forces continued on to advance north of An-Nasiriyah. British artillery destroyed Iraqi mortars and guns that had opened fire on Iraqi civilian areas in Basra. A British soldier from the Black Watch was killed in action at Az-Zubayr. In a separate incident, two more soldiers were killed when their Challenger 2 tank was accidentally hit by another Challenger 2 during an engagement with Iraqi forces.

After six days of conflict, the Coalition had made steady progress towards its objectives. The Al-Faw peninsula, Umm Qasr and the southern oilfields had been secured, and Iraqi resistance in those areas overcome, with 3 Commando Brigade in control allowing the US 15th Marine Expeditionary Unit to return to the 1st Marine Expeditionary Force, which was now heading towards Baghdad. Indeed, British forces had made a key contribution towards the objective of ensuring that the essential economic infrastructure was kept in working order, and that was vital to operations that now lay ahead.

The UK Naval Task Group command faced a number of major challenges on the maritime front. The biggest by far was to provide safe access to Umm Qasr port to allow logistics personnel and humanitarian aid to flow quickly into southern Iraq. Although 3 Commando Brigade had brought relative calm to the entire area, the threat of mines in the seagoing approaches and in the 44-mile stretch of waterway was very real and the sea had to be made safe for shipping, and particularly RFA *Sir Galahad*, which was waiting to come in with 500 tons of humanitarian relief.

The port of Umm Qasr is a city similar to Southampton and the country's major access route for supplies. A Mine Countermeasures Task Group, under Royal Navy command and including American and Australian elements, was drawn together to encompass all the skills available, including the equipment aboard three minehunting vessels, underwater vehicles, mine-clearance divers and even the American unit of dolphins trained to sniff out mines.

The task was made all the more hazardous because the extent of Iraqi minelaying was simply unknown, and the waterway was littered with 74 wrecks dating back to the Iran–Iraq war.

Royal Navy divers operating from the mine-countermeasure vessels concentrated on the clearance of Umm Qasr port while the Fleet Diving Group, who describe themselves as the 'down and dirty' side of the business, covered depths where almost fingertip searches were necessary in the mud and silt, enlivened by sewage outfalls, and up to ten to 13 feet deep. In such conditions, visibility was often zero. The same divers were part of a joint force that had earlier carried out reconnaissance of beaches earmarked for an amphibious landing. They discovered a large number of anti-personnel mines, which they made safe, later removing mines, booby traps and other explosives from the southern oilfields. With a potent mix of high explosives and thousands of gallons of fuel and gas, the whole operation was filled with danger. The deconstruction of these hazards became a joint mission, calling up the careful hands and expert eyes of Royal Engineers, the Royal Logistics Corps and RAF teams, as well as naval personnel.

Given the inherent difficulties, coupled with appalling weather and sandstorms five days into the war, the mine-clearance operations necessarily descended into a slow process made worse on Day Six by the discovery of two more mines, although by then an area 40 miles long and two miles wide had been cleared, with more than 100 items blown up.

But just seven days after fighting raged for this town of 40,000 people and its port, *Sir Galahad* was finally called in to unload her cargo, escorted by British and Australian mine-countermeasure ships and armed launches, watching for any threat from hostile speedboats. Unfortunately, the whole backbreaking operation then took on the air of a PR operation, with media in attendance. On the dockside were Royal Marines, waiting to welcome the first British ships into this port for more than 20 years. Although run down and neglected, the cranes and derricks were all still operational, and *Sir Galahad* soon became a hive of activity as personnel from the ship's home base, Marchwood military port on Southampton Water, worked around the clock to unload and deliver the aid provided by the people of Kuwait, which included

345

water, sugar, lentils, chickpeas, rice, tea, milk powder, 2,400 blankets and 8,200 packs of rations. It was a welcome package, but insignificant in terms of the appalling conditions already existing in southern Iraq, and soon to be experienced throughout the country. Given that the United Nations estimated that 60 per cent of Iraq's 27 million people were already dependent on food aid even before the war began, a very substantial humanitarian operation was called for, and the arrival of a single ship, symbolic though it was, would resolve little. It did, however, highlight what would otherwise have been a largely unnoticed area of UK forces' operations in the Gulf in clearing the aspect and making the port and the seaway safely navigable. First Sea Lord Admiral Sir Alan West was laudatory in his assessment of the operations with which his people were concerned:

> I do want to go on record straight away and say how amazingly proud I am, first of all of the UK servicemen altogether but – you would expect me to say this as the First Sea Lord – of my own boys and girls. I have been amazingly impressed by what they have done. Just before operations started, I sent a signal to them all. In part of that signal I said: 'I do not underestimate the difficulties and challenges of the task ahead, but I am also aware you are fully trained, well equipped and ready. The spotlight of world attention will be on you, and I have no doubt of your courage and determination to see the job through. Equally, let humanity and victory be our guiding principle.' And I have to say I think that has been absolutely the case. All of those things have been met, and I am very proud of my people.
>
> We had a relatively large force out there. We have had about 33 units of mine deployed east of Suez, including two SSNs [nuclear-powered submarines] and one of those, *Turbulent*, had been away from the United Kingdom for 300 days, in which time she has been fully involved in the global war on terror, doing all sorts of things that we wouldn't even speak about because they are very sensitive, but they are very helpful for the safety of the people in this country, and, of course, was involved in T-LAM [Tomahawk Land-Attack Cruise

Missiles] shoots against Iraq. I have been through those
T-LAM shoots, looked at the firing; they were all very
accurate, and the ship's company were very keen to know and
find out that these things were accurate because the aspect of
humanity and victory is an important thing and they didn't
want to feel that they were fully involved in something that
was being shot all over the place.

So what was the maritime contribution in those three
weeks? Well, we kicked the door open effectively. You saw the
picture of a Royal Marine jeep knocking down a door; well,
we rather did that in terms of letting people into the country.
We were using T-LAMs from sea, and we fired a considerable
number of those, and they were all very accurate and went on
the sorts of regime targets I wanted to hit.

In the amphibious operations in the Al-Faw peninsula, our
expertise was recognised by the Americans, and we actually
took an American battalion effectively under command of
my Commandos so we could do that attack, and by doing
that attack slightly early we actually got to all the oil infrastructure, various parts of which were wired up to be
exploded. We arrived before they could be blown up, and that
was a very successful outcome. We had support for those
forces, with naval gunfire support from the sea. I had three of
my ships doing 17 fire support missions, which generally
made the Iraqi positions surrender. So it was all very successful, and they were operating, if you imagine these ships, with
less than six feet under their keel in those rather badly charted
waters, again which I think shows the sort of professionalism
in the sort of things we practise regularly.

We conducted operations really across the littoral; we
supported our Marines from sea both in terms of logistic
supply and close air support, attacking enemy tanks and the
like, and the Commando Helicopter Force was there to
provide mobility, which was carried out with exceptional skill,
given the amount of traffic. We enabled and delivered
humanitarian aid, we carried out mine clearance in the waterways, we did a lot of explosive ordnance disposal and we
really were the lead people in all that, with the Americans

helping us, along with some Australian divers, and, of course, the world-famous dolphins from America which seem to have caught everyone's attention. Further, we provided medical support from sea with the hospital ship RFA *Argus* [which included treatment for wounded POWs]. All this was done in a joint environment, but I am very proud of what our people did.

The result was that within the UK area of operations we saw a quite dramatic sense of return to normality. I think you can find certain areas – and this is always a danger when you are involved in an incident – that seem to you something huge and immense, but sometimes you have to stand back and look at the overview. In terms of movement of forces, 3 Commando Brigade took over all of the southern oilfields in the Basra area, [while] the 7th Armoured Brigade was responsible in the town of Basra, and the 16th Air Assault was rather north of there.

And on the maritime side we still had a lot of work in the approaches to Umm Qasr and the move up to Az-Zubayr to enable a large amount of shipping to get in there for a huge amount of enabling operations. 539 Assault Squadron was able to operate up all the various waterways. The area is very much like marshland, with huge waterways in all directions and [we were already aware of the problems we would face] . . . in fact, I had sent an MCM [mine countermeasures] force out into that theatre in September 2002, because things were looking a bit tense out there, and it is always best to be ready in case something does happen. So they had been out there really quite a long time; they got to know the area and were used to working there. And our [covert] survey people had been operating out there and doing very, very good survey work, again for the safety of marines altogether.

And so when the MCM operations started on 22 March, we had US helicopters minesweeping, we had other minehunters available. We destroyed 11 mines that were laid, but we were very lucky in that we had gone a day early and we caught them before they laid another 76 mines, which we found in ships ready to be deployed. And a week after

22 March we had a channel safe all the way up to Az-Zubayr, quite a small one, and we broadened that and widened it to about 1,000 metres wide and then continued with operations, not just removing mines that might have been laid now, but ones that were laid in past wars and getting rid of explosive ordnance in that region.

In Umm Qasr itself, our Commando Regiment handed that over to 102 Logistic Brigade and 17 Port and Maritime Regiment, who did a lot of work in the port there, and we began recruiting a lot of Iraqis who used to work there to get the port up and running again. We were using experienced people. I had a Royal Naval Reserve Commander, who is the Port Manager of Southampton, who found himself there, giving advice. The infrastructure was largely intact, and indeed our plan, which we went through in immense detail in terms of kinetic targeting, was to leave it intact, and that has by and large been amazingly successful; we have not taken out these things. But, of course, an awful lot of it was in a very, very poor state because the regime didn't look after it and wasn't focusing its resources in the right way.

We always said that when forces were not required, not essential for the operation, we would pull them back, not least to give the people a break. I mentioned *Turbulent*, which had been away from the UK for ten months. We needed to recharge these people's batteries. We are in a very dangerous world; there is a global war on terror, and we need forces available should they be required to look after the people of the United Kingdom and we want them refreshed, ready to do whatever they might need to do . . .

However, the scaling down of the maritime operations as the land forces continued their dash to Baghdad did not signal a prompt return home for all the navy vessels in the Gulf. With their guns hardly cooled, several ships that had contributed much to covering the seaborne landings and supporting the ground troops with bunker bombardment were immediately given orders to proceed not to home ports but in the opposite direction: to join an operational exercise as part of the Five-Power Defence

Arrangement (FPDA), designed to safeguard the strategically vital waters around Singapore and Malaysia. The FPDA comprises ships from the UK, Australia, New Zealand, Malaysia and Singapore. First Sea Lord Admiral Sir Alan West explained:

> It is the only organisation like that in the region, and there are dangers of instability, as we know from the Bali bombing within Indonesia. The UK has more investments in that region than any other country in Europe, and indeed in a number of the countries more than America, and so stability is important, not just for us, actually, but for the rest of the world. There is no doubt that having these forces in those areas does add to stability.

Other ships were returned immediately to the Royal Navy's long-standing commitments, including NATO's Mediterranean Naval Force, made up of ships from Allied nations, training and operating together, with command rotating on an annual basis among the nations contributing ships to the force. Although the force was set up in 1992, since the terrorist attack on the Twin Towers in New York on 11 September 2001, it has been permanently engaged in Operation Active Endeavour in the eastern Mediterranean, monitoring both strategic shipping routes from the Far and Middle East that enter it from the Suez Canal en route to Europe and local traffic from the Black Sea, the Near East and North Africa.

Warships monitor the busy shipping lanes while also providing an overt presence in the area, constantly alert to any terrorist-related activity, which could include movements of arms and explosives as well as the terrorists themselves. Then ships are maintained on permanent patrol and at high alert, ready to deal with any threat that might materialise. The British navy also contributes substantially to its sister organisation, the NATO Atlantic Force, which continues its permanent peacetime role. Comprising destroyers, cruisers and frigates from the navies of various NATO nations, the force operates, trains and exercises as a group, providing day-to-day verification of current NATO maritime procedures, tactics and effectiveness.

Created in 1967, the Atlantic Force has since involved a total of over 500 ships and more than 150,000 serving men and women, participating annually in a series of scheduled NATO and national exercises aimed at providing a visible, practical demonstration of transatlantic cooperation, although in the case of the Iraq work no other NATO member apart from Britain felt inclined to join the American forces sent to oust Saddam Hussein, a task that was completed with surprising speed.

And so, as the rapid collapse of the Iraqi regime was witnessed minute by minute on television screens around the world, the Royal Navy began to scale down its presence in the Gulf. As an amphibious mission, it had undoubtedly been a highly successful operation. Men were landed fast and safely. Casualties had been far below expectations, and, of course, considerably fewer than in the Falklands. As already noted, *Turbulent* was the first to return to her base port of Devonport, Plymouth, after completing the longest-ever deployment of a nuclear submarine in Royal Navy history. It was an occasion that attracted a formal welcome from defence chiefs and politicians from Westminster. Commander Andrew McKendrick, the submarine's commanding officer, said: 'In the last ten or so months, *Turbulent* has been from 15 degrees west longitude to 145 degrees east longitude, so we have truly been halfway around the world and back. The crew have been faced with some difficult and demanding tasks and have performed as true professionals throughout. We are thrilled to be at home again with our families and friends who have supported us so magnificently.'

Undoubtedly, the Iraqi adventure proved to be a major test for British armed forces across the board, and the Royal Navy in particular. In recent times, there had been much media speculation on the decline of British naval power since the Second World War, due in part – if not all – to the frequent changes in government policy and the continual onslaught against defence spending by successive governments. The navy became a prime target for cuts, and in the year of the Queen's Golden Jubilee it became a matter of considerable controversy that only a handful of ships was available for her review of the fleet, compared with the hundreds that had been assembled on such occasions in the past. In fact, quantity in shipping numbers is no longer a virtue. The era of the

Grand Fleet and battleships bristling with big guns died with the advent of the atomic age. They were hugely expensive deathtraps then, and would be even more so today. What was seriously lacking over the second half of the twentieth century, however, was a forward-looking cohesive policy for Britain's maritime forces that was laid down and adhered to, enabling ships to be built and operated in accord with a long-term plan, instead of the made-for-the-moment vision of some newly promoted minister in government or penpusher in Whitehall whose objectives were often attuned to the party line and budgets, rather than to future needs.

Political shenanigans and foolhardy decisions in the past undoubtedly cut the effectiveness of the Royal Navy. When major reductions were being made back in 1980, for example, and the new *Invincible*-class carriers were threatened with the axe even before they were completed, Argentina decided it would be a very opportune time to invade the Falklands, and consequently the navy had to hire in a large number of ships to mount its Task Force to eject them. The carriers stayed, and they have since proved a godsend to the navy in a difficult era when defence policy was firmly nailed to the requirements of NATO and the Cold War.

The possibility of so-called 'out-of-area' engagements requiring floating airfields was considered to be of minimal risk but, as the Falklands quickly demonstrated, this was not the case, nor would it be in the future. The end of the Cold War was seen as a further opportunity in Westminster to wield the axe, and the Royal Navy once more suffered and was left struggling to meet commitments both in manpower and equipment when global terrorism re-emerged in the 1990s. Naval professionals must have been tearing their hair out in frustration, emanating from half a century of stop-go policies.

At last, however, a more sustainable and realistic view of the future has been laid down under the Labour administration of Tony Blair. By necessity, the Royal Navy has finally been allowed to cut away from the Cold War focus on the single-minded adherence to the North Atlantic- and European-based policies. As the twenty-first century approached, the navy had been pressed with operations in every corner of the globe. Deployments varied in strength and versatility, from single ships or submarines to amphibious Task Forces capable of every maritime discipline, constantly at work defending the United Kingdom's interests worldwide, and they will be very much part of future operations.

Although the focus has returned to bigger carriers capable of carrying substantial armoury, transport and aircraft, destroyers and frigates still play key roles, essential in any conflict and providing air and sea defence. In general, however, the Royal Navy's capabilities are designed around three core assets: carrier-borne aircraft, submarines and amphibious forces, all supported by escorts and other vital support units. At the top of the pile are the *Vanguard*-class submarines SSBNs (Ship Submersible Ballistic Nuclear) on patrol, maintaining the strategic nuclear deterrent 24 hours a day, 365 days a year, and in the navy's visionary plan for the future *Vanguards* will be joined over the next 15 years by some powerful additions.

The nuclear-attack submarines SSNs (Ship Submersible Nuclear), such as *Turbulent*, are fast, highly flexible and powerful instruments of government policy. They are able to maintain high speeds, capable of covering 600 nautical miles per day with no need to refuel. They may be first on the scene, overtly or covertly, where they are then available for inserting Special Forces, for which they are often used, or early denial of the sea to an enemy. The T-LAMs are their weaponry, as used in Kosovo, Afghanistan and Iraq. They have the dual role of gathering critical intelligence through electronic means and can remain at sea independent of outside support for at least 90 days.

During the first decade of the twenty-first century they will be joined by the *Astute*-class SSNs, a new breed of hunter-killer submarines, to replace the ageing *Swiftsure* and *Trafalgar* boats, with a power plant that will allow them to complete a lifespan of 25 years without refuelling.

Next are the aircraft carriers that have certainly proved their value in the last ten years: *Ark Royal*, *Invincible* and *Illustrious* and the Commando helicopter carrier *Ocean* have all been very fully engaged, and with refits will remain in service until two new aircraft carriers are available in 2012. The replacements are massive 60,000-ton floating airfields costing £2.9 billion.

Along with them comes the new ghost-like destroyer, Type 45, to gradually replace the current Type 42. She will be equipped with the sophisticated and lethal Principal Anti-Air Missile System (PAAMS), which is capable of controlling several missiles in the air at any one time, each one of which could engage individual targets, preventing attackers from swamping the fleet's air defences. It is also intended that the Harrier force be completely replaced by a new combat aircraft, which is due to enter service in 2012 and be operated from the new carriers.

Indeed, the whole outlook, although still distant, is for a Royal Navy that will have the benefit of greater foresight in planning, design and ships' architecture than for many years past. Events have shown that submarine warfare is as relevant as it has ever been and, quite apart from the security aspect, interesting times are ahead as the Royal Navy's future falls into place with a new generation of multi-faceted, multi-disciplined ships manned by smaller crews surrounded by Star Wars technology.

# APPENDIX

## Royal Navy: Principal Ships, 2003

The current stock of ships and submarines operational at the time of writing is listed below. It will be seen that they vary in age from the early 1970s. The list does not include the newest warship, HMS *Albion*, an 18,500-ton assault ship, one of the most sophisticated of its type which can carry 700 Royal Marine Commandos and up to 60 vehicles, ranging from trucks to battle tanks, and eight new landing craft. *Albion* came into service in July 2003 and was built in four years in Barrow-in-Furness by BAE Systems as part of a £500 million programme to replace *Fearless* and *Intrepid*. Her sister ship *Bulwark* was due for delivery in 2004. The two new ships will be based in Plymouth along with the navy's other front-line amphibious warfare vessels, including the helicopter carrier *Ocean*.

| Ship Name and Pennant No. | Launch Date | Displacement (Tonnes) | Total Crew |
|---|---|---|---|
| **Aircraft Carriers** | | | |
| INVINCIBLE (RO5) | 1977 | 20,600 | 1,051 |
| ILLUSTRIOUS (RO6) | 1978 | 20,600 | 1,051 |
| ARK ROYAL (RO7) | 1981 | 20,600 | 1,051 |
| **Amphibious Assault Ship** | | | |
| OCEAN (L12) | 1995 | 21,758 | 265 |

| Ship Name and Pennant No. | Launch Date | Displacement (Tonnes) | Total Crew |
|---|---|---|---|
| **Type 42 Destroyers Batch 1** | | | |
| NEWCASTLE (D87) | 1975 | 3,560 | 253 |
| GLASGOW (D88) | 1976 | 3,560 | 253 |
| CARDIFF (D108) | 1974 | 3,560 | 253 |
| **Type 42 Destroyers Batch 2** | | | |
| EXETER (D89) | 1978 | 3,560 | 253 |
| SOUTHAMPTON (D90) | 1979 | 3,560 | 253 |
| NOTTINGHAM (D91) | 1980 | 3,560 | 253 |
| LIVERPOOL (D92) | 1980 | 3,560 | 253 |
| **Type 42 Destroyers Batch 3** | | | |
| MANCHESTER (D95) | 1980 | 3,880 | 301 |
| GLOUCESTER (D96) | 1982 | 3,880 | 301 |
| EDINBURGH (D97) | 1983 | 3,880 | 301 |
| YORK (D98) | 1982 | 3,880 | 301 |
| **Type 23 Frigates** | | | |
| NORFOLK (F230) | 1987 | 3,500 | 181 |
| ARGYLL (F231) | 1989 | 3,500 | 181 |
| LANCASTER (F229) | 1990 | 3,500 | 181 |
| MARLBOROUGH (F233) | 1989 | 3,500 | 181 |
| IRON DUKE (F234) | 1991 | 3,500 | 181 |
| MONMOUTH (F235) | 1991 | 3,500 | 181 |
| MONTROSE (F236) | 1992 | 3,500 | 181 |
| WESTMINSTER (F237) | 1992 | 3,500 | 181 |
| NORTHUMBERLAND (F238) | 1992 | 3,500 | 181 |
| RICHMOND (F239) | 1993 | 3,500 | 181 |
| SOMERSET (F82) | 1994 | 3,500 | 181 |
| GRAFTON (F80) | 1994 | 3,500 | 181 |
| SUTHERLAND (F81) | 1996 | 3,500 | 181 |
| KENT (F78) | 1998 | 3,500 | 181 |
| PORTLAND (F79) | 1999 | 3,500 | 181 |
| ST ALBANS (F83) | 2000 | 3,500 | 181 |

| Ship Name and Pennant No. | Launch Date | Displacement (Tonnes) | Total Crew |
|---|---|---|---|
| **Type 22 Frigates Batch 3** | | | |
| CORNWALL (F99) | 1985 | 4,200 | 250 |
| CUMBERLAND (F85) | 1986 | 4,200 | 250 |
| CAMPBELTOWN (F86) | 1987 | 4,200 | 250 |
| CHATHAM (F87) | 1988 | 4,200 | 250 |
| **Antarctic Patrol Ship** | | | |
| ENDURANCE (A171) | 1991 | 6,500 | 112 |
| ***Castle*-Class Patrol Vessels** | | | |
| LEEDS CASTLE (P258) | 1980 | 1,427 | 45 |
| DUMBARTON CASTLE (P265) | 1981 | 1,427 | 45 |
| ***Island*-Class Patrol Vessels** | | | |
| ANGLESEY (P277) | 1979 | 925 | 35 |
| GUERNSEY (P297) | 1977 | 925 | 35 |
| LINDISFARNE (P300) | 1978 | 925 | 35 |
| **Ocean Survey Vessel** | | | |
| SCOTT (H131) | 1996 | 13,500 | 63 |
| **Coastal Survey Vessels** | | | |
| ROEBUCK (H130) | 1985 | 1,477 | 46 |
| GLEANER (H86) | 1983 | 25 | 5 |
| ***Sandown*-Class Minehunters** | | | |
| SANDOWN (M101) | 1988 | 450 | 34 |
| INVERNESS (M102) | 1990 | 450 | 34 |
| WALNEY (M104) | 1991 | 450 | 34 |
| BRIDPORT (M105) | 1992 | 450 | 34 |
| PENZANCE (M106) | 1997 | 450 | 34 |
| PEMBROKE (M107) | 1997 | 450 | 34 |
| GRIMSBY (M108) | 1998 | 450 | 34 |
| BANGOR (M109) | 1999 | 450 | 34 |
| RAMSEY (M110) | 1999 | 450 | 34 |
| BLYTH (M111) | 2000 | 450 | 34 |
| SHOREHAM (M112) | 2001 | 450 | 34 |

| Ship Name and Pennant No. | Launch Date | Displacement (Tonnes) | Total Crew |
|---|---|---|---|
| **Hunt-Class Minehunters** | | | |
| BRECON (M29) | 1978 | 615 | 45 |
| LEDBURY (M30) | 1979 | 615 | 45 |
| CATTISTOCK (M31) | 1981 | 615 | 45 |
| COTTESMORE (M32) | 1982 | 615 | 45 |
| BROCKLESBY (M33) | 1982 | 615 | 45 |
| MIDDLETON (M34) | 1983 | 615 | 45 |
| DULVERTON (M35) | 1982 | 615 | 45 |
| CHIDDINGFOLD (M37) | 1983 | 615 | 45 |
| ATHERSTONE (M38) | 1986 | 615 | 45 |
| HURWORTH (M39) | 1984 | 615 | 45 |
| QUORN (M41) | 1988 | 615 | 45 |
| **Archer-Class P2000 Fast Training Boats** | | | |
| ARCHER (P264) | 1985 | 49 | 11 |
| BITER (P270) | 1985 | 49 | 11 |
| SMITER (P272) | 1985 | 49 | 11 |
| PURSUER (P273) | 1985 | 49 | 11 |
| BLAZER (P279) | 1988 | 49 | 11 |
| DASHER (P280) | 1988 | 49 | 11 |
| PUNCHER (P291) | 1988 | 49 | 11 |
| CHARGER (P292) | 1988 | 49 | 11 |
| RANGER (P293) | 1988 | 49 | 11 |
| TRUMPETER (P294) | 1988 | 49 | 11 |
| EXPRESS (P163) | 1988 | 49 | 11 |
| EXAMPLE (P165) | 1985 | 49 | 11 |
| EXPLORER (P164) | 1985 | 49 | 11 |
| EXPLOIT (P167) | 1988 | 49 | 11 |
| TRACKER (P274) | 1998 | 49 | 11 |
| RAIDER (P275) | 1998 | 49 | 11 |
| **Vanguard-Class Submarines** | | | |
| VANGUARD (S28) | 1995 | 15,900 | 135 |

| Ship Name and Pennant No. | Launch Date | Displacement (Tonnes) | Total Crew |
|---|---|---|---|
| VICTORIOUS (S29) | 1995 | 15,900 | 135 |
| VIGILANT (S30) | 1995 | 15,000 | 135 |
| VENGEANCE (S31) | 1998 | 15,900 | 135 |
| *Swiftsure*-Class Submarines | | | |
| SOVEREIGN (S108) | 1973 | 5,000 | 116 |
| SUPERB (S109) | 1974 | 5,000 | 116 |
| SCEPTRE (S104) | 1976 | 5,000 | 116 |
| SPARTAN (S105) | 1978 | 5,000 | 116 |
| SPLENDID (S106) | 1979 | 5,000 | 116 |
| *Trafalgar*-Class Submarines | | | |
| TRAFALGAR (S107) | 1981 | 5,208 | 130 |
| TURBULENT (S87) | 1982 | 5,208 | 130 |
| TIRELESS (S88) | 1984 | 5,208 | 130 |
| TORBAY (S90) | 1985 | 5,208 | 130 |
| TRENCHANT (S91) | 1986 | 5,208 | 130 |
| TALENT (S92) | 1988 | 5,208 | 130 |
| TRIUMPH (S93) | 1991 | 5,208 | 130 |

# Index

Location references for footnotes have an 'n' suffix.